walking
in the
WORD

walking
in the
WORD

A FAMILY JOURNEY FROM GENESIS TO REVELATION

Carolyn Wells

AMBASSADOR INTERNATIONAL
GREENVILLE, SOUTH CAROLINA & BELFAST, NORTHERN IRELAND

www.ambassador-international.com

Walking in the Word

A Family Journey From Genesis to Revelation
© 2016 by Carolyn Wells
All rights reserved

ISBN: 978-1-62020-508-2
eISBN: 978-1-62020-412-2

Cover Design & Typesetting by Hannah Nichols
Ebook Conversion by Anna Riebe Raats

AMBASSADOR INTERNATIONAL
Emerald House
411 University Ridge
Suite B14
Greenville, SC 29601, USA

www.ambassador-international.com

AMBASSADOR BOOKS
The Mount
2 Woodstock Link
Belfast, BT6 8DD, Northern Ireland, UK
www.ambassadormedia.co.uk

The colophon is a trademark of Ambassador

This book is dedicated to the memory of my parents, Louis and Kitty Howson. I am grateful for the privilege of being brought up in a family where God's Word was read daily.

And to my three children, Heather, Andy, and Euan, who were the inspiration for this book.

ACKNOWLEDGEMENTS

I would like to express my deepest appreciation to all those who have supported me in this venture. My husband Alan has been an encouragement to me to keep going and without his constant support this would never have made it to print. Thank you to Heather, Andy, and Euan, my three children: your encouragement has been appreciated and the sacrifice of time on the Xbox so I could write in the dining room has been noted boys! Thank you! To the many friends and family whose constant encouragement to carry on has been invaluable, I would like to express my appreciation. Thank you to the staff of Ambassador International for making this possible. Most of all I am grateful to my Heavenly Father for the vision He gave me for this book and for His constant, unchanging love.

CONTENTS

NEW TESTAMENT

INTRODUCTION

This series was born from a desire to take my own family through the Bible from start to finish, allowing them to see how it all fits together. There are many great devotional books for families, and we have benefited greatly from them. However, I feel there is a need for Christian families to walk through the Bible together, to know God's story as a part of history and see how it applies to our lives today. Each day has a passage to read from the Bible. These can be read from a version of the Bible that suits the age of your children.

This study can be used in whatever way suits your family best. You can choose to study a section from the Old Testament followed by one from the New or simply go through it from beginning to end. The sections are flexible for you to use as suits your lifestyle and stage of family life best. It is important that we encourage each member of our families to put what is learned into practice, difficult bits and all!

I would encourage you to make the most of the opportunity to listen to what your children have to say and guide them to apply God's Word to their lives and situations. Some days give an opportunity for parents to be very open and share experiences from their past. These times can be of great benefit in drawing us close together and allowing our children to learn from our mistakes. Some days provide an opportunity for the family to do something practical in applying what they have learned. This is a chance for the family to work together in their walk with God.

Throughout the book, there are verses or short passages to memorize. Select those activities as they suit or as an occasional extra. The goal is to train your children to apply the whole of God's Word to their lives and to encourage each other (and you) in our walk with God.

On the Way: This section is an introduction to the day's reading and will fill in the story as much as possible—a guide.

Checkpoint: Here we stop each day and discover the lessons and challenges from God's Word to us.

Prayer Stop: Pointers to encourage the family to pray together.

I pray that as you walk through the Bible, you will walk into a deeper relationship with God and each other and that you will gain strength from the Lord to stand firm in your faith as a Christian family in today's diverse society.

FROM THE START

GENESIS

The word *Genesis* means "origin." This is very suitable for the first book of the Bible, which maps out the beginning of Creation, of human history, and also the beginning of Israel. It is believed to have been written by Moses.

DAY 1

On the Way: The first chapter in Genesis describes Creation. It shows us the power of God's Word that brought our universe into being. On the first day, God created light and darkness; on the second day, the sky. On the third day, He made dry land, plants, and trees; on the fourth day, the sun and moon; the fifth day, God created birds and sea creatures; and on the sixth day, He created animals and man.

After God finished His work of Creation, He set aside the seventh day to rest. It is His plan that we also have a rest from our work, and so He has given us a day of rest. That's why we have Sunday as a special day to worship Him and rest.

READ GENESIS 2:1–9

Then the LORD *God formed the man from the dust of the ground (v7a).*

Checkpoint: Six times in Genesis chapter 1 it mentions, "And God saw that it was good." God was pleased with what He had created. He created so many different things with so much variety. How many different colors can you name? God created them. Look at the different flowers, vegetables, and fruit. How many of each can you name? He created so many different animals that we are still discovering new ones and new facts about them. Each time scientists discover something new about how creation works, remember that God already knew it; He created it that way! It is so amazing to think that our God did all this.

He has created a good world for us to live in, and we should do our best to look after it.

Today we read about God creating man, the only part of God's creation to have the breath of God breathed into it. We are uniquely created.

- *How can we look after God's world?*
- *Think of at least two ways that your family can look after God's creation and try to put these into practice.*

Prayer Stop: Praise God for His wonderful creation. Think of your favorite animals, food, and plants and thank God for these. Ask God to show you how to help look after creation.

DAY 2

On the way: God created man and placed him in the Garden of Eden. He also created woman by causing Adam to fall into a deep sleep and forming her from one of his ribs. Adam called her Eve. She was created to be a helper for Adam. God gave them the job of looking after the garden.

READ GENESIS 2:15–25

> *You may freely eat the fruit of every tree in the garden—except the tree of the knowledge of good and evil* (vs16b–17a).

Checkpoint: God gave man the gift of life and a purpose for his life in verse 15. God has a purpose for each one of us. As His children, we should ask Him to show us that purpose and obey Him. In verses 16–17, we read of the rules that God set for Adam and Eve to live by. There was only one: not to eat from the tree of knowledge of good and evil. He also gave them the reason to live by this rule. Can you find it in verse 17?

God gives us boundaries for our lives throughout His Word. We will discover some of them as we go through these studies. By accepting God's boundaries for us, we will discover the purpose He has for our lives and learn how to be content no matter what we face.

Our parents also set boundaries for us. (Usually with good reason!) It is God's will that we honor and obey them.

- *Discuss with your family what you found difficult about living by the boundaries your parents gave you. Ask your children what they find difficult about living within the boundaries you have set. Perhaps you could discuss the reasons for those boundaries.*

- *Discuss with your family how you have changed boundaries for your children from those you had as a child.*

- *Remember it is one of God's rules to obey our parents. Look it up in Ephesians 6:1–3. What reason is given?*

Prayer Stop: Thank God for the guidelines in His Word. Thank Him for your parents. Ask God for help as a family to live by His boundaries and for wisdom as you live by the boundaries set in your family.

DAY 3

On the Way: Adam and Eve were given the "Freedom of Eden." God's purpose for them was to live and work in this beautiful garden. He wanted them to enjoy it and be satisfied in it. But Satan had other ideas.

READ GENESIS 3:1–13

> *She saw that the tree was beautiful and its fruit looked delicious, and she wanted the wisdom it would give her. So she took some of the fruit and ate it. Then she gave some to her husband who was with her and he ate it too* (v6b).

Checkpoint: Satan made Eve doubt what God actually said when God told them not to eat of the tree of knowledge of good and evil. As she spoke with him, her focus moved from God to the fruit, and she saw that it looked good. Sin is like that; it looks good. Satan knows we will not go for horrible, boring things, so he makes it look great fun with lots of benefits for us. But BEWARE. If what we are being tempted to do is against God's Word, it is sin. Therefore, it is very important for us to know God and His Word and stay focused on what we learn from Him. God wants us to be free to enjoy the good things He has for us, so we need to follow His guidelines in His Word.

- *Is there anything that is taking your focus away from God at the moment—as a family or as an individual?*

- *Take a minute to think about your life. Are you being tempted to do something that you know is against God's Word? Perhaps you are not sure what God's Word says about it; if your family feels reluctant to discuss this together, you could encourage them to talk about it with a suitable leader at church.*

Prayer Stop: Ask God to help you understand what is right and wrong as you look at His Word and listen to others. Pray for each member in your family to be aware when Satan is trying to tempt them. Pray that God would give them strength to resist.

DAY 4

On the Way: Adam and Eve have two sons. When they are grown up, Cain, the eldest, becomes a gardener; his younger brother, Abel, becomes a shepherd. They have obviously been taught by their parents the ways of God because both are working men, and we see them bringing an offering to God (v3–4). We want to have a look at their attitudes today.

READ GENESIS 4:1–12

> *You will be accepted if you do what is right. But if you refuse to do what is right, then watch out! Sin is crouching at the door, eager to control you. But you must subdue it and be its master* (v7).

Checkpoint: Cain brought some fruit to offer to the Lord as a sacrifice. There doesn't seem to be anything special about it; it doesn't even seem to be the first of his crop. He does not seem to have put much thought or preparation into it. Abel brought some fat portions from the firstborn of his flock. They were specially selected as those born first, and he would have had to sacrifice the lambs to prepare the special offerings of fat. This would have taken some thought, preparation, and sacrifice on his part. Cain, it seems, brought whatever was at hand to offer God; Abel prepared his sacrifice. We can see immediately the difference in their attitudes. God was more interested in what was in their hearts than what was in their hands. God is more interested in our hearts too, not the words that come out our mouths or the fact that we attend church.

- *What is our attitude like when we go to church to worship God? Do we prepare our worship, or do we not give it a thought?*

- *How are you when you leave your place of worship? Abel found favor with God (Genesis 4:4), but Cain was angry and resentful, which led him into further sin. (See today's key verse.)*

Prayer Stop: Thank God for our churches where we can worship God with other Christians. Pray that God would help us look into our hearts and check our attitudes as we go to worship next and also as we leave that place of worship.

DAY 5

On the Way: We have moved on a good few years from Adam and Eve now and come to the time of Noah. Before we do, take a quick look at Genesis 5. See if you can find the name of the oldest person mentioned. How old was he?

We see that the number of people on the earth have increased and that sin has also increased.

READ GENESIS 6:9–22

> *Noah was a righteous man, the only blameless person living on earth at the time, and he walked in close fellowship with God* (v9b).

Checkpoint: Noah was different from those around him. He walked with God. Others were intent on pleasing themselves and not God. So much so that verse 6 tells us God was sorry He had made man. God was going to wipe mankind from the face of the earth because they had become so wicked. He knew that Noah was righteous and so gave him and his family a way in which they could be kept safe from destruction. Noah believed God and acted on His word. Those around him just laughed; in the end, they were destroyed.

Our society is just as it was in Noah's day. People prefer to please themselves rather than pleasing God. As God's people, we are called to be different from those around us, just as Noah was. God gave Noah a way to be saved. He has given us a way to be saved from sin's curse. Not by building a boat but by accepting Jesus as our Savior and asking His forgiveness for our sin.

- *What things in your community do not please God?*
- *How can you be seen in your community to be different from those around?*
- *If there are members in your family who have not accepted God's way of salvation for themselves, you may want to talk about this with them or encourage them to speak with a suitable church leader.*

Prayer Stop: Pray that we would stand out in our neighborhood as people who walk with God. Pray for two people in your community or school who do not know God and ask God to give you a chance to share His way of salvation with them.

DAY 6

On the Way: Just as God had commanded him, Noah built the ark and took the animals and his family onto it with him. God sent the floodwaters over the earth for forty days and forty nights, destroying everything on the face of the earth. It took over a year for the earth to dry out, and Noah remained in the ark all of that time (Gen. 7:11 and Gen. 8:13–14). How do you think Noah felt all this time?

READ GENESIS 8:15–22; 9:12–16

> *I have placed my rainbow in the clouds. It is the sign of my covenant with you and with all the earth* (9:13).

Checkpoint: God told Noah when it was the right time to leave the ark. He came off and immediately worshipped God. God made a promise that He would never again destroy all the earth with a flood. He gave Noah a sign of that promise (the rainbow in the sky). He also gave Noah instructions for his future (Gen. 9:1–7).

I'm sure Noah felt a little uncertain during his year on the ark, wondering what would happen next and where and how the ark would come to rest. As God showed him each stage, I'm sure Noah's faith in God was strengthened, and in the end, we see him worshipping his God and being given a mighty promise from God and a bright hope for his future. Sometimes we can feel uncertain about the direction of our lives, not knowing what is ahead, but we can be sure that God has a plan.

- *When we are not sure of what God is doing in our lives or of the way ahead, how do we react? Have you ever been in a situation like this? Talk about how it felt.*

- *What can we learn from Noah's reaction?*

Prayer Stop: Pray for those you know are finding it difficult to know what God is doing in their lives. Pray that their faith will be strengthened. Pray that we will remember God's promises to us when we are finding it hard to see the way ahead in our own lives or our family.

DAY 7

On the Way: Noah and his family came out of the ark and were scattered throughout the earth (Gen. 9:19). Today's reading tells us how this came about. God had already destroyed the earth by the flood because of man's sin. A few generations later, we see man rebelling against God's plan again, this time by building a tower, probably a ziggurat. These were religious buildings, 3–7 stories high, and looked a bit like a huge wedding cake.

READ GENESIS 11:1–9

> *In that way the* Lord *scattered them all over the world, and they stopped building the city. That is why the city was called Babel, because that is where the* Lord *confused the people with different languages* (v8–9a).

Checkpoint: Verse 4 tells us why man wanted to build this tower:

1. They wanted to reach the heavens.
2. They wanted to make a name for themselves.
3. They wanted to stay close together.

In making their plans, they had not given God His place. God acted by confusing their language so that they couldn't understand one another and therefore couldn't carry out their plans. Instead, they were spread all over the earth.

Sometimes we forget to ask God to show us His way when we make plans. We forget that on our own we cannot possibly reach God: it is God who reaches out to us. Sometimes we are very keen to make ourselves seem important in the things we do. Sometimes God has to remind us that He is the Mighty God, and His plans and ways are best.

- *Are there any plans you or your family are making just now? Perhaps you are looking for a church in which to worship together, looking for a new house, or planning a holiday. Discuss what you think is important when looking for God's will and plans for our lives.*
- *Discuss how you might know that plans you are making or things you are doing are not God's will.*

Prayer Stop: Pray for God to guide you so that you will know His will for you as a family. Pray for any specific plans you are making.

DAY 8

On the Way: The end of chapter 11 gives us the family tree of Noah's son, Shem. It leads us to Abram, who we will be studying this week. In verse 31, Terah, Abram's father, is traveling with Abram and the rest of his family. They are heading for Canaan. However, they don't make it there and settle in Haran instead.

MEMORY VERSE

"My thoughts are nothing like your thoughts," says the Lord. *"And my ways are far beyond anything you could imagine. For just as the heavens are higher than the earth, so my ways are higher than your ways and my thoughts higher thaan your thoughts."*

~ Isaiah 55:8–9

READ GENESIS 12:1–9

Then the Lord *appeared to Abram and said, "I will give this land to your descendants." And Abram built an altar there and dedicated it to the lord, who had appeared to him* (v7).

Checkpoint: Abram was told by God to leave his father's family and go where He would show him. However, Terah, his father, was traveling with him and they settled in Haran instead. The passage does not tell us why Terah was with him. Did Abram take him? Perhaps he decided to go with Abram when he heard he was leaving. We don't know, but the result is that Abram was hindered from fully obeying God's command. It can be the same today. Other people may think that they know God's will for our lives better than we do (or even better than God does sometimes). But we must seek God's will for our lives and fully obey it. It is wise to ask older Christians to pray with us and for us as we make these decisions. Once we know God's will, we should not let anyone or anything deter us from obeying. It is only once Terah dies that Abram sets out again on his journey to Canaan. When he arrives, God reminds him of the promise given to him, and Abram worships the Lord.

- *What things/people in our lives may hinder us from fully obeying God's will?*
- *Is there anything you have started in your life that you have been distracted from and need to get going again?*

Prayer Stop: Pray about the last discussion point. Pray for those you know who are looking for God's guidance in their lives right now. Mention some people by name if you can.

DAY 9

On the Way: Having reached the land that God was giving him, Abram experiences a test of his faith in God. There is a famine in that land. Abram has a choice; he can stay in the land and trust God to provide for his family, or he can head off to Egypt where there is plenty of food but is not where God wants him to be. He chooses to head to Egypt, where he gets into a terrible scrape with Pharaoh. (Gen. 12:10–20). He is banned from Egypt and journeys back to where God wanted him to be.

READ GENESIS 13:1–18

> *So Abram settled in the land of Canaan, and Lot moved his tents to a place near Sodom* (v12a).

Checkpoint: At the start of today's passage, we see Abram going back to where he had left off from God's will to head to Egypt. When we stray from God's will, it is important to go back to that point and ask God to forgive us and take us on from there. We need to recognize when we started to do our own thing. Having learned more about his faith in God, Abram then gives his nephew Lot the choice of where he would like to stay. Because they had become so wealthy, they would have to separate in order to support their flocks. Lot saw that the land toward the east looked richer and opted to go there. He settled toward Sodom, renowned for its evil. In chapter 14, we read of the mess this choice made for him and his family. Lot chose the land that looked good, but as we learned on day 3, sin usually does look good in the beginning. It is important that we choose the right way and not just what looks good. Remember, it was Abram who received God's blessing.

- *How do we find what God wants us to do?*
- *Abram's trip to Egypt taught him more about God and his faith. Talk about events in your life that have taught you more about God.*

Prayer Stop: Pray that we will not be tempted to disobey God just because something looks good. Pray that we will learn more about Him in every circumstance of our lives.

DAY 10

On the Way: Abram settled in Hebron and worshipped the Lord there. He returned to Sodom to rescue Lot from its destruction. He and his wife, Sarai had no children, but God promised him many descendants, and Abram believed God's promise. As time goes on and they still had no children, Sarai, suggested that he marry her servant. (That was the custom in those days.) Abram agreed to this and soon had a son named Ishmael when he was 86 years old. This caused problems in his family a few years later.

READ GENESIS 15:1–5; 17:1–8

> *I am . . . God Almighty. Serve me faithfully and live a blameless life. I will make a covenant with you, by which I will guarantee to give you countless descendants* (17:1b–2).

Checkpoint: At the beginning of chapter 17, Abram is 99 years old. Thirteen years have passed since God first spoke to him, and God appears to him again confirming His promise. He tells Abram, whose name He changed to Abraham, that his wife Sarai, now to be called Sarah, will have a son. The first time God gave His promise to Abram he had no problem believing it (Gen. 15:6). However, after waiting thirteen years, Abram seems to find it harder to believe. What was his response this time? (Gen. 17:17).

It is very hard to wait for things to happen when we know they are going to happen. (E.g., Christmas: Will I get the present I asked for?) Abram must have felt like this. He believed God but as the years passed, it became harder to wait and so when he saw a way to solve the problem himself he did. This led to lots of trouble for him.

- *Do we believe God's promises to us and then try to sort things out ourselves? Can you think of any circumstances as a family when you have had to wait for God to do something?*
- *Have you had the experience of trying to do things your own way instead of God's? How did this affect the outcome?*
- *What lessons can we learn from Abram's experience?*

Prayer Stop: Pray for patience to let God work out His purposes in your lives.

DAY 11

On the Way: In chapter 21, we read that Abraham and Sarah had a son at the very time God had promised him. He was called Isaac. As he grew, however, there was tension between him and Ishmael, the son Hagar had borne Abraham. This resulted in Hagar and Ishmael being sent away.

In our reading today, we take up the story some time later when Isaac had grown into a young man.

READ GENESIS 22:1–19

> *"God will provide a sheep for the burnt offering, my son," Abraham answered.*
> *And they both walked on together (v8).*

Checkpoint: Abraham's faith is tested by God in the hardest way imaginable. He was told to go on a three-day journey and sacrifice Isaac as an offering to the Lord. How do you think Abraham felt about this? What questions do you think he may have been thinking? In verse 3, we see his response. He got up and prepared to obey the Lord immediately. He did not question God or say, "But you said . . ." He had such great faith in God that he knew God would provide an answer. Hebrews 11:19 tells us that he reasoned God could raise the dead if He was asking Abraham to sacrifice his only son. His trust in God's promises did not waver.

- *Has God been asking you to do something that you feel is too hard? Perhaps He has been asking you to speak to a friend or neighbor about Him or to give up watching an inappropriate program on TV. Perhaps He has been asking your family to move to a new church or home or even school, but you feel it is too big a thing to do? Can you learn anything from Abraham's response?*
- *God provided a ram for the sacrifice in place of Isaac (Genesis 22:13). What does this picture speak of to you?*

(Note to parent: Discuss with the family the picture of God providing His Son Jesus as a sacrifice for our sins.)

Prayer Stop: Ask God for strength to obey Him in whatever He is asking you to do. Spend time thanking Him for sending Jesus to be our Savior. Pray for those you know who have not accepted Jesus as their Savior yet.

DAY 12

On the Way: After their experience on the mountain with God, Abraham and Isaac returned to the servants and stayed in Beersheba. In chapter 23, we read of Sarah's death and of Abraham buying a cave as a grave for his family. In chapter 24, we now meet with Abraham who is very old and thinking about the future of his son. He sends his servant to his hometown to find a wife for Isaac.

READ GENESIS 24:10–21

> *He [the Lord] will send his angel ahead of you and he will see to it that you find a wife there for my son (v7b).*

Checkpoint: Abraham was sending his chief servant back to his home country to find a wife for Isaac. Let's look at how the servant went about his task and see what we can learn from it. First of all, in verse 10 we see him getting ready to go, taking provisions from Abraham's livestock and gifts for the woman and her family. Then we see him praying, asking the Lord to guide and lead him to the woman which He had chosen for Isaac. We read about that prayer being answered in our reading today, and in verse 27 we see him thanking and worshipping the Lord for His answer.

It is important to remember that God will give us all we need to do the job He has for us. Before we start, we should pray and ask God to guide us. We need to prepare as much as we can for the job, just as the servant did. When we see God answering our prayers, let's remember to give Him the praise and glory.

- *How do you think the servant felt when he heard the woman say the exact words he had prayed about?*

- *Talk about an experience you or anyone you know has had of God answering your prayers specifically like this. How did it feel? Did you remember to thank Him for the answer?*

Prayer Stop: Think of some answers to prayer your family has had recently and take time to praise Him for these answers just now. Is there a task that you feel God is asking you to do? Take time to ask Him to guide you as you go ahead and do it for Him.

DAY 13

On the Way: Isaac and Rebecca marry, and Abraham marries a woman called Keturah after Sarah's death. He lives to be 175 years old! After his death, Isaac and Ishmael bury him with Sarah.

READ GENESIS 25:19–34

> *As the boys grew up, Esau became a skillful hunter. He was an outdoorsman,*
> *but Jacob had a quiet temperament, preferring to stay at home* (v27).

Checkpoint: Isaac and Rebekah's twin boys, Jacob and Esau, are born. Our key verse shows us that they grew up to be completely different from each other. Isn't it funny how brothers and sisters, even twins, can be so very different? All of us are unique: we like different things, are good at different things, and achieve different things. Sadly, sometimes this can bring about problems in the family as it did in Isaac's family (Gen. 25:28). However, if we as parents accept each of our children as unique gifts from God and teach them to love and respect their differences, our families will be blessed. After all, it is not by accident that we have been put together by our Creator.

The second half of our passage highlights the different characters of the two men. Esau reacted quickly to the smell of food and just wanted to eat it. Jacob saw this as an opportunity to gain the upper hand and devised a scheme to trick his brother. This caused major problems in the family, as we will see. It is never good to use our differences against each other.

- *Talk about the differences in your own family members. What is good about having so many different characteristics in one family?*

- *Be honest with each other and discuss if there are times you feel there is favoritism shown in your family. What steps as a family can you take to help make sure that each member is loved and accepted by both parents and siblings?*

Prayer Stop: Thank God for each member of your family. Think of two things unique to each person and say thanks to God for these. Pray that as a Christian family you will grow closer to each other as you grow closer to God.

DAY 14

On the Way: Isaac became very wealthy and was known and feared by the kings and rulers of the lands he lived near. Today's reading brings us to a point at the end of Isaac's life when he is old and frail and cannot see anymore. He calls Esau to prepare him a feast and bring it to him so that he may give him his blessing, as was the custom for the oldest son in those days. Rebekah overheard this plan and decided to take matters into her own hands so that Jacob would receive the blessing rather than Esau.

READ GENESIS 27:5–23

Then take the food to your father so he can eat it and bless you before he dies (v10).

Checkpoint: The lies and deceit we read of today is a result of the favoritism shown by Isaac and Rebekah. They both had their favorite son, and there was tension between Isaac and Rebekah, Jacob and his father, and Jacob and Esau. This does not make for a very happy family. It is important that as a Christian family we keep our relationships strong and completely honest and open with each other. Perhaps Rebekah panicked when she heard Isaac's plan since she knew it was God's plan for Jacob to be the leader (Gen. 25:23). So she decided to fix the problem herself. God does not need our help to bring about His plans. He uses us to achieve His purposes, that is certainly true, but He often works in ways that we can never understand. We must be willing to be used by God but allow Him to work in us and through us in whatever way He chooses. To do it our own way brings only tension and stress.

- *Have you ever had the experience of waiting for God to work out a plan and not knowing how it was possibly going to work?*
- *How does Isaiah 55:8–9 help us to understand this principle?*
- *Are there tensions in any of your family relationships that need to be brought into line with God's will?*

Prayer Stop: Pray that God would give you patience to wait for Him to work out His plans for you in His way. Pray that God would strengthen your family relationships and help you to be completely honest and open with each other.

DAY 15

On the Way: Just as Isaac had finished blessing Jacob, Esau returned from hunting. Having prepared the meal as his father had asked, Esau took it to him. Isaac realized he had been tricked and started to tremble. Esau was furious and pleaded with his father to bless him also. He was so angry that he vowed to murder Jacob after his father died. Rebekah heard of this plan and told Jacob to run away to her brother's home and stay with him. She told Isaac that he was going to find a wife. (More lies!) Jacob is on his way to Haran and stops for the night.

MEMORY VERSE

But God showed his great love for us by sending Christ to die for us while we were still sinners.
~ Romans 5:8

READ GENESIS 28:10–22

What an awesome place this is! It is none other than the house of God, the very gateway to heaven! (v17b).

Checkpoint: As Jacob settles down for a night's rest, God comes to speak with him in a dream. When we look at Jacob's life so far, full of lies and deceit, it is hard to imagine a holy God wanting to speak to him. He not only speaks to Jacob but also assures him that God will be with him to protect him and bless him. This is a picture of God's grace and mercy. Grace is God giving us the blessings we do not deserve. Mercy is God not punishing us for our sin in the way we deserve. We see Jacob's reaction in our key verse: "How awesome is this place."

God has shown us grace and mercy by sending His Son Jesus to die in our place and giving us the opportunity to have a relationship with Him through Jesus. Read this week's memory verse, Romans 5:8. It was while we were (like Jacob) living in our sin that Christ came and died for us.

- *Have you accepted God's gift of grace and mercy by asking Him into your life? If so, what is your reaction?*

- *In what ways does God speak to people today? Talk about any ways God has spoken to you.*

Prayer Stop: Thank God for His grace and mercy shown toward us and worship Him for it. Pray that you would hear clearly what God is saying to you as individuals and as a family.

DAY 16

On the Way: Jacob carried on with his journey after meeting with God and came to where his mother's family lived. He met Rachel at a well while she was giving her dad's sheep some water. She is the daughter of his mother's brother, Laban. Rachel runs to tell him of Jacob's arrival, and he brings Jacob to his home to live with them. Jacob works for Laban and falls in love with Rachel. He asks Laban for Rachel to be given to him as his wife in return for seven years work. Our reading today tells the story of the wedding. In chapter 30, we read of the birth of his first eleven sons and his daughter, Dinah.

The story of his family relationships is one that is full of jealousy, frustration, and stress.

READ GENESIS 29:16–30

"What have you done to me?" Jacob raged at Laban. "I worked seven years for Rachel! Why have you tricked me?" (v25b).

Checkpoint: Jacob does not seem to have grown much as a result of his experience with God, which we read of yesterday. He has not let it affect his relationships either in his work or at home. We need to let our experiences with God affect the way we live our lives at home and school or work.

Today's reading tells the story of Laban deceiving Jacob and giving him Leah instead of Rachel as his wife. Can you think of someone else who played a similar trick on a relative in one of our readings recently?

Jacob, who had deceived his father, experienced trickery and did not like it!

- *Read Galatians 6:7–9. What principle can we learn from Jacob's experience and from these verses?*

- *Discuss the things you have been learning from God's Word and how you feel they should be affecting your family and school/work relationships.*

Prayer Stop: Thank God for the lessons He is teaching you as a family or as individuals and pray for each other that you would put these into practice. Pray for your own family relationships and for other families you know, especially any whose relationships are strained at the moment.

DAY 17

On the Way: A few years later, after his children have been born, Jacob feels it is time to go back home. However, Laban knows that it is because of Jacob he has become so wealthy, and he persuades Jacob to stay. They agree what his wages will be, and Jacob settles down to work again for Laban. We take up the story today some six years later when Jacob's own flock has become large and healthy, and Laban's has become weaker.

READ GENESIS 31:1–9, 17–21

> *So Jacob took all his possessions with him and crossed the Euphrates River,*
> *heading for the hill country of Gilead* (v21).

Checkpoint: Jacob notices that relationships with his in-laws are changing. Both Laban and his sons seem to be full of jealousy for Jacob because his flocks were greater. The Lord told him it was time to move on; Rachel and Leah agreed. When God is leading us, we will find, like Jacob, that our circumstances will confirm what God's Word is saying to us. In the last chapter, we saw Jacob wanting to move but his circumstances did not work out accordingly. God's time had not yet come for him to go. We may feel convinced that God wants us to do something specific for Him. He will confirm it through His Word, through our circumstances, and through the confirmation of those close to us.

However, we must be careful to fully obey God's plans for us. Look at the way Jacob left Laban's land (Gen. 31:20). Do you think this was a godly way of going?

It is important that we not only fulfill God's plans but that we also do it in His way.

- *Think about how you are treating your family members. Is there anything in your relationships that needs sorted?*

- *Do you feel God is telling you to do something specific at the moment? What does His Word say? What about your circumstances and those close to you?*

Prayer Stop: Thank God for His perfect timing in our lives and pray for patience as you wait for His timing to work out. Pray for your family relationships that they would be conducted in a godly way and so bring glory to God.

DAY 18

On the Way: Having left Laban, Jacob heads toward his home country and sends messengers ahead of him to Esau. When they return, they tell him Esau is on his way to meet him. They don't mention how their meeting with Esau had gone, and so Jacob automatically assumes the worst and devises a plan in case Esau turns nasty. Then he prays! This is the first time we see him pray. That shows us that he is growing more dependent on God. Jacob carries on with his plan, and when everything is in place, he finds himself alone with God.

READ GENESIS 32:22–32

"I will not let you go unless you bless me" (v26b).

Checkpoint: Jacob was afraid of meeting Esau because of his past history with him. These issues had to be sorted while he was alone with God. We too may have things or people that we are afraid to face because of events in the past. We need to get alone with God to sort out these issues and ask His forgiveness first.

God could have simply overpowered Jacob immediately, but He wrestled the whole night with him, waiting for him to willingly surrender. In the end, God had to disable him so that Jacob might experience His blessing. God is patient with His children. He does not simply overpower us and make us do His will. He wants us to surrender willingly and so He has patience with us. Sometimes we can be very stubborn, and God takes action to make us stop and listen to Him so we can know His blessing.

- *Discuss some ways that God may make us stop and listen to him. Perhaps you or someone you know has had a particular experience you could share.*
- *Talk about some ways that you can "get alone with God" to find out how to sort difficult things you might be facing.*

Prayer Stop: Take time to thank and praise God for His patience with us. Ask God to show you if there are things in your lives right now with which you are struggling against Him. Be willing to give these things to Him and so receive His blessing fully in your lives.

DAY 19

On the Way: Jacob sets off on his journey and sees Esau coming toward him. He immediately starts planning and scheming, organizing his family so that Rachel and Joseph are at the back and least likely to come to harm if that was Esau's intent. He himself went on ahead.

READ GENESIS 33

> *God has been very gracious to me. I have more than enough* (v11b).

Checkpoint: Jacob is fearful and full of schemes to try to soften Esau's heart, but Esau just runs to hug his brother. Things have gone well for Esau, and he no longer seems to be thinking of murdering his brother. Jacob, however, has not forgotten the past and is fearful of their meeting. The things that happened all those years ago are still very fresh on Jacob's mind and influence his reactions now. When hurtful things happen in our families, we must move on from them and not let them affect the way we live our lives. We need to respect each other's differences and discuss the difficulties that arise between us. This will help us to forgive each other quickly and not be like Jacob.

Although Jacob seems to be the same as far as his scheming is concerned, he recognizes that it is because of God's grace that he has all he needs (Gen. 33:11b). Esau, on the other hand, does not seem to recognize God's grace in his life at all (Gen. 33:9b), but he is the one who seems to have moved on from the past. God works at different times and in different ways in all of our lives. Let us encourage one another to allow God to work in each of our lives and so become the people He wants us to be.

- *Are there issues in the past that are affecting your family? It may be as recently as yesterday or as far away as a year or more. Ask God to help these be resolved in His will.*
- *Discuss ways to help avoid bearing grudges against others.*

Prayer Stop: Thank God for all the differences in your family. Praise Him for each person and even for the things that you find difficult to cope with some-times! Pray that you will not hold grudges and that the past will not affect your relationship with each other or the Lord.

DAY 20

On the Way: At the end of chapter 33, we see even more deceit in Jacob's life. Will he ever learn? He told Esau he would join him in Seir, but instead he went to Succoth. This brought terrible problems to his family. In chapter 34, his sons take over the role of making important family decisions; Jacob does not take his responsibility as family leader. However, God is not finished with Jacob yet. It is amazing that after all the times Jacob has let God down, God still keeps His promise to him and keeps guiding him.

READ GENESIS 35:1–15

> *We are now going to Bethel, where I will build an altar to the God who answered my prayers when I was in distress. He has been with me wherever I have gone (v3).*

Checkpoint: In verse 1, God speaks to Jacob, and Jacob leads his family into God's will again. First, he tells them to get rid of the false gods they have gathered. He buries them as a sign that they are no longer part of their lives. Then he moves on with his journey to Bethel. It is important that the head of our families leads us in God's will. This can be a difficult task for them if we complain and make life difficult for them. Jacob's household seemed to be willing to follow his lead (Gen. 35:4), and this brought them to the place God wanted them to be.

- *Are there things in our lives that we need to get rid of like Jacob's family? Perhaps we have some belongings that are not right for us to have, need to change our TV-watching habits, or perhaps have a wrong attitude in our hearts.*
- *What things can we do to encourage the head of our family in their task of leading us in God's will? Talk with them about what they feel God wants you as a family to be involved in at the moment. If you are the head of the family, share what God has been putting on your heart with your family.*

Prayer Stop: Pray that God would show you the things in your life that He wants to change and that you would be willing to obey Him in this. Pray for the head of your family, that they will lead the family in God's will and that the family will be willing followers!

DAY 21

On the Way: Jacob and his family return to settle on his father's land. On the way, Rachel died while giving birth to Joseph's younger brother, Benjamin. Isaac also died after Jacob arrived home. Jacob stayed on in his father's land, and we take up the story when his son Joseph is seventeen.

READ GENESIS 37:1–11

Do you actually think you will reign over us? (v8b).

Checkpoint: We can sense family tensions already in this chapter. Jacob grew up in a family where favoritism caused tensions. You would think that he would have learned by the mistakes of his parents. Sadly not. He made the same mistake! Joseph was his favorite. This obviously caused problems within the family. Joseph had a hard time growing up because his brothers hated him so much. He didn't let this stop him from telling them his dreams. He almost seems to gloat while telling them that his sheaf of corn rose up above theirs and that the sun, moon, and stars bowed down to him. It seems as if he made things worse for himself by going on about it. You get the feeling that he was almost deliberately trying to annoy them. Do you ever do that? Sometimes it is wiser to say nothing and let things work out than to upset people by appearing to show off. When we are young, we often feel we must always prove that we are right. As we get a little older, we realize that sometimes it is better to stay quiet and keep our thoughts to ourselves as we see Jacob doing in verse 11.

- *Parents sometimes make the same mistakes as their own parents, even when they say they won't! Perhaps you need to give this some thought. Our parents also did lots of things right! What do you do in your family because your parents did it with you? What do the children think of this?*

- *Often in families, some members deliberately provoke each other. Discuss ways that you can keep this from happening in your own family.*

Prayer Stop: Pray that as a family you will follow God's leading. Pray for your family unit that God will show you how to love and support each other and not deliberately wind each other up.

DAY 22

On the Way: Jacob's older sons were grazing their flock, and Joseph was sent to see how they were getting on. Angry and jealous of their father's favorite, they were not pleased to see Joseph and made plans to kill him. The oldest brother, Reuben, tried to encourage them not to kill Joseph but to put him in a pit; he was planning to rescue him secretly later.

MEMORY VERSE

May the words of my mouth and the meditation of my heart be pleasing to you, O lord, my rock and my redeemer.

~ Psalm 19:14

READ GENESIS 37:23–36

Joseph's brothers pulled him out of the cistern and sold him . . . for twenty pieces of silver (v28b).

Checkpoint: As we read the way the brothers chat together, we can see what leads to family tension and destruction. Reuben tries to rescue Joseph and suggests an action that would seem to be punishing Joseph, but secretly he intended to rescue him later. He is unable to be completely honest with his brothers. Verses 21–23 reveal deceit—cold, hardhearted treatment of their father. Verses 26–29 show selfishness and greed in the hearts of the brothers. Judah wants to make money from their underhanded act, while Reuben appears again and is immediately concerned, not for Joseph, but for what his father would say to him. They pretend to comfort their father, all the while knowing exactly what had become of Joseph. Dishonesty, selfishness, greed, deceit, and hypocrisy—these don't lead to a very happy family.

- *What character traits do the conversations in your family show? (They can be positive ones!) Where do you think all these horrible feelings started in Jacob's family? How can the memory verse help us guard against these things in our own family?*
- *What happens in Jacob's family as a result of jealousy and anger not being worked out properly? What does James 1:20 tell us about anger? We will all be angry at some point with each other. How can we be sure that this will not create lasting problems in our family?*

Prayer Stop: Make this week's memory verse your prayer for your family. List the positive character traits you see in your family and take time to thank God for them today.

DAY 23

On the Way: Joseph is taken to Egypt and sold as a slave to the captain of the king's guard, Potiphar. He was a very powerful man in Egypt. Joseph worked hard, and Potiphar noticed he was to be trusted and so gave him more and more responsibility over all that he owned.

READ GENESIS 39:6–23

> *With Joseph there, he didn't worry about a thing—except what kind of food to eat!* (v6b).

Checkpoint: Joseph devoted himself to serving God in this difficult situation. He could have become bitter and angry; he had seen that happen a lot in his family. Instead, he chose to honor God by his reaction. How do we react in difficult situations? We do have a choice, and we should choose to honor God. Joseph was promoted as a result of his wise reaction. However, it was not all easy for him. He was working with people who did not have the same high standards in their lives. His boss's wife tried to trap him. Joseph knew that this was not what God wanted and so refused to be close to her. Again, he chose to honor God by his reaction. As a result of this, the woman told lies that landed him in prison. Joseph did not even try to defend himself; instead, he turned his attention to living for God in the prison. When life seems unfair to us, the first thing many of us do is complain. Joseph teaches us that we have a choice in how we react.

- *How do you react to being treated unfairly? What can we learn from Joseph about our attitude and reaction to these situations and our attitude to our work?*

- *The people we live and work among have different standards for their lives just as it was in Joseph's day. What difficulties and temptations have you faced because of this? What can we learn from Joseph about our reaction and attitude to those situations?*

Prayer Stop: Pray that you will react correctly when you are treated unfairly. Pray that God will give you the strength to stand up for His standards. Pray for Christians in other countries who are being put in prisons and treated unfairly just because they follow Jesus.

DAY 24

On the Way: In prison, Joseph was given more responsibilities because he could be trusted. One night Pharaoh's cupbearer and baker, both prisoners, had dreams. With God's help, Joseph told them the meaning of those dreams. The cupbearer was to be forgiven and given his job back, but the baker was to be hanged. Within three days, those foreseen events occurred. As the cupbearer leaves to return to his job, Joseph asks him to mention him to Pharaoh. It's the first time we see Joseph trying to sort out his own circumstances instead of trusting God. When we are in tough circumstances, it is tempting to try to sort things out ourselves. Joseph had to learn patience. It was not until two years later that the cupbearer actually did remember him. This was because Pharaoh had dreams that his wise men couldn't interpret. Joseph was brought before Pharaoh and with God's help told him a famine was coming. Joseph is then promoted to second in command in Egypt.

READ GENESIS 41:41-57

Pharaoh said to Joseph, "I hereby put you in charge of the entire land of Egypt" (v41).

Checkpoint: Joseph is given a position of great power in Egypt. He started out as a slave with nothing. This did not affect his attitude to how he carried out his responsibilities; he worked hard and served God even when he was treated unfairly. This was all in God's plan for him. He did not know that thirteen years after arriving as a slave in Egypt, he would be second in command to Pharaoh. He was given an Egyptian name and wife, but he did not forget God's hand in his life. Sometimes it is easier to remember God when things are difficult. We forget Him when things are easy. Let's learn from Joseph to honor God no matter what our situation.

- *Look up 1 Samuel 2:30 and Isaiah 55:8-9. Is there any situation in your life that is hard to understand just now? How do these verses help us?*
- *Have you ever been tempted to feel sorry for yourself and try to sort out your own situation?*

Prayer Stop: Pray that in every situation we will remember to give God glory in our lives. Pray this too for Christians you know in high positions.

DAY 25

On the Way: The famine spread throughout the world and when Jacob heard that Egypt had food, he sent his sons to buy some. Joseph recognized them immediately, but before he identified himself, he tested them to see if their attitudes had changed. He kept Simeon prisoner and returned their money to their sacks, telling them not to return unless they brought Benjamin with them. On discovering the money, they were terrified and felt God was judging them for what they had done to Joseph previously. They knew they had done wrong. Jacob would not allow them to return with Benjamin initially, but eventually relented and sent them back with him to get food. They brought gifts for Joseph and the money that had been returned to them. They were taken to Joseph's house and given a feast there. Joseph tested their attitude to Benjamin. Would they abandon him as they had done to Joseph? He had his silver cup put in Benjamin's sack, and when they discovered that, they were sick with worry. They all returned to Joseph, and Judah, who had been the ringleader in selling Joseph, offered to take Benjamin's place. Joseph could wait no longer: he let them know who he was.

READ GENESIS 45:1–10

It was God who sent me here ahead of you to preserve your lives (v5b).

Checkpoint: The brothers, having admitted they were wrong and shown they had changed their ways, were now facing Joseph, whom they had intended to harm. Joseph is quick to point out that it was God who had been in control of his life all along. It was God who had placed him there in order that their lives might be preserved. God blessed Joseph so that others could be blessed through him. Joseph was ready and willing to forgive his brothers and so a great reunion took place. What do you think would have happened if Joseph decided to treat them the same way they treated him?

- *When others do wrong to us how do we react? Do we see where God can use it for good?*
- *What similarities can you see between the way Joseph treated his brothers and the way God treats us?*

Prayer Stop: Pray that we will always be willing to forgive those who do wrong to us. Thank God for His mercy to us.

DAY 26

On the Way: Pharaoh heard Joseph's news and instructed him to bring his whole family to live in Egypt. Can you imagine their journey home? You can read about Joseph's reunion with Jacob in Genesis 46:29–30. Joseph introduced his family to Pharaoh. They were shepherds, regarded as the lowest among men in Egypt, but Joseph did not hold this back from Pharaoh. He was honest about his family, and Pharaoh accepted them and gave them the best of the land. The family settled in Goshen and cared for their flocks there. Joseph continued to rule in Egypt. Today we move seventeen years ahead. Jacob is reaching the end of his life, and Joseph brings his sons to visit him.

READ GENESIS 48:1–11

But now God has let me see your children, too! (v11b).

Checkpoint: When Joseph brings his sons to visit Jacob, he tells them about both the times when God had blessed him and the low points. He is amazed that God allowed him to see Joseph again and also his grandchildren. The boys have been brought up in a very privileged family: the second most powerful family in Egypt. They were raised as princes and yet Joseph brings them to see their grandfather who is a shepherd and therefore not respected in Egypt. This does not matter to Joseph. He honors and respects Jacob because Jacob is his father; Joseph has not let his position stand in the way of family relationships.

We can learn so much from our grandparents. They have so much experience, and we should give them the respect due to them. Even though Joseph honored God himself and would have shared this with his sons, he still brought them to his own father to let them spend time with him and receive the blessing only he could give them.

- *Are there any places where you would be embarrassed to introduce your family? Why? Think about how Joseph dealt with his family who were very different to those he lived among. What can we learn?*
- *Talk about the things you have already learned from your grandparents both about life in general and spiritually.*

Prayer Stop: Pray that your family members will honor and respect each other. Pray for your grandparents. Thank God for them. Remember especially anyone you know whose grandparents have died.

DAY 27

On the Way: After Jacob had blessed Joseph's sons, he called for his other sons and blessed each of them appropriately. He instructed them to bury him in Canaan not Egypt. When Jacob had finalised these things, he died and was mourned as someone of great esteem in Egypt. After this mourning was over Joseph, his brothers, and a whole company of Egyptian officials went to Canaan to bury Jacob as they had vowed.

READ GENESIS 50:15–26

> *You intended to harm me, but God intended it all for good. He brought me to this position so I could save the lives of many people (v20).*

Checkpoint: After Jacob had been buried, the brothers start to think that Joseph might take revenge on them now. So they devised a plan (here they go again!). They sent him a message saying that Jacob had instructed that they ask him to forgive them for what they had done to him. Why do you think Joseph wept when he heard this?

If Jacob had been worried about this, he would have told Joseph before he died. The brothers do not see that Joseph had already forgiven them. They still have a guilty conscience about what they did. This is so like us sometimes. We ask God to forgive us, but we do not accept His forgiveness. We keep worrying about what we have done and find it hard to forgive ourselves.

It always seems easier to deal with tricky situations if we ask someone to "test the water" first. If there is a good response, it is easier for us to face those we have offended. However, what do we do if there is not a good response? Does this mean that we should not ask them to forgive us? It is best to be completely honest and remember to honor God with our reactions.

- *How should we react if we have done wrong to someone?*
- *Have you been in a situation where you have had to ask someone to forgive you and you didn't know how he or she would react? How did you feel?*

Prayer Stop: Pray that God would give us courage to ask others to forgive us when we hurt them. Pray that God would help us to forgive ourselves and to accept His and others' forgiveness.

EXODUS

This book covers the time in Israel's history when God brings His children out of Egypt and starts them on the journey back to the land He had promised them.

DAY 28

On the Way: After Joseph and his brothers died, the Israelites became so numerous that they seemed to be taking over the land! The king who had honored Joseph also died, and the new king did not know who Joseph was. So he planned to get rid of those people who seemed to be taking over his land. He instructed the nurses who attended the birth of the babies to kill any boys that were born. However, the nurses feared God more than Pharaoh and let the boys live. His next plan was to have baby boys thrown into the Nile.

READ EXODUS 2:1–10

So the girl went and called the baby's mother (v8b).

Checkpoint: Today we read of a couple who had a baby boy. His mother knew he was no ordinary child and hid him for three months. She took time to think about the best thing to do. This boy's mother risked everything for three months in order to work out the best way forward. In the end, she did obey the law by placing her son in the river, but in a waterproofed basket. The family was godly and would have walked with God in their daily lives. I have no doubt that they would have spent some time during the three months asking God for wisdom in what to do with their son.

So often, when we are faced with difficult decisions we panic and make wrong choices. Yet we have a God who wants us to come and ask Him for wisdom. Sometimes this takes time and does not work out as quickly as we would like, but it is important to wait for God's timing in our decision making.

- *Discuss a time when you had to make a difficult decision and didn't know what to do.*
- *How do you think Moses' mother reacted when she was asked by the princess to look after her own child?*
- *How can Ephesians 3:20–21 guide us in how we deal with and react to difficult decisions?*

Prayer Stop: Pray about difficult decisions you or your family have to make at the moment. Ask God for wisdom and patience to deal with the situation according to His plan. Pray about missionaries who have to make difficult decisions. Pray for any you know personally.

DAY 29

On the Way: Moses grew up in the palace and was educated by the Egyptians. When he was forty, he went to his own people and killed an Egyptian he saw fighting with an Israelite. The next day, seeing two Israelites fighting, he tried to stop them. They asked if he was going to kill them as he had the Egyptian. When Pharaoh heard, he tried to kill Moses, but Moses ran away to Midian. He stayed with the family of a priest there and married one of the priest's daughters. A long time later while he was in the desert with his father-in-law's flock, he noticed a bush on fire. The bush was not burning up, and so he went to investigate. It was then that God spoke to him from the bush and called him to go back to Egypt to set His people free. Moses had a few questions for God.

READ EXODUS 4:1–17

Now go! I will be with you as you speak, and will instruct you in what to say (v12).

Checkpoint: God gave Moses clear instructions and some really convincing signs to prove to him and the Israelites that it was God who had sent him. Moses tried several excuses to avoid this mission. God promised to teach him what to say, but in the end, God sent Moses' brother Aaron with him. Moses' hesitation to do God's will angered God. God had spent a long time getting Moses ready for his task and was not going to let his insecurity put him off. After all God had told him and shown him, Moses still did not seem to be brave enough to serve God in this way. God is patient with His children, but there comes a time when He requires us to simply obey Him. This was what He was asking Moses to do. He had explained his task fully and encouraged him, and still Moses tried to get out of it.

- *What excuses do we make to get out of doing what we know God wants us to do?*
- *Why do you think Moses had all these questions for God? Was he wrong to ask?*
- *Is there anything you have been putting off doing for God?*

Prayer Stop: Thank God that He prepares us for His tasks and that He will not leave us to do it alone.

DAY 30

On the Way: After receiving God's message, Moses left to return to Egypt with his family. He met his brother Aaron in the desert and having told him all that God had planned they went together to the Israelite elders as God had commanded Moses. Aaron spoke to them and performed the signs God had given them. When the elders heard that God was concerned for them, they worshipped Him and believed what they had been told. They then took God's message to Pharaoh but he did not want to let the people leave their work.

READ EXODUS 5:6–23

Why have you brought all this trouble on your own people, Lord? (v22b).

Checkpoint: Encouraged by the positive response from their own people, Moses and Aaron set off to see Pharaoh. He was not so positive. But God had told Moses that this would happen (Exod. 4:21), so it was no great surprise. They did not expect Pharaoh to work the Israelites even harder though, and this made them grumble against Moses. How quickly they had changed from wanting Moses and Aaron to lead them, to moaning at them when the going got tough. Sometimes we can be a bit like that with the leaders in our churches. We are happy when things are going well, but if things don't go the way we like, we quickly start to complain.

They weren't prepared for extra trouble and neither was Moses. God had told him to go to Egypt to rescue the people from slavery. He had told Moses that He would harden Pharaoh's heart and that Moses would have a tough time with Pharaoh, but God had not mentioned having a tough time with his own people!

- *Why do you think God didn't tell Moses this? How can not knowing every detail of God's plan strengthen our faith?*

- *Are there leaders you know of who are having a difficult time doing what God has called them to do? Think of two things that you can do this week to encourage them, such as sending them a card to let them know you are praying for them.*

- *Is there anything in your attitude toward your church leaders that you might need to change?*

Prayer Stop: Pray for your church leaders by name: ask God to encourage them. Pray that your church will actively encourage and respect the leaders God has given you.

DAY 31

On the Way: The Israelites' attitude discouraged Moses. So he asked the Lord, "Why?" It is natural to ask this when things don't go as we planned. However, God does not always give us the answer to our question. Instead of answering Moses, He reminds him of the past: of how God had kept the promises that brought the Israelites to this point in their history (Exod. 6:2–4). He knows what is going on in the present. He has heard the Israelites groaning (Exod. 6:5), and He reminds Moses of the promises for their future (Exod. 6:6-8). Moses was encouraged by this and reported it to the Israelites. They were so fed up they did not want to listen. Moses then went back to God.

READ EXODUS 6:28–7:7

When I raise my powerful hand and bring out the Israelites, the Egyptians will know that I am the Lord (7:5).

Checkpoint: Moses' confidence had been shaken. Things had not gone according to plan, and now the people were complaining to him. He immediately turned to talk to God about it, and when they still would not listen to him, he goes back to speak to God. Having reminded Moses of His promises the first time around, He now reminds him of the job he had to do. This time we see Moses and Aaron do exactly what God commanded (Exod. 6:6). Moses had not managed to rally the people, so he fixed his eyes on the Lord and continued to talk with Him and obey His commands personally.

- *Why do you think Moses' confidence was shaken after meeting Pharaoh the first time? In what or whom do you think Moses placed his confidence?*

- *In what ways do you think it may have been more difficult for Moses to return to Pharaoh again? What do you think made him able to obey God this time? Read Hebrews 11:24–28 to help answer this.*

- *What things do people put their confidence in today? In what do you have most confidence?*

Prayer Stop: Pray that you will learn to have faith in God even when the going gets tough. Pray for those you know who are discouraged at the moment. Pray that they will fix their eyes on Jesus and have confidence in Him.

DAY 32

On the Way: When Pharaoh refused to set the people free, Aaron performed the signs God had given him. Pharaoh's wise men were also able to turn their staffs into snakes. When Aaron's staff ate the others, Pharaoh was still unmoved and would not let them go. This was the beginning of the plagues sent by God to show His mighty power to the Egyptians. First, their water was turned to blood, and then they were invaded by frogs, followed by a plague of gnats and then flies. The animals and people were affected next when they broke out in boils. Locusts then swarmed in to destroy all Egypt's crops, followed by solid darkness for three days. Pharaoh's magicians turned water to blood and conjured up frogs, but after that, they could not keep up and imitate God's plagues. Each time Pharaoh said the people could go, but then his heart was hardened. The last plague, after which Pharaoh would let the people go, would affect every household in Egypt, from the palace to the slaves. God would pass through Egypt and kill the firstborn of every household. God gave instructions on how the Israelites were to be protected.

READ EXODUS 12:1–14

> *But the blood . . . will serve as a sign . . . When I see the blood, I will pass over*
> *you* (v13a).

Checkpoint: The story of the plagues gives us a picture of God's great patience. He will try again and again to turn His people's hearts to Himself. After nine opportunities, Pharaoh's heart is still against God; therefore, God will bring a final judgment on Egypt. He does provide a way out for His people. It is by obeying these instructions that the Israelites will be saved from death when the angel passes over Egypt. It is only by sacrificing a lamb that the Israelites will be saved.

- *In what way does this mirror what Jesus has done for us?*
- *In verse 14, God instructs the people to remember this through the generations. What are the similarities within Luke 22:19?*
- *Why is it important to remember what God had done for us?*

Prayer Stop: Take time to remember the sacrifice Jesus made for us and thank Him for the gift of salvation. Pray for those you know whose hearts are hard against God.

Practical Application: Perhaps you would like to spend time as a family, celebrating communion together.

DAY 33

On the Way: The Israelites obeyed the Lord's instructions and made preparations to leave. At midnight, the Lord struck down the firstborn of all Egyptian families and animals. Then Pharaoh sent for Moses to send the people away. The Egyptians gave them lots of goods and wealth to take with them. God gave them instructions so that they would remember His rescue regularly and be able to tell their children about God too. He led them out of Egypt; He gave them clear direction (by cloud and fire) but He did not lead them in the most direct route. After the Israelites left, Pharaoh changed his mind and chased the people. When they saw the Egyptians, the people were terrified and moaned to Moses.

READ EXODUS 14:13-28

> *The LORD himself will fight for you. Just stay calm* (v14).

Checkpoint: God often leads us in ways that don't make sense to us. Sometimes we have problems that seem too big and we cannot see an answer. Like the Israelites in today's reading, we start panicking and complaining. Verse 14 reminds us that God is in control. We need to trust Him to show us the way ahead. It is easy to get bogged down with our problems but in verse 15, God tells the people to move on. Stop focusing on the problem and get on with moving toward the answer! We often have to take the first step in faith and obedience to God. Moses had to stretch out his hand over the sea, and God took it from there! God did not expect Moses to part the sea. He required only that Moses obey Him by taking the first step. God does not expect us to do the impossible either. We need only to take the first step in obedience to God, and He will do the impossible.

- *Why did the Israelites have to face the Red Sea experience? (Exodus 14:18, 25)*
- *What lessons do you think they learned through it? (see also Exodus 14:31)*
- *Are you facing something that seems impossible at the moment? What lessons can you learn from today's reading?*

Prayer Stop: Spend time worshipping God for the fact that His ways are so much greater than we can ever understand. Pray for guidance and wisdom to get through the tough things you are facing just now.

DAY 34

On the Way: The Israelites had seen God rescue them in a truly amazing way. Can you imagine what it would have looked like to see the ocean divide in two like that? What words would you use to describe God and how would you feel about Him after He had shown His power like that? This made them turn to God in a great song of praise. The first half tells what God did, how He rescued them. We read the second half in our reading today.

MEMORY VERSE

With your unfailing love you lead the people you have redeemed. In your might, you guide them to your sacred home.

~ Exodus 15:13

READ EXODUS 15:9–18

Checkpoint: This whole praise song is centered on God. What He has done for them (Exodus 15:1–10), what He is, and what He will do (Exodus 15:11–18). The people sing of God's power and unfailing love in all He does. In verse 13, they declare that they trust Him to lead them into the special place He has for them. After their amazing rescue, it is no wonder they are so happy and full of praise for Him. It is important to remember to praise God when He rescues us or leads us through a difficult problem. So often we forget. When you sing a praise song, think about the words you are singing. It is easy to remember a happy tune and forget the words, but it is important to remember the words we sing to God. In doing this, we give Him glory, which is our aim as His children.

- *How do we react when we see God work in a miraculous way in our lives?*
- *Share some amazing things God has done for you. Has He rescued you from anything? (The most important thing He has done is send Jesus to rescue us from sin.)*

Prayer Stop: Praise God specifically for some things He has done in your lives as a family or as individuals.

Practical Application: Choose one of your favorite praise songs and sing/read it together. Individually or together, try to write a song/poem praising God for what He has done in your life. Try to do this over the next week.

DAY 35

On the Way: It does not take long for the people to start moaning after being so full of praise to God! A little bit of hunger and they grumble and wish they were back in slavery in Egypt! However, God does not hold this against them and miraculously provides meat and bread for them in the form of quail and manna. He gives them specific instructions for gathering food. Each person had as much as they needed. You would think that this would teach the Israelites to trust God, but look what happens in the reading today.

READ EXODUS 17:1–7

Then Moses cried out to the LORD, "What should I to do with these people?" (v4a).

Checkpoint: My son once described someone as a "moan-a-lot." I think this is a good way to describe the Israelites at the moment. They have so much to thank God for, and yet they still find something to moan about.

Sometimes we can be a bit like that. We come up against a little problem in our lives, we think God has forgotten about us, and we moan! I'm sure if the Israelites stopped to think what God had done for them already instead of worrying about being a little hungry or thirsty, they would have realized God would not let them down. They would realize they needed to trust Him and see what He would do. God sometimes allows hard times in our lives to teach us to trust Him more and to help us grow closer to Him.

- *Is there something in your life at the moment that you are moaning about because you are not getting things as you want them? Stop and think of all the good things God has done for you in the past. Put your trust in Him to work things out for you in His way.*
- *Talk about things God has provided for you in a miraculous way, either as individuals or as a family.*

Prayer Stop: Take time to think if there is anything you are moaning to God about just now and ask His forgiveness. Praise Him for the things He has provided in the past and ask for help to trust Him now.

DAY 36

On the Way: Soon another test came along for the Israelites. The Amalekites started a war with them. Moses ordered Joshua to choose some men to go and fight, while Moses would stand at the top of the hill and pray with his arms stretched out to God. As long as he held up his hands, the Israelites would be winning, but if he lowered his hands, the Amalekites would start to win. So Aaron and Hur helped him to keep his hands up until the battle was won by the Israelites. Moses praying for the people was an important part of his leading them. In today's reading, we see another important job he did as leader.

READ EXODUS 18:13–24

They will help you carry the load, making the task easier for you (v22b).

Checkpoint: Moses was trying to help everyone on his own. This was far too much for him to do and his father-in-law noticed this and gave advice. Moses wisely listened and looked for others to help in the job of leading the people. Sometimes we can think no one else is good enough to help us, but that is not God's idea. He put us in families and also in church families that we might help each other. It is important in our churches that we do our bit to serve God and not leave the jobs to others. If we do nothing, someone else will be doing extra. As we saw in today's reading, that is not good for anyone.

- *Think about the people in your church. Is there someone who seems to be too busy? Is there anything you could do to help?*

- *Think of the things you are involved in. Is there anything you could perhaps ask someone else to help you with?*

- *Why is it helpful to share jobs in a church setting?*

Prayer Stop: Pray for your church leaders that others will be willing to help in the church. Pray that God will show you the correct things to be involved in and be willing to give anything else up for someone else to do.

DAY 37

On the Way: The Israelites travel on and come to the Desert of Sinai where they set up camp. Moses climbs the mountain where God speaks with him and again reminds him of the promises He made to the Israelites. Moses reminds the people of this and they vow to be obedient to God. It is after this that God gives Moses what we know as The Ten Commandments, and we will read those today.

MEMORIZE THE TEN COMMANDMENTS
OVER THE NEXT FEW DAYS

READ EXODUS 20:1–21

> *"Don't be afraid," Moses answered them, "for God has come in this way to test you, and so that your fear of him will keep you from sinning" (v20).*

Checkpoint: When the people saw the power of God as He met with Moses on the mountain they were frightened. (I think I would have been too!) They realized how holy God was and that they were so sinful they could not meet Him face to face. They asked Moses to speak with God for them. We call this being a mediator: someone who can speak on our behalf. Moses spoke with God for the Israelites and gave them God's message.

Moses reminded the people that God did not want them simply to be terrified of His power, which they saw that day. He wanted them to know how powerful He was and so remind them to keep His laws and not sin. God wants us to remember His power also, to know that we can trust Him and that we should fear Him and be obedient to Him. He is the same God today as He was in the days of Moses—a holy and powerful God.

- *Moses came to God on behalf of the Israelites. Who comes to God on our behalf? Moses is a picture of how Jesus stands before God on our behalf.*
- *What does it mean for us to fear God?*
- *What should our behavior be like if we truly do fear God?*

Prayer Stop: Praise God that He has given us a way to come to Him through Jesus. Pray for those you know who do not know Jesus that they will come to God through Him. Pray for each other that you would learn to truly fear God.

DAY 38

On the Way: Moses is given much more than just the Ten Commandments while he is on the mountain with God. God gives him laws concerning every area of life. Concerning property, relationships, how to treat servants and foreigners, laws for being fair to others and many more things. He also gives them instructions about the Sabbath and festivals they should celebrate every year. God was interested in every area of their life. After Moses had told the people all these things, he spent time with the priests and elders worshipping God. God called him up to the mountain again. This time he was there for forty days and nights. God gave him special instructions concerning building a place of worship.

READ EXODUS 25:1-8

Have the people of Israel build me a holy sanctuary so I can live among them (v8).

Checkpoint: God wanted His children to have a place where they could focus specifically on Him as they travelled, so He gave Moses instructions on how to build what was known as the Tabernacle (a portable church)! God was so interested in every detail of this right down to the curtain hooks (Exod. 26:32). The people were to provide the materials to build this by giving offerings to God. God is still interested in every area of our lives. He wants us to be part of a church family, which helps us focus on Him and become more like Him. It is right that we look after the church building that we are part of. To do that, we need to be willing to give some of what God has given us.

- *Talk about your giving as a family. Parents may explain what principles are used to give to the church and God's work. Do you feel this needs to be revised?*

- *Not everyone has much money to give. In what other ways can you help look after the church building?*

Prayer Stop: Praise God that He is interested in every area of our lives. Pray that God will show you what He wants you to do to look after your church building and be ready to do it.

DAY 39

On the Way: On the mountain God gave Moses tablets of stone with the Law and commandments written on them. There was so much detail in what God had told Moses that I'm sure he was glad to have it written down to avoid missing anything God had said. It is a good idea to write down what we feel God saying to us then we can easily look back to see if we have obeyed God fully and remember what He has done for us.

In today's reading, we see that God is not only interested in the way we live but also that He picks out jobs especially for us to do.

READ EXODUS 31:1–11

> *I have filled him with the spirit of God, giving him great wisdom, ability, and expertise in all kinds of crafts* (v3).

Checkpoint: God not only had plans for how to build His place of worship, but He had also picked and prepared certain people to do it. He had picked Bezalel and Oholiab and had given them the skills they needed to do the job. I'm sure they didn't suddenly become good at these things. They would have grown up being taught them and worked hard at learning them. Now they were ready to be used by God in a special way.

We can be sure that God has picked us and is preparing us for a specific job too. We may not understand why our parents keep nagging us to practice that instrument or insist we learn to cook a meal or anything like that. It may be that God is preparing us to do a special task for Him. So work hard at increasing the skills you have the opportunity to learn just now and let God use you for His special purposes.

- *What skills do you have that you may need to work at now so that you can be ready to use them when God wants you?*

- *Thinking about God using our skills. What should our attitude be to learning and keeping those skills?*

Prayer Stop: Pray that God would help you to be willing to work hard at developing the skills He wants you to have. Pray that you would be willing to use those skills for Him when the time comes.

DAY 40

On the Way: The people became impatient waiting for Moses to come down the mountain. They began grumbling again and wanted to worship something they could see, something to which they could feel a connection. I'm sure they saw the cloud on the mountain that Moses disappeared into, but they didn't know what was going on in there and didn't feel it was anything to do with them. They asked their high priest to make them a god they could see. Aaron went ahead with their plan. He carved a calf for them from gold they gave him. He then realized he was wrong and tried to make it look better by arranging a feast to God in front of the calf. Moses' reaction was very dramatic when he came down from the mountain!

READ EXODUS 32:19–26

What did these people do to you to make you bring such terrible sin upon them? (v21b).

Checkpoint: Aaron was the spiritual leader of these people, and he let them make plans against God. What was worse was when Moses asked him what had happened; he blamed the people and lied about his involvement in it. Moses realized that Aaron had failed in his responsibility as priest of the people. It is important to know that even godly leaders get it wrong sometimes and need to be reminded of God's will. We should be ready to encourage our leaders to stand firm in obeying God and not make their job harder than it is. When mistakes are made and they are truly sorry for them, we should be ready to forgive them. Aaron was quick to blame the people for what he did wrong. Often we blame someone else for our sin, but we must learn to take responsibility for what we do wrong and be ready to make it right.

- *Why was Moses so angry with Aaron?*
- *In verse 19, the tablets of the Law are broken. How does this describe what the Israelites were doing? (By worshipping another god, they had broken the whole Law of God.)*
- *It is hard to admit when we are wrong. How does it feel when you are in this situation?*

Prayer Stop: Ask God to help you to admit when you are wrong and to avoid blaming others. Pray that God would help your leaders do what God wants them to do.

DAY 41

On the Way: The Lord was angry at the Israelites. He told Moses that He would no longer go with these people. However, Moses knew that unless the Lord went with them there was no use in going anywhere. So he pleaded with God to forgive them. At this, the people wept and demonstrated that they were truly sorry. Moses spent some time worshipping God and asking Him to guide them as a nation again. God instructed him to carve out more stones like the ones he broke and climb back up the mountain; there he met with God again for forty days and nights. God wrote the Law again on the tablets of stone, and Moses went back down the mountain.

READ EXODUS 34:29–35

And the people of Israel would see the radiant glow of his face (v35a).

Checkpoint: Since the golden calf event, Moses has spent a lot of time praying and asking God for help with these difficult and stubborn people. He feels as if God has not given him any help with his task. He asks God to assure him that he is doing the right thing. God reassures him and encourages him to carry on. Sometimes doing God's will is difficult, and other people make it difficult for us too. Like Moses, we can keep going to God and telling Him how we feel and how difficult we find it. God will give us help as He did with Moses, even if it is telling us to keep on going! In today's reading, Moses has just spent forty days and nights with God on the mountain. His face was shining. It was obvious to all that he had a special experience with God. Now he shares his experience with them. When we have been in God's presence, it should affect our lives. People should notice the difference in us.

- *Talk about a time when you have found it hard to do God's will. Was it because others were making it difficult? How did you deal with it?*

- *What difference does spending time with God make in your life? How does it affect others?*

Prayer Stop: Pray for anyone you know who is finding it hard to obey God right now. Pray that others will be able to see the difference God has made in your life.

LEVITICUS

The third book in the Old Testament focuses on the God's Law given to Moses. It lists the things that the people are required to do to worship at the Tabernacle and also how the priests were to live their lives before God and others. The book covers every area of life, emphasising God's holiness. We will look only at a few areas in our devotions but you may want to read some more on your own.

DAY 42

On the Way: In Exodus, we saw Moses spending a lot of time with God in the "Tent of meeting." In Leviticus, the things God instructed Moses about are written down. The instructions were mainly about the offerings and sacrifices required by God to pay for the sin in peoples' lives. Offerings were to be offered in thankfulness to God as well.

READ LEVITICUS 6:1–7

> *Through this process, the priest will purify you before the L*ORD*, making you right with him, and you will be forgiven for any of these sins you have committed* (v7).

Checkpoint: At the start of this book, God gives Moses very clear instructions on how offerings and sacrifices were to be made. Sin offerings involved an animal being sacrificed to make amends for sin in people's lives. Other offerings required people giving a part of what they had to God in worship. There were special regulations on how this was to be done highlighting God's holiness and requiring that people put some thought into what they offered to God. These offerings to say sorry for sin had to cost the people something, and they were part of their worship to God. Jesus has paid the price we need to have our sins forgiven, and we should worship Him for that.

We notice in today's reading that God is interested in every area of our lives, no matter how small it may seem to us. He cares if we cheat or lie. However, He always gives His children a way in which they can show they are sorry and come back to Him.

- *Think about ways in which you have sinned against God. Have you lied or cheated anyone? (You may want to use this as reflection time rather than open sharing.)*

- *In what way has God made it possible for us to be forgiven?*

- *How can you give some more thought to the way in which you worship God? Put your thoughts into practice this week.*

Prayer Stop: Take time to confess your sin and ask God's forgiveness. Thank God for sending Jesus to die so that we may be forgiven.

DAY 43

On the Way: Yesterday we saw how God was concerned with every area of our lives. He gave the Israelites special people to help them worship and offer sacrifices in the correct way. These people were called priests and were especially chosen by God from the tribe of Levi. Aaron (Moses' brother) was to be chief priest and his sons were to assist him. Others from the tribe were given special jobs to do at the Tabernacle.

READ LEVITICUS 9:5–8, 22–24

> *Then Moses said to Aaron, "Come to the altar and sacrifice your sin offering*
> *and your burnt offering to purify yourself and the people"* (v7a).

Checkpoint: Just as there were special people to help with worship and work at the Tabernacle, so we have people who serve us in a similar way in our churches. No matter what our part is in church it is important that each person confesses their sin and asks God's forgiveness. In verse 6, Moses taught Aaron and his sons that they must offer sacrifice for their own sin before they offered any for the people. In this way, they would be able to hear clearly what God was saying. Leaders must confess their sin to the Lord so that they can hear clearly how God wants them to lead His people. This does not just mean ministers or elders but any leader of God's people. We are never too young to start this habit of confessing our sin to God. We need to be aware of the things in our lives that don't please God.

- *Think of all the leaders in your church. How many can you name?*
- *How can we make their role as leaders easier for them?*
- *What things do you think may make their role more difficult?*
- *Think of two things you can do this week to encourage the leaders of groups in which you are involved.*

Prayer Stop: Pray for the leaders in your church that God will help them live Godly lives and that they will lead in God's will. Pray that they will be encouraged in their ministry.

DAY 44

On the Way: In Chapter 10, the sons of Aaron disobey God in the way they carry out their duties as priests. They died because they did not respect the Law of God. In the following chapters, God sets out His Law for His people. Chapters 11–20 deal with these in detail and involve every area of life as we mentioned in Day 38. In today's reading, we discover the reason God gave these Laws to the Israelites.

READ LEVITICUS 20:22–26

> *You must be holy because I, the LORD, am holy. I have set you apart from all other people to be my very own* (v26).

Checkpoint: There was a reason that God's people were given these laws to live by. God just didn't decide He was going to make life extra difficult for them! He gave them His Law so that they would stand out among the nations as different: set apart as His people. When the Israelites lived by God's Law, others looked and saw the way in which God blessed them and were amazed at how great He was. They would often be afraid of what God would do to their people if they came against the Israelites. Sadly, the Israelites did not always follow God's Law, and this got them into deep trouble, as we will see in the following weeks. As God's children today, we have also been given His Word to live by, to set us apart as people who belong to God. It is when we live our lives in line with God's Word that others notice the difference and discover how great God is.

- *Read Titus 2:11–14. What things are mentioned that set us apart as God's people? Use these verses as your memory verses for this section.*

- *How can we be different from those around us and yet still be involved with them?*

Prayer Stop: Pray that God will help you to obey the Word of God and so show that you are set apart for God. Pray for other Christians you know (mention some by name) that they too would show they are God's children by the way they live. Pray that others would be attracted to Christ because of our lifestyle. Mention some friends or family by name.

DAY 45

On the Way: God gave the priests specific Laws for the way they were to carry out their duties. He set out a plan for special days of worship and festivals so that the people did not forget to take rest and remembered to worship Him.

READ LEVITICUS 23:3; 25:4, 11–12, 18–22

> *Be assured that I will send my blessing for you in the sixth year, so the land will produce a crop large enough for three years* (25:21).

Checkpoint: God is interested in the whole of creation resting, both people and land. It would seem strange to the people that they were to rest the land and every fifty years set things back to the way they were. God promised blessing if they obeyed; He promised to provide for them miraculously. He wanted a fair and stable society. The year of Jubilee ensured that the poor were properly looked after and had a fair chance to provide for their families.

Some nations have ways of helping the poor today, but they don't usually involve rich people sharing out what they have with others! God is interested in establishing an unselfish society in which we all take an interest in each other.

God also wants His people to have time to rest and worship Him. Jesus taught that we were to keep the Sabbath to rest and worship.

- *How can you help the society in which you live become fairer? Perhaps you need to write to your congressman (in the USA) or your member of Parliament (in the UK) to ask about putting new policies in place.*
- *Some people need to work on a Sunday, which would be the day normally set aside to worship. Is it wrong to work on Sunday? How can we make sure that we have a true "Sabbath rest" even if we have to work Sunday?*

Prayer Stop: Pray that government will create a fair and stable society by the laws they pass. Pray for Christians who have to work Sundays, that they would find time to have a true Sabbath rest.

Note: The Christian Institute and CARE are Christian organizations who keep in touch with policy making in government. They send out newsletters and keep others up to date with specific points for prayer. They can be contacted through their websites if you are interested in being involved in prayer/action for the society our government is creating.

DAY 46

On the Way: As we come to the last chapter of Leviticus, we see God emphasizing obedience to His Law in Chapter 26. Now in Chapter 27, we read about giving to God out of thankfulness for what He has done for us.

READ LEVITICUS 27:28–34

Anything devoted in this way has been set apart as holy, and it belongs to the LORD (v28b).

Checkpoint: We have learned a little about the sacrifices required of the people by God's Law. These were offerings to be made regularly to God to ask His forgiveness for sin and to show that they were His children. As we come to the end of this book, we learn of another form of giving: giving a special gift to God to say a special thank you over and above what the law required. Nothing else could replace these things; once they were vowed to God, they belonged to Him, and no one could change that.

Today we bring money as an offering usually taken at church. Perhaps you or your family give money to other Christian organizations or missionaries as part of that offering too. These are good and necessary habits to get into as Christians. However, often when we feel a special closeness to God or want to show Him how thankful we are we may want to give a little more. It does not necessarily need to be money: it could be anything, as we see in the last chapter of Leviticus. People dedicated their houses or servants, animals or even children to God.

- *What things can you think of that may make you want to dedicate a little more than the usual to God? Have you or your family experienced a time like this?*

- *Other than money, what else could you devote to God?*

Prayer Stop: Take time to thank God for all that He has done for you. Mention some things specifically. Pray that God would show you if there is anything He wants you to dedicate to Him in a special way and ask that you be given a willing heart to be obedient.

NUMBERS

The book of Numbers is an account of the Israelites' journey from Mount Sinai, where they received God's Law, through the desert to the borders of the Promised Land. Having been rescued from Egypt, you would think they would be thankful; however, throughout this book we will see them being stubborn, disobedient, and rebellious.

DAY 47

On the Way: Just over a year after the Lord brought Israel out of Egypt, He told Moses to count the number of men in the community who were able to serve in the army and to make a list of each of their names. He gave Moses a list of people who were to help him in this task. The results of this census are printed in Numbers 1:20–43.

READ NUMBERS 1:44–54

So the Israelites did everything just as the LORD had commanded Moses (v54).

Checkpoint: The Levites were not counted in the first census because they were not to serve in the army. They had a special task to perform, looking after the Tabernacle, which was the place of worship. Within the Levite tribes, each family group is given a specific task to carry out in the Tabernacle and given instructions where to set up their tents to live. In the following two chapters, God gives instructions to the rest of the nation regarding where they must set up home.

God paid attention to every detail of their lives, and He pays attention to these details in our lives also. He is concerned about where we live and work and how we use the special talents He gives us to serve Him. He has plans for every detail in every day of our lives. He calls people to work for Him in the church, but He also calls people to work for Him in other jobs as well. We need to ask God to show us His plans for us and make sure we obey them fully.

- *Sometimes we do not like where we live or the jobs we have to do. Read Psalm 139:16. How does this help us accept the situation we are in?*

- *What specific tasks do you think God has asked you to do in your area or church?*

Prayer Stop: Thank God for placing you in the area you live and in your church. Pray that you will know what God wants you to do and that you will be faithful in doing it.

DAY 48

On the Way: Moses had given God's instructions to the people concerning where they were to set up camp and what they had to do. God also gave clear instructions on their lifestyle. We looked at some of these in Leviticus. After the census was complete and the Tabernacle set up, Moses had a special ceremony of dedication.

READ NUMBERS 7:1–11

> Then the LORD said to Moses, "Receive their gifts and use these oxen and wagons for transporting the Tabernacle" (vs4–5a).

Checkpoint: Each tribe brought their offerings to the Lord, and God gave Moses instructions as to what had to be done with them. They were to be given to the Levites so they could carry out the work God had given them to do. We do not usually bring oxen as our offering today! However, what we do bring should be used for God's work in our church and to help others carry out the task God has given them to do. This could be to pay the pastor or support a missionary you know to enable them to carry out the work God has for them. It may be to help with a special project locally or abroad. Each tribe brought an offering. Even the leaders had to bring their offering to the Lord. It is the responsibility of each one of us to bring an offering to the Lord. If we are part of God's people, we should be giving from what we have to help God's work. This includes everyone, those who are rich or poor, who are leaders or not, all should give something to support the work of the Lord.

- *What areas of God's work does your church support with the offerings given? Who decides how this is spent?*

- *What things besides money could we give to God as an offering? How could this help others do God's work?*

Prayer Stop: Pray for those in your church who decide how the offering is spent. Pray that they will be wise and honest with their task. Ask God to help you know exactly what He would have you give as your offering to Him.

DAY 49

On the Way: Today we are going back a little in time as we come to chapter 9. This takes place about one month before the census we have spoken about over the last two days. The first Passover was celebrated one year before in Egypt. Now God tells the Israelites to celebrate it again.

READ NUMBERS 9:1–14

Moses answered, "Wait here until I have received instructions for you from the Lord" (v8).

Checkpoint: Moses gave the Israelites God's command to celebrate the Passover. However, some of them brought a problem to him that he did not know how to answer. He immediately took the problem to God. Moses did not tell the people what he thought or what a possible solution might be. He wanted to give them only God's answer. This is the sign of a wise leader. Sometimes we are tempted to give our own opinions, but our opinions are not necessarily God's ideas, and we should always ask Him first.

God gave Moses the answer. The people were given another date, one month later, in which they could celebrate the Passover. They were unclean because of a dead body, and although they wanted to celebrate the Passover, they had to show that they could not draw near to God because of their impurity. However, God shows us that this is not a permanent thing; He gave them another time in which they could come.

Our sin separates us from God. But He has given us a way in which we can come to Him, through accepting His Son Jesus as our Savior.

- *What is your first reaction to others when they ask you for an answer to a problem? What can we learn from Moses?*
- *The Passover was put in place to remind the people what God had done for them. What do we celebrate today that reminds us what God has done for us?*
- *The people recognized that their impurity separated them from God. What should we do before we celebrate communion with others? Read 1 Corinthians 11:28.*

Prayer Stop: Praise God that our sin does not need to separate us from Him forever. Take time to confess any sin to Him now.

DAY 50

On the Way: After having established the Passover celebration again, Moses set up the Tabernacle. As we read in chapter 7, the tribes brought their offerings to the Lord. Earlier when the Lord led them out of Egypt, He led them by a cloud during the day and a pillar of fire at night. Now that the Tent of Meeting was set up, God gave them evidence of His presence by a cloud settling over the tent by day, and at night that cloud looked like fire.

READ NUMBERS 9:15–23

And they did whatever the LORD told them through Moses (v23b).

Checkpoint: The verses that we read today show us that the Lord very clearly gave His children guidance. He showed them where to set up camp, how long to stay and when and where to move to. There is a very strong emphasis in this passage about the Lord's command. As God's children, we should obey the Lord and follow His guidance wherever He leads us. The Israelites did not know how long they would be in one location, but as soon as the cloud moved, they knew it was God's sign for them to move as well. It may have been unsettling to think that as they set up camp, they might be moving again tomorrow. However, this passage tells us that they obeyed regardless.

God has a time and a place for us also. Sometimes we must stay in the one place for a very long time. My dad lived in the same house for 78 years! However, God calls some people to move to different areas more often.

- *How would you feel if God asked your family to move to another area? Perhaps you are already facing this. Remember, the Israelites wanted to be where God's presence led them.*
- *God does not lead us by clouds today. How can we know if God is leading us somewhere else?*

Prayer Stop: Pray for anyone you know facing a move to a new area. Perhaps a missionary family you know. Pray that you would know God's guidance clearly in your life.

DAY 51

On the Way: The children of Israel had been given the Law and had set up their camp. They had the Tabernacle set up, but now they are on the move. They set out from Mount Sinai toward the Promised Land. This is the start of their 38-year journey in the desert.

READ NUMBERS 10:29–36

They marched for three days after leaving the mountain of the LORD (v33a).

Checkpoint: The first leg of the journey was short. Just three days. It would have been a huge task for all the people to move, and as they were not used to moving camp it may have taken them a while to pack. I'm sure that after 38 years, they would have had it down to a fine art and learned to travel light! Moses invited his brother-in-law to travel with them. He knew the area and would be a valuable person to have as a scout in the desert as they traveled.

God provides those with the right skills to help us in the tasks He gives us to do. Moses was the leader of the people, but he needed help in areas in which he was not confident. When God first called Moses, he lacked so much confidence that God gave him his brother Aaron to be his spokesperson. Here he invites Hobab to be his eyes! With Aaron, Moses was trying to get out of what God had planned for him. However, he was not trying to shirk his responsibility by asking Hobab to come along. He realized that Hobab had the necessary knowledge of the area to help him, and he was not too proud to ask for that help.

Sometimes we can be slow to ask for help because we think we should be able to handle things ourselves, but God gives others skills we don't have, and we are wise to use them.

- *Are you struggling to do something that you could ask someone else to help you with? What is it, and who will you ask?*
- *Is there something you could help one of your leaders at church with?*

Prayer Stop: Ask God to show you who to ask for help if you need it. Pray for your church leaders that they would be given help in the areas they need.

DAY 52

On the Way: In chapter 9, we saw how important it was for the Israelites to obey the command of the Lord. Now in chapter 11, we see the complaining start. They are fed up with the same food every day; they want meat, not manna. They remembered the variety of food they had in Egypt but had obviously forgotten the hardships they suffered as slaves there.

READ NUMBERS 11:16–23, 31–34

> *Then the LORD said to Moses, "Has my arm lost its power? Now you will see whether or not my word comes true!" (v23).*

Checkpoint: Sometimes we can find ourselves in situations that seem impossible. Like how do you provide 600,000 men with meat for one month in the desert? You can hear the frustration in Moses' comment in verse 21. It all seems too much for him. The people are complaining, he doesn't have any means to provide them with meat, and so he cries out to God, not for help but in complaint! God hears and gives him an answer.

God knows when His children can go no further, and He will send help. He gave Moses people to help him and provided meat for everyone in the camp . . . so much that they made themselves sick with it! Moses was so caught up in his complaint to God that he seemed to forget the mighty deeds God had done in the past for the Israelites. He seemed to doubt God's strength. The people were so caught up in their difficulties that they also forgot God's past mighty deeds. They allowed their desires to take over, and this proved disastrous for them in the end.

- *When you face impossible situations, what is your reaction? What can we learn from today's reading?*
- *God gave Moses seventy elders to help him. In what ways can you help your church leaders?*

Prayer Stop: Are there things that you complain about regularly? Ask God to help you with your attitude. Pray for your church leaders that they would find strength to lead God's people.

DAY 53

On the Way: Complaining seems to have taken root in the camp! Not only were the people complaining about the food and Moses complaining about the people, now we find Miriam continuing the theme with Aaron by complaining about Moses!

READ NUMBERS 12:1–16

> *The Lord was very angry with them, and he departed* (v9).

Checkpoint: Oh, how quickly a complaining spirit can affect others! It spread throughout all the Israelites. Now we see it threatening family relationships with Moses and his brother and sister. Miriam started attacking Moses' personal life, but it would seem that she was really jealous of his public ministry, how he served God, and the recognition he got for that.

Often when we are jealous of what others are doing, we bring up everything that annoys us about them. This is very unhelpful and certainly not how God would want us to handle things. It can end up hurting more people. Miriam involved Aaron, and God acted at once to put a stop to it. He made it clear to Miriam and Aaron that He was angry at their outburst and acted to remind them of His power.

He also shows us His great mercy here as He allows Miriam to be healed. Although she has consequences to take, at the end of seven days she will be restored to the people and to God. When we complain against our leaders, we need to remember that our attitude can affect others too. When we allow our attitudes to become out of line with what God wants, then He will take action to remind us of His holiness. Sometimes these are hard lessons to learn.

Note that Moses did not react to Miriam's outburst or hold a grudge against her.

- *How do you react when others criticize you? What can you learn from Moses in this example?*
- *Talk about ways that Miriam could have handled her feelings better. What can you learn from her mistakes?*
- *What is Miriam's restoration a picture of?*

Prayer Stop: Pray for your family that God would protect you from a complaining spirit. Pray for strength to react in a godly way when others criticize you.

DAY 54

On the Way: The Israelites moved on, and the land that God was going to give them came into view. God told Moses to send some men to explore the land. So Moses sent twelve men, one from each tribe, to investigate and report what the land, the people, and the crops were like. The men returned to give Moses a report on what they found.

READ NUMBERS 13:25–14:4

> *But Caleb tried to quiet the people as they stood before Moses. "Let's go at once to take the land," he said. "We can certainly conquer it!"* (13:30).

Checkpoint: The men started giving a truthful account of what they had seen in the land. However, as they describe what they saw, the story becomes exaggerated by their fear. Caleb realizes this and stops them by saying, "We can certainly do this." He realized that they were not on their own. The others seemed to forget that God was on their side. They let their fear take over. They had forgotten the miraculous way God had dealt with them in the past. They did not listen to Caleb and started spreading their fear around the camp until the people were so paralyzed that they wanted to go back to Egypt!

Our fearfulness can affect others. If God is asking us to do something that seems too big for us, whether personally or in our church, we must remember to trust Him and not allow fear to blind our faith. We must also be aware that others may be speaking with the voice of fear rather than truth and not let the fearfulness of others affect us.

- *Have you ever felt God asking you to do something that worried you or made you fearful? How did you respond?*

- *When others try to make us fearful, what resources do we have to help us through?*

Prayer Stop: Pray that you would not listen to the voice of fear but of truth and that God would give you faith to believe that "[you] can do everything through Christ who gives [you] strength" (Phil. 4:13).

Suggestion: Listen to Casting Crowns' song "Voice of Truth."

DAY 55

On the Way: They were so scared that they wished they were back in Egypt! They had forgotten how awful it had been there. By forgetting God and rebelling against Him, they were sinning, and Moses had to plead with God not to strike them down there and then. God listened to his prayer. However, because of their attitude, He will not let them see the land He was giving them. That privilege was to be left for their children. They would be shepherds in the desert for forty years and would die in the desert.

MEMORY VERSE

You were running the race so well. Who has held you back from following the truth? It certainly isn't God, for he is the one who called you to freedom.

~ Galatians 5:7–8

READ NUMBERS 14:36–45

But Moses said, "Why are you now disobeying the Lord's orders to return to the wilderness? It won't work" (v41).

Checkpoint: The consequences of the Israelites' sin seem very unforgiving. However, we must remember that God had displayed patience many times over. He had provided for them and shown them His mighty power in many different ways. They refused to learn from their experiences and instead preferred to panic and listen to the opinion of those who were not speaking God's Word. It wasn't until they saw the destruction their unfaithfulness brought that they thought it might be better to do what God had said.

We must remember that God is holy. He cannot be "messed" with. If we choose to be disobedient to Him, we must take the consequences. He wanted to give His children a great land to live in, but because they looked at it from a human standpoint, they missed God's blessing. Don't be like the Israelites; make every effort to be obedient to the Lord no matter how hard it seems. Remember, He has the strength to get you through.

- *How does the memory verse help us understand the Israelites' situation?*
- *How do you think Moses felt about the Israelites' behavior?*
- *How do you think the Israelites felt in the end?*

Prayer Stop: Pray that God would help you to be obedient to Him. Pray for those you know who are finding it hard to do what God is asking them to do. Think about ways you could encourage them.

DAY 56

On the Way: As soon as the events of the previous chapter are over, God encourages His children by giving them hope for their future by giving them instructions for when He does bring them to the land He has promised. They should have started preparing their families for the future. You would think *now* the Israelites would have learned their lesson, but they seem to have gone deeper into rebellion! They not only rebel against God's discipline, they start blaming Moses for their predicament! Some of the leaders start saying that God has not called Moses and Aaron to lead the people. Moses leaves it to God to judge, and these men are instantly destroyed in front of the whole assembly. God now gives instructions to show whom He has chosen as the spiritual leader of His people.

READ NUMBERS 17:1–13

> *Place Aaron's staff permanently before the Ark of the Covenant to serve as a warning to rebels* (v10b).

Checkpoint: We get a picture of God's patience in this passage. The Israelites had given Moses and Aaron (and God) a terrible time with their rebellious spirit. Moses loses patience with them, but God patiently continues disciplining and teaching. He makes it clear to everyone that He has chosen Aaron to be the spiritual leader of His people and leaves them that reminder in case they start rebelling again. In our journey with the Israelites so far God has spent a lot of time reminding them of the things He has done for them in the past, but they never seem to remember for very long! Sometimes we can be guilty of forgetting the things God has done for us. It is important that we learn from the Israelites and remember what God has done so that we can trust Him in the future.

- *God appoints people to be leaders of His church today. Can you think of things that may make life difficult for them in that role? Check that you are not guilty of a rebellious spirit against your leaders.*
- *How can you be an encouragement to them?*
- *Talk about ways that you have experienced God's patience with you.*

Prayer Stop: Pray for your church leaders that they may be encouraged by the attitude of their congregations. Praise God for the times He has shown His patience to you.

DAY 57

On the Way: Chapter 18 gives instructions to Aaron and the Levites regarding their duties and responsibilities as spiritual leaders, and Chapter 19 provides instructions about maintaining purity among the people. Chapter 20 brings us back to the Israelites' journey and seems to signal the end of their forty years in the desert. Moses and Aaron have led them all these years. There is little record of the years spent wandering in the desert.

READ NUMBERS 20:1–13

> *Because you did not trust me enough to demonstrate my holiness to the people of Israel, you will not lead them into the land I am giving them!* (v12b).

Checkpoint: Moses did not fully obey God on this occasion. He became very frustrated with the people of Israel at this point, so much that he spoke rashly to them (Num. 20:9) and acted in frustration by striking the rock (Num. 20:10). This was not what God had commanded him to do. He seemed to let his heart become angry with the people. He became focused on their rebellion rather than leaving their behavior for God to deal with and focusing on being obedient to God himself.

Sometimes when we work with other people, we become distracted from the task that God has given us. We can become entangled in frustration about others' behavior and allow our focus to be on the wrong thing. God wants us to be obedient to Him no matter what others are doing. We must trust Him to deal with other people's shortcomings and not focus on them ourselves.

- *What emotions do you think Moses and Aaron were feeling when they realized that they were not to bring the Israelites into the Promised Land?*

- *We do not read of Moses' reaction to God here, but what do you imagine Moses saying to God? What do you think the right attitude would have been?*

Prayer Stop: Pray that God would help you to have the right attitude in being obedient to Him. Not focusing on other people but focusing on God alone. Pray for your church leaders that they would keep their focus on what God wants them to do.

DAY 58

On the Way: The Israelites faced opposition as they traveled toward the Promised Land and camped across the Jordan from Jericho. During this time, Aaron died, and they continued to complain against the Lord. When they arrived in Moab, the king (Balaak) was afraid and sent for a diviner from a nearby land to curse the Israelites. After refusing to come initially, he was eventually persuaded but would not commit himself to cursing the Israelites.

READ NUMBERS 22:21–35

Go with these men, but say only what I tell you to say (v35b).

Checkpoint: Balaam was a pagan prophet who had an encounter with God in the verses before our reading today. Balaam would have known of the Israelites' God and was perhaps afraid of His power. He may also have been afraid of Balaak because he was king. After what seems like some confusion, God told him to go. On the road, he has an amazing encounter with his donkey. Eventually when the donkey speaks to him, Balaam answers its question! (I think I may have had a question or two for it first!) Balaam was considered a wise man and donkeys considered dumb animals, yet it was through his donkey that God chose to speak to Balaam in a way that he would never forget, so that he would remember to be obedient to God and not be tempted to go after the reward promised by the king instead.

Sometimes, like Balaam, we can become a little confused about the right thing to do. We have God's Word as our guide and must remain faithful to it. God showed Balaam His power in a way that he would not forget and reminds us of this as we read His Word today.

- *What do you think you would have done if you were Balaam? Why do you think God chose to warn Balaam in this way?*

- *What effect do you think this experience would have had on the rest of Balaam's life?*

- *Balaam was asked to curse God's children. This errand was dramatically changed on the road. Can you think of another destructive mission that was dramatically changed on a road? (Acts 9:1–19)*

Prayer Stop: Think of those persecuting God's children today (both governments and individuals) and pray for their salvation. Pray that you would be obedient to God's Word in every decision you have to make.

DAY 59

On the Way: When Balaam arrived in Moab, he could not curse the Israelites even though Balaak made him try several times. Instead, he blessed them. However, this did not keep the Israelites from turning away from God again by becoming involved in wrong relationships with Moabite women. As a result, they were tempted to worship their false gods. God disciplines His children for this.

God's desire for His children then was for them to marry other Israelites. It is still God's desire that His children should marry other Christians and not be tempted to put other things or people before Him. Moses continues to lead and teach the people.

READ NUMBERS 27:12–23

> O Lord . . . Please appoint a new man as leader for the community . . . so the community of the Lord will not be like sheep without a shepherd (v15b–17).

Checkpoint: Moses had led the Israelites for forty years, through all kinds of circumstances. They had often tested him beyond what he could bear. Yet, as he faces the end of his life, his concern is that they not be left without a leader. I'm sure at times he would have loved to walk away from them and leave them to their rebellious ways, but he stuck at it for forty years, reminding them of God's provision and promise to them. When we serve God in leadership, sometimes other people can make this a challenge for us, and we may feel like giving up. Learn from Moses and keep focused on the task that God wants you to do. He will provide someone to take over when the time is right; He had already picked Joshua out to succeed Moses.

- *What does Moses' prayer show us about how he felt for these people?*
- *What do you think would have happened if Moses died and there was no leader for the Israelites?*
- *What can we learn from Moses about Christian leadership? What can we learn from the Israelites about following?*

Prayer Stop: Pray that if you are (or become) a leader of God's people, you will be faithful and be concerned for those you lead.

DAY 60

On the Way: In the last few chapters of Numbers, we read of Moses presenting Joshua to the priest in preparation for leadership and of the final instructions God was giving His people through Moses. These were instructions for worship and instructions for allocating and governing the Promised Land when they arrived there.

READ NUMBERS 33:50–56

Take possession of the land and settle in it, for I have given it to you to occupy (v53).

Checkpoint: We have seen some of Moses' faults and frustrations as we have looked at the journey of the Israelites to the Promised Land. We now see him about to hand over the leadership to Joshua, but he has not given up yet! He is determined to finish the task that God had given him to do. It would have been easy for him to let Joshua get on with the job. He had been working closely with Moses anyway, and Moses may well have said, "I'm about to die, and you will be responsible for the people in the Promised Land, so I'll just let you get on with it!" Instead, he was determined to do just what the Lord instructed him. He not only prepared Joshua for leadership but also left all the instructions from God for how to order their life in the Promised Land and confirmed to the people the vision of a land of their own (Num. 33:53).

It is important to finish our God-given tasks well: not simply give up on them when we feel tired or we know we will be handing them over to someone else soon. We must give those who come after us a vision to carry on.

- *In what ways do you think Joshua's takeover was made easier by Moses' attitude?*
- *Yesterday we talked about things we can learn about leadership from Moses. What things can we learn from his attitude in these last few chapters of Numbers?*
- *What could Christian leaders today do to help prepare others for leadership?*

Prayer Stop: Pray that Christian leaders would train others to take up leadership in the next generation. Ask God to show you what role He has for you. Make sure you are committed to *finishing* that task well.

DEUTERONOMY

We have come to the last book of the Pentateuch. This is the name given to the first five books in the Bible written by Moses. Deuteronomy means "repetition of the law." It is a collection of Moses' closing words to the Israelites as he prepares them for entering the Promised Land. The end of the book brings us to the end of Moses' ministry and life.

DAY 61

On the Way: Throughout this book, Moses reminds the people of God's faithfulness to them and of the Law given to them. He reminds them of God's promises and that they needed to obey God. It is his personal farewell message to them. In the first four chapters, he reminds the people of their story so far.

READ DEUTERONOMY 1:1–8

Look, I am giving all this land to you (v8a).

Checkpoint: Moses' introduction to the Israelites was to remind them of God's promise to them, the promise of a land of their own. This would encourage them to keep going. So far, it had taken them forty years to travel an eleven-day journey! This was because they had disobeyed God. When we disobey God, it keeps us back from carrying out God's will right away. God has to teach us to honor Him and make His will our priority before we can carry on. God will still work out His plans for us, but we can make it much more complicated for ourselves if we do not completely obey God.

Sometimes when we find things hard, it is good to remember God's promises to us. They can carry us through difficult times. Moses reminds them of the journey so far, the good times and the tough patches. At certain points in our lives, it is helpful to look back at our own story and see how God has led us to this point. This can encourage us to keep trusting God for the future. It can also remind us that God is faithful even when we do things wrong like the Israelites. We can learn from hard times too.

- *How do you think the Israelites felt as they heard Moses retell their story?*
- *At what times in our lives may it be helpful to reflect on our story so far?*
- *When can it be helpful to reflect on our mistakes? Do you think it could be harmful to do this sometimes?*

Prayer Stop: Praise God for His promises and for the way He has guided you so far. Pray that you will be obedient to Him.

DAY 62

On the Way: Many of those who gathered to listen to Moses would not have been alive when the Israelites left Egypt. They had been born as their families wandered in the desert for forty years. God had said no one alive when the ten spies frightened them away from the Promised Land would be allowed to enter the land. It was important for the people to hear and understand clearly the things Moses was telling them. Having gone over the story so far, Moses now goes on to talk about the Law and reminds the people that they must remember to obey the Lord.

READ DEUTERONOMY 4:1–14

Obey them so that you may live (v1b).

Checkpoint: Moses reminds the people of how important God's Law is. In our key verse and in verse 6, he gives two reasons why they should live by this Law. In verse 1, he tells them obeying God's Law has a personal benefit—"that you may live." In verse 6, he tells them of the benefit to those around them—"this will show others your wisdom." God's children are set apart by God to be different from those around, and their obedience to God's Law will show others the difference and the benefits.

In verse 9, Moses warns the people to be careful and watch closely so that they wouldn't forget the things God had done for them. He had just reminded them from their history that they were prone to forget, and he urges them to be careful to teach these things to their children. He was encouraging them to remember to be obedient.

We often need to be reminded of this. We need to remember the Bible verses that encourage us to be obedient to God and remember what He has done for us.

- *Read Psalm 119:105. What is the personal benefit to obeying God's Word mentioned here?*
- *Read Matthew 5:16. What is the benefit to others mentioned here if we obey God's Word?*
- *How do we keep God's Law in our minds?*

Prayer Stop: Praise God for His Word that guides us. Pray that God would help you to obey His Word so that others may see the difference and praise Him.

DAY 63

On the Way: Moses moves on from reminding the people to obey the Law to reminding them about who gave them the Law. He reminds them that it was God's voice they heard at Mount Sinai. They did not see Him; they only heard Him. Moses reminds them that they must not worship any idol made by man but only the Living God. He led them forty years in the desert and knows that they tend to be unfaithful. He urges them to stay faithful to God but reminds them again of God's mercy and grace toward them when they do wander away.

READ DEUTERONOMY 4:32–40

> *He showed you these things so you would know the* Lord *is God and there is no other* (v35).

Checkpoint: More reminding! This time it's a call to remember that the Lord their God is the only true God. He has shown them this by all the miraculous signs He gave them when rescuing them from Egypt and guiding them in the desert. He had chosen them and set them apart from other nations. No other god has ever done anything like this! Moses says, "There is no other" (Deut. 4:39).

This God is our God. He has set us apart to be His children, and He provided a way of salvation for us. It is only through Jesus, His Son, that we can be saved. He has promised eternal life to those who trust Him. The history of Israel is a picture of the church. God has rescued us from sin as He rescued Israel from Egypt, and He is leading us to His "Promised Land" where we will be with Him forever. It is good for us to be reminded of this and worship God for it.

- *List the similarities between the Israelites being led to the Promised Land and God's people (the church) today.*

- *Read Acts 4:12. What does this mean for you?*

- *Look at Exodus 34:6–7. How had Israel experienced God's mercy? How have you experienced God's mercy?*

Prayer Stop: Thank God for His plan of salvation and for His Son, Jesus, who died for us. Take time to worship God; He is the true God; there is no other God.

DAY 64

On the Way: Moses goes from reminding the Israelites about God's greatness to reminding them of the Law God gave them. He has taken them through the whole of their history since coming out of Egypt, which was before most of the assembled people were born. However, he reminds them that they were actually there when God gave them the Law at Mount Sinai. He recalls the awesome meeting with God and challenges them to love their God with all their being.

READ DEUTERONOMY 6:1-9

> *And you must love the LORD your God with all your heart, all your soul, and all your strength* (v5).

Checkpoint: Moses urged the Israelites to make these laws a central part of their life. The Law was given to prepare them for life in the Promised Land, and now that land was in sight. The Law was given that the people might fear the Lord and know God's blessing on their lives. Our key verse encourages the people to love the Lord with every part of their being, to keep the laws in their heart, and to make sure their children knew and understood them. They had to be part of everyday life.

God's instructions to us come through the Bible. It prepares us for life here on earth and tells us how to be ready for eternity, life after we die. If we obey God's Word to us, we will learn more of God's promises to us, and we will have peace with God and be with Him forever. It is important that our families know and understand God's Word and His way of salvation. That is why it is good to spend time together as a family reading and studying the Bible. As we do this, our love for God will grow.

- *What do you think it means to love God with all your heart, soul, and strength?*
- *In Mark 12:30 and in the other Gospels, Jesus quotes this verse but adds "mind" also. Why do you think He did this?*
- *Read Psalm 119:11. What will knowing God's Word by heart help us with? How will it do this?*

Prayer Stop: Pray that God would help you as a family to love Him with all your being. Pray that you will be able to share His Word with those of your family who do not know Him yet.

DAY 65

On the Way: Moses warns the Israelites not to be tempted to worship the gods of the nations around, nor to intermarry with those who worship those gods. He reminds the Israelites that God chose them to be His children and encourages them to trust Him when the nations around seem too strong for them.

READ DEUTERONOMY 8:1–5, 10–11

> *When you have eaten your fill, be sure to praise the LORD your God for the good land he has given you (v10).*

Checkpoint: The Israelites' experience in the desert was difficult. At times, they were hungry and thirsty. They had no way of providing food and water for themselves so they had to depend totally on the Lord. Verse 2 tells us that God did this to know what was in their hearts. God, who knows everything, would have known their reaction without doing so, but the experience would show the people themselves their own hearts. Sometimes they did not respond very well to God's provision, and they had to learn repeatedly that it was God who was in control. God provided for them miraculously for forty years. Their clothes did not wear out (imagine wearing the same clothes for forty years), and He looked after them physically. They had to learn that they needed to be dependent on God. God was now bringing them into a land in which they would have plenty. They would want for nothing. Moses warned them that they should remember this also comes from God.

Sometimes it is easier to remember we are dependent on God for everything when we have nothing and need Him to provide. Often when we have plenty and can buy whatever we need, we forget that all we have comes from God. We, like the Israelites, need to learn that our lives are dependent on God no matter how many material blessings we have.

- *Why does Jesus use the words of verse 3b in Matthew 4:4?*
- *Why is it easy to forget to thank God when things are going well for us?*
- *Think of some difficult times that you may have gone through. What did God teach you then?*

Prayer Stop: Take time to praise God for all the blessings He has given you. Ask God to help you remember that all you have always comes from Him and to forgive you for the times you have failed to acknowledge His blessings.

DAY 66

On the Way: Having reminded the Israelites of God's provision to them in the desert and exhorted them to teach these things to their children, Moses now turns to their attitude upon entering the Promised Land. He warns them against thinking they earned it because of the good things they had done.

READ DEUTERONOMY 9:1–6

> *You must recognize that the* LORD *your God is not giving you this good land because you are good, for you are not—you are a stubborn people* (v6).

Checkpoint: Moses reminded the Israelites that they didn't deserve the blessings God had for them in the Promised Land; they had been disobedient and rebellious through the years in the desert. He warned them not to be tempted to think that they had done anything to deserve such a blessing. The blessing came about because of the wickedness of the nations they were driving out and because God had promised this land to their ancestors. God's promise could not be changed, but the blessings the Israelites would know in the land would depend on them obeying God. In Titus 3:5 of the New Testament, we are reminded that it is not because we have done anything to deserve eternal life that we are given it but because of God's mercy and love for us. This is a promise in His Word: whoever believes on the name of the Lord will be saved. As with the Israelites, it is in being obedient to God's Word that we will know deeper blessing in our lives. We must not be tempted to think we deserve salvation or can earn it; no, it is a gift from God. What was happening to the Israelites was a picture of what would happen in the future to those who believe in Jesus, God's plan of salvation.

- *Three times Moses mentions to the Israelites that it's not because of their righteousness that they are being given this land. Why do you think he stressed that so much?*
- *Why did God give the Israelites this land?*
- *Read 1 Peter 2:9. Why have we been chosen by God?*

Prayer Stop: Thank God for His gift of salvation and praise Him for His great mercy to us. Praise Him for the gift of His Word that teaches us His plan of salvation.

DAY 67

On the Way: Moses continues to remind the Israelites of their rebellion against God and continues to encourage them to obey God, warning them of the consequences of disobedience. Today's reading is the end of his general teaching on what God has done for them so far.

READ DEUTERONOMY 11:18–25

> *Teach them to your children. Talk about them . . . when you are going to bed and when you are getting up* (v19).

Checkpoint: Moses emphasized some things repeatedly in order to show the Israelites how important they were. He knew these people and knew how easy it was for them to forget the things God had done and turn away from Him. So in today's reading and in the verses that follow, we see Moses telling the Israelites to not forget to tell their children of all that God had done for them. He reminds them that they have seen things that their children have not seen, and it is important to teach their children about all the mighty things God has done. The children also needed to learn of the discipline of God so that they might avoid the mistakes of their parents. This had to be a natural part of their daily family life.

God has placed us in natural and church families. We must make it our responsibility to teach our children what God has done for us. We must teach what the Bible teaches and share the lessons we learned so that our children may learn God's way of salvation and perhaps avoid the mistakes we ourselves have made. This should be part of our daily conversation with our children at home and those in the church who may not have Christian parents.

- *When we share what God has done in our lives, how does this benefit and encourage us as we share and those who hear?*
- *Perhaps you can think of a specific time God has taught you something and share it now.*

Prayer Stop: Pray that you would learn to be open and honest in sharing what God has done in your life so that others can be encouraged and perhaps warned. Pray for those young folk in your church who do not have Christian families. Perhaps you could make time to share with young Christians who don't have Christian families.

DAY 68

On the Way: Moses now moves from speaking generally of the importance of obeying God's Law to teaching specific commandments from God—teaching the people exactly what God's Law required of them.

MEMORY VERSE

So be strong and courageous! Do not be afraid and do not panic before them. For the Lord your God will personally go ahead of you.

~Deuteronomy 31:6a

READ DEUTERONOMY 12:1–11

> *Rather, you must seek the LORD your God at the place of worship he himself will choose from among all the tribes—the place where his name will be honored (v5).*

Checkpoint: God's people were to be different from the nations around as a sign that they were special to God. It was important that they not worship in the same way the nations around them worshipped. They had to seek out the place God had for them to worship and then bring their offerings to that place. It was in obeying this that they would know God's blessings in their family life.

As God's children today, we too must look for the place God has for us to worship. A place where we can worship as God requires. There are many churches around today, many with different ministries. As a family, if you are not already committed to a church, I would encourage you to look for the place God has for you to worship and serve Him—where you can use the gifts He has given you. If you are part of a church, make sure you are using your gifts to serve God there and not just attending the services. God's people were required to be active in bringing their tithes and offerings to the place of worship. If we too are active, we will grow in our faith and experience God working in our lives.

- *What things should we make a priority when looking for a church to join?*
- *Read Romans 12:1–2. What does it mean to offer our bodies as living sacrifices? What result will this have in our lives?*

Prayer Stop: Thank God for your church family and pray that God would show you how to serve Him in your church, no matter what age you are. Pray for those you may know who are looking for a church to serve God in.

DAY 69

On the Way: Moses continues to give the people very specific instructions for worship so that they will have no doubts regarding what God requires of them. He then moves on to warning them about people who may teach them lies.

READ DEUTERONOMY 13:1–5

Serve only the LORD your God and fear him alone (v4a).

Checkpoint: Moses was concerned that people from other nations would try to trick the Israelites into following false gods by performing miracles or predicting events. By seeing evidence of these things, the people might think that others had power from God and follow them. Moses warned the Israelites not to follow such men but to follow the Lord. They were to keep His commands, serve Him, and hold fast to Him. If they were doing this, they would be focused on what the Law of God taught and be able to recognize when false teachers were trying to trick them away from God.

Unfortunately, there are people today who do just the same. They teach things that are not in line with God's Word and try to convince people that it is the truth. These people often have many rules made up by man, which they expect others to follow. What they do and teach points to another person and not God. If we are doing as Moses encouraged the Israelites to do—to keep God's commands, serve Him, and hold fast to Him—we too will be able to see that these people are not teaching the truth and are trying to trick us into following them or another person. We must be on our guard, checking everything we are taught with God's Word and being sure that we follow only His commands and not those made up by man.

- *Read 1 John 4:1–3. What guidance do these verses give us about deciding what is truth?*

- *Talk about some ways that people may try to trick us today into worshipping "false gods."*

Prayer Stop: Praise God that His Word is truth. Pray that you would be aware of anyone teaching what is against God's Word and ask God for help in standing against it.

DAY 70

On the Way: When teaching about God's Law, Moses mentions every area of life—even preparing them for the future when they will demand a king like other nations (Deut. 17). He continually warns against following the practices of other nations, encouraging them to stand apart and follow the Lord. He reminds them to praise God for all that He has given them.

READ DEUTERONOMY 26:8–15

> *Afterward you may go and celebrate because of all the good things*
> *the LORD your God has given to you and your household* (v11a).

Checkpoint: In all of his speech, Moses constantly reminds the people to praise God for all He has done for them, to remember where they came from and how God rescued them, to teach these things to their children, and to keep God's Law. They are to realize that everything they have comes from God, and they are to give some of that back directly to be used in God's service.

In today's reading, we see specific areas that this offering is to be used for. What does it say in verse 12? First, it was to be given to the priests, those who served God in the Temple and so had no other income, then to the vulnerable people who were poor because of their circumstances.

We have people just like this in our society today. We have people devoted to teaching and sharing God's Word in our churches and as missionaries. There are people in our cities and around the world who are very poor because of circumstances. We as God's children should be ready to share what we have with them as an act of our worship and thankfulness for what God has given us.

- *Look up 2 Corinthians 8:1–2, 7, 12, and 9:7. Is it only when we have spare money that we should consider giving to God's work? What should our attitude be in giving?*

- *Regarding your own giving, do you set aside money for God's work? Perhaps you need to think about who or what to support with your income even if you are giving from a small amount of pocket money.*

Prayer Stop: Praise God for all that He has given you. Pray for those you support financially and ask God for guidance in how you should use your income for His glory.

DAY 71

On the Way: Moses has led the Israelites for forty years and knows how quickly they turn away from God. As he comes to his final words to them, he lists the blessings that come from obeying the Lord and the curses that come from disobedience. He urges them to remember the journey so far and remember God's faithfulness to them even in their unfaithfulness. He calls them to recommit themselves to the covenant God made with them.

READ DEUTERONOMY 29:1–13, 29

But he provided for you so you would know that he is the LORD your God (v6b).

Checkpoint: By reminding the people, again, of all that God has done for them, Moses is hoping that they will wholeheartedly commit themselves to follow God. He points out that while all the miracles were happening in Egypt and God was providing for them in the desert, they did not really understand that it was God working for them. They often had their minds set on going their own way. By reminding them of this now, Moses is hoping that at last it will sink in. God did not abandon them but was leading, guiding, and providing even through the hard times. They may not have understood how God was doing it or even why God was doing it but they could certainly know that it was God who was protecting them and providing for them. Verse 29 teaches that we are responsible for doing the things we know are in line with God's Word and let God deal with the things we do not understand. This way we bring glory to Him, grow in our faith as we look back, and see the way He has led, protected, and guided us.

- *Why do you think it is difficult sometimes to see God at work in our lives? In what ways can we be like the Israelites in this?*

- *Read Isaiah 55:8–9. How can these verses help us deal with things we do not understand?*

- *Look back over your life and share some of the ways you can see God has led, guided, or protected you in the past.*

Prayer Stop: Take time to thank God for guiding your lives and commit yourselves to obeying Him. Pray for those who are finding it hard to see God at work in their lives just now.

DAY 72

On the Way: Having reminded the Israelites of all that God had done for them and urged them to keep on remembering these things, Moses hopes that in the future they will remember to obey God, having learned from the mistakes of their past. Now in today's reading, he gives them a choice.

READ DEUTERONOMY 30:11–20

> *No, the message is very close at hand; it is on your lips and in your heart so that you can obey it* (v14).

Checkpoint: Moses gives the Israelites a very "black and white" choice; the choice is life or death. He spells out very clearly the results of either choice and again urges them to choose life by obeying the Lord. This is not an impossible thing for the people. They have God's Law written down, and he has already encouraged them to make it part of their everyday life by talking about it at home and knowing it in their heart. He reminds them of that in verse 14.

We too have a choice to make between life and death, between following the Lord or not. The Bible clearly tells us the results of both choices, and I would urge those who have not yet chosen to choose life by accepting Jesus as their Savior. As we read and memorize God's Word, we can learn how to be obedient to Him. God has made it possible for us to choose life and be obedient to Him. As the Israelites had the Law, we have been given His Word and must use it to help us make the right choices.

- *Look up John 5:24 and Romans 10:9–10. How can these verses help us make the right choice?*

- *How does knowing and memorizing God's Word help us live in the right way? Psalm 119:11 may help you answer.*

- *If you have not already chosen Jesus as your Savior, you may want to think about this now and talk to someone about it.*

Prayer Stop: Pray for those you know who are thinking about accepting Christ as their Savior; pray that they will make the right choice. Praise God that He has given us His Word to help us be obedient to Him.

DAY 73

On the Way: Moses' speech to the Israelites is coming to an end. He has reminded them of the past, guided them to the present, and warned them for their future. He presents Joshua to them as their next leader and encourages him to be strong and courageous as he leads these people. He reminds him that God is with him. Moses and Joshua go together to the tent of meeting; there God tells Moses how it will be in the future with the Israelites. The story does not change: God knows they will turn their backs on Him again when all is going well for them. God instructed Moses to write a song to teach the Israelites as a warning to them.

READ DEUTERONOMY 31:23–30

For I know how rebellious and stubborn you are (v27a).

Checkpoint: Moses had done all in his power to help the people choose to follow the Lord. He had taught them God's Law, written it down, reminded them of it, and now he even taught them a song about it. How do you think he felt when God told him in his final meeting along with Joshua, that the people would rebel again? They just didn't seem to learn. Often we too can be very stubborn—forgetting the lessons we have learned and continuing to disobey God. As He did with the Israelites, God often has to remind us of the lessons we learned previously. No matter what our Christian leaders do to remind us of God's Word, the choice is our own: will we follow God's way or go our own. I pray that we will not be rebellious and stubborn like the Israelites, but will remember the lessons learned from our past and from our leaders and choose to obey the Lord.

- *We thought about how Moses may have felt upon hearing the Israelites would rebel again. Joshua was with Moses; how do you think he would be feeling, knowing that he was the new leader?*
- *How did God encourage him especially?*
- *Think on two things you can do to encourage your leaders this week.*

Prayer Stop: Thank God for His Word and your church leaders. Ask God to show you whether there is anything you must do to be obedient to Him right now.

DAY 74

On the Way: Moses taught the people the song God instructed him and again urged them to pay attention to God's Law which are not just words but are their life. God has prepared Moses for the end of his life and now gives him instructions to climb Mount Nebo telling him he will die there. Moses blesses each of the tribes and then does as God commanded.

READ DEUTERONOMY 34:1–12

> *There has never been another prophet in Israel like Moses, whom the LORD knew face to face* (v10).

Checkpoint: The first part of this chapter seems sad. Moses, after all he had been through, goes to the top of the mountain, looks over to the Promised Land, and dies there, seemingly alone. However, it was God who had led him there. God was with him on the mountain, and it would seem that it was God who buried him. God was his constant strength through the forty years he led the people. God did not leave him in the end, even though Moses got it wrong sometimes.

As we live our lives, no matter where God leads us, we should make God our constant friend and guide. He will not leave us even though other people will let us down. Verse 10 states that there was no other prophet in Israel like Moses. God had used him for a special purpose and performed mighty miracles through him. He was remembered for these even though the people he led were rebellious and did not always do right. God's purposes for us will work out; other people will not be able to stop that.

It was because of Moses' own reactions that he did not enter the Promised Land. It is easy to become distracted by other people, but we must keep our focus on God and be obedient to Him alone.

- *In what ways can you compare and contrast Moses in the Old Testament to Jesus in the New Testament?*
- *Do you think Moses would have been sad at the top of the mountain before he died? Why/why not?*
- *Talk about the main lessons you have learned from Moses' life.*

Prayer Stop: Pray for any older people you know, that they will be aware of God's presence with them. Pray that God will help you to keep focused on Him and not on others.

THE HISTORY BOOKS
OF THE OLD TESTAMENT

From Joshua through the book of Esther, we read more about the story of God's people as they settle into the land that God had chosen to give them, as they turn away from God, and of the measures that God takes to bring them back to Himself. We learn about the different leaders God sends to lead His people.

JOSHUA

Joshua was the leader God chose to take over from Moses and lead His people into the land He was going to give them. The book of Joshua tells the story of how the Israelites conquered and settled in that land to make it their home.

DAY 1

On the Way: Toward the end of Deuteronomy, Moses presented Joshua to the Israelites as their new leader, the man God had chosen to take the place of Moses. Joshua had been Moses' assistant and knew something of the job that was before him.

In today's reading, we meet with Joshua at the very start of his journey, as the leader moves forward without Moses.

MEMORY VERSE

This is my command—be strong and courageous! Do not be afraid or discouraged. For the LORD your God is with you wherever you go.

~ Joshua 1:9

READ JOSHUA 1:1–11, 16–17

Checkpoint: Imagine how Joshua is feeling. Moses is gone, and now it is up to him to lead the people. He may have been feeling very alone and scared. It was a big job he had to do. Then God speaks to him, encouraging him and assuring him that there is no need to be afraid. Moses may have gone, but God was not going away. He assured Joshua, more than once, that He was there to stay with him. However, Joshua was given a task to do; he could not just sit back and be the boss. In verses 6–8, God tells Joshua that he must be strong and courageous and meditate on God's Law, not turning away from it. He had to keep God the center of his life and leadership. After meeting with God, Joshua goes out and gives the people instructions to get ready to move on.

The people respond very positively in verses 16–17. Joshua had spent time listening to God before he went out to give the people instructions. They saw that God was with him as He was with Moses and were willing to support him as their leader now. Sometimes changing leaders can be hard. Perhaps you have had a change of leadership in your church or youth group recently.

- *Think of ways you could encourage a new leader.*
- *What things may they find difficult?*
- *What do verses 6–8 tell us is important for leaders to do?*

Prayer Stop: Pray that your leaders will remember the importance of spending time with God. Pray that they will be strong and courageous and obey God.

DAY 2

On the Way: Joshua was getting ready to lead the people across the Jordan into the Promised Land. He wanted to be prepared, so he sent two men ahead to spy out the land. In our reading today, we arrive in Jericho with the men who are staying at the home of a woman called Rahab.

READ JOSHUA 2:2–24

> *For the LORD your God is the supreme God of the heavens above and the earth below* (v11b).

Checkpoint: Rahab came from a nation that did not worship God. However, she had heard of all the things that the God of the Israelites had done, and she had come to believe that the God of the Israelites was indeed the Living God. She was prepared to risk her life to protect the spies because she knew that God was on their side. The spies gave her a promise that if she did as they asked, she and her family would be safe. When they were gone, she wasted no time but immediately tied the red cord to her window. In Joshua 6:25, we read that because of what she had done, she was saved when the Israelites conquered Jericho.

In a nation that was shaking in fear, this one woman, Rahab, put her trust in God. When things in the world are making others afraid, we can trust in God. We do not need to be afraid. Remember the memory verse from yesterday. God has given us a way to be saved. If you have not already accepted Him as Savior, you can do this now. Do not wait; respond immediately, as Rahab did.

- *Rahab believed because she heard of the things God had done. What things has God done for you that you can tell others about?*

- *Rahab would have had to tell her family of the way they could be rescued. To be safe, they would have to be in her house at the time of the attack. Do you have family who are not Christians yet? Make sure you tell them the way they can be saved. But remember, the decision is theirs.*

Prayer Stop: Pray for those you know who do not know Jesus. Pray that you will have the chance to share the gospel with them and that God will speak to them.

DAY 3

On the Way: The people were ready to cross the Jordan. Joshua gave them instructions to follow the priests as they carried the Ark of the Covenant into the river. God had told them that as the priests entered the river, He would stop the river flowing so that they could cross over on dry ground. This was to confirm to the people that God was with Joshua as He was with Moses. Joshua asked each tribe to choose a man and in today's reading, we learn what their special task was.

READ JOSHUA 4:1–8, 15–18

These stones will stand as a memorial among the people of Israel forever (v7b).

Checkpoint: The Israelites would have heard about the Red Sea parting, but none of them would have been alive when that happened. Their families had wandered in the desert for forty years afterward. It is always more effective when we experience things firsthand and not just hear the story. God gave this new generation of Israelites a personal experience. They knew God was powerful, they had heard the stories, but now they saw it for themselves. To prevent them from forgetting and to help their children remember, the twelve men chosen had to carry stones from the riverbed, setting them up in camp to be a constant reminder of the power of God and how He brought them to the place they were now living.

It is important for our parents to teach us about God, but it is more important that we know and experience God in our lives ourselves.

- *What things do you have that are constant reminders of all that God has done for you? (Things like the Bible, or perhaps more personal stories to your family.)*

- *Read Psalm 145:1–4, 13. What are some of the mighty acts of God that we can teach to our families?*

- *If parents have stories of wonderful things God has done in their lives, share them with your children.*

Prayer Stop: Praise God for some of the things that you have spoken about today. Pray that you will be faithful in teaching every generation of your family about God.

DAY 4

On the Way: God brought His people safely across the Jordan River to the land He had promised them. However, there was a slight problem . . . there were people already living in that land! God had promised that He would drive these people from the land. The first city they come to is Jericho.

READ JOSHUA 5:13–6:5, 20—21

Take off your sandals for the place where you are standing is holy (v15b).

Checkpoint: Joshua had a problem called Jericho. He did not know what to do. However, God knew and came to meet with him as he was nearing Jericho. As Joshua realizes that he is meeting with God, he bows down to worship, asking to hear what God has to say. We are reminded of the story of Moses as Joshua is asked to remove his sandals. I am sure Joshua would remember all the mighty acts of God he had seen and heard of through Moses.

Joshua didn't start telling God how big the problem of Jericho was. He simply asked to hear the message God had for him. God gave him the answer to Jericho. What do you think Joshua might have thought about this war strategy?

Sometimes when we face big problems, we spend a lot of time telling God about the problem. Let's learn from Joshua. When he met with God, he bowed in worship and asked to hear what God had to say. He then obeyed. We don't read of him mentioning to God that this is rather an unusual way to go about invading a city. He simply obeys.

Sometimes God's answers to our problems are not what we think will work. He sometimes asks us to do things a little differently. Are you willing to obey and see more of God's mighty acts at work in your life?

- *Have you or your family ever had a problem that you did not know what to do about? How did God help you solve it?*

- *How would the Israelites have felt when they saw the walls of Jericho fall down?*

- *How do you think those in Jericho felt when they saw the army marching around their city?*

Prayer Stop: Pray that God will help you to hear what He has to say about answering the problems you face just now. Pray for others you know who are facing hard things now also.

DAY 5

On the Way: God instructed the Israelites to destroy everything in Jericho when they took it over and to keep none of the spoils for themselves. He warned them that disobeying this would bring destruction on themselves as individuals and would make the whole of Israel liable to trouble. After they had captured Jericho, Joshua sent men to Ai to see what that land was like.

READ JOSHUA 7:2–7, 10–12, 20–26

> *I will not remain with you any longer unless you destroy the things among you that were set apart for destruction* (v12b).

Checkpoint: Joshua could not understand why God would have brought them this far only to allow them to be defeated. However, we discover that because one man disobeyed God, the whole community suffered. This is a picture of what happened back in the Garden of Eden, when Adam disobeyed God and the entire human race suffered. Just as Achan's sin had to be dealt with before God would rescue the people from their enemies again, so our sin needs to be dealt with before we can have free access to God again.

As God had commanded before the Israelites entered Jericho, the result of Achan's sin was his death. The result of our sin too is death. However, God has loved us so much that He has given us a way to be saved. Jesus came to die in our place for our sins. So if we believe in Him and ask His forgiveness for our sins, we will be rescued from the effects of our sin. In the same way that disobeying God meant that Achan had to die, we too will be separated from God forever if we do not accept His way to be saved.

- *Read Romans 5:8, 6:23, and 10:9. What do these verses tell us about the result of sin and the way God is willing to rescue us from it?*

- *If someone reading this with you has not accepted Jesus as their Savior, you may want to chat about this with them or encourage them to speak to a suitable person in church.*

Prayer Stop: Thank God that He sent His Son Jesus to die for our sin. Pray for those you know who have not asked Him to be their Savior yet.

DAY 6

On the Way: After Achan's sin had been dealt with, the people could then move on with God leading them again. Joshua and the whole army then moved to attack Ai and God gave them the city this time. Joshua then built an altar to the Lord and read the whole book of the Law to all the people. When the kings in the surrounding countries heard what had happened to Jericho and Ai, the joined together to go to war against Israel. However, the Gibeonites decided on a different tactic.

READ JOSHUA 9:3–16

So the Israelites examined their food, but they did not consult the LORD *(v14).*

Checkpoint: The Gibeonites were trying to save themselves and their country so they tricked the Israelites into making a vow of peace with them. If all that they were told was true, the idea of a peace treaty would have been good, but these people were not telling the truth.

Sadly, today there are some people who would do the same for us as Christians. They try to tell us that it doesn't matter which god you believe in, as long as you believe; they try to convince us that just telling a white lie to save face is okay. However, the Bible is very clear that these things are not okay, and we must not be tempted to follow other people's ideas without first finding out what God has to say on the issue.

That was where the people of Israel went wrong: they did not ask God. As a result, the Gibeonites lived and worked among them, bringing their own traditions and gods. This in turn led the Israelites away from God. It can happen to us too. If we start to listen to ideas that are not in the Bible it can start to turn our hearts away from God.

- *List three ways that we can find out what God wants us to do today.*
- *Read Proverbs 3:5–6. How do these verses help us in finding out what God's will is?*
- *Talk about any experience you have had of others trying to get you involved with things that may not be right.*

Prayer Stop: Pray that you will know what is right when others ask you to do things. Pray that you will be able to stand up against being tempted to do the wrong thing.

DAY 7

On the Way: Israel was making progress in taking the land God was giving them. They were learning that they had to seek God and obey Him every step of the way. Each encounter was different. Jericho was taken by a miracle, Ai by planned war, and Gibeon surrendered to them. Now the king of Jerusalem was fearful and planned an attack of revenge on Gibeon along with four other kings from the area. They banded together and attacked Gibeon.

READ JOSHUA 10:6–15

Surely the LORD fought for Israel that day (v14b).

Checkpoint: The Gibeonites needed help. Joshua headed off with all his fighting men to fight for Gibeon. The army marched all night and must have been exhausted. However, they arrived at Gibeon in the morning, fought, and defeated the enemy army. They continued to fight all day until they had completely beaten them. As they were doing this, note what was happening in verses 10, 11, and 13. Our key verse sums this up nicely: Surely the Lord was fighting for Israel.

The Israelites could not have done this alone. They did what they were able to do—what they were trained for—and God did the rest. Often when we face difficult situations, there are certain tasks we are able to do and as we do them, we will see God act in amazing ways to help us.

- *The Gibeonites witnessed confusion, hailstones, and the sun staying still in the sky for almost a day. What do you think they learned about the God of Israel?*

- *Read Psalm 44:3. Why do you think God did not simply allow the Israelite army to beat the enemy by fighting alone?*

- *Have there been times when you have seen God come and help you in difficult situations as you do what you are able to do?*

Prayer Stop: Thank God that He is able to help us get through difficult situations. Ask Him to give you wisdom to do whatever you are able to do. Pray for anyone you know facing difficulties just now, that they would see God working on their behalf and give Him praise.

DAY 8

On the Way: After the Israelites had defeated the five kings that attacked Gibeon, they continued to move on to take the rest of the land that God was giving them. In the chapters that follow, we read lists of all the defeated kings. This did not all happen at once; it took a number of years. When Joshua was very old, God revealed that He would drive the remaining nations from the rest of the land. Then the land would be divided up among the tribes as promised in the time of Moses.

READ JOSHUA 19:49–51; 21:43–45

> *Not a single one of all the good promises the* LORD *had given to the family of Israel was left unfulfilled* (21:45a).

Checkpoint: The people of Israel had not known peace since leaving Egypt. They had wandered in the desert for forty years and had been capturing cities since they moved into the land that God was giving them. Now, however, God gave them rest. They were able to enjoy the land that God had given to them; each tribe had been given a certain area and settled in it. Joshua and Caleb were also given areas to settle as commanded by God through Moses. This part of their journey was finished.

There are times in our lives when it is right to stop and enjoy the blessings that God has given us. Often we think that we should be constantly busy, working for God. It is God's will that we sometimes take time to reflect and praise Him for how He has led us so far before we embark on the next exciting part of the journey and discover the new things He wants us to do.

- *The Israelites were able to reflect and see that none of God's promises had failed. Look back at your lives and think about how God has been faithful to you and your family.*
- *When do you find it hard to trust God's promises?*

Prayer Stop: Take time to praise God for the blessings you have in Him. Pray that God will give you strength to trust in His promises even when it is hard.

DAY 9

On the Way: Each tribe was given an area of land to call their own. The priests were given towns to live in and land to pasture their flocks. As we read yesterday, Israel was given a time of peace and was able to settle into the land that God had given them. God also provided a way for those who accidently killed someone to be protected.

MEMORY VERSE

So now there is no condemnation for those who belong to Christ Jesus.

~ Romans 8:1

READ JOSHUA 20:1-9

Now tell the Israelites to designate the cities of refuge (v2a).

Checkpoint: God was very aware of the character of His people. He knew that they were likely to take justice into their own hands. So if someone accidently killed another person, God knew that the relatives were likely to take revenge and so be guilty of a greater crime. God wanted to protect His people from such things and provided cities of refuge.

This is a picture of what happened in the New Testament when Jesus came to die for our sins. God knew there was no way we could ever set ourselves right before Him and that we are prone to taking things into our own hands, judging others more severely than we do ourselves. So God gave us a refuge in Jesus. So that whoever believes in him will not die but have eternal life(John 3:16). It is only through what God has done that we can have eternal life. We cannot do anything ourselves but must make use of the provision God has given us.

If the guilty person just stayed at home, then he would have no protection. He would have to carry out the requirements in the Law if he wanted that protection. So it is with us today. We must accept the gift of salvation from God if we want to have His gift of eternal life.

- *Read Romans 8:1-2. How do these verses describe the protection we have through Jesus?*
- *Look at Joshua 20:9. What kind of people does God want to protect? What does this show us about the kingdom of God?*

Prayer Stop: Thank God for His gift of salvation. Pray for those you know who have still to become part of God's kingdom.

DAY 10

On the Way: You may remember that when the Israelites came to the Jordan, at first the tribes of Reuben, Gad, and the half tribe of Manasseh asked to stay on the east of the Jordan because the land there was suitable for their flocks. Moses permitted this on the condition that they help their fellow tribes to conquer the land they were to inherit across the Jordan. This was completed now, and Joshua sent those tribes back home. We join them on the way back.

READ JOSHUA 22:10–12, 24–27, 30–34

Today we know the LORD *is among us* (v31b).

Checkpoint: Have you ever done something, intending it to be helpful or good, only to have someone else take it completely the wrong way? It may have caused a great upset and perhaps took you by surprise. In today's reading, we see the tribes returning home, wanting a reminder that they were part of the Israelites because the Jordan River was now between them. They built a huge altar. The rest of the tribes jumped to the wrong conclusion over this innocent act and prepared to go to war. But first, they sent the priest to meet these tribes before engaging in battle and discovered that their motives for building the altar were indeed good. The priest took back a full report, battle was avoided, and in fact there would be unity among the tribes because of this.

When we are tempted to react to someone's actions, we should stop and find out if we understood it correctly. By doing this first, we can avoid unnecessary quarrels and hurt, and we can keep the unity that God wants us to have with other Christians.

- *Have you overreacted to someone's actions (or perhaps someone overreacted to yours)? What happened?*

- *Read Hebrews 12:14–15. How can this verse help us practice what we learned today?*

Prayer Stop: Pray that you will be wise and sensitive in how you react to other people's actions. Pray that God will keep your church from quarrels.

DAY 11

On the Way: When the tribes of Reuben, Gad, and Manasseh had settled back in their lands, the Lord gave Israel rest for a good few years. Now Joshua was very old. He would die soon and wanted to prepare the Israelites for that and encourage them to carry on with the mission God had given them. We will look at three different parts of his farewell speech over the next three days.

READ JOSHUA 23:1–13

So be very careful to follow everything Moses wrote in the Book of Instruction (v6a).

Checkpoint: Joshua realized that he had completed the task that God had given him, and he prepared the people for the next step of their journey. He wanted them to focus on the fact that it was God who had brought them this far, and if they were faithful, God would continue guiding them. They were God's children and had to continue living as God's children with new leaders.

Sometimes our leaders are called to serve God in a new location, or perhaps they retire. It is important to remember that our churches do not depend on the leader but on God. He will provide new leaders, and we will continue to be the people God wants us to be and continue with the mission that He has given us. It may be difficult to say goodbye to great leaders. I am sure the Israelites were a little afraid and uncertain; however, Joshua reminded them that God was not leaving them and would continue to guide them. Their job was to remain faithful to God. God has also been our guide and will continue to do so. Our task, like the Israelites, is to remain faithful.

- *How do you think the Israelites were feeling as they listened to Joshua? Have you ever had to say goodbye to a leader you loved? How did you feel?*

- *Read Jeremiah 29:11. How can this verse encourage us in such circumstances?*

Prayer Stop: Pray for your church to depend on God for guidance and that your church family will be faithful to Him. Pray for your leaders in church to depend on God to guide them.

DAY 12

On the Way: Joshua was God's appointed leader, and now at the end of his life, he calls Israel together to remind them of what God had done so far and to encourage them to remember their special promise to serve only Him. The Israelites would perhaps have known that this would be the last time Joshua would speak to them, and so you can imagine them listening carefully to every word.

READ JOSHUA 24:1–7, 14–15

But as for me and my family, we will serve the LORD (v15b).

Checkpoint: Joshua takes the people on a trip down memory lane. He goes right back to the time of Abraham. Though none of the people would have been alive during Abraham's time, they would have heard the story. Joshua reminds them of their journey so far. At the end of today's reading, he states that as a result of looking back and remembering what God had done, he and his household were choosing to stick firmly with following God.

It is good to look back and see how God has brought you to where you are today, to remember the people who have taught you about God, perhaps the people who God sent at just the right time to help you in difficulty, to remember the exciting things you have seen God do in your own life or in the life of others. As we do this, it should encourage us to tell God again how much we love Him and that we will choose, like Joshua, to stick to firmly following His ways.

- *Take time to think about your life so far. Think about the people who have been important to you and your family, and the times you have seen God do amazing things in your lives. It is as we look back that we can give God praise for all He has done.*

- *Find the person who has been a member longest in your church and ask him or her to share memories. Perhaps you could invite them for dinner or coffee. Together, praise God for all He has done in your church.*

Prayer Stop: Praise God for all you have talked about in Question 1. Pray that God will help you to commit your life to follow Him.

DAY 13

On the Way: Having reminded the people of their history and how God had worked in their lives to bring them to this point, Joshua challenges them to commit themselves again to serving God. He lets them know that he is fully committed to serving God. We join them as they commit their lives to serve God.

READ JOSHUA 24:16–27

> *You are a witness to your own decision . . . you have chosen to serve the* Lord *(v22).*

Checkpoint: As we mentioned yesterday, it is good to look back and remember all that God has done for us. It is just as important to move forward. We shouldn't just focus on what has happened in the past but should look to the future and what God has planned for us to do. Joshua challenges the people to commit their lives again to serving the God who has been faithful to them all these years.

As we look back, it is important to give God praise, but we must also use this to make a commitment to Him for our future, looking forward to the exciting work He will continue to do for us and through us. Joshua marked the people's new commitment with a stone. By writing the promise down, in the future others could look back, praise God for what He continued to do, and commit their lives also to serving God.

The people needed to get rid the false gods they had collected to show their new commitment to the Living God. Perhaps there are some things in your lives that have crept in that are not really pleasing God.

- *Having spent time yesterday looking back, take time today to commit yourselves to serving God in a new way. How could you mark this occasion so that in the future you can look back and remember it?*
- *Take time to reflect on the things in your life, the way you spend your time, what you watch on TV, etc. Are there things that need to change to reflect your new commitment to God?*
- *Are there any new things that you feel God may be leading you into?*

Prayer Stop: Pray that God would make clear to you the things He has planned for you to do for Him. Commit yourselves to obey Him.

DAY 14

On the Way: And so we come to the end of the book of Joshua. Joshua has obeyed God and brought the Israelites to their new country. He led the people and taught them the way to live so that they might continue to please God after Joshua's death. The closing verses of the book are our reading today.

READ JOSHUA 24:28–33

> *The people of Israel served the Lord throughout the lifetime of Joshua and of the elders who outlived him—those who had personally experienced all that the Lord had done for Israel* (v31).

Checkpoint: Joshua did all he could to ensure that the people of Israel were prepared to serve God once he was gone. We can see from today's key verse that as long as there were people alive who could remember firsthand the things God had done, they did serve God. In the books we read next, we will see that did not remain the case. However, Joshua had been faithful in his mission. God had not given him the job of looking after Israelites forever, just as long as he was alive.

We need to be faithful in the things that God has given us to do in our lives. We cannot be responsible for the choices others make in the future. We must do all we can to prepare our families to follow God and trust Him to help them make the right choices when we are no longer with them.

- *Talk about your childhood and what affect your upbringing has had on the choices you make today. Even if you did not have Christian parents, your parents' principles or priorities may affect how you make decisions today. If you did not have a happy childhood, how has that affected your decisions for your family?*

- *Ask your children what they see in your family life that will prepare them to make wise and godly choices in the future.*

Prayer Stop: Pray that you will continue to make wise decisions to help your families serve God. Pray the same for other families in your church.

JUDGES

The people of Israel were without a leader now that Joshua had died. Things became a little confused as they settled into the land. They started to disobey God and worship the gods of the local people. God gave them other leaders, called judges, and we are going to learn about some of them over the next few days.

DAY 15

On the Way: Under Joshua, the Israelites had conquered most of the land God was giving them, but they still have work to do. They ask God for guidance. In the past, Joshua told them what God was saying, but now they hear God's messages through the priest.

READ JUDGES 1:1–16, 19

When the men of Judah attacked, the Lord gave them victory over the
Canaanites and Perizzites (v4a).

Checkpoint: The tribe of Judah set out to fight against the Canaanites. They were the strongest of the tribes, but they asked for help from the Simeonites. It is good to have help from others, regardless of our own strength and confidence. God has put us in families and in His family to help and support one another.

The story of King Adoni-Bezek is gruesome! However, in verse 7 we see that he had done the same thing as had happened to him to seventy other kings. He reaped what he sowed and learned that God does act justly. Sometimes we do not see what God does to those who mistreat us, but we know that we can trust Him to do what is right.

The men of Judah seemed to stop once they had taken the hill country because they did not have the right chariots. God's command to them was to take the whole land. Thus, we see the first seeds of disobedience creeping in. They had seen and heard about God's mighty miracles, and yet they let the wrong kind of chariots put them off obeying God completely. This led to all kinds of trouble.

- *How can 1 Corinthians 12:14–20 encourage us to help others even when they seem to have much more than us?*

- *Talk about some instances you know of where you or others have been treated unjustly. (Think about those in other lands who suffer for their faith.)*

- *Because of the wrong equipment, Judah chose not to fully obey God. Are there things that God may be asking you to do but that you feel you don't have what it takes?*

Prayer Stop: Pray that God would show you those who perhaps need your help in some way. Pray for those who are being treated unfairly because of their faith. Pray that you won't let anything put you off obeying God.

DAY 16

On the Way: After Judah had conquered Canaan, the other tribes took the land God had given them. However, they did not drive the nations completely from the land as God had commanded. As a result of this, the people were influenced by the false gods of the other nations. Their hearts were turned away from the Lord.

MEMORY VERSE

Jesus replied "You must love the LORD your God with all your heart, all your soul, and all your mind. This is the first and greatest commandment."

~ Matthew 22:37–38

READ JUDGES 2:10–22

And they refused to give up their evil practices and stubborn ways (v19b).

Checkpoint: This new generation of Israelites had forgotten the ways of the Lord that their families had taught them. They started to worship the false gods of the foreign nations. This angered God because they kept doing it in spite of the way He constantly showed them His love and favor. So God was not with the Israelites when they went to war. When they were defeated, they felt great distress.

God was angry; the people were distressed. When we forget to give God the top place in our lives, like the Israelites we may face distress as God allows consequences to happen to remind us of Him.

God shows His willingness to forgive His children by providing them with judges to lead them again in His ways. However, when each judge dies, the people quickly forget the Lord and become more and more involved in worshipping false gods. They refused to give up their evil ways (v19). God provides us with leaders to teach us and show us His way and His Word. It is right that we respect and learn from them, but we should also remember their teaching when they are no longer with us.

- *The Israelites stopped having victory over their enemies. What things might God use in our lives to remind us that He wants us to follow Him? Have you had personal experiences with this?*
- *How does God show His willingness to forgive us? Romans 5:8 may help you here.*

Prayer Stop: Pray that God will help you to live in ways that please Him, making you aware of the things that need to change in your life. Pray for your leaders.

DAY 17

On the Way: The Israelites who lived in the land now had not yet been born when God gave their ancestors victory in Joshua's day. So God allowed the foreign nations to stay among them so that they would learn to rely on God in warfare. The people are constantly rebelling against God, one minute crying out to Him and the next disobeying Him. We are now introduced to some of the judges God used to save His people from their enemies. The first was Othniel, who ruled for forty years. In today's reading, we meet Ehud.

READ JUDGES 3:12–25

I have a message from God for you! (v20b).

Checkpoint: When Othniel died, the Israelites very quickly allowed their hearts to rebel against God again. God sends Eglon, the Moabite king and enemy to Israel, to take control over them in order that they might turn back to Him.

Eventually, as the children of Israel plead with God to help them, God uses Ehud to rescue them. Ehud is chosen to take the annual offering from the people to Eglon; God gives him a special task of overcoming the king who had taken control of the Israelites.

God rescued the Israelites. The story of how Ehud led the people to victory is unusual (if not a little gruesome). God helped him carry out this plan so that the children of Israel would see that God had not forgotten them and that He would fight for them if they turned to Him.

Perhaps God has given you special talent or will give you a special opportunity, as He did for Ehud, so that you may be able to help those of God's children who are oppressed today. (You will not have to do anything like Ehud did; warfare is very different today!)

- *In what ways could you help God's children who are being oppressed today?*
- *What might your message from God be for today's oppressors?*
- *The Israelites rebelled when they had no leader. Why do you think this happened?*

Prayer Stop: Pray for organizations like Release International and Barnabas Trust who help oppressed Christians today.

Practical Application: If you don't get a regular prayer diary from one of these or similar organizations, perhaps you could look into doing so.

DAY 18

On the Way: After Ehud died, true to form, Israel rebelled against God again. This time, Jabin, king of Canaan, had victory over them and oppressed them for twenty years. They cried out to God for help again. We take the story up with Deborah.

READ JUDGES 4:4–10

I will go, but only if you go with me (v8).

Checkpoint: Deborah, a godly woman, is now leading Israel. As she is going about her daily routine of giving direction to those who ask her for help, God gives her a message that will rescue Israel from their enemies. When Barak hears God has chosen him to carry out His mission, he wants Deborah to come with him. The Bible does not tell us why, but he must have felt certain he would win with Deborah by his side. Perhaps he wanted her to "keep him right," in case he did something that was against God's plan.

It does not seem to bother Barak that he will not get the honor for rescuing Israel from Jabin himself. That honor will go to a woman. (In the last half of chapter 4, we read of Jael killing Sisera, the commander of Jabin's army.) It seems that Barak wanted to be sure he was doing things the right way and was not afraid to ask for support and advice from others. The fact that someone else would get the honor did not bother him. He wanted to make sure he did the job right.

- *When God calls us to do something for Him, do we try to do it all alone without accepting help or advice in order that we might get the honor for it? What is the most important thing when serving God?*
- *Can you think of examples in the Bible when people asked for help and advice?*
- *It may seem that Barak didn't trust God to go on his own. When you find it hard to trust God, who do you go to for help and advice?*

Prayer Stop: Pray that God will give you courage to do the things He asks you to do. Thank God for godly people who can give us support and advice. Pray that God will have the glory in everything you do.

DAY 19

On the Way: God gave the Israelites power over Jabin and his army. On that day, Deborah and Barak sang praise to God. It is always good to praise God when He helps you and gives you victory.

In chapter 6, the Israelites rebel again! This time the Midianites conquered the Israelites and treated them so cruelly that they were left hiding fearfully in the rocks and caves. The Midianites ruined all their crops and livestock. Today we meet Gideon, threshing wheat in a winepress to try to hide it from the Midianites.

READ JUDGES 6:12–24, 36–40

Mighty hero, the LORD is with you (v12b).

Checkpoint: All Israel is living in fear, trying to find some place to keep livestock and grow crops that the Midianites will not destroy. Gideon hides in a winepress to thresh some grain when an angel appears and tells him God is with him! Not only that, the angel calls him a "mighty hero." Nothing could seem further from the truth! God saw in Gideon something that he could not see himself. What did Gideon do?

1. He asked some questions (Judg. 6:13, 15). "If God is with us, then why is all this happening?" "How can I save Israel?" The angel did not answer him directly but told him that God was sending him and to go in God's strength.

2. He worshipped God (Judg. 6:19). It was as he offered his sacrifice that he realized it was indeed the Lord who had appeared to him.

3. He asked God for assurance (Judg. 6:36–40). God was patient with Gideon as he looked for more assurance that he had heard God correctly.

If God is asking you to do something that you do not feel brave enough to do, do not be afraid to ask God questions or ask Him for assurance in special ways. In doing so, remember to worship God and know that He will give you the courage you need to do what He wants you to do.

- *Imagine how Gideon was feeling when the angel first spoke to him.*
- *How do you think he felt in verse 40 after God had answered him a third time?*
- *What do you think happened to Gideon's faith in between?*

Prayer Stop: Pray for courage to obey God. Worship God for His holiness and power.

DAY 20

On the Way: God continued to speak to Gideon, telling him to pull down the altars to Baal and build an altar to the Lord. Fearful of what his family and fellow citizens would do, he did this at night. Even though God was speaking to him, he remained afraid of others. God did not stop working through him. Gideon gathered an army together in order to fight the Midianites and continued to ask God for guidance. We meet him and his army in our reading today.

READ JUDGES 7:2–15

> *When Gideon heard the dream and its interpretation, he bowed in worship*
> *before the LORD (v15a).*

Checkpoint: Gideon had gathered an army suitable for facing a mighty enemy, but God had a different plan. He wanted Israel to know that they had a mightier ally. God would fight for them and give them victory, and they would be in no doubt about that. Gideon continued to be fearful, but God continued to give him courage.

In verses 10–14, God provides encouragement for Gideon even before Gideon asks! Gideon kept on with the mission, obeying God through his fear. God knows our character and sends encouragement when we need it. When God asks us to do something for Him, He will give us the courage we need. We should not let our fear of failure or fear of others stand in our way.

I'm sure Gideon wondered what God was doing, leaving him with just three hundred men to fight such a might enemy. God's ways are not the same as ours. He is able to do anything because He is God. He asks us to obey, and it is exciting to be part of the miracles that God does.

- *How does Isaiah 55:8–9 relate to this story? How can we relate it to our lives?*
- *When you are fearful, what is your normal reaction? What can you learn from Gideon?*
- *Have you heard or been part of something that God has done when it seemed like the plan could never work? How does that feel?*

Prayer Stop: Pray especially for any situation you are facing that makes you feel afraid. Ask God to help you obey Him despite your feelings.

DAY 21

On the Way: After defeating the Midianites, there was unrest in the nation of Israel itself. Gideon tried to encourage the people to worship the Lord again, but he refused to rule over them, saying that the Lord should be their ruler. However, he did ask for an offering out of which he made a gold breastplate that the priests wore. Even this became like an idol to the people. After Gideon died, his son Abimelech set himself up as leader in the nation, killing the other seventy sons of Gideon. He did not do what pleased the Lord. After him came other judges to rule the land. The Israelites constantly struggled with the nations around them and struggled to remain faithful to God.

MEMORY VERSE

You saw me before I was born. Every day of my life was recorded in your book. Every moment was laid out before a single day had passed.

~ Psalm 139:16

READ JUDGES 13:2–14

For he will be dedicated to God as a Nazirite from birth (v5b).

Checkpoint: Rebellion this time meant that it was the Philistines who oppressed the Israelites. Every generation of Israelites seemed to make the same mistakes. They were always tempted to follow the gods of the nations around them and forget that they were God's chosen nation. God never gave up on them; He gave them more than one "second chance." When they called to Him, He answered them.

We are sometimes like the Israelites. We forget to give God the top priority in our lives, but He never gives us up.

Today we read of the angel of God visiting a couple and telling them they will have a son. God had special plans for this baby boy. He has plans for all of us too. Not just when we are older and ready to work, but for all of our lives.

- *Read Psalm 139:13–16. How does this make you feel as a person? How does it make you feel as a parent concerning your children?*
- *Having lived for forty years under the Philistines, how would Manoah and his wife have felt when the angel of God appeared to them?*

Prayer Stop: Praise God that He knows what every day of your life holds for you. Pray that you will keep making God top priority in your life.

DAY 22

On the Way: The couple we read of yesterday had a son whom they called Samson. They would have brought him up according to the plan the angel told them. However, as he grew up, he began to make choices for himself. Not all of them were wise.

READ JUDGES 14

His father and mother didn't realize the Lord was at work in this (v4a).

Checkpoint: Samson is now old enough to make his own choices, and he begins to make decisions that would not be in line with the plans God had set out for him before he was born. God knew exactly the decisions Samson would make, and He used them to bring about His purposes anyway.

As we grow up, we don't always make the wisest of decisions. Sometimes they are completely opposite of God's perfect plan for us; however, we must never feel that we have moved too far away from God's plan. God can use even the sinful choices we make to bring about His plans and purposes. This does not mean that we should make sinful choices deliberately. NO. It just shows us how merciful God is, willing to use us even when we sin against Him.

Samson's parents encouraged him to marry a Jewish woman, but he would not listen. They knew his choice was against God's perfect plan, but because of his age and perhaps his attitude, they were unable to change his mind. He was intent on following his own heart, but as we follow the story, we see that God did not leave him. He continued to use Samson even though Samson made mistakes. As parents, we need to trust our children and the decisions they make to God.

- *If mercy means "not getting what we deserve," how do we see God's mercy to Samson in today's reading?*
- *How do we see God's mercy toward us?*
- *How do you think his parents felt about his behavior? How do your behaviors and decisions affect your parents?*

Prayer Stop: Praise God that He does not treat us as we deserve but shows us mercy. Pray for your family and ask God to help you make wise and godly decisions as you grow older.

DAY 23

On the Way: Yesterday we saw Samson's great physical strength and his weakness. He insisted on marrying a Philistine woman and giving in to her, but this brought great trouble to him and his people. The trouble continued, but so did the display of God's power in him through the things he did. He caught three hundred foxes and used them to set the Philistines' crops alight by tying torches to their tails. He attacked the Philistines because they killed his wife and her family; he killed one thousand men on his own just by using the jawbone of a donkey, and he escaped from the Philistines by lifting the city gates from their hinges!

READ JUDGES 16:4–22

But he didn't realize the Lᴏʀᴅ had left him (v20b).

Checkpoint: Samson has fallen in love again with a woman who is not Jewish. She tries to trick him into revealing the secret of his strength. At first he tells her lies, but when she clearly won't give up, he gives in and tells her the truth. It is at this point that we read in verse 20 that he did not know that the Lord had left him.

Samson fought the Philistines, perhaps thinking his strength was his own and not from God. He did not seem to care about the fact that God had set him apart from birth and had a special plan for him. He lived as if God's plan did not matter.

Although God had used him to lead his people, there came a time when—as a result of Samson continuing to do things his own way—God left him, and Samson had to take the consequences of his own decisions. He had not learned from his first mistakes.

When we continue to sin, not learning from our mistakes, then sometimes God will allow us to face the consequences of our actions.

- *In what ways do we see Samson deliberately disobeying God? (Deuteronomy 7:3–4 will give you one clue.)*
- *Why is it important that Christians marry Christians? (2 Corinthians 6:14)*

Prayer Stop: Thank God for His patience with us and pray that you will learn from your mistakes and not be like Samson. Confess any sin to God that He has brought to mind.

DAY 24

On the Way: We may feel rather sad that Samson deliberately chose to disobey God and follow his own sinful desires. It seems pitiful that a man with such opportunity should end up grinding corn just like the animals. However, God is not finished with Samson.

READ JUDGES 16:22–34

Oh God, please strengthen me just one more time (v28b).

Checkpoint: The Philistines were celebrating: they now ruled the Israelites with no threat of trouble from Samson. It seemed that they used him as entertainment. They enjoyed seeing this man, once so powerful, now blind and helpless. You can imagine them shouting at him as he ground the corn perhaps even alongside the oxen. Because of his continued rebellion against God, he had brought himself to this. However, Samson now had time to think about his actions and their consequences. When the Philistines were together celebrating and laughing at him, he used the opportunity to pray and ask God for strength for one more victory over Israel's enemies. Samson now realized that his strength came from God, and he wanted God to have the victory over the Philistines. So as they praised their god for their victory, even though they had paid Delilah to find out the answer to Samson's strength, Samson asked the Living God for strength and gained victory over the Philistines—though he died with them.

When Samson had no strength left, he turned to God and asked for help. No matter what we have done, if we turn back to God, He will forgive us and restore our relationship with Him. Samson did not have the glory and honor among his people that he could have had if he honored God all his life, but his story demonstrates that we have a God who is willing to forgive if we turn back to Him.

- *Think of some times that you have felt far away from God. How did it feel when you started talking and listening to Him again?*
- *What do you think Samson felt when he asked to have his hands placed on the pillars?*

Prayer Stop: Thank and praise God that He is forgiving and merciful. Pray for those you know who have perhaps turned away from God, that they would repent and return to Him.

RUTH

After the book of Judges comes the little book of Ruth. It is only four chapters long but tells the story of King David's great-grandmother, who is also included in Jesus' ancestors.

DAY 25

On the Way: Ruth was from Moab, one of Israel's enemies. The story begins in Judah. During the time that judges ruled, there was a great famine there. A man called Elimelech took his wife Naomi and their two sons to live in Moab, which had plenty of food. Sadly, while living there, Elimelech died. His two sons married women from Moab, but then the sons also died. This left Naomi alone in a foreign land with two daughters-in-law. She heard God was providing food again for Judah and set out to go back. Both her daughters-in-law started out with her, but Naomi encouraged them to return to their own people, telling them they would be able to marry again there. We start reading as Orpah decides to return to her home.

READ RUTH 1:14–22

> *I went away full, but the* Lord *has brought me home empty* (v21a).

Checkpoint: Elimelech's decision brings nothing but heartache for his wife. Women in those days depended very much on their husbands for their living. Now, not only is Naomi left with nothing, but also the two Moabite girls who married her sons are left with nothing.

When we go through difficulties, God wants us to rely on Him more, not run away to where it might look easier but is not in His will! When we do that, we can bring difficulties not only on ourselves but also on those near us.

Naomi decides to go back to her own people; there she may be able to find relatives to help her. She realizes that before they left, she and her husband had so much because they had God, but having chosen to leave the country God had given them, they ended up with nothing.

Orpah listens to Naomi and decides to go back to her own land. Ruth, however, shows total commitment not only to her mother-in-law but also to her people and to God. Ruth was not thinking of herself. She didn't have much hope going to live in Judah, but neither was she going to abandon her desolate mother-in-law.

- *From this story, what can we tell about Ruth's character?*
- *Does Naomi seem happy to be back among her people?*
- *How do you feel when you do something that is not God's will?*

Prayer Stop: Thank God that He welcomes us back when we wander off. Thank Him for forgiving us.

DAY 26

On the Way: Ruth and Naomi are back in Bethlehem and have to find food and shelter. Verse 1 of chapter 2 introduces us to a man called Boaz, who is a relative of Naomi's husband. Ruth takes the responsibility to provide food for her and Naomi. She asks Naomi to let her go and pick up the grain left behind the harvesters in the fields. As she sets off to do this, she finds herself working in a field belonging to Boaz.

Boaz notices immediately that there is a stranger working in his field and asks who she is. He then makes sure that his hired workers look out for her and goes to speak to her personally.

READ RUTH 2:8–20

And as it happened, she found herself working in a field that belonged to Boaz (v3b).

Checkpoint: Ruth is in a dangerous position; she is a stranger in the land and needs food for herself and Naomi. Any of the landowners could have been nasty to her or harmed her, but she found herself working in the field of Naomi's relative. He is a kind man who, we can tell from our reading today, looks after his workers and who takes note of the kind things others do. How amazing! God guided Ruth to the very place where He knew she would be safe and looked after. She had no idea who Boaz was. She was willing to take the risk to provide for her mother-in-law, and God gave her an extra blessing of protection and extra food as well.

Sometimes we think things "just happen," but we need to remember that we have a God who knows *everything* from the very start to the very end of all time. Nothing just happens to Him.

- *How do you think Ruth felt when Boaz came to speak to her? (Ruth 2:10)*
- *What are the similarities in Ruth and Boaz's characters?*
- *Ruth later discovered that Boaz was their near relative. How do you think this would have affected her view of God?*

Prayer Stop: Think of some amazing surprises in your life and thank God that nothing is a surprise to Him. Pray for those in difficult situations, that they will look back and see how God rescued them.

DAY 27

On the Way: Ruth lives with Naomi and continues to work in Boaz's field until the end of harvest. One day Naomi talks to Ruth about finding another husband. Ruth is still young, and when Naomi dies, she will be left in a foreign country with no family unless she marries. Naomi has seen how Boaz treats Ruth and how he treats his workers. She knows he is fair in all he does, and to sum it up, she tells Ruth to go and ask him to marry her! It seems a bit odd to us today, but Ruth was happy to follow Naomi's advice.

READ RUTH 3:5–18

I will do everything you say (v5a).

Checkpoint: It was an ancient tradition that if a man died without children, his nearest male relative would buy his land, marry his widow, and have a family with her. This was known as being a "kinsman-redeemer": someone who would stand in for the man who had died to protect his family and land and to make sure that the widow is provided for. This tradition seems strange to us, and it may have been strange to Ruth too, who came from Moab, not Israel. However, she was willing to listen to her mother-in-law. She knew Naomi and had a good relationship with her. It is always good as a Christian to have someone older whom we can go to and receive wise advice.

In verse 13, Boaz shows Ruth (and us) that he is committed to doing the right thing before God. He commits himself to finding the right future for Ruth, if not with the man who is next in line, then by marrying her himself. Naomi tells Ruth that he can be trusted to do the right thing (Ruth 3:18).

- *What parts of Boaz and Ruth's character would you look for in a godly husband/wife? Parents may talk to their children about what they saw in each other.*

- *If you don't have someone already, think of a suitable older Christian you could ask for advice and guidance.*

Prayer Stop: Pray for your or your children's future husband or wife! Thank God for your parents' marriage. Pray for those you know who are getting married soon. Thank God for older Christians with godly advice.

DAY 28

On the Way: In those days, courts were held at the city gates, and important matters were decided there with the city elders. Boaz went there to have the future of Naomi's family decided. In chapter 4, he approaches the nearer relative at the gates and asks if he would buy the land for Naomi. The man would have bought the land, but he could not marry Ruth. So he let Boaz have the land and Ruth as his wife. This was agreed in front of the city elders as witnesses.

READ RUTH 4:9–17

Praise the LORD who has now provided a redeemer for your family! (v14b).

Checkpoint: At the end of this lovely story, we see God continuing to bless Naomi, Ruth, and Boaz. Naomi's family lived in Judah, but when times were hard, they took their family to a place that seemed better. In Moab, her husband died, as did her sons after marrying Moabite women. Naomi was left with nothing and no way of providing for herself. However, God had other plans, and today we see her praising God because she now had a grandson. Her family grew in a way she had not thought possible. As Naomi turned back to God and to His people, God blessed her, not only by providing what she needed but also by giving her close relationships with Himself and others. She had a caring daughter-in-law who was committed to looking after her.

Ruth had committed her life to God even though it seemed that she would have nothing, living in a foreign land. Her priority was to look after Naomi and to do what was right in God's sight. When we make pleasing God our priority, He promises to never leave us. We may not always be rich in money, but we will be rich in God's blessings.

- *What blessings did God give to Ruth and Naomi?*
- *What blessings has God given you?*
- *Some Christians have lots of possessions, and others not as much. Who do you think has the most blessing from God? Why?*

Prayer Stop: Thank God for all the blessings He gives you. Pray that God will help you to use the possessions you have to honor Him.

Practical Application: Think of something that you or your family could do to be a blessing to someone in need this week.

1 SAMUEL

This book was probably written by Samuel himself, recording his life as the last judge of Israel. It also covers the reign of Saul, who was the first king. We are also introduced to David in this book.

DAY 29

On the Way: In chapter 1, we meet Elkanah. He has two wives, one called Penninah, who has children, and Hannah, who has no children. Each year he took his family to worship God in Shiloh, giving gifts of meat to his children and wives. Penninah taunted Hannah because she had no children; it became so bad that Hannah was unable to eat. Elkanah could not understand why Hannah was so upset, because she knew that he loved her very much.

MEMORY VERSE
Give all your worries and cares to God, for he cares about you.

~ 1 Peter 5:7

READ 1 SAMUEL 1:9–20

But I am very discouraged, and I was pouring out my heart to the Lord (v15b).

Checkpoint: Elkanah's family is far from perfect. God's ideal from the start was for a man to have one wife. At that time in history, though, it was socially acceptable to marry another woman, especially if the first wife was unable to have children. It is worth noting that, in the Bible, when a man had more than one wife, there is trouble in his family. Although Elkanah's family was not perfect, he still made it the tradition that they worshipped God together. Even though our own families are not perfect and may not agree on everything, it makes a big difference if we can worship God together. It helps us accept the things we find hard in family relationships.

Hannah desperately wanted a baby of her own and begs God to answer her prayer. Verse 18 tells us that after she had done this, she was able to rejoin the family, start eating, and not feel sad anymore. She knew God cared for her and had heard her cry for help. This is a good example for us; when we feel discouraged and down, we need to put our memory verse into practice and carry on like Hannah, knowing that God cares and has heard our prayer.

- *When do you find it hard to pray or worship with your family? What do you do when you feel like this?*
- *What things are discouraging you just now?*

Prayer Stop: Praise God for your family and ask Him to help you with any difficult family relationships. Bring the things that are discouraging you to God.

DAY 30

On the Way: God answers Hannah's prayer, and Samuel is born. Hannah also keeps her vow to God; when she has weaned him (between the ages of 3–5), she takes Samuel to the temple to live there, helping Eli the priest. Eli's sons were also priests but were wicked, disobeying God and not heeding Eli's warnings. God told Eli that they would both die, and God would provide another honest and godly priest to serve in their place. Samuel continued to grow, and each year his parents would visit him and bring him new clothes to wear. He learned about God and was popular with the people.

READ 1 SAMUEL 3:1–18

Here I am (vs5b, 6b, 16b).

Checkpoint: Samuel was doing what he normally did in the temple when he heard his name. He responded immediately, thinking it was Eli, only to discover that Eli did not call him. Again, he hears the voice and does the same. He has a willing heart, ready to respond even at inconvenient times during the night! When this happened three times, Eli realized that it must be the voice of God and tells Samuel how to respond.

Although Samuel had lived in the temple, he never had a personal experience of God speaking to him directly, and Eli does not seem to have prepared him for it. We can sometimes be so busy doing things for God that we don't realize we don't have a personal relationship with Him. He wants us to be willing to listen to Him, not just do things for Him. We also need to help those who are younger or have not been Christians long to learn how to listen for God speaking to them.

Samuel knew how to respond the next time God called; he was willing to learn. Are we willing to respond to help others even when it is inconvenient? Are we willing to learn to respond to God when He speaks to us even though what He asks us may be difficult, like it was for Samuel?

- *In what ways does God speak to us today?*
- *Talk about a time you knew God was saying something very clearly to you. How did you know?*

Prayer Stop: Praise God that He still speaks to us today. Pray that you would have a willing heart to respond to Him.

DAY 31

On the Way: We read yesterday of the difficult message that God had given to Samuel about Eli and his family. After that, God continued to speak to Samuel, and the people of Israel recognized that he was indeed a prophet from God, because all that he said was reliable. Relationships between the Israelites and Philistines were always strained, and we see them at war again.

READ 1 SAMUEL 4:1–11

Why did the Lord allow us to be defeated by the Philistines? (v3b).

Checkpoint: When the Israelites were defeated by the Philistines, they realized that God had something to do with that defeat. So, to solve this problem, they brought the Ark of God to the battlefield. They did not understand that the Ark was a picture of God's presence with them. It contained the Law of Moses by which they were meant to live. However, they were using the Ark as a "magic charm," thinking that simply having it with them would guarantee them victory. They did not think that it was their behavior toward God that was the problem. They needed to change their hearts. Eli's sons, who were with them, failed to stop them from using the Ark in such a way. Again the Israelites are defeated, and the words of Samuel came to pass. The people seem surprised that they were defeated and ran back to their tents in fear. Their magic charm had not worked.

We must make sure that we do not put more importance on the symbols of our faith in God than in God Himself. Our attitude and behavior must show that we are His children rather than the fact that we carry a big Bible or go to church.

- *Why were the Philistines afraid when they heard the Ark had come to the Israelite camp?*
- *How does this compare with the Israelites' attitude?*
- *How can our attitude toward religious objects give people the wrong impression of God?*

Prayer Stop: Pray that your attitudes and behavior would show others how powerful God is. Pray that God would show you anything in your heart that needs to be changed and ask Him to help you with this.

DAY 32

On the Way: A messenger runs from the battle to tell those at home about the defeat. When Eli hears the Ark has been captured, he falls backward from his chair and dies from a broken neck. His daughter-in-law, who is expecting a baby, goes into labor and gives birth to a son. She names him *Ichabod*, meaning "the glory has left Israel." After this, she dies.

At first, the Philistines put the Ark in their god's temple, but every morning they find the statue of Dagon fallen, so they move it to another town. Wherever the Philistines put the Ark, God causes diseases and death. Eventually, they find a way to send it back to the Israelites.

READ 1 SAMUEL 6:1–3, 10–21

Who is able to stand in the presence of the LORD, this holy God? (v20a).

Checkpoint: The Philistines realized that the Ark represented the Living God of the Israelites. Knowing the truth did not make them want to turn away from their own gods; it just made them want to get rid of the Ark.

Even though the Philistines did not worship God, they accepted His power and respected Him. People today can do this. They may not believe they need God, but they know God is powerful and respect Him.

The Israelites did the opposite. They did not treat the Ark with the proper respect, and as a result, seventy men died. They were God's children, but they did not give Him proper respect. Sometimes when we have known God for a long time or heard Him talked about since we were little, we can forget how holy God really is. We treat Him with less respect than we should. Knowing that God is holy and powerful does not make Him our God, as we saw from the Philistines. The Israelites were God's children, just as we are if we are Christians today, but they had still to remember that God is holy and deserves all of our respect.

- *How did the Israelites react when they were reminded of God's holiness?*
- *How do we as Christians sometimes treat God with less respect today?*
- *Is there anything you need to change to give God proper respect in your life?*

Prayer Stop: Take some time to worship God for His holiness. Pray for anyone you know who respects God but does not know Him as their Savior yet.

DAY 33

On the Way: The Israelites moved the Ark to the home of Abinadab and made his son a priest to look after it. They felt God had abandoned them throughout those years. Samuel urged them to get rid of their false gods and return to God. He gathered them at Mizpah to pray for them. While they were there, the Philistines tried to attack them, but God caused the Philistines to become confused and gave Israel the victory. Samuel grew old and retired, making his sons judges. They did not please God, and so the people came to Samuel and asked him to give them a king to rule them instead.

READ 1 SAMUEL 8:6–20

We want to be like the nations around us (v20a).

Checkpoint: The people had returned to God under Samuel's leadership and enjoyed peace instead of war. When Samuel's sons became judges, the people asked Samuel to give them a king to rule them instead. They were looking at how other nations were ruled and thought a monarchy would be good for them. They forgot that God was their King. He led them in times of trouble before and had given them great victories over their enemies. Though God warned them of the dangers of having a man rule over them, they still insisted on being like other nations.

Sometimes in our churches today, we try to do things we see other organizations doing. We forget that we are not running a business; we are the family of the Living God. We are called to be different. God is our Father and head of His church. We can look and see the good things in other organizations, but if those things make people and ideas more important than God, then we are making trouble for ourselves.

- *In what ways should our churches be different from charitable organizations?*
- *How do you see this practiced in your own church?*

Prayer Stop: Praise God that we are part of His family. Pray that your church will show that God is their Father in the way it is led.

DAY 34

On the Way: Samuel prays about the request the people have made, and God tells him to listen to them. In chapter 9, we are introduced to Saul. One day his father's donkeys were lost, and Saul was sent to look for them. When he couldn't find them, his servant suggested they go to ask the prophet where they might be. God had told Samuel to expect a visitor and that would be the man God had chosen to be king. So when he saw Saul coming, he knew this was the man. He treated Saul with special honor, giving him a great feast with thirty invited guests. He invited him to stay the night and in the morning told him to return home because the donkeys were safe. It was as they were leaving that Samuel told Saul that God had appointed him to be king over Israel. Saul kept quiet about this when he went home.

READ 1 SAMUEL 10:9–11, 17–26

> *This is the man the Lord has chosen as your king* (v24b).

Checkpoint: Can you imagine what was going through Saul's head when he met Samuel? He was simply looking for donkeys but instead received word that he would be the nation's first king! It is easy to understand why he kept quiet about it at home. When the time came for the nation to learn who God had chosen for the job, Saul was hiding. He did not want to be king.

God has a plan for everyone. We don't know what that exact plan is from the start of our lives, but as we go about our normal routines, God will bring a circumstance that leads us in a surprise direction. God uses the ordinary things in our lives to bring about the extraordinary things in His plan for us and in His kingdom.

- *Why do you think Saul hid?*
- *Has God asked you to do something that makes you fearful?*

Prayer Stop: Praise God for the plans He has for you. Pray that you would have courage to accept God's will and obey Him.

DAY 35

On the Way: The Ammonites came and besieged the Israelite city of Jabesh Gilead. They were threatening them with violence and captivity. The people in the city were unable to fight on their own and sent for help from the other tribes in Israel. When Saul heard this, he became very angry and rallied all the men of Israel to help. The people in Jabesh Gilead were delighted, and 330,000 men went to the Ammonite camp and destroyed the army. After this, the people confirmed Saul as their king before God.

READ 1 SAMUEL 12:12–24

*The L*ORD *will not abandon his people* (v22a).

Checkpoint: Samuel speaks to the people, reminding them of all the amazing things that God had done for them in the past. He shows them that by insisting on having a human king, they were rejecting God as their leader, and this was a sin. When they were reminded of God's great power, they realized that they needed to turn away from their sinful behavior. God was willing to forgive their sin, but they had a part to play in what happened next. They had to stop deliberately sinning; they had to genuinely worship God again and trust in Him.

When God forgives us, we cannot continue deliberately sinning. Like the Israelites, we must show that we are truly sorry by our attitude; we must make every effort to turn away from the sin.

Samuel continued to serve the people as God wanted him to, even though they had been disobedient. He was also willing to forgive them. When we see others sin, we should not hold it against them, but be willing to forgive, realizing that we too are sinners and don't always do things correctly.

- *Read 1 John 1:9. How does this verse relate to today's reading? How does it encourage you?*

- *Samuel was going to continue teaching and praying for the people. Who does the same for you? Take time this week to contact them to say "thank you."*

Prayer Stop: Thank God for the people who pray for you and teach you God's Word. Pray that God will show you anything in your life that is sin at the moment.

DAY 36

On the Way: Saul became king when he was 30 years old and reigned for 42 years. He chose 3,000 men to help him fight the Philistines and sent the rest home. His son Jonathan took 1,000 of these men and attacked a Philistine outpost. When the Philistines heard about it, they were angry and rallied an enormous army to fight back. Saul summoned the Israelite army to meet him at Gilgal.

READ 1 SAMUEL 13:6–15

You have not kept the command the Lord your God gave you (v13b).

Checkpoint: The Israelite army began to look around. Seeing the size of the enemy, they became scared and began to run away. They forgot the great things that God had done for them in the past, because the present situation seemed too big for them.

It was the priest or prophet's job to make the sacrifices for the people. This was a special task given to them in the Law of Moses and the way in which God had chosen to accept offerings from the people. But when Saul saw his men becoming fearful, he became impatient and took it upon himself to do Samuel's task. He reacted without stopping to think it through or ask God what to do.

Sometimes when we feel afraid, we would rather run away than face the situation. But we need to remember God has promised never to leave us. He is able to do amazing things. If we become impatient and try to do things our own way, then we may miss seeing the great things God has planned. Saul would miss out on the good things God had planned for him and his family.

- *Can you think of other times in the Bible when people faced scary situations and saw God rescue them in amazing ways?*

- *What things might you be afraid to face today?*

Prayer Stop: Thank God for His amazing power that can rescue us and give us strength when we are scared. Pray for those who may be facing a scary situation (for example, a serious illness or a bully).

DAY 37

On the Way: Samuel left Saul. Saul, his son Jonathan, and the 600 men left with him camped at Gibeah; the Philistines camped at Michmash and sent out raiding parties. They had superior weapons to the Israelites because the Israelites did not have the skills to make swords like the Philistines. Only Saul and Jonathan had swords. Jonathan knows that they have to do something; they cannot just sit around waiting on the enemy to attack, so he suggests to his armor bearer that they should go over to spy out the Philistine camp. He did not tell his father.

READ 1 SAMUEL 14:6–15

Nothing can hinder the LORD. He can win a battle whether he has many warriors or only a few! (v6b).

Checkpoint: Jonathan knew that something had to be done, and he was willing to take the lead in this. He had confidence that God would give him the guidance he needed at the right moments. All he needed to do was be willing to go and have the courage to trust God. As a result of this, God gave him an amazing victory. He could not have done it on his own, but because he was willing to do his part, God did the rest.

Sometimes we can face things that seem too big for us to handle. We can choose, like Saul, to sit back and hope God gives us a message, or we can start to tackle the problem with what we know, relying on God to guide us and take care of the parts that are too big for us. It does not matter to God what size the problem is or how much we are able to do, because he is able to do anything.

- *How do you think Jonathan and his armor bearer reacted when they felt the earthquake?*
- *Talk about a time you have seen God do something that you could never have imagined.*
- *Are you facing something that seems too big at the moment? Do the things you are able to and be amazed at the things God will do.*

Prayer Stop: Praise God for His great power that is available to us as His children. When you have a problem that seems too hard, pray for courage to trust God and guidance for the things you should do.

DAY 38

On the Way: While Jonathan and his armor bearer were routing the Philistines with God's help, Saul is desperately trying to decide what to do. Great confusion follows. In his desperation to show his leadership, he makes his men vow not to eat anything until he has full revenge on the Philistines. This rash vow causes them great distress, as they have no energy to fight. Jonathan was not present for that command and ate some honey. This gave him energy. When it was discovered that he had not kept his father's vow (because he was unaware of it), his father intended to kill him, but the soldiers spoke out and rescued Jonathan. In today's reading, we see Saul acting on impulse again.

READ 1 SAMUEL 15:1–15

I am sorry that I ever made Saul king, for he has not been loyal to me and has refused to obey my command (v11b).

Checkpoint: Saul was given very clear instructions from God. He started off well; however, he did not complete the commands from the Lord. When Samuel questions him about it, he blames his soldiers! He fails to see that as leader he had responsibility to make sure his soldiers knew the correct instructions; he seems to have left them to do as they wanted. He did not realize that by only obeying a little, he was actually being disobedient. In verse 12, we see how his heart has changed; he has built a monument to himself! He has become proud of his position and taken the glory away from God.

When we start to think that obeying just part of God's Word is enough, then we are in danger of letting other things have God's place in our hearts. Like Saul, we may be in danger of thinking more of ourselves than we should. God wants us to fully obey Him, not out of fear but because we love Him.

- *Are there areas where you sometimes don't obey God completely?*
- *Read John 14:15. What does this tell us about what our attitude should be in obeying God?*

Prayer Stop: Worship God because He is holy. Pray that you would love and obey God completely.

DAY 39

On the Way: When Samuel confronted him, Saul stubbornly stated that he had obeyed God's instruction. He had allowed the animals to be taken as a sacrifice to God; this was not what God had told him to do. Samuel reminds him that God is more interested in our obedient attitudes than in what we can be seen doing. As result of Saul's attitude, God rejects Saul as king, and Samuel leaves Saul. Samuel is very sad about all that has happened, but God tells him to go and anoint another king from Bethlehem, one from the family of a man named Jesse.

MEMORY VERSE

The Lord doesn't see things the way you see them. People judge by outward appearance, but the Lord looks at the heart.

~ 1 Samuel 16:7b

READ 1 SAMUEL 16:1–13

Checkpoint: Samuel has to move on from the sadness he feels about Saul's behavior and anoint another king that God has chosen instead. Saul did not turn out as Samuel had expected.

The new king chosen by God did not fit with tradition! Normally, the eldest son would be given a position of authority before the youngest, but God reminded Samuel that it was not tradition or looks that mattered but what the thoughts and intentions of a person's heart were. After all, Saul had been the most handsome man around, and look how that turned out!

People will let us down, no matter what position they hold. We must be willing to forgive and move on from disappointing situations. God is not restricted to doing things the "normal" way. He is still more interested in our hearts than in our age or what we seem to be on the outside. We should be more interested in attitudes than looks as well!

- *Have you ever felt let down by someone in an important position? How does Romans 3:23–24 help us accept this?*

- *How can we make sure our attitudes and intentions please God?*

Prayer Stop: Thank God for those leaders who are great examples of people who have the right attitude. Pray that God will protect them. Ask God to show you anything you need to change in your heart.

DAY 40

On the Way: Samuel anoints David as king and then leaves, but God's plan continues. Saul has become depressed and needs some relaxation. His aides suggest harp playing may help, and someone happens to have heard a shepherd boy in the hills playing well, so they send for him. David finds himself in the palace playing the harp for the king! This gives him firsthand experience of palace life and kingly responsibility.

When God calls us to do something, He also prepares us for it. We see David again when the Philistines prepare for battle against Israel. They send out their prize fighter who is over nine feet tall! All the Israelites are terrified, but David, who is just visiting his brothers on the battlefield, volunteers to face the giant.

READ 1 SAMUEL 17:38–51

> *I come to you in the name of the Lord of Heaven's Armies* (v45b).

Checkpoint: David shows courage when everyone else, including King Saul, is terrified! What is it that makes the difference? It is his faith in God and the preparation that God has already given him. He has fought wild animals when looking after his father's sheep; David knows that with God's help, he was able to overcome them. He sees Goliath as the same kind of challenge, and with God's help, Goliath can be conquered. David took the weapons he knew how to handle, not what Saul tried to give him, and faced the enemy.

When we face scary challenges, we need to remember that God has promised to go with us and that He has prepared us to face them. We need courage to trust in God and not succumb to fear. We need to listen to how God wants us to handle these things and not give in to how others expect us to handle them.

- *Why do you think Saul and his army were afraid?*
- *Are you facing something that seems too big to handle just now? Can you think of ways God may have already prepared you to face this?*

Prayer Stop: Praise God that He prepares us to face difficult times and does not leave us. Pray for courage for those you know who are facing difficult times.

DAY 41

On the Way: After David killed Goliath, Saul took more notice of him. David spent more time at the palace and became firm friends with Jonathan, the king's son. The people praised David for the victory over the Philistines, and Saul became jealous of David's popularity and the fact that God was with him. Saul tried several times to kill David himself or to organize that he be killed. Each time he failed. David married Saul's daughter, Michal, and she also helped David escape from her father. When David went to Ramah to see Samuel and stay with him awhile, Saul was so determined to kill him that he followed him there, but God confused his efforts.

READ 1 SAMUEL 20:1–7, 12–15, 35–42

May the LORD be with you as he used to be with my father (v13b).

Checkpoint: Saul knew that if David continued to live, he would be king and not Saul's own son Jonathan. Jonathan could see that his father's behavior had changed and God was not leading him anymore. Although he did not believe that his father wanted to kill David, he knew that David would be king one day rather than him.

Look at the difference between the two men's attitudes. Saul was trying every way he could to keep the kingdom in his family. Jonathan was willing to risk his life to save David, who would be king in his place. Jealousy destroys character. We can see how it did that to Saul. He overreacted and struggled with temper and must have been horrible to live with! Jonathan, on the other hand, kept a loyal friendship with David.

- *How do you think Jonathan felt as he walked back to the palace after David left?*
- *Have you ever experienced being jealous of someone, or someone being jealous of you?*
- *What helps us to avoid jealousy? (1 Corinthians 13:4) What was it that kept Jonathan from being jealous?*

Prayer Stop: Ask God's forgiveness for any jealousy you may feel and ask Him to help you truly love your friends. Pray for those who treat you badly, perhaps because they are jealous.

DAY 42

On the Way: David left Jonathan and went to Ahimelech the priest. He told Ahimelech that he was on a mission for the king and was given Goliath's sword and the special bread at the temple for his men. They went from there to Gath, where David feared for his life and pretended to be insane to escape. He escaped to the cave of Adullam, where all his family and some other discontented men came to him. There were about four hundred men with him. God told them to go back to Judah, where Saul, when he heard of David's arrival, continued to chase him relentlessly.

READ 1 SAMUEL 24:3–21

May the LORD therefore judge which of us is right and punish the guilty one (v15a).

Checkpoint: This is an amazing story showing what strong character David has. He has had to hide in the wilderness and live in caves to escape from Saul. Yet at the very moment he could easily kill Saul and be free of him forever, he does not act on it. He realizes that Saul is still the king, a position given to him by God. Until God takes it away from him, David was going to respect Saul's position. When Saul realizes that David has spared his life, he is amazed and accepts at last that indeed David will be king.

When we are persecuted by others, it is best to leave God to deal with them. We can then have a clear conscience before God and others, knowing that we have done the right thing. If we allow God to deal with problems His way, His name will be honored.

- *How do you think David felt when he was able to speak to Saul in the cave?*
- *When you feel someone is persecuting you, what is your usual reaction? What can we learn from David's response?*

Prayer Stop: The Bible tells us to pray for those who persecute us. Pray for those who are making life difficult for you in some way today. Pray for those who are persecuting people because they are Christians. Pray too for those Christians, that God would give them wisdom to know how to respond.

DAY 43

On the Way: Saul returned home. Samuel died and was buried at his home. David went off to the wilderness of Maon, where a rich but unruly man called Nabal lived. David sent a message to ask him to provide a few provisions for his men. Nabal refused and aroused David's anger. He set off to take revenge, but Abigail, Nabal's wife, heard and quickly arranged some provisions for the men. She met David on the way and thus stopped him from taking revenge into his own hands. When Nabal heard of the news, he had a stroke and died. David married Abigail.

Saul again tries to chase and kill David, and again (1 Sam 26), David spares Saul's life. Then David goes to the Philistines, asks for their protection, and lives among them. David and his men prepare to go and fight Israel with the Philistine army, but the Philistine commanders do not trust them and send them home, where they find their town has been raided and their families captured.

READ 1 SAMUEL 30:9–24

No, my brothers! Don't be selfish with what the LORD has given us (v23b).

Checkpoint: Two hundred of David's men were too tired to continue the pursuit of the Amalekites and so stayed to guard the equipment. The others continued and recaptured their families and possessions. Those who went with David complained that those who stayed behind should not get any of the plunder. However, David reminded them that they were all part of the team, playing different parts but deserving an equal share of the blessing God had given them.

When we are part of a team, each member has different duties, but all aim for the same goal. Each role is needed. Some people are able to do more than others, but that does not make what they do more important.

- *How do you think those who stayed felt when they heard the others complain?*
- *In what ways can we experience the same kind of attitude among members of any teams we are part of?*
- *At the end of 1 Samuel, what great leadership qualities do you recognize in David?*

Prayer Stop: Thank God for any team that you are part of. Pray that your team will show acceptance to everyone in it, no matter what part each one plays.

2 SAMUEL

The second book of Samuel records the reign of David as king. It shows him as a great leader of God's people whose desire was to follow God. This does not mean that he was perfect: his sinful human nature is shown in this book too, along with God's forgiveness.

DAY 44

On the Way: At the end of 1 Samuel, the Philistines attacked Israel and killed Saul's three sons, Jonathan, Abinadab, and Malkishua. Saul was wounded in battle, and chapter 31 tells us that he then fell on his own sword to avoid capture from the Philistines. The Israelite army fled and deserted their towns, so the Philistines moved into them. Three days after David had returned from defeating the Amalekites, a man from Saul's camp came to him. The man was obviously in mourning.

READ 2 SAMUEL 1:4–15

> *They mourned and wept and fasted all day for Saul and his son Jonathan,*
> *and for the Lord's army and the nation of Israel, because they had died by the*
> *sword that day* (v12).

Checkpoint: The man's story of Saul's death is different from what we read in the last chapter of 1 Samuel. It may be that he thought David would be so pleased that Saul was dead that he would be rewarded. However, we know from previous events that David respected Saul's position because God had chosen him for it, and until God removed him, David would do all he could to respect Saul, despite his attempts to kill David. David knew that one day he would be king, but he was willing to wait and let God work it out rather than take matters into his own hands.

When we hear of our enemies suffering hard times, it is hard not to feel a little bit of pleasure and think that they have what they deserve. David provides a good example of how those who love God should react, and his men followed his example.

- *Read Matthew 5:43–45. How did David put this into practice?*
- *Have you ever had an experience like David? How did you react?*
- *What are some ways you can show that you love your enemies?*

Prayer Stop: Pray that you will be able to practice Matthew 5:43–45 when you need to. Pray for those who persecute Christians, that God would stop them from doing so and that He would protect His children.

DAY 45

On the Way: David moved to Hebron in Judah with his family, and the men of Judah made him their king. Meanwhile, the commander of Saul's army, Abner, took Saul's only surviving son, Ishbosheth, and made him king over the rest of Israel. Israel and Judah battled, and David's men won. This was the start of a long war between the two: Saul's men became weaker, but David's army grew stronger. After a row with Ishbosheth, Abner defected to David but was then killed by Joab, the commander of David's army, without David's knowledge. When Ishbosheth heard of Abner's death, he and all of Israel were afraid. One night as he slept, two of his own men crept in and killed him. They thought David would be pleased, but as he did with the messenger who told him of Saul's death, David also put these men to death.

READ 2 SAMUEL 2:1–7; 5:1–7

You will be the shepherd of my people Israel. You will be Israel's leader (5:2b).

Checkpoint: In today's reading, David became king first of all over Judah and then after some time he was crowned king of all Israel. David knew that God had a plan for him to be king; he also had several chances to make that happen himself by taking Saul's life, which he chose not to do. He waited on God's timing instead.

Sometimes when we know that God has a special purpose for us, we desire to know how it will work itself out. Often we are unable to see the way ahead, and we try to work things out ourselves. This was a lesson in trusting God for David, and we can learn it too. We cannot know the way God will work things out, but He wants us to trust Him and know that He will work out His plan for us. His ways are best.

- *Have you ever had the experience of knowing God wanted you to do something but not seeing how it would come about?*

- *Read Proverbs 3:5–6. What should we do when we find it hard to wait for God?*

Prayer Stop: Praise God that His plans are perfect and too great for us to understand. Pray that you will have patience to let God work out His plans.

DAY 46

On the Way: David led his army to fight against Israel's enemies. He asked God for wisdom in these battles, realizing that he needed God's help. He also started to bring the Ark of God back to Jerusalem. It was put on a new cart pulled by oxen, but one of the oxen stumbled. A man named Uzzah put out his hand to steady the Ark. Only priests were allowed to touch the Ark. Uzzah was not a priest and died because he had done this. This made David angry with God and afraid to have the Ark near him, so he had it taken to the home of a man called Obed-Edom. God blessed the man and his family, and eventually David brought the Ark to Jerusalem with great celebrations and worship.

READ 2 SAMUEL 7:1–17

Your house and your kingdom will continue before me for all time, and your throne will be secure forever (v16).

Checkpoint: David was enjoying peace from his enemies, and it seemed a good time to build a permanent temple for the Ark of God. The priest Nathan told David to go ahead, but God had other plans. David would not be famous for having built a temple but for something far greater—God promised that David's kingdom would never end! David's family did stop ruling Israel, however, Jesus as a descendant of David is the one God promised would be ruler forever. What an amazing thing God had in store for David's family. He did promise that David's son would also build the temple.

David's idea of a temple was good, but it was not God's plan for him. Sometimes we too will have a good idea that seems right, but we need to be willing to accept God's "no" if it comes and be willing to let Him work out the greater plans He has for us.

- *If David had gone ahead with his idea, what might he have missed in the future?*
- *Have you ever wanted to do something for God that did not work out, and you had to watch someone else do it? How did you feel? What might you have missed out on if you had gone ahead?*

Prayer Stop: Praise God that His plans are for our good. Pray that you will be willing to accept it when God says no.

DAY 47

On the Way: David was looking for ways he could continue to serve God in the time of peace. As we saw in the last reading, God had different plans for David. God explained this to Nathan the priest, who then told David what God's plans were. Today we will look at David's response.

MEMORY VERSE

Trust in the LORD with all your heart; do not depend on your own understanding. Seek his will in all you do, and he will show you which path to take.

~ Proverbs 3:5–6

READ 2 SAMUEL 7:18–29

You made Israel your very own people forever, and you, O LORD, became their God (v24).

Checkpoint: On hearing the message from God as Nathan told him, David goes immediately to spend time with God. He doesn't give Nathan a message for God but brings it to God himself. When we hear God speak to us through others, perhaps at church or in youth group, we need to make that personal response to God and spend time letting God know what is on our hearts. David praises God for all the amazing things He has done for him already; He brought him from being a shepherd to being the king of a nation. He has done the same for the nation, bringing them from being slaves to being free in their own land.

What God did for Israel, He has also done for us; He has made us part of His family by saving us from our sins. What is your response to God for this? Do we realize, like David did, that there is nothing we have done ourselves that has made this happen? Do we give God praise for what He has done already? Like David, we need to remember that what God has done is only part of His promise. There is still more to come. God's promise to us will continue forever as we live with Him in His kingdom.

- *Look back and think about how God has led you so far in your life.*
- *Read 1 Corinthians 13:12. How does this make you feel about what God has for our future with Him?*

Prayer Stop: Praise God for all the blessings in your life so far and for the blessings He still has to give you! Worship Him for this amazing fact.

DAY 48

On the Way: The Lord gave David victory over all his enemies. David became famous throughout the land because God gave him victory wherever he went. In today's reading, we see more of his godly character being shown.

READ 2 SAMUEL 9:1–13

> *I intend to show kindness to you because of my promise to your father,*
> *Jonathan (v7b).*

Checkpoint: Traditionally, a new king could kill all of the conquered ruler's family, but that was never David's desire. We already know he did not take Saul's life when he had the chance, and now we see him not only allowing Saul's grandson to live but also showing him kindness. David remembered the promise he had made to Jonathan and wanted to fulfill it. It seems to be a few years since Jonathan's death, and we don't know why it is only now David wants to carry out his promise; perhaps he was distracted by all that happened in his own life. Even if we are distracted by life, it is always right to keep our promises, no matter how late!

Mephibosheth would have known what David could do to him and so perhaps felt some fear as he went to see him. David reassured him that he didn't need to be afraid. David wanted to show God's kindness to him (v3) and not just by treating Mephibosheth fairly. David blessed him and gave him back what belonged to his family. David was aware of the kindness that God had shown him and wanted to show that same kindness to others. It is this same kindness that God wants us to show others, not just to treat them fairly but also to bless them with the same generosity with which God has blessed us.

- *Read Romans 5:6 and 1 Peter 5:10. How do these verses explain how generous God's kindness is to us?*

- *Is there someone you can show God's kindness to today? Perhaps it is someone who has made your life difficult before; God may want you to show His kindness to them.*

Prayer Stop: Thank God today for the kindness He showed you by sending Jesus to die for you. Ask Him to show you someone to share His kindness with today. Pray for those you mentioned in the second point above.

DAY 49

On the Way: In the spring, when kings usually led their men to war, David sent Joab, his commander, to fight, while he stayed behind in Jerusalem in his palace. One day he noticed a beautiful woman bathing on her rooftop. When he asked who she was, he discovered that her husband Uriah was fighting in his army. He sent for the woman, Bathsheba, and slept with her. Later she sent him news that she was pregnant. David then planned to have her husband brought home so that they could be together, and it would cover up his sin. However, Uriah refused to sleep in the comfort of his own home when his fellow soldiers were out fighting, so David arranged to send him back to the battlefield with instructions to put him at the most dangerous place so he would be killed.

READ 2 SAMUEL 11:26–12:9

But the LORD was displeased with what David had done (11:27b).

Checkpoint: David had sinned; he had allowed himself to give in to temptation. First of all, he was not leading his men as he should have been; he had left that responsibility with Joab. When we do not take our responsibilities seriously, we begin to compromise in other areas. That is what seemed to happen to David. When he saw Bathsheba, he could have turned away, but instead he allowed temptation to dwell in his heart, leading to disaster. The Bible encourages us to guard our minds and hearts so that we avoid sin.

Nathan was given the task of making David aware that God knew what he had done and was angry with him. Nathan needed courage to do this since David was the king. God gave him the words so that David understood the message. When we need to confront others about sin, we need to ask God for the right way to do it. Sometimes it is the way we say things that has more effect than what we actually say.

- *What things can we do that will help us avoid temptation?*
- *Galatians 6:1 describes what Nathan did. Think about how you might speak to someone to bring him or her back to God.*

Prayer Stop: Pray that God would make you aware of sin in your life. Praise Him for the gift of forgiveness.

DAY 50

On the Way: Although David was truly sorry for his sin and God forgave him, he would have to take the consequences of sinning. The son Bathsheba gave birth to became ill and died. David and Bathsheba had another son and called him Solomon. God told David that murder would not be far from his house.

David had many wives and therefore many children. One day his oldest son, Amnon, assaulted his half-sister Tamar. When David's son Absalom heard of this, he plotted to kill Amnon. He did so two years later and then fled to Geshur to stay with his grandfather for three years. By law he was a murderer and should have died, but David allowed him to live. When he returned to Jerusalem, he did not see his father the king for another two years.

READ 2 SAMUEL 15:1–12

> *After this, Absalom bought a chariot and horses, and he hired fifty body-guards to run ahead of him (v1).*

Checkpoint: Absalom deserved to die: he had murdered his brother. However, perhaps because God had spared David's life after his plot to murder Uriah, David allowed him to live. Unlike his father, Absalom was not sorry for what he had done. With pride and arrogance, he demanded to see the king, and then he bought horses and chariots, giving himself a position of importance so people noticed him. He criticized the way his father reigned and wanted to have the position of judge so he could be popular. His lifestyle did not show that he was fit to be a judge; it was just his ambition.

Often those who have the ambition for positions of power are not those who are best suited for it. Absalom continues to scheme to get himself into a position of power. However, this just brings trouble on himself and his father's family.

- *Compare the way David gained the throne with the schemes of Absalom. Which honors God?*

- *How can ambition get in the way of doing God's will in our lives?*

Prayer Stop: Check the attitude of your heart and ask God's forgiveness for any pride there. Pray that any selfish ambition will not stop God's good plans for you.

DAY 51

On the Way: David had to flee from Jerusalem. Even some of his advisors had defected to Absalom, but those who were left, along with 600 men from Gath, went with David. David sent the priests back to Jerusalem so they could send him reports. He also sent his friend Hushai back. Absalom returned to Jerusalem; all Israel was with him. David's advisor Ahithophel advised Absalom to pursue his father and kill him. However, Hushai advised a different plan, and Absalom went with it. Hushai then sent the priest's sons to warn David what was happening.

READ 2 SAMUEL 18:1–5, 9–15

"For my sake, deal gently with young Absalom." And all the troops heard the king give this order to his commanders (v5)b.

Checkpoint: David was being chased by his own son who wanted to have him killed. As a result of his deliberate sin with Bathsheba, God had told him his own household would rebel against him. David did not rebel against God over this; he repented and carried on, trying to lead his people in the right way. He commanded his troops to deal gently with Absalom. He still longed for his son, though Absalom was leading a rebellion against him. This is a picture of the way God treats us: even though we rebel and sin against Him, He is patient with us and gives us every chance to return to Him.

We meet Absalom in the battle, but he seems to be alone with no men around him. He does not seem to have organized his army but is determined to personally see his goal met. As he meets David's men, he shows no courage to fight them, but turns to escape and is caught by his hair in a tree. Sometimes, like Absalom, we can become so obsessed by getting what we want that we don't realize there is no one there to help us. Our pride can stop us from being wise.

- *Do you think Joab was right to take Absalom's life?*
- *Read Proverbs 16:18. How do we see this in Absalom's situation? Have you had personal experience of this?*

Prayer Stop: Thank God for His patience with us. Pray that pride would not have a place in your heart.

DAY 52

On the Way: As he waits at the city gates for news of the battle, it would seem that the only news David is interested in is that of the fate of his son Absalom. He shows no interest in the rest of his army. When he hears that Absalom is dead, he goes into a room and weeps uncontrollably, shutting himself off from other people. The army returns but instead of returning with joy at their victory, they creep back into the city because they have heard of the king's grief.

READ 2 SAMUEL 19:5–8

You seem to love those who hate you and hate those who love you (v6a).

Checkpoint: David was so heartbroken at the death of his son he seems to have forgotten all the incidents surrounding his death. He has forgotten that his army had risked their lives to defend him and had defeated his enemy. If Absalom had not died, David's own life and the lives of the rest of his family would be at risk. Joab took it upon himself to make the king face this reality.

Sometimes we can become so taken up with events that affect us, thinking only of our own feelings that we cannot see things from any other point of view. David listened to the advice of Joab and took his place among the people again. His heart was still broken because of Absalom's death, but he could see that his reaction was not helping the nation he ruled.

It is right that we grieve when someone we love dies. David was obviously going to be upset at the death of his son. However, he was unable to think how his army must have felt when he practically treated them as if they had run away.

- *Have you ever been so upset about something that you forgot others were involved?*
- *How were you able to face life again? Was there someone like Joab to help you?*

Prayer Stop: Praise God for people who are willing to help us see things from other points of view. Pray for those who have had a family member die. Pray that they will know God's comfort and be able to face life again.

DAY 53

On the Way: David returned to Jerusalem. Those who had followed Absalom started to follow David again. David forgave Shimei, who had openly cursed David, and was restored to Mephibosheth. A man called Sheba led another rebellion against David but was defeated by David's army. For three years, there was a famine and when David asked God why, God told him it was because of the way Saul had treated the Gibeonites. To put things right, the Gibeonites asked for seven of Saul's relatives to be handed over to them. After those men were buried with Saul, God ended the famine.

READ 2 SAMUEL 21:15–22

These four Philistines were descendants of the giants of Gath, but David and his warriors killed them (v22).

Checkpoint: The Israelite army was facing giants again. This time David is cornered and about to be defeated by one of the giants when one of his younger soldiers steps in and kills the giant. At the start of David's story, we see him facing Goliath with great faith and enthusiasm. Now he is much older, has had a lot of battle experience, and is simply worn out. During this war with the Philistines, we read of three other giants being killed by the Israelites. No longer is the army frozen with fear when facing giants, as they were in 1 Samuel 17; now the men have learned from their leader and are able to step in and handle the responsibility that David is unable to handle physically.

Sometimes in our lives, we can face situations that seem impossible to us; they seem like giants and make us afraid. God has put people in our lives who can be examples to us. We can learn from them and put what they teach us into practice. We can learn how to face the giants in our lives and begin to teach others as well.

- *Are you facing any giants at present?*
- *Who might be able to help you deal with them?*
- *How do you think David felt when he saw his men fighting giants?*

Prayer Stop: Thank God for the people in your life that can teach you how to face the "giants." Pray for any situation you or others are facing right now.

DAY 54

On the Way: The close of 2 Samuel presents a song of praise written by David and a list of the mighty warriors in David's army and some of their amazing victories. As David thinks about all that, his heart is turned from focusing on God. He decides to count how many fighting men he has. Joab tries to talk him out of it, but David insists. However, as Joab brings him the results, David realizes that he has sinned and asks God's forgiveness. God sends the prophet Gad to give David the message that He will send His judgment, and David has to choose famine for three years, fighting for three months, or plague for three days. David wants to rely on the mercy of God rather than of man and so God inflicts Israel with a plague. As the three days are coming to a close and Israel has suffered great loss, David sees the angel of the Lord.

READ 2 SAMUEL 24:17–25

> *I will not present burnt offerings to the LORD my God that have cost me nothing* (v24b).

Checkpoint: I wonder what Araunah thought when he saw the king coming to his property. David could have demanded anything from him, yet he offered to buy his threshing floor. Araunah generously offered it to the king, as well as all he would need to offer sacrifices. He had a generous spirit and was willing to give from what he had. When people ask us for help, how do we respond?

David insisted on paying for it. He did not want to offer a sacrifice to God that did not cost him. When we serve God, do we try to do things as cheaply as possible or with the least effort? A sacrifice is giving up something we value; are we willing to give up what we value most for God? All the material things we have come from God, and it is right that we honor Him with them.

- *In what way can you honor God with what you have?*
- *Read Romans 12:1–2. What should our sacrifice to God be? How will this cost us?*

Prayer Stop: Praise God for the sacrifice He made in sending Jesus to die for us. Pray that God will help you be willing to give up the things you value for Him.

1 AND 2 KINGS

These books tell the story of the kings of Israel from the end of David's reign. It covers the kingdom being divided into Judah and Israel. Some of the kings followed the Lord, and others refused to follow Him. We can see the contrast throughout these books. We also read of how God used His prophets at this time.

DAY 55

On the Way: David was old, and his son Adonijah decided he would be the next king. So he prepared himself by buying chariots and horses and gathering advisors. Joab, David's army commander, and Abiathar the priest went with him, but the others refused to follow him. He invited all his brothers except Solomon and set out to become king. Nathan the prophet asked Bathsheba, Solomon's mother, to go and alert the king. She asked David why Adonijah was king when he promised that Solomon would reign after him. Nathan confirmed that this was true. Immediately, David arranged for Solomon to be crowned king that day with great celebration.

MEMORY VERSE
People who accept discipline are on the pathway to life, but those who ignore correction will go astray.

~ Proverbs 10:17

READ 1 KINGS 1:5–9, 32–36, 41–43, AND 49–53

Now his father, King David, had never disciplined him at any time (v6a).

Checkpoint: Like Absalom, Adonijah wanted to be king. However, it was up to David as king to choose his successor, but he had not done so officially yet. Adonijah attempted to take on a role that had not been given to him. Chapter 1 verse 6 tells us David had never disciplined his son, and so Adonijah had done as he pleased as he grew up. His lack of discipline and respect was evident in his behavior. Although David was a godly king, he was an unwise father. As parents, God gives us responsibility to teach and train our children. As children, we are wise to listen to the wisdom of our parents.

When Adonijah's plans were discovered, he went running for protection to the altar, the holy place where people came for forgiveness. If he had truly bothered to consider what God wanted, he would have gone there before he put his plans into action! It is always best to ask God what His will is before we make a mess of things ourselves.

- *Read Proverbs 19:18 and Ephesians 6:1, 4. How do you see these verses at work in your family life?*
- *How do you think David felt when he heard of Adonijah's plot?*

Prayer Stop: If you have Christian parents, praise God for them and pray that they would have wisdom to lead the family. Pray that others will see how your family honors God because of the way you treat each other.

DAY 56

On the Way: David had already chosen Solomon as king but ended up having to crown him in a hurry. He had not told his advisors or the rest of his family what his plans were. So as he grew frailer, he hurriedly crowned Solomon as king. In today's reading, we hear what he has to say as he hands the throne over to Solomon.

READ 1 KINGS 2:1–12

Observe the requirements of the Lord *your God, and follow all his ways* (v3a).

Checkpoint: Knowing he is about to die, David gives Solomon some advice and instructions. He gives him a good rule to live and reign by in verse 3 and tells him to be strong and brave. The result will be that God would keep His promise to David's family. Although God made this promise to David, it depended on his descendants personally choosing to follow God. This is good advice for us too, to bravely live by God's Word. But unless we personally choose to do this, we will not experience the blessing it will bring in our lives even though our parents lived this way.

David also gives Solomon some instructions to follow. He asks him to finish off some things he perhaps was not brave enough to do. He calls on Solomon's wisdom to act in the right way. At the end of David's life, we recognize that although he was a godly man, he was not perfect. He had let his family down, and he had let God down. No matter how wise and godly people are, we need to remember that they, like us, are sinners and will sometimes let us down. We need to be ready to forgive them and realize that we can learn lessons from their weakness as well as their wisdom.

- *How do you think Solomon felt as David spoke to him?*
- *How do you feel when older Christians give you advice?*
- *If an older Christian asks you to do something that you are not sure is right, what would you do?*

Prayer Stop: Thank God for those older, wise Christian people in your life and pray that God would protect them from temptation. Pray for anyone you know who is perhaps near the end of their life. Pray for strength for them and their families.

DAY 57

On the Way: Solomon secures his reign. Adonijah asks for a favor from him and quickly meets his death. Joab, who had joined Adonijah's rebellion, was also killed, and the priest Abiathar was sent back to his hometown. Solomon gave the commander's post to Benaiah, and Zadok became priest. Having dealt with all his rivals, Solomon settled in as king.

READ 1 KINGS 3:1–14

> *Give me an understanding heart so that I can govern your people well and know the difference between right and wrong* (v9a).

Checkpoint: Marriages between royal families was common in Solomon's day, and it generally meant the king would be at peace with the nation from which his bride came. By marrying a princess of Egypt, Solomon was securing peace with Egypt; however, as we will see further on, he was also bringing trouble on himself. God had set a standard for marriage among His own people then, and He sets that standard for us also. It is important that as Christians we marry a Christian because they will have the same priorities as ourselves. This encourages us to be able to work through difficulties together without having to compromise the values we have in life and helps us grow in faith.

When given the chance, Solomon could have asked for anything at all, but he asked God for wisdom so that he could lead the people and make right decisions—so that he could do what God wanted him to do. We can ask God for wisdom so that we can do what God wants us to do correctly and in the best way.

- *Read 2 Corinthians 6:14–17. This verse can mean all kinds of close relationships. In what ways did Solomon fail to practice this truth?*

- *How can we put this into practice in our own lives?*

- *Have you ever felt that something God wanted you to do was too difficult? What did you do? Would you do anything different now?*

Prayer Stop: Praise God for the standards He gives us to live by and ask for help as you build relationships with others, that those relationships will honor Him. Pray for wisdom to do what God wants you to do.

DAY 58

On the Way: Solomon was faced with two women who both had a baby. One child had died in the night, and his mother had swapped him with her friend's living baby. When the other mother woke up, she realized the dead baby beside her was not her child. The women argued over whose baby had died and brought their argument to the king. Solomon suggested giving half of the baby to each mother. This made the real mother plead for its life and revealed which woman was truly the baby's mother. The people were amazed at the wisdom God gave Solomon.

READ 1 KINGS 4:24–34

During the lifetime of Solomon, all of Judah and Israel lived in peace and safety (v25a).

Checkpoint: Solomon's reign was a peaceful one; there were no wars to fight. His father David had been a warrior king, but Solomon seemed to spend much of his time learning. He learned about the world around him, and as we look at the book of Proverbs, we see he learned a lot about the fear of the Lord as well. Solomon was wealthy, and the people seemed to be well off, able to provide what the king required for his household. It seemed a very happy time.

It is great to have a time in our lives when everything is going well and everyone in our family seems happy and content. We can thank God for these times. However, when things are going smoothly, we are in danger of becoming smug, thinking we have it all sorted. We must remember that all we have and all we go through are in God's hands. When things are going well, we need to look out especially for the little things that creep in and turn us away from God.

- *Look up Deuteronomy 17:16–20. Although all seemed well for Solomon, where can you see things start to go wrong?*
- *When we have peace in our lives, what can we do to make sure we still give God top priority?*

Prayer Stop: Praise God for the trouble-free times and praise Him that He is with us in the hard times. Pray that, no matter what, you will always give God top priority.

DAY 59

On the Way: King Solomon received a message from one of his father's friends, the king of Tyre. He replied, explaining that he was about to start building the Temple his father David had been unable to build. God had told David his son would build it. Solomon asked King Hiram if he could buy wood from him. Hiram agreed, and Solomon sent workers to help as well as food for the king's household in payment.

READ 1 KINGS 5:13–6:1; 6:7–13

> *During the fourth year of Solomon's reign . . . he began to construct the Temple of the LORD* (6:1b).

Checkpoint: Though Solomon was neglecting to follow all God's ways, we can see that he continues to have wisdom in the things he does. Let's look at two wise choices from today's reading.

1. He hired enough workers so that they could work in shifts and not be away from home too long (1 Kings 5:14). This gave the men a break and let them be home to take part in family life. When we work, it is important that we do not let it take over our life. We need to have the right balance, or every area of our life will suffer. We will not be healthy, our family relationships will suffer, and we will not actually be able to give our best at work either.

2. There was no sound of iron tools at the building site (1 Kings 6:7). Solomon wanted to build the house of God with respect, without the constant noise of chisels and hammers. How do you treat the place you worship? We must never make the building more important than God. After all, it is not the building itself that is holy but the God we worship in it. However, if we have little respect for our place of worship, this can reflect our respect or lack of respect for God.

   - *Think about your family's work and home life balance. Is there anything you need to change to keep priorities right? Talk about how each person feels.*

   - *How can we show respect for God in the place we worship? Do you think it matters how we treat the house of God?*

Prayer Stop: Thank God for our families and pray that you and others you know will keep the balance right.

DAY 60

On the Way: Solomon put a lot of detail into the building of the Temple and into the way it was decorated and furnished. He then built himself a grand palace. It took thirteen years to build! When he had finished the buildings, he called the elders of Israel together and had the Ark of the Lord brought to the Temple by the priests. When they placed it in its position, a great cloud filled the Temple. Solomon praised God in front of the whole nation; he prayed for them and dedicated the Temple to God.

READ 1 KINGS 8:54–66

> *Praise the LORD who has given rest to his people Israel* (v56a).

Checkpoint: As Solomon prays, he does not pray for the building he has just completed and is dedicating to the worship of God; he prays for the people who will use the Temple, both those standing before him and those in the future. The whole congregation spends two weeks celebrating and worshipping together and went home joyful and glad.

As we saw yesterday, though the place we worship should be treated with due respect, it is by far the congregation and their dedication to God that is more important. Solomon prays that they will know God is with them, want to do His will and obey Him, will know God's help daily, and that others will come to know the Lord. We can pray this prayer for our own congregation as well.

They spent two weeks together worshipping and celebrating. It is a good thing when we can spend more than just the usual times together worshipping. Perhaps you could suggest or organize a special celebration for your church (perhaps not two weeks)!

- *Why is the congregation more important than the building? (Read 1 Corinthians 3:16–17)*
- *Why do you think the members of the congregation were joyful when they went home? How do you feel when you leave your congregation?*

Prayer Stop: Praise God for the church that you are part of and pray for the members of it. Pray for those in other countries who cannot meet with other Christians and know the joy of being part of a congregation.

DAY 61

On the Way: Over the last few chapters, we have seen Solomon rise to the top of his power. He has shown that he fears God and has led the people to worship God: he has achieved great things in building and gaining knowledge. However, as we saw a few days ago, there are certain things that God required of kings that he seems to have missed. Even though he is great, he is not perfect—none of us are. God appears to him again, reminding him that if he obeys, then God will carry out His promises for His people.

MEMORY VERSE

The LORD detests the use of dishonest scales, but he delights in accurate weights.

~ Proverbs 11:1

READ 1 KINGS 9:10–14, 24–28

It took Solomon twenty years to build the LORD's Temple and his own royal palace (v10a).

Checkpoint: As Solomon finishes building, he seems to be in need of extra money and so sells some towns to King Hiram, who does not seem too pleased with what he has been given for his money! It seems in these verses that Solomon is focusing on gathering wealth and building luxury palaces for his wives and himself. He seems to have so many horses that he needs to have towns to house them! It seems he had not read God's guidelines for kings (Deut. 17:15–20) every day as was required. If he had done this, he would be aware that some of his practices were against God's plan.

When we become happy and secure in our situation, as Solomon was, it is important that we keep our eyes fixed on God and His will for us. He has given us guidelines to live by, and we should read them daily so that we can be aware of the things in our lives we need to change before it is too late.

- *Proverbs 11:1 was written by Solomon. Do you think he practiced this when dealing with Hiram?*

- *What dangers do Christians face when we are secure in our situations?*

Prayer Stop: Thank God for His Word to guide us. Pray that you would obey it. Pray that God would help you to always treat others fairly.

DAY 62

On the Way: Chapter 10 brings us an amazing account of Solomon's wisdom and wealth. It is almost too much to imagine. He seems to be running a great shipping business, making lots of money, and using the wealth he gains from that to decorate his palaces. People came to hear the wisdom God had given him and brought him gifts. In some ways, his wealth seems to have become greater than his wisdom.

READ 1 KINGS 10:1–9, 13

> *Praise the LORD your God, who delights in you and has placed you on the throne of Israel* (v9a).

Checkpoint: Solomon's reputation had traveled to other countries, so the queen of Sheba arrived to test him and see if what she had heard was true. She was overcome by all she saw and heard. Solomon was able to answer all her hard questions, and as a result she declared that God had been so good to Israel by giving them a king such a Solomon.

It does not appear that Solomon spoke of God much to the queen. She seems to think that Israel is blessed by a great king, not that Solomon has been blessed by God. She is impressed by all that she sees in his household, even his religious offerings.

People often want to ask us questions to test us because we are Christians. Do not be afraid to tell them the story of what God has done for you. When we give them answers, it is important our answers help them understand more about God and not just think we are very smart! Solomon does not seem to have told the queen the story of how his wisdom came about. She seems to think that it is all his hard work and that he fits God in with his sacrifices.

- *Read Micah 6:6–8. How do these verses fit in with Solomon's story so far? How would Solomon's life have been different if he walked humbly with God?*

- *Do you find it hard to tell people who do not know God what He has done for you? Why/Why not?*

Prayer Stop: Praise God for all He has done for you, pray that He will help you tell people about it. Pray that others would see God's love in you.

DAY 63

On the Way: The king's guidelines written in Deuteronomy 17 state that the king must not gather a large stable of horses or send people to Egypt to buy them, and he must not gather large amounts of wealth for himself. So far, Solomon has done both of these. The third guideline is that the king must not marry many wives. In our reading today, Solomon has done just that, so we can understand why things have been going a little "pear-shaped" for Solomon!

READ 1 KINGS 11:1–13

> *The LORD was very angry with Solomon, for his heart had turned away from the LORD* (v9a).

Checkpoint: Solomon had many wives! This did not just happen in a week or two; we can be sure that all through the story thus far, Solomon has been marrying foreign women and disobeying God. Solomon had done many good and wise things during his reign; however, he had obviously been making some mistakes as well! We read about them today. As he dedicated the Temple, he told the Israelites "to be completely faithful to the Lord . . . and always obey his decrees" (1 Kings 8:61). We know now that as he was saying this, his heart was being turned from God by his foreign wives. Other people may have looked at Solomon, seen his wisdom, and believed he had a close relationship with God, but the truth was less favorable. Eventually, the problems begin to show. It was not always like this; at first, Solomon was sincere about obeying God, but he let his own sinful nature take over. It seems that he was not aware he was disobeying God.

When we do not keep a close watch on our actions or the things we say or even think we can often become unaware of the sin in our lives. That is why it is important we know God's Word and live our lives by its standards. We need to be sure that we are putting into practice the things we read in God's Word, not just telling others about them.

- *Read Isaiah 29:13. How was this true for Solomon?*
- *What things may turn your heart away from God? How can we guard against that?*

Prayer Stop: Praise God for His Word and its guidance. Pray that God would help you be obedient.

DAY 64

On the Way: Throughout Solomon's reign, there has been peace. However, now, because Solomon has continually disobeyed God, things begin to change for him. We see a few enemies rising up. Some of them are from surrounding nations, relatives of some of his wives, but one of them, Jeroboam, is one of his own officials.

READ 1 KINGS 11:26–40

> *I am about to tear the kingdom from the hand of Solomon and I will give ten of the tribes to you* (v31b).

Checkpoint: God is working out His plan; because of Solomon's sin, He cannot allow Israel to continue to be ruled by his family. However, because of God's promise to David and because David had honored God, Solomon would reign until he died. God does not break His promises. Even if we are not faithful, God will always keep His promises. David, Solomon, and now Jeroboam were all given promises from God about their reign, but they also had a part to play in this promise. We know that both David and Solomon made mistakes in their lives. The difference between them is that David admitted his sin and turned back to God. God forgave him; although he had to bear the consequences of his sin, God continued to bless him. We do not read of Solomon asking God to forgive him; he does not seem to be sorry for so obviously disobeying God, so God takes action against him. Solomon had so much going for him, but because of unwise choices, his family lost out.

There is nothing we can do to make ourselves right with God. God has done that for us by sending Jesus to die for our sins. However, our lives as Christians can be affected by the choices we make. We can become proud and think we have "made it" like Solomon, or like David we can be aware that we need to keep confessing our sin to God and asking for His help. The way we deal with our sin will also have an effect on those close to us.

- *Read 1 John 1:9–10. What is God's promise to us and what is our part of that?*
- *How may our families be affected if we do not confess our sin?*

Prayer Stop: Take some time to confess any sin to God. Praise Him for His forgiveness.

DAY 65

On the Way: After such a magnificent reign, with wealth and luxury, not much is said about Solomon's death. His son Rehoboam takes over his throne, and Jeroboam returns from Egypt. Jeroboam and the Israelites ask King Rehoboam to reduce the taxes and heavy work that Solomon had forced on them. Solomon's older advisors agree with the people, but Rehoboam's friends urge him to show his power and increase the load. The Israelites turn against Rehoboam and make Jeroboam their king. Only the tribe of Judah stays loyal to Rehoboam. This was what God had said would happen.

READ 1 KINGS 12:25–33

Unless I am careful, the kingdom will return to the dynasty of David (v26b).

Checkpoint: In 1 Kings 11:31, God told Jeroboam that he is going to be given the rule of ten of the tribes of Israel. This was a position given by God. Jeroboam was not part of the royal family and therefore not a natural heir to the throne. It appears that he may have tried to take Solomon's throne after hearing this message from God and so had to escape to Egypt. Now we see him as king, making his mark as a ruler of the people. Everything in our reading today was Jeroboam's ideas. He doesn't think to ask God for guidance and follows unwise advice from others. He does not keep his side of the promise God gave him. He even leads the people to worship other gods.

When we serve God, we need to ask for God's help in carrying out our duties. This pleases Him. We cannot rely only on our own ideas or strength. Often God will use our ideas and abilities, but they must always agree with what we read in God's Word. Jeroboam's actions were all centered on what he himself could do to protect his kingdom. He forgot it was really God's kingdom. When God gives us a job to do, we need to leave the results to Him and be faithful in doing what He asks.

- *What things might we be tempted to worship instead of God?*
- *How can we guard against this?*

Prayer Stop: Thank God that we can serve Him and pray that you will stay in God's will. Pray also that your church leaders will stay focused on God's will.

DAY 66

On the Way: God sends a prophet from Judah to Bethel with a message of judgment for Jeroboam just as he is about to burn incense on the altar he had built. Jeroboam points to the man and orders he be seized, but as he does, his hand becomes paralyzed. At the same time, the altar splits and the ashes pour out. This was the sign that the prophet gave. Jeroboam asked the prophet to pray that his hand would be restored and asked him to stay for food, but God had told the prophet not to eat there and to go home a different way. So he left.

READ 1 KINGS 13:11–25

You have defied the word of the LORD (v21b).

Checkpoint: The prophet from Judah had obeyed God in a very difficult task. He went to another kingdom to give God's message of judgment to the king. God gave him a sign to prove His message was true. When the king asked him to eat, he obeyed God's instructions. It was clear he could not eat with the king to whom he had just given God's judgment. However, when another prophet asks, he becomes uncertain. The prophet from Bethel lies, tricking him into disobeying God. We don't have room here to speculate on why the prophet lied, so let's concentrate on one thing: God's message does not change. The man from Judah knew what God had told him was true. He had seen it happen, yet he was still tricked into disobeying God.

It is important that we obey God in the small details as well as the large ones. This prophet started out well. However, when the prophet from Bethel came along, he let himself be led astray. If we are sure of what God has told us, and what is asked of us is not against the Bible's teaching, we need to obey God. If others tell us something different, we need to check it carefully before going ahead and doing as they say, especially if we do not know them very well.

- *How can 1 John 4:1 help us understand what the prophet should have done?*
- *How can we test what others tell us is from God?*

Prayer Stop: Praise God that He speaks to us as individuals. Pray for wisdom to know what God is saying to you.

DAY 67

On the Way: Because he had disobeyed God, the prophet from Judah died on his way home. Jeroboam did not listen to the warning from God and continued to do evil. When his son became sick, he asked his wife to go to the prophet Ahijah disguised as someone else. As she did so, God told Ahijah that she was coming and gave her a message that the child would die and that Jeroboam's kingdom would be taken from his family because he had sinned against God. And it was so.

READ 1 KINGS 14:21–31

> *The people of Judah did what was evil in the LORD's sight* (v22b).

Checkpoint: This is a sad story. Not only had the people of Israel sinned under Jeroboam's reign, King Rehoboam of Judah did not lead his people in God's ways either. Both of these kings did evil in the eyes of the Lord. They allowed and encouraged the worship of foreign gods in their kingdoms. The people in Jerusalem, where Rehoboam reigned, began to copy the ways of the nations around them (v24b). This made the Lord angry because He had called these people to be different: He had rescued them from Egypt and promised to be their God. Yet none of that seemed to matter to them, and they began worshipping the gods of the nations around them.

God has called us to be different from those around us too, to show that we are His children. He has rescued us from our sin, and if we are Christians, we should show Him and others that we are thankful by the way we live.

- *How might we start to copy the way those who are not Christians live? How can we guard against doing so?*

- *Read 1 Peter 2:9. How can we show others the goodness of God? Why is it important we do?*

Prayer Stop: Thank God that He has called us to be His children. Ask God to show you someone to show His goodness to, especially this week. Pray for that person and the opportunity to open up.

DAY 68

On the Way: The kings of Judah remained in David's family line because of God's promise to David, but only Asa pleased God among them. The kings of Israel become more and more evil. During the reign of Ahab, who was more evil than the others, we meet Elijah. He followed the Lord and told Ahab that God was going to stop the rain for the next few years. God sent Elijah to hide by a brook and sent ravens with food for him. Then the brook dried up.

READ 1 KINGS 17:8–24

> *Now I know for sure that you are a man of God, and that the* LORD *truly speaks through you* (v24b).

Checkpoint: Imagine how this widow felt when Elijah came and asked her for bread. Her god, Baal, had let her down; she had no food and no hope. Now this stranger was asking for bread and making promises about how the God of Israel will provide for her. It made no difference to her. If she refused, she would have one more meal and die; if she did as asked, she might still end up with no food and die anyway. It really was her last hope. Because she did as Elijah asked, she was able to see the mighty power of God at work. Imagine how she felt now! I am sure she was convinced about the true God.

Sometimes God brings us to extreme situations that we have no way of solving so that we can see His power at work for us. Each situation in life is different, and we must never think that seeing God at work in one area of our lives means that we will never face another tough situation. This woman's son died. This was another test of her new faith in God, another chance for her to keep on depending on God and not just keep looking back to the first time she met Him.

- *Look at Elijah's prayer in verse 20. How do you think he was feeling? (It is always okay to tell God how we feel.)*

- *Have you ever had God do something amazing in your life? How did you feel? How do you feel now?*

Prayer Stop: Praise God for His mighty power. Pray for anyone you know going through a tough time just now. Pray that they would be able to trust God.

DAY 69

On the Way: Three years into the drought, Elijah went to King Ahab and told him to bring all Israel to Mount Carmel along with the 450 prophets of Baal. He would prepare an altar to the Lord, and they would prepare one to Baal. Whichever god sent fire to the altar was the real God. They did this, and although the 450 prophets cried all day to Baal, nothing happened. Elijah had twelve large jars of water poured over his altar before he prayed, and God sent fire that burned up everything, even the water in the trench around. The people then turned to God, and the prophets of Baal were seized. Elijah prayed that God would send rain, and He did.

READ 1 KINGS 19:1–18

I have had enough, Lord (v4b).

Checkpoint: Elijah is exhausted after Mount Carmel and has not had time to recover when he faces a threat from Jezebel. So he runs away, afraid. It seems too much for him to deal with. It can be exhausting when we feel that we are the only Christian in our group and others try to catch us out with difficult questions. Elijah had faced a huge test on Carmel and now needed some rest so that he could see things as they really were. He felt alone, and he just wanted to die.

Feeling alone can be a terrible thing and may make us feel as if life is not worth living. However, God knew what Elijah needed and provided it. God knows what we need too and will provide it for us. Elijah felt alone, but God reminded him there were others (7,000 others) in Israel who followed him. Sometimes we need to remember that we are not following God on our own. It helps to find another Christian to talk to.

- *Read Ephesians 6:12–13. How was this true for Elijah? How is it true for you?*
- *Have you or anyone you know become exhausted from serving God? What did you/they do?*
- *Think of someone you know who may be a bit weary just now. What can you do to encourage them?*

Prayer Stop: Thank God that He knows when we are tired and how to help us. Pray for the person you are going to encourage this week.

DAY 70

On the Way: God sent Elijah to the wilderness in Damascus, instructing him to anoint a king in Aram and in Israel too. He was to find a man called Elisha and anoint him to take over as prophet. Elijah found Elisha ploughing in the field and threw his cloak over him. This was a sign that he was chosen to take over from Elijah. Elisha accepted this offer by burning his plough and killing his oxen for a feast before setting off to be Elijah's assistant. King Ahab eventually listened to the warnings God gave him and humbly turned to God. God forgave him. As we move into the second book of Kings, we come to the end of Elijah's ministry.

READ 2 KINGS 2:1–18

Please let me inherit a double share of your spirit and become your successor (v9b).

Checkpoint: Elijah seems to have been told by God that his life on earth was coming to an end. Elisha, aware of that, was determined not to leave Elijah, although he did not want to talk about it with the prophets who spoke with him. When something we dread is about to happen, often we do not want to talk about it, but some people are the opposite—they want to talk about it all the time! It is perhaps best to be somewhere in the middle.

It seems that both Elijah and Elisha knew what was about to happen, so we can assume they had spoken about it and were prepared for it. Perhaps it is not wise to talk to just anyone about how you will cope with a dreaded event, but it is wise to speak with someone close you can trust to help you prepare. God puts us in families and church families, and we can often find support for difficult events in our lives within these groups.

- *How do you react when something you dread is about to happen?*
- *Have you ever had to face the news of someone dear to you being terminally ill? How did you prepare for that?*
- *Who might you talk to if you receive difficult news?*

Prayer Stop: Thank God that He is always with us, especially at difficult times. Pray for someone you know who is facing a dreaded situation just now.

DAY 71

On the Way: Before Elijah was taken, Elisha asked that he be given "a double share" of the spirit of Elijah. The firstborn son inherited a double share of possessions by law when a man died. Elisha was not asking for a greater ministry than Elijah but that he would be his successor. So his ministry begins. The kings and leaders consult him to find out the will of God, and Elisha gains the reputation of being a man of God.

MEMORY VERSE

And God will generously provide all you need. Then you will always have everything you need and plenty left over to share with others.

~ 2 Corinthians 9:8

READ KINGS 4:1–7

What can I do to help you? . . . Tell me what do you have in the house (v2).

Checkpoint: This woman, whose husband was a man of God known by Elisha, had been left with some debt when her husband died. She had nothing left in the house to sell in order to pay the debt, and her sons would have to become slaves. So she went to Elisha for help. He doesn't just provide what she needs; he gives her the ability to take care of it herself and the opportunity to grow in her faith. He instructs her to use the only thing she has left. As she goes home and shuts the door, it is only she and her sons who experience God's miracle firsthand.

If the woman had followed Elisha's instructions to borrow jars but had not actually started pouring the oil into them, she would never have experienced this miracle. If we want to see God work in our lives and in what we do, we need to put His Word into practice. If we don't do that, His Word will have no effect on our lives.

- *How would this event have affected the woman's faith?*
- *What might she do if she has a need in the future?*
- *How would it be different if Elisha had just given her money?*

Prayer Stop: Thank God that He is able to provide all we need. Pray for those in your town who have nothing to live on. Can you help them in their need?

DAY 72

On the Way: After this event, Elisha goes to Shunem, where he raises a child who had died. There is a famine in the land. During a visit to some prophets, Elisha asks them to make a stew. Something poisonous was put into the stew, but after Elisha threw some flour into it, it became fit to eat. When someone brought Elisha a gift of barley loaves during the famine, he instructed that the loaves be given to the people to eat. There was plenty for everyone and some left over. So Elisha gained the reputation of being a prophet.

READ 2 KINGS 5:1–16

Now I know that there is no God in all the world except in Israel (v15b).

Checkpoint: Naaman was a very important man, but he suffered from leprosy, a skin disease with no cure in those days. If you had leprosy, you were put out of your job and home because others were afraid of catching it. Even though Naaman was important and wealthy, he was unable to do anything about having leprosy. It attacked him the same way it would the poorest person in town.

The Bible compares leprosy to sin. No matter our importance, wealth, or intelligence, sin affects us all the same way. There is nothing we ourselves can do about it.

It was a servant girl who gave Naaman the answer. She was not afraid to speak about what she knew of God, and Naaman was not too proud to listen to her. No matter our age, whether young or old, God can use us to share His good news.

Naaman was not happy about what he had to do, but his servants encouraged him to obey. We too have only one way that we can deal with the sin in our lives: it is God's way. We need to ask Him to forgive our sin and accept Him as our Savior.

- *How would you feel about telling a government official the good news of Jesus?*
- *Leprosy can be treated today. There are missions who help treat folk in poorer countries. Perhaps you might like to look them up on the Internet at www.leprosymission.org.uk.*

Prayer Stop: Praise God that He has given us a way to be forgiven. Pray for those suffering from leprosy today and for those helping them.

DAY 73

On the Way: Elisha would not accept any gift from Naaman after he was healed. Elisha's servant, Gehazi, was not pleased about this and tricked Naaman into giving him the gifts. Elisha became aware of his actions, and because of his dishonesty, Gehazi then received the leprosy from which Naaman had been healed. Elisha continued to serve the Lord and the king.

READ 2 KINGS 6:8–17

O LORD, open his eyes and let him see! (v17b).

Checkpoint: Elisha stayed faithful to God and was loyal to the king. God used him to help protect the Israelites from attack by the king of Aram. He was able to use the gift that God had given him for the protection of God's children.

When we become Christians, God gives each one of us a gift (often more than one). These gifts are given to us so that we can help each other (1 Cor. 12) and so that God's family will be encouraged.

The king of Aram kept trying to find a weak spot in the Israelites' defense, but God did not stop protecting His children. He continued as long as His enemy kept it up. Our enemy is Satan, and he will try to find a weak spot in our character, trying to trip us up and tempt us to sin. God is greater and knows all of the devil's tricks; He is able to help us withstand them.

The king's attack became a bit more personal. He wanted to get rid of Elisha in order to have victory over Israel. When Elisha's servant saw all the forces, he panicked. Elisha had eyes of faith and knew that God was protecting him. He prayed that his servant would have those eyes of faith so that he could see God's protection.

When we feel weak and afraid at the things Satan is doing, we need to pray that God will strengthen our faith so that we can stand against our enemy.

- *Read Ephesians 6:12. How does the servant's vision of the chariots of fire and horses give us comfort in this?*
- *How can we stand against the devil's schemes?*
- *What gift has God given you to help His children?*

Prayer Stop: Praise God for His mighty power and protection. Pray for anyone you know who is afraid at the moment. Pray for strength.

DAY 74

On the Way: The Arameans gave the land of Israel peace for a while. Then they besieged Samaria again, causing a famine in the land. The king became angry with Elisha and wanted to kill him, and again the Lord protected Elisha and gave him a message for the king that he would provide plenty for the people to eat. The king did not believe it, but it did happen the next day.

As the kings of Israel and Judah came and went, God continued to guide them. Though some did evil in God's sight, there were others who pleased God by what they did.

Elisha died and was buried. We take the story up again with King Hezekiah.

READ 2 KINGS 18:1–8

He remained faithful to the LORD in everything (v6a).

Checkpoint: Hezekiah was a young man who led the people in God's way. He did not merely show them by example and allow them to make up their minds if they wanted to follow. He actively got rid of the things that were turning their hearts away from God. Even the serpent that God had told Moses to put up in the desert was broken up because the people were starting to worship it. This was meant for good, a symbol of a time when God had saved them, but it had become something that turned them away from God, so Hezekiah got rid of it.

No matter what age we are, we can be aware of things around us that take our minds and hearts away from God. We should make every effort to rid our lives of those things. As parents or leaders, we should be active in protecting our families from such things. There may even be things that started off helping us follow God but have now been given the wrong place in our lives. We need to remove anything that turns our hearts away from worshipping God alone.

- *What things can turn our hearts away from God?*
- *Can you think of anything that is meant to help us worship God that may take our hearts away from Him if we give it the wrong place in our lives?*

Prayer Stop: Praise God for those who help keep us focused on God. Pray nothing will turn us away from Him.

1 AND 2 CHRONICLES

These two books record the history of Israel and Judah. They record much of the same events as 1 and 2 Kings, although they were written much later on. Because we are a bit limited for space in this study, we have mainly looked at the events as recorded in Kings, but so that we look at all the books in the Bible, we are going to finish Hezekiah's story in the book of 2 Chronicles! Perhaps as a challenge after you have completed this study, you could read 1 and 2 Chronicles and find the differences between the events recorded in Kings and Chronicles.

DAY 75

On the Way: As we saw from 2 Kings 18, Hezekiah encouraged the people to worship God again and pleased God in all he did. In 2 Chronicles, we read in a bit more detail how Hezekiah set about doing this: he reopened the Temple and re-appointed the priests to perform their duties there as they should have been doing. He invited the people to celebrate the Passover together again. He showed great wisdom in all he did. After all of this, the king of Assyria invaded Judah. Again, we see Hezekiah act with wisdom and strong leadership.

READ 2 CHRONICLES 32:1–8, 20–21

*We have the L*ORD *our God to help us and to fight our battles for us!* (v8b).

Checkpoint: Hezekiah had been faithful to God in all he had done, and yet Judah was still invaded. Being faithful and obedient to God does not mean that bad things will never happen to us. However, because Hezekiah knew God, he was able to act wisely and lead the people through this difficulty.

Our relationship with God is important when difficult times happen. Hezekiah did what he could do; he repaired the walls and cut off the supply of water to the enemies, and he took advice from his advisors and organized the people. He encouraged the people and prayed for God to rescue them. When we face difficult times, often there are things that we can do for ourselves: it is important that we do these things and leave the things we cannot do to God, remembering that He is greater than anything we face. Hezekiah was able to lead the people wisely in this situation. When we see others facing difficulties, we can encourage them to act wisely and pray with them too.

- *How did Hezekiah encourage the people and give them a good example to follow?*
- *What practical things can you do to help someone who needs encouragement this week?*

Prayer Stop: Thank God that He is greater than any problem we face. Pray for wisdom to act wisely in difficult situations and to encourage others to do the same.

DAY 76

On the Way: The king of Assyria teased the people of Judah and insulted God. Hezekiah did not respond to the Assyrian king but encouraged his people, as we saw yesterday, and prayed. This is a good lesson for us to learn when people tease us for being Christians.

In the end, the Assyrians were defeated by the Lord. The people of Judah did nothing but get ready. God destroyed the Assyrian army.

READ 2 CHRONICLES 32:24–33

God withdrew from Hezekiah in order to test him and see what was really in his heart (v31b).

Checkpoint: In 2 Kings 20, we read in more detail about God healing Hezekiah and giving him fifteen years more to live. He confirmed this by making the shadow move ten degrees backward on the sundial. God had shown him a great kindness, and yet after all we have seen Hezekiah do for God, he now becomes proud. We are not told specifically what made him proud, but we can surmise that it may have been because of the miracle God had shown him.

Our God is a great God and is able to do amazing wonders for His people. When we see this happen, we must be careful not to put our focus on the miracle but on the God who can perform it. Although Hezekiah has been tempted to become proud, he confesses his sin to God and is forgiven. Although Hezekiah did what pleased God, he was not perfect and still had sin in his heart. We, too, will always struggle with sin in our hearts until we are with the Lord in heaven. We need to be ready to confess that sin and be forgiven like Hezekiah. Sometimes God will allow things to happen in order to show us what our hearts are really like. He allowed Hezekiah to see that there was pride in his heart as he showed the officials around his palaces.

- *How can being proud of what God has done for us become a sin?*
- *Read Psalm 138:6. How can this help us understand verse 31?*
- *What things are you tempted to be proud of?*

Prayer Stop: Thank God that He does show us the sin in our hearts. Confess any you are aware of to Him now. Pray that you would always give Him honor for the things He has done for you.

DAY 77

On the Way: Hezekiah's son Manasseh became king after him. Sadly, it is recorded that he encouraged the people to worship false gods again. The Lord warned him, but Manasseh did not listen. Then the commander of the Assyrian army took him captive. In distress, Manasseh turned to God; he restored the Temple and encouraged the people to worship God again. When he died, Amon, his son became king. He did not seek God like his father had but his son, Josiah, became king at age eight and did what was right before God.

READ 2 CHRONICLES 34:14–21, 31

When the king heard what was written in the Law, he tore his clothes in despair (v19).

Checkpoint: Although Josiah was a king who pleased God and encouraged the people to worship Him, he was only doing what he had learned from the past and from what he felt was right in his heart; he did not have the Law before him to live by. When they found the book and read it, Josiah realized that as a nation they were a long way from God's standards. He then vowed to live by what was written in the Law.

We have something far greater than the book of the Law: we have the complete Word of God, and it should be our priority to live by that Word. Do you read it regularly and live your life by what you read in it? In front of the elders of Judah and Jerusalem, the king committed himself to do what was written in the scroll (2 Chron. 34:29). It is often good to have people who can ask you whether you are reading the Bible or who can provide you with guidance when you don't understand it. Today's study will remind you that it is important to read God's Word and will encourage you to do it.

- *What difference would it make in your life if you did not have a Bible to read?*
- *What things encourage you to read your Bible? Is there anything that makes it difficult?*
- *Who can you ask to encourage you to read God's Word more?*

Prayer Stop: Thank God for the gift of His Word. Pray for those in the world who do not have a Bible or are not allowed to read it.

Practical Application: See if you can help to supply some Bibles to places that have none.

DAY 78

On the Way: Josiah died in a battle against the king of Egypt, and his son Jehoahaz became king. The king of Egypt deposed him and placed his brother on the throne instead. Then Nebuchadnezzar, the king of Babylon, captured Jerusalem and took captives and treasures back to Babylon. Eventually, under the reign of King Zedekiah, because the people kept sinning, God allowed the king of Babylon to completely destroy Jerusalem.

MEMORY VERSE

But you, O Lord, are a God of compassion and mercy, slow to get angry and filled with unfailing love and faithfulness.

~ Psalm 86:15

READ 2 CHRONICLES 36:14–21

He had compassion on his people and his Temple (v15b).

Checkpoint: As we have looked at the history of the children of God, we have seen that they repeatedly turned away from Him. No matter what happened, they were easily led to worship false gods and to disobey God. God had sent them messengers to warn them, but they ignored the warning and made fun of the messengers, adding to their sin. As a result, God allowed them to be taken into exile, and Jerusalem was destroyed.

We can be guilty of continuing to sin against God. As we see from our key verse, God has a very deep love for His children and is very patient; He will send us messengers to help us face our sin and give us a chance to repent. We should respond by learning the lesson quickly and confessing our sin. We should not be like the Israelites who ignored God's warning.

It was in God's Law that every seven years the land should not be farmed; it should be given rest. This Law had not been followed in the nation and so, when the people were exiled, the land was given that rest. God will work out His purposes. No person or thing can stop Him.

- *What things or people has God used in your life to make you aware of sin?*
- *How did God show His compassion and patience with the people? How does He show it to us?*

Prayer Stop: Praise God for His patience with us and that nothing can stop His plans. Pray that you will be quick to learn the lessons God wants to teach you.

EZRA

The book of Ezra covers the story of the Israelites returning to the land God gave them after their capture and exile in Babylon. It starts when some of them return to rebuild the Temple, which had been burned down. Ezra was a scribe and recorded these things for us.

DAY 79

On the Way: Jeremiah had given the people God's message that they would be in Babylon for seventy years. At the end of this time, King Cyrus of Persia told his entire kingdom that God had put it in his heart to build a temple for the Living God in Jerusalem. He wanted those who had been in exile in Babylon to return to Jerusalem to do this. So they set out, and their neighbors helped them by giving them valuable gifts. King Cyrus also gave them the articles from the Temple that Nebuchadnezzar had taken. When they arrived, they started to rebuild the altar.

READ EZRA 3:1–4, 3:11; 4:5

We alone will build the Temple for the Lord the God of Israel (4:3b).

Checkpoint: Though they were afraid of the local people, the people made it their priority to build the altar first so that they could offer sacrifices to the Lord and worship Him. When we move to a new place to live, it is important that we find a place to worship God with other Christians. Even when we start out on a new adventure and may feel afraid, we should make it our priority to put God first.

In chapter 4, we see some people trying to stir up trouble. They pretended to be true worshippers of God. The local people were against the workers and tried to stop them from completing the temple. When we serve God and are involved in work that builds up His church, we will come across people who will try to stop us. There will be people who make things difficult and even threaten or frighten us, perhaps people who are against Christianity. There may also be people who try to come and help us but who secretly want to make trouble for us. We need to be wise and pray that God will protect His work from those attacking it from both the outside and the inside.

- *Why do you suppose the older people were weeping? (Ezra 3:12)*
- *What sort of things can frustrate us when we serve God?*
- *Is there anyone new in your area? Perhaps you could invite them to your church.*
- *Does your church have any new members? What could you do to make them feel welcome?*

Prayer Stop: Praise God for the people in your church family. Pray that any new members will feel welcome.

DAY 80

On the Way: The local people continued to try to stop the rebuilding of the temple. Years later, when King Artaxerxes reigned, the people wrote a letter to him, and he ordered the building to be stopped until King Darius took the throne. Even then, people were still trying to have the work stopped. Darius looked back in the records and noted that they had been permitted to build by King Cyrus. He then issued a rule that let the Israelite people build without any obstruction. The Temple was finished and dedicated.

READ EZRA 7:1–10

The gracious hand of the LORD his God was on him (v6b).

Checkpoint: Today we are introduced to Ezra, who is a scribe. This was someone who was well educated and had learned all he could about a certain subject. Ezra was an expert in the Law of Moses. The people had forgotten the details of the Law and did not live by them, but while living in Babylon, Ezra had become an expert in this Law. Ezra was a captive but had used his time in Babylon to learn and obey God's Law.

Sometimes we can feel like a captive. Perhaps illness keeps us isolated from others. We can use such times, like Ezra, to learn more of God's Word.

When Ezra was able to go back to Jerusalem, he was ready to teach the Law of Moses to his fellow citizens. This was not just something that happened. In verse 10, we read that he had made up his mind to do this. The first thing he did was learn the Law of Moses, then he obeyed it himself, and then he was ready to teach it.

We cannot teach something that we do not live ourselves. Make up your mind today to learn and obey God's Word. Then you will be ready to teach it to others when God gives you that chance.

- *When you are stuck and feel like a captive, how do you react? What can you learn from Ezra?*
- *How can you encourage others to learn more of God's Word?*
- *Read Psalm 119:105. How does this relate to Ezra?*

Prayer Stop: Thank God for those who teach you God's Word. Pray for time to learn more about it.

DAY 81

On the Way: The king sent a decree to the governors in the province of the Euphrates to provide Ezra with whatever he required for the Temple and also to allow any of the people of Israel to return to Jerusalem with him. So Ezra set off with the volunteers. He fasted and asked God for protection along the way. When they arrived safely, they made sacrifices to God and worshipped Him.

READ EZRA 9:1–8, 10

> *I blush to lift up my face to you. For our sins are piled higher than our heads* (v6b).

Checkpoint: As we learned yesterday, Ezra was an expert in the Law of Moses. We might say he knew it "inside out." So when the leaders came and told him that the men had been marrying women from the outside of God's chosen people, he was very upset. He knew what God's Law said about this and understood why God did not want them to do so, and he knew how great a sin this was against God.

When we get to know God's Word and grow closer to God, we begin to recognize the sin in our lives and in the world around us. We know that our sin caused Jesus to suffer and die on the cross, and we should not take that lightly. Ezra was embarrassed to come to God because of the sin of his people. How do you feel when you know you have sinned?

God did not want His children to marry outside of His people because He knew that this would cause His children to turn away from Him. It is the same for us; we should marry one who loves the Lord and will encourage us to stay close to Him rather than one who may turn us away from Him.

- *Why do you think Ezra was so upset at the people's sin? How do you feel about sin in the world?*

- *Ezra prayed for his nation. What sinful things do you see in your nation that you might pray for?*

Prayer Stop: Thank God that He shows us our sin through His Word. Pray for your nation, that God would provide wise and godly leaders to make wise and godly decisions.

NEHEMIAH

Nehemiah was a Jewish exile serving in King Artaxerxes' palace in Babylon. He heard that the wall of Jerusalem still needed rebuilt and asked the king for permission to take some of his people and help to rebuild the walls. This book tells that story. It seems to have been written by Nehemiah himself, but Ezra may have had some input.

DAY 82

On the Way: Some of the Jews had already returned to Jerusalem when King Cyrus of Persia deemed he should let the exiled people return to build the Temple again in Jerusalem. Ezra returned a few years after this with another group of Jews returning to Jerusalem. However, some still remained in Babylon. We see Nehemiah as one of these people serving in the king's palace.

READ NEHEMIAH 1:1–11

Things are not going well for those who returned to the province of Judah (v3b).

Checkpoint: People were free to move between the two nations. Nehemiah's family had come to visit but had told him of the difficulties they were facing in Jerusalem. The people of God had returned to the land that God had given them, but they were struggling to rebuild. Nehemiah's response was to pray, not just to say a prayer, but to cry out to God and also fast.

When we hear of difficulties in our nation or in our churches, what is our first response? Often we analyse the problem and try to decide why it happened or who to blame. Let's learn from Nehemiah; we should turn to God and pray. By the end of his prayer, we get the impression he is about to do something. He asks God that the king would be kind to him.

When we pray for situations, we need to be willing to be part of the answer. Nehemiah was to be part of the answer for the nation of Israel. Whether it is a national problem or a more personal problem, God may want us to be part of the answer.

- *What problems are happening nationally or internationally at the moment? In what practical ways can you help?*

- *What lessons can we learn from Nehemiah's prayer when we pray for our nation?*

- *Are you part of an active church? Perhaps there are churches nearby who need help rebuilding; can you or your church help in any way?*

Prayer Stop: Praise God for often using us as part of the answer to our prayers. What national/international crises need your prayer today? Pray for any church you mentioned in the third question above.

DAY 83

On the Way: Nehemiah was a cupbearer for the king. He would regularly be in the king's presence, and therefore the king would notice if there was anything different about him. The king's servants were to appear happy before the king and keep personal problems away from their work. However, Nehemiah could not hide his feelings from the king.

READ NEHEMIAH 2:1–10

The gracious hand of God was on me (v8b).

Checkpoint: The start of our reading is about three or four months after Nehemiah's prayer in Chapter 1. He had not received an immediate answer to his prayer. When we pray, we often expect God to answer right away. We become impatient when an answer doesn't come quickly. God's timing is not like ours! He is patient and works everything out according to His will. He sees everything that is happening around the whole situation, not just what we see and understand. So we need to be patient and wait on God to answer in His time.

The end of verse 2 tells us Nehemiah was terrified, but he answered the king anyway. He knew that God had given him this opportunity, and he was not going to waste it. He did not let his fear stop him from doing as God wanted.

We can sometimes be afraid of what God asks us to do. We need to remember that God is much bigger than our fear. We need to trust Him and not allow our fear to hold us back from serving Him.

Nehemiah was able to pray at the same time as talk to the king. We have that access to God at any time and can talk to Him anywhere. No matter what we are facing or when, we can pray. Nehemiah had to wait until the king asked him what was troubling him, but he did not have to wait to bring his worries to God.

- *Have you experienced times when you felt God forgot to answer your prayer?*
- *Read Romans 8:15. How can knowing we have God's Spirit in us give us courage?*
- *Have you ever been in a situation where, like Nehemiah, you have had to pray on the spot?*

Prayer Stop: Thank God that we can come into His presence to pray. Pray for courage to obey God.

DAY 84

On the Way: Nehemiah arrived in Jerusalem. No one knew his plans until he had looked at what needed to be done. He went out one night to look round the walls and then told the city officials how God had put it on his heart to rebuild them. They supported this idea, but some officials from surrounding areas laughed at them.

READ NEHEMIAH 3:1–5, 8–12

Then Eliashib the high priest and the other priests started to rebuild (v1a).

Checkpoint: This chapter shows us the people who were involved in rebuilding the wall. The sections we read show us the variety of people who took part.

The high priest started the work. In the community everyone looked up to him, but he did not think he was too important to rebuild the city walls. We read of individuals helping, including people from the towns of Jericho and Tekoa. The leaders of Tekoa refused to work under the supervisors (Neh. 3:5). They seemed to think they were above such guidance and did not work as part of the team. In the second section, we read of district leaders and perfume makers building as well. They were people who normally did something very different, willing to do their part in the rebuilding process.

When we lead others, we should lead by example, like the high priest and district leaders. No work should be below us; we should be willing to work beside those we lead. When we help others with a task, we should be willing to work under their guidance, not like the leaders from Tekoa. When we refuse to work as part of a team, we hold the work back instead of moving it forward.

The perfume makers would not have used stone and cement very often, but they were willing to do their part. We should be willing to help out even in things we do not normally do in order to serve God and build His kingdom.

- *Can you think of examples of leaders who led by example?*
- *What difficulties crop up when people do not work as part of a team?*
- *How do you feel about offering to do something you have never done before?*

Prayer Stop: Praise God that you are part of His family and that we all have different strengths. Pray that God would show you what He wants you to do to build His kingdom.

DAY 85

On the Way: Everyone in the city and some from outside the city did their part to rebuild the wall. Nehemiah had shared his vision, and the people had taken it on to make it happen. People took responsibility for their own section of the wall, and so the work kept going. When things are going well, we need to be careful; that can be when difficulties start to happen.

MEMORY VERSE

But we have this treasure in jars of clay to show that this all-surpassing power is from God and not from us. We are hard pressed on every side, but not crushed; perplexed, but not in despair; persecuted, but not abandoned; struck down, but not destroyed.

~ 2 Corinthians 4:7–9

READ NEHEMIAH 4:1–14

Don't be afraid of the enemy (v14b).

Checkpoint: The work is going well, but problems start to crop up. Sanballat starts to mock the Jews for what they are doing. Tobiah comes along and demoralizes them by making them think their work is weak. Then these two men talk about attacking them. This had an effect on the people of Israel. In verse 6, they had enthusiasm, but by verse 10, they had started to complain. They were weary with all the hard work and the threats from the enemy. As if this was not enough, some of their own people started to make them fearful of enemy attacks.

When we serve God and things are going well, we need to be on the lookout for the enemy's attack. People can laugh at what we do; they can make us think our work is useless, or they can actively try to stop us. This does make us feel weary and exhausted. It can slow us down as it did the builders. They had to guard against attacks as well as build, and that impeded their progress.

Look at Nehemiah's reaction to all of this: he prayed. He did not answer back at all. He reminded the people of how great God is and kept going with the work in hand. This is what we should do too.

- *How do you feel when people attack the work you are doing for God?*
- *What can you learn from Nehemiah's response?*

Prayer Stop: Praise God for leaders who can encourage us to keep going. Pray for those who attack you for serving God.

DAY 86

On the Way: When Nehemiah heard of the enemy's plan to attack, he was able to change the work force and place a guard on the wall. This meant that work could continue, even though it was perhaps a bit slower. Nehemiah prepared for attack while the work went on. He let the people know the plan: if they heard the trumpet, they would rush to where it was and rely on God to help them. They worked long days to get the walls built; they didn't even change their clothes!

READ NEHEMIAH 5:1–13

What you are doing is not right (v9b).

Checkpoint: The Jewish nobles were forcing their fellow Jews to pay heavy taxes that they were unable to afford, so they had to sell their children into slavery and take loans out in order to pay the taxes. The rich Jews were becoming richer, while those who were less well off were becoming poorer. This is what we call *social injustice*. Nehemiah was angry. It is right to be angry at social injustice. The people who suffer in this way are often powerless to do anything about it, just as the Jews in our reading today.

Although Nehemiah was angry, he did not just go and shout about it to the nobles. He gave it some thought. Before we take action against anyone who is guilty of this behavior, we must think about what we will say and what we will do. Nehemiah showed them that what they were doing was wrong and told them how to put it right. He showed them by example; he did lend fellow Israelites money, but he did not charge them interest.

- *What examples of social injustice do you see today?*
- *What can you do to help the situation? Perhaps you could take some action by writing to the government or signing a petition.*
- *Read Acts 2:42–47. How did the early church deal with social injustice? What lesson can we learn from this?*

Prayer Stop: Praise God for all that He has given you and pray that you will be wise with what you have. Pray for any social injustice you are aware of.

DAY 87

On the Way: The walls were finished 52 days after the work had begun! The enemies were not happy about this and plotted to harm Nehemiah. They tried every trick they could think of, but God protected Nehemiah and gave him wisdom to deal with them. Nehemiah set up a watch around the walls and registered the people. He was governor of the city. When everyone was settled, they asked Ezra to read the book of the Law. They confessed their sins and vowed to obey God. Nehemiah discovered that the high priest had given rooms in the Temple to Tobiah when they should have been used for the things of God. He also discovered that the Levites and priests were not being provided for as they should have been. He put all this right.

READ NEHEMIAH 13:15-22

Why are you profaning the Sabbath in this evil way? (v17b).

Checkpoint: This was an obvious disobedience of the Law. God had given clear instructions to His people that they must keep the Sabbath holy and do no work. When God gave the commandments to Moses, He said we had six days in which to do ordinary work. The seventh day was a day to rest and remember God in a special way. It was not even the foreign people in Jerusalem who were guilty of this; it was men of Judah themselves.

This standard is one that is taught in the New Testament too. Jesus reminds the religious leaders that the Sabbath was created for man to rest and worship God (Mark 2:27). The leaders in Jesus' day had made it a thing that was bound by rules so strict that no one could do anything! These are two extremes, and we need to think how God would have us treat His special day. Some people have to work on Sunday, but we need to realize that rest and worship are important for us to stay healthy both in body and spirit!

- *How is our nation the same as Jerusalem in Nehemiah's day?*
- *How can you keep the Sabbath special in your life?*

Prayer Stop: Thank God that He has given us time to rest. Pray that you would spend your day of rest wisely.

ESTHER

We do not know who wrote the book of Esther; some say Mordecai, Ezra, or Nehemiah. It tells of how the Jewish people were nearly annihilated but were rescued by the brave acts of Esther, who was queen in Persia at the time.

DAY 88

On the Way: King Xerxes of Persia held a huge banquet for all his officials and governors; this lasted 180 days. At the end, he held another banquet for all of the people, this one lasting a week. During this time, Queen Vashti offended him. He was so angry he took the position of queen away from her. He sent his officials to look for beautiful young women in the provinces and had them bring them to the palace. One of them would be his new queen.

READ ESTHER 2:5–12, 16–20

> *This man had a very beautiful and lovely young cousin, Hadassah, who was also called Esther* (v7a).

Checkpoint: In our reading today, we get a picture of Esther as a person. Her situation in life would have meant she did not have much going for her; she was a Jewish exile living in Persia, and her parents had died, so she was living with her cousin. However, she is described as "beautiful and lovely." She was not only beautiful to look at but lovely in personality; the king's official was impressed with her and treated her well. She continued to follow Mordecai's advice even though she lived in the palace—even after she had become queen. She pleased the king more than any of the other women. No matter what situation she was in, her character still remained the same: she was humble, willing to take advice, and unwilling to let her position go to her head.

When we are in situations that put us under pressure or that put us in a position of power, how do we behave? It is good to learn from Esther that whether we are in a low position just living our lives or in a position where we have power over people, our character should be constant, showing the love of God to others.

- *How do you think Esther felt as she entered the king's palace to begin all the beauty treatments?*
- *Why do you think Mordecai wanted her to keep her nationality secret?*
- *How do you react to different situations in life?*

Prayer Stop: Praise God for the character He has given you and pray that you will show His love in every situation you face.

DAY 89

On the Way: So Esther had been made queen. She continued to communicate with her cousin at the palace gate, and she still took his advice and treated him with respect, as she had done when she was living in his family. Mordecai seemed to have a position in the king's court, as he was there every day and was on duty when our reading starts.

READ ESTHER 2:20–3:6

> *But Mordecai refused to bow down or show him respect* (v3:2b).

Checkpoint: Today we are going to look at Mordecai's character. He was doing his job at the king's gate and discovered two of the king's guards plotting to kill Xerxes. Mordecai was able to let Esther know, and she warned the king. Although it was written in the king's diary that Mordecai had revealed the plot, he was not given any thanks for it at this point. He did what was right even though no one else knew what he had done. When the king made Haman prime minister, Mordecai did what was right again, even though this time it could have cost him his life. He refused to bow to anyone on earth; he would bow only to God. When his friends tried to persuade him to do otherwise, he stood firm and would not be persuaded. He had courage to do the right thing even when everyone else urged him to do the opposite.

We should always do what is right, whether others know what we have done or not. We need to remember that God always knows, and we should always live to please Him. We should always give God the top priority in our lives, as Mordecai did. This may mean that we have to stand up to people who try to turn our hearts from God; this takes courage, but God has promised to give us courage when we need it.

- *Read Mark 13:11. How do you see Mordecai living this out in his life? How does it encourage you to do what is right?*

- *Why did Mordecai tell Esther to keep her nationality a secret, but he told people he was Jewish?*

Prayer Stop: Thank God for giving us courage to stand for Him when we need it. Pray for those who are persecuted because they are Christians today.

DAY 90

On the Way: When Haman learned that Mordecai was a Jew, he determined in his rage not to punish only Mordecai for not bowing to him but to punish all Jews. He had dice thrown to help him decide when this punishment would happen, and it was decided that the next year would be best.

READ ESTHER 3:8–4:3

Then the king and Haman sat down to drink, but the city of Susa fell into confusion (3:15b).

Checkpoint: Today we get a picture of the characters of Haman and the king. Haman flew into a rage when Mordecai would not bow down to him. He was proud of his position and intolerant of those who felt differently, so he was determined to get rid of them. He was able to influence the king by convincing him that the people were out to cause trouble by disobeying him. The king did not investigate the claim but gave Haman his authority to do as he pleased. The king did not take his responsibility seriously. After all this was done, the king and Haman had a drink together. What they had planned would cause turmoil in other people's lives, but they were not concerned.

These men are not the kind of men you would want as leaders. Haman manipulated things to get what he wanted, the king did not take his responsibilities seriously, and yet both seem to have all the power.

Some Christians live in countries like this today; they are persecuted because they are Christians, and they are powerless to do anything about it. There are people who do not tolerate others thinking differently from themselves. Paul wrote in 1 Corinthians that he tried to find common ground with everyone in order to share the good news of Jesus; Jesus calls us to be peacemakers. This should help us to find ways to work with others, respecting them as people even if we cannot agree with their beliefs.

- *Find out what you can about Christians who are persecuted for their faith. Visit www.releaseinternational.org for information.*

- *How do you react when someone thinks differently from you?*

Prayer Stop: Pray for Christians who are persecuted for their faith. Pray that God would help you to be tolerant of others but strong in your faith.

DAY 91

On the Way: We read yesterday how upset Mordecai and all the Jews were when they heard the law that they were to be killed. They cried, fasted, and went into mourning. It was a tradition that when people were mourning, they wore sackcloth and put ash on their heads. Mordecai did this and went to the king's gate; everyone around could see him, and Esther was told about it.

READ ESTHER 4:4–17

Who knows if perhaps you were made queen for just such a time as this? (v14b).

Checkpoint: Esther could see Mordecai was upset but didn't know why. So she sent him clothes to put on instead of the sackcloth. When he refused, she sent someone to find out the reason for his behavior. Having been told about the decree she thought that the problem was too big for her to solve.

When we become aware of problems affecting us or other Christians, sometimes we try to sort it out in the easiest and most simple way, doing something that would make it seem like the problem has gone away, a bit like Esther sending Mordecai clothes to wear.

Mordecai told Esther everything about the decree so that she understood how serious it was. He told her that, as queen, she could do something about it. Esther did not know what would happen when she went to see the king, but she was willing to take that risk for her people.

Problems sometimes seem far too big for us to even think about solving. When we come across a situation like that, we must do what we can do and ask God to do the rest. That might mean we have to take a risk, like Esther did. God knows what will happen in our lives from start to finish. He will work out His plans. Perhaps you will be the person in the right place one day to be able to stand up for God's people.

- *Why is it important that we get to know all the details of a problem before we try to solve it?*

- *What problems face Christians today that you may be able to do something about?*

Prayer Stop: Thank God for allowing us to help work out His plans. Pray that you would be willing to take the right risks for God.

DAY 92

On the Way: After asking all the Jews to fast with her for three days, Esther prepared herself with special robes to go into the king. When he saw her, the king was pleased and asked her what she wanted. He was very generous; he would have given her up to half the kingdom! However, Esther simply asked that he and Haman attend a banquet. She would explain her request at the banquet.

MEMORY VERSE

Wise people think before they act; fools don't—and even brag about their foolishness.

~ Proverbs 13:16

READ ESTHER 5:9–14

He bragged about the honours the king had given him and how he had been promoted (v11b).

Checkpoint: In today's reading, we can see the difference between being wise and being foolish. Esther prepared herself to go to the king. She fasted and then gave some thought to how she should come to the king and what she should say. We are not told why she did not ask for what she wanted straight away, but she obviously felt this was what God wanted. Haman's behavior is the opposite. He thinks so much of himself that he invites his friends to listen to him boast about how great he thinks he is! There is only one thing making him unhappy, and that is the way Mordecai is treating him. His wife and friends suggest that he should kill him, so he plans to do this the next day. It seems as though Esther's plan will be too late to save Mordecai.

We cannot understand God's plans; sometimes things don't make sense, but if we are acting wisely, asking God to guide us and doing what we can, we need to trust that God knows the whole of the story and will do what is best.

Haman was proud because of his position, and he used his power to get what he wanted. When we are in such a position, we should act wisely to help others, as Esther did; this is what pleases God.

- *Why do you think Esther invited the king and Haman to a banquet?*
- *What are the differences between Esther and Haman?*

Prayer Stop: Thank God for His wisdom. Pray that God will give you wisdom in any problem you are facing just now.

DAY 93

On the Way: That night, the king couldn't sleep and had his diaries read to him. When his servants read the part where Mordecai had uncovered the plot to take the king's life, he realized that Mordecai had not been rewarded. Then Haman came to the king's court to ask him to have Mordecai killed. While the king is looking for a way to reward Mordecai, Haman is seeking to have him killed! The scene that follows is quite funny. The king asked Haman how he should honor someone who pleased him and Haman, thinking it was for himself, gave the king his best idea.

READ ESTHER 6:10–7:10

> *You will never succeed in your plans against him* (6:13b).

Checkpoint: Here we see the downfall of Haman. His pride and scheming have eventually caught up with him because God is at work. Haman plans to kill Mordecai the very night the king can't sleep and discovers he needed to reward him. Haman had to parade Mordecai round the city, giving him honor. Haman's wife and friends realized that Mordecai had God on his side. All this occurred just in time for Esther to tell the king about Haman's evil plot.

As we have seen in the book of Esther and may also have experienced ourselves, we cannot outsmart God! God has His plans worked out and will bring justice to those who plan evil, though it may seem that they are getting away with their evil plans. God may not work in the way we would expect, but He will work, and we need to trust Him. This does not mean that everything will always turn out happy or easy for us. God is more interested in our being faithful to Him and trusting Him no matter what. Esther was willing to take the risk regardless of the outcome.

- *Read Psalm 10:13–15. Would you ever think of praying for your enemies like David does in verse 15? Why/why not?*

- *How do you feel when you see someone getting away with doing wrong?*

- *How can Acts 17:31 help us deal with this?*

Prayer Stop: Praise God that His plans work out and are way beyond what we could ever think of. Pray for your enemies. Remember that Jesus tells us to love them.

DAY 94

On the Way: Now Haman has been put to death. The king gives his property to Esther, who gives Mordecai the job of looking after it. However, the decree against the Jews still stands because it was made in the name of the king, and the laws of Persia could not be withdrawn. So Esther went into the king again to ask for the lives of the Jews to be spared. As the king could not withdraw the first law, he gave Mordecai and Esther authority to send the Jews a decree telling them whatever they wanted. They were able to give the Jews permission to defend themselves against anyone who would attack them because of Haman's decree.

READ ESTHER 8:13–9:4

For Mordecai had been promoted in the king's palace (9:4a).

Checkpoint: The end of this story is full of opposites! Mordecai is now the prime minister instead of Haman. He is given the king's ring, as Haman was, and had used it to issue a decree to help his people against the evil Haman had planned for them. The people were full of joy at Mordecai's decree but full of fear when they heard Haman's. Because of all the good Mordecai did, people honored him because they wanted to, unlike being told to honor Haman by the king. Even after all of this, the people were not guaranteed success; they could only prepare as best they could and trust God to do the rest.

We have come across this lesson a few times in Esther. God wants us to be active in standing up for what is right, to do our part and then to trust Him for the answer. God did rescue the Jews. In the story, we can see Him working through the lives of His people, who were in the right place for the right time.

- *When you have done all you can in a circumstance, how easy do you find it to trust God with the rest?*

- *Read 1 Samuel 2:30. How do you see this worked out in Esther's story?*

- *Are people for whom you can take a stand being treated unfairly around you?*

Prayer Stop: Use 1 Samuel 2:30 as a point to praise God. Pray for those who are facing unfair treatment at the moment.

PSALMS AND BOOKS OF WISDOM

This section includes books of worship and books of wise sayings from leaders who followed God.

JOB

Job is part of what are called the Books of Wisdom in the Old Testament. It deals with the question of suffering and helps us understand more about it. It does not give us a definitive answer as to why people suffer but shows us that we are unable to understand the ways of God.

DAY 1

On the Way: Job lived in the land of Uz. The Bible tells us he feared God in everything. He was a very wealthy man with seven sons and three daughters and was well known and respected in the whole area around where he lived. His family was used to a life of luxury and spent a lot of time having parties in their homes. Job would pray for them and ask God to keep them from sinning.

READ JOB 1:6–22

> *The LORD gave me what I had and the LORD has taken it away. Praise the name*
> *of the LORD (v21b).*

Checkpoint: It is easy when things are going well to praise and thank God for all that we have. Satan knows this and pointed out to God that things were going so well for Job it was no wonder he praised God. But God knew His servant Job and knew his heart was fixed on serving God no matter what. It is hard to imagine so much happening to one person in such a short space of time. While each servant was giving Job his message, the next messenger arrived with more bad news. All of Job's livestock was destroyed, and then his children were killed. He had nothing left. This makes Job's response remarkable. He realizes that everything he had, including his family, came from God's hand, and he accepted that God had now allowed it all to be taken away.

This is an important lesson for us to learn. We can become so attached to the things we have, that we forget it all comes from the Lord. When these things are taken from us, we can get into such a state. It's much better to focus on God on these occasions, as Job did. This is particularly hard when the people we love are affected, not just things.

- *How can our key verse help us have the right attitude to the things we have in life (including our families)?*

- *Talk about how Job might have felt on receiving so much bad news.*

- *Have you or your family had to deal with receiving bad news? What was your reaction?*

Prayer Stop: Pray for anyone you know who has lost something or someone special. Pray that God would help you to be steadfast when you go through hard times.

DAY 2

On the Way: Job has now lost his business and children. As God knew, he did not turn against Him because of that. Job did not sin by his reaction to this loss. Satan was not satisfied with this and challenged God to allow Job's health to suffer; then Job would turn against God.

READ JOB 2:6–13

Should we accept only good things from the hand God and never anything bad? (v10b).

Checkpoint: It is harder to praise God when we are going through hard experiences. Job's wife is an example of how people sometimes treat God when they are suffering. They react angrily and blame God; they don't accept that a loving God would allow suffering. Job reacts differently; he is obviously suffering very much from his illness and yet accepts that God has allowed it. He challenges his wife to think differently. She thinks he would be better off dead. Her life has been deeply affected by Job's trouble, but her reaction is very different. She is unable to bring comfort to her husband because she is suffering too. Job's friends come and sit with him for a whole week without saying anything. They were very upset when they saw how ill Job looked, but they stayed with him.

Often it is important to just be with those who are suffering and not to be put off by their horrible circumstances. Friends can be a real comfort at such times when family members are overwhelmed. Words, as we will see later, can be so meaningless.

- *In what ways had Job's wife been affected by Job's suffering? Why would it be difficult for her to comfort her husband?*
- *How can we comfort others who are suffering? Think of some practical things you could do.*
- *When we are suffering, how should we react to God?*

Prayer Stop: Pray for anyone you know who is suffering and that God would show you the right ways to help them. Pray that when you face difficult circumstances you will not turn against God.

Suggestion: Perhaps you could make a card and send (or take) it to someone who is going through difficult circumstances this week.

DAY 3

On the Way: After having the company of his friends for a whole week, Job ventures to speak. He seemed to feel that as they had been with him all that time and had seen how much he suffered that he would now tell them how he felt.

READ JOB 3:1–7, 23–26

> *Why is life given to those with no future, those God has surrounded with difficulties? (v23).*

Checkpoint: Job pours it all out! He is in such agony he wishes he had not been born; in fact, he wants to die. That seems to be the only way he can think of getting relief from his pain. Between verses 11 and 23, he asks why he didn't die when he was born and why it is not possible for him to die now.

Often when we suffer illness or difficulties, we look for something that might bring us relief. It is important to be honest about how we are feeling. We need to be real. Job was not about to blame God for all his suffering, but he was not going to pretend it was great either! Of course, Job was feeling miserable, and he let his friends know it here. In verse 23, Job is almost saying, "Life is not fair; why am I not allowed to die and find relief from my suffering? Why has God not given me a way out? He seems to have put a hedge up to keep me in this suffering."

No one enjoys suffering; it is only natural to look for ways out. Although we may feel like God has abandoned us, we must remember His promise to be with us always.

- *Knowing what kind of man Job was, how do you think his friends might have felt when they heard Job speak?*

- *Many things in life that we have no control over don't seem fair. Can you think of some? Perhaps some come to mind from current news reports.*

- *How do these things make you feel?*

Prayer Stop: Praise God that He has promised never to leave us or abandon us. Pray for those who feel that He has.

DAY 4

On the Way: From chapter 4–37 we have a conversation between Job and three of his friends. They think they have the answer to Job's problem and all three of them give their opinion of what they think Job should do. Job replies to them, but no one seems to hear what he is saying.

READ JOB 4:7–11; 8:1–7; 19:21–25

I know that my Redeemer lives and he will stand upon the earth at last (19:25b).

Checkpoint: Our first reading gives us a flavor of what Job's friends think is the problem. To them it seems obvious. Job has sinned, and God is punishing him for that. So the answer to them is also simple: repent, and God will restore your health and wealth. (Job 8:6–7).This seems to have been their experience of God so far. Job knows that he has not sinned and therefore does not understand why God has allowed this suffering. This is a new experience for him, and his friends are finding it difficult to accept.

When we are comforting those who are suffering, it is important to remember we do not know all the answers to solve their problems. We may think we understand the reason behind their difficulties, but it is important to listen and hear what they are saying. Job's friends were not listening to him (Job 12:1–2). They were giving him what we call *pat answers*, things that everyone knows about God: He is holy and punishes sin, etc.

But Job's circumstance did not fit into their knowledge and they refused to accept that God is so great that indeed there may be another reason for Job's suffering. In Job 16:2–3, Job is fed up with their empty words and finds no comfort in his friends' presence. He pays no attention to what they say but makes a statement (Job 19:25) showing that no matter what happens, his faith will not be shaken.

- *When we do not understand what others are going through, how can we bring true comfort to them?*
- *How could knowing Isaiah 55:8–9 help us in a situation like Job's?*
- *Reflect on what your reaction might be if you were suffering like Job. Would you be able to make his statement in Job 19:25?*

Prayer Stop: Pray that God would help you be a true comfort to those who are suffering.

DAY 5

On the Way: In chapter 32, we meet Elihu. He has been there all the time, quietly waiting for the older men to have their say. He listens to their reasoning, all the while becoming angry at the empty and seemingly pointless words of these older men. We meet him at the start of his speech.

READ JOB 32:6–9; 34:5–15

Truly, God will not do wrong. The Almighty will not twist justice (34:12b).

Checkpoint: Elihu can wait no longer and suddenly blurts out what he is think-ing. He thinks he has something new to say but actually, as we read in chapter 34, his thoughts are pretty much the same as the others. He thinks Job has sinned and needs to repent. He emphasizes God's power, might, and holiness, but he does not then conclude that if God does not do wrong, then God must have His reasons for Job's suffering. His understanding of God is limited, the same as his three friends. God, in their opinion, has to act in a certain way. It is true that God gives wisdom in spite of age (Job 32:8–9), but there is no evidence of God's wisdom in Elihu's speech.

Paul, in his letter to Timothy, says, "Don't let anyone think less of you because you are young. Be an example for the believers" (1 Tim. 4:12a). Young people can have wisdom and understanding of situations given to them by God, but this will show itself in the way you speak and live. Elihu seemed to be nothing more than an obnoxious bag of wind! We must be careful when we speak that we are displaying God's example of love and humility toward others. It is then that we will be listened to and be able to be God's messenger, no matter what age we are.

- *Read 1 Timothy 4:12. What practical ways can young people set an example for older believers? Talk about some specific examples.*

- *In what way does Elihu's attitude differ from this?*

- *Can you think of an occasion when God has acted in ways beyond your understanding? How can Job's experience help us in reacting to these situations?*

Prayer Stop: Use 1 Timothy 4:12 to pray for the young people in your family and church. Pray for God to give you wisdom and understanding to help and comfort others.

DAY 6

On the Way: At last, God speaks to Job in response to his request that the Almighty would answer him (Job 31:35).

READ JOB 38:1–18

Where were you when I laid the foundations of the earth? Tell me, if you know so much (v4).

Checkpoint: We can almost feel the sense of relief when we read verse 1 in chapter 38, "Then the Lord answered Job." We look forward to Job having his questions answered and gaining a full understanding of his situation. We look forward to his friends being shown how wrong they were and apologizing. However, as we read the next four chapters, all we see is God asking Job a string of questions. These questions all relate to who is in control of the earth and all that goes on in it to keep it functioning that we may live on it. God asks him questions about the wild animals and how much knowledge he has of their lives. The only conclusion we (and Job) can reach from these questions is that God is indeed all-powerful. His understanding and knowledge is far above all we could ever dream of and that He is in control.

Often we do not get the answers we are looking for from God. Remember the verse we looked at a couple of days ago in Isaiah 55? God's ways are far above anything we can imagine or understand. He is not confined to our human reasoning. The questions God asks Job could be asked to us. What would your answer be? In Job 40:4, Job replies that he is *nothing*. His response is to worship God in His greatness. When things in our life seem beyond our understanding, let's respond like Job and worship our all-powerful God, trusting Him with the situations we cannot begin to understand.

- *Read Psalm 139:5–6. Look at some of the questions God asks Job in chapters 38–41. Use the verses from Psalm 139 as praise in response to these.*

- *Put into your own words how these questions make you feel about God.*

- *How do you think Job's friends felt at this point?*

Prayer Stop: Spend some time worshipping God for His great power. Pray for yourselves or others you know who are in situations they cannot understand right now.

DAY 7

On the Way: Today we come to the end of Job's story. We read his response to God, and at the end, we see how God blessed his life even more after his suffering than He had before. He never learns the reason for his suffering, but that has not hindered him from trusting more fully in God.

READ JOB 42: 1–17

I had only heard about you before, but now I have seen you with my own eyes (v5).

Checkpoint: After lots and lots of talking and questioning, God has spoken directly to Job, and Job is almost left speechless. He doesn't have a lot to say! When God has spoken to him, he realizes how dependent he is on God, how mighty God is, and how little he knew God before this. He realizes that he had known about God before, but now he has experienced God in a deeper way in his life and realizes that he cannot possibly stand against God and His plans.

If we keep our focus on God when we are going through times of difficulty, He can use these times to bring us closer to Him and teach us more about His character, things we may never have discovered had we not had tough times.

God did not forget Job's friends. He also spoke to them, correcting them and allowing them a second chance. He did not condemn them for their foolish and limited thinking. I'm sure they left Job knowing God in a deeper way also.

We can grow closer to God by learning from our mistakes. He is patient with us. At the end of the story, we see Job enjoying a full and happy life once again. His suffering did not last forever.

- *What lesson can we learn from Job about when we face difficult times?*
- *What can we learn from his friends?*
- *What can we learn about God?*

Prayer Stop: Pray that you will grow to know God more in every tough situation you face. Pray that you will be willing to learn from your mistakes and ready to repent. Thank God for His patience and willingness to forgive.

PSALMS

This is a collection of songs and prayers used by God's people throughout their history. King David wrote many of them at various stages in his life. In this book, we see God's children talking to God and letting Him know how they feel about events in their world or life. Emotions range from joyful to sad to angry. They show us a way to tell God how we feel and help us to worship Him also.

DAY 8

On the Way: We are not told who wrote this psalm or in what circumstances it was written. However, it is a great introduction to the book as a reminder that those who make obeying God's Word a priority in their lives will be truly happy. The rest of the Psalms echo this in many different ways.

MEMORY VERSE
Try to memorize as much of Psalm 1 as you can for this section.

READ PSALM 1

For the LORD watches over the path of the godly, but the path of the wicked leads to destruction (v6).

Checkpoint: This psalm records the different results from a life lived in God's way and a life that is not lived by God's standards and Word. In verse 1, we are told of three things that the person over whom God watches does not do. In verses 2–3, we are told of three things they do. Can you spot them?

Here is an explanation of what they mean:

Verse 1: He doesn't take advice from those who are against God. He doesn't deliberately keep company with those who are doing wrong. He is not comfortable in the company of those who make fun of God's ways.

Verse 2: He enjoys reading God's Word. He thinks deeply about it constantly.

Verse 3: As a result, he reacts suitably to the different circumstances of life (a tree . . . that bears its fruit in season).

A person who lives in the right way before God will be strong when things are difficult. He or she will be able to enjoy the good things from God and will know that God is watching like a caring parent.

- *Contrast this with what happens to those who do not follow God. What does the psalm say will happen to them?*

- *What do you think it means to meditate on God's Law? Explain how you could make room for this in your own life, either individually or as a family.*

Prayer Stop: Praise God that His Word can have such a positive effect on our lives today. Pray that you would learn as a family to meditate more on God's Word. Pray for someone you know who does not walk in God's way.

DAY 9

On the Way: Psalm 4 is an evening prayer of David's written during a difficult time in his reign and family. The men of Israel rebelled against him with his son Absalom (see 2 Sam. 15). David must have been sad and perhaps a bit unsure of what to do, but this psalm shows us that his faith in God does not waver.

READ PSALM 4

> *Don't sin by letting anger control you. Think about it overnight and remain silent. Offer sacrifices in the right spirit and trust the LORD (vs4–5).*

Checkpoint: Throughout this psalm, we are given some important pointers on making sure we have peace from God when times are tough. David pours out his heart to God and asks for an answer to his problem. Often we just moan about our problems or worry about them and forget to tell God how we feel. David urges his people not to sin when they get angry (Psa. 4:4-5); to search their hearts and listen to God; to worship Him correctly and trust Him to rescue them. He has personal experience of God rescuing him in this way (Psalm 139:23). Having brought all this to God, he then goes to bed and has a good night's sleep(Psa. 4:8).

When we face difficult situations, we too must check out our attitudes. We need to tell God exactly how we feel and ask for an answer. It is easy to become angry with those who are causing us problems, but this psalm tells us not to, but rather to trust the Lord instead. When we do this, we can sleep peacefully as David did.

- *What does it mean to worship God with a pure heart?*
- *Has there been a time when anyone in your family has had problems sleeping because of a worrying problem? Talk about how they got over it and what this psalm could teach them.*

Prayer Stop: Pray about any difficulty you or your family is facing at the moment. Make sure you tell God all about it and ask for His help. Pray that God will help you to learn to leave problems in His hand and not worry about them.

DAY 10

On the Way: Psalm 8 encourages us to think of God's greatness and power compared to our own. You can imagine David sitting, perhaps at night, looking at the sky with the stars and the moon and all of a sudden feeling very small compared to the vast heavens above him. This psalm would be a record of his reaction to this. It also leads us to think about God's greatness and to praise Him for it.

READ PSALM 8

> *O LORD, our Lord, your majestic name fills the earth* (vs1, 9).

Checkpoint: There is nowhere on earth or in heaven where God's greatness is not seen. Take a moment to think about it; even where there would appear to be evil and no good, there is still God's own creation that shouts out His glory. No matter where we are, we can always see evidence of God's glory. This should make us feel like dancing!

Verses 1b–2 tells us that it is not only in the high and lofty things of the universe that we can see God's amazing design but also in the things that would appear little and sometimes insignificant, like the gurgles of a baby. No matter what age you are, you can show God's greatness by praising Him. This fact leaves the enemies of God speechless. They have nothing to say about that.

When we think about all of God's works in this universe and where man fits into it, it is amazing that God gives us such a responsibility to look after His world. Yet that is what He has done. This is a gift from God, not something to which we have an automatic right. As Christians, we should make every effort to take this responsibility seriously and look after our world.

- *Name some things in God's creation that you find absolutely fascinating.*
- *What is your reaction when you "consider the heavens" (Psa. 8:3)?*
- *What things can you do to help look after God's creation?*

Prayer Stop: Pick some of your list of fascinating things and praise God for them. Pray that you will be able to do the practical things you have spoken of to look after the world. Pray that the government will introduce laws that will be good for the environment and help look after creation.

DAY 11

On the Way: In today's psalm, David asks a question and then answers it in the verses that follow. It is as if he has been thinking about how holy and mighty God is and wonders who would ever be acceptable to come into God's presence. From verse 2, he gives us the answer, setting out a list of character traits of the person who can come into God's presence.

READ PSALM 15

Such people will stand firm forever (v5b).

Checkpoint: The list from verses 2–5a is pretty impressive. I can't think of any person I know who would fulfill every one of these characteristics! This emphasises how holy and perfect God is and what it takes to live in His presence. Go through the psalm a phrase at a time and put into your own words the kind of person who can approach God. List the things they do and the things they don't do. Try to give a practical example of each thing.

This is a challenge to us to become the kind of people God wants us to be. There has only ever been one person who was able to fulfill every one of these characteristics: Jesus Himself. He is our example. We are to strive to be like Him in every way. We will never be perfect on this earth, but we can keep becoming more like Jesus as we let Him change us through His Word.

Note the last part of verse 5. If we continue to be changed into the person God wants us to be, our lives will become more and more secure and we will not be shaken when life gets hard.

- *What area of your life is God challenging you to change at the moment? List some practical things you can do to help strengthen this in your life.*

- *Can you think of godly people in the Bible who trusted in God and were not shaken when the going got tough? What about some people you know?*

Prayer Stop: Pray for your family that you will each allow God to work in you to change you more into what He wants you to be. Praise God for the example we have in Jesus and the fact that because He was a perfect sacrifice, we can come into His presence before we are perfect.

DAY 12

On the Way: This psalm divides nicely into three parts. Verses 1–6 speak of the heavens showing the Glory of God. Verses 7–11 speak of God's Word directing us. Verses 12–14 is a prayer after David has considered God's greatness in His world and Word. As the greatness of the heavens can lead us to know about God, the greatness of His Word can lead us to *know* God.

READ PSALM 19

> *The commandments of the LORD are clear, giving insight for living* (v8b).

Checkpoint: There are six things mentioned in verses 7–11 that God's Word can do for us. Can you find them? Try to put them into your own words. I think most people want to have these things in life. However, just as knowing the recipe for chocolate cake doesn't automatically give you a chocolate cake (one must follow the recipe and bake the cake first), so knowing God's Law doesn't automatically give you these things in life. We must put God's Word into practice for it to have an effect on our lives.

I have sometimes tried a new recipe only to find that it doesn't turn out the way I thought it should. God's Law is described as perfect, trustworthy, right, clear, true, and more desirable than gold. We can fully depend on God's Word to bring about the results it promises. Usually, I change a recipe because I think I know better than the instructions. This can have devastating results! So it is with God's Word. We must obey God's Word in God's way to get God's results.

- *Have you ever tried to follow God's instructions in your own way? Share the results with the family. Can you think of any examples of people in the Bible who did this? (E.g., Abraham, Jonah, Peter)*
- *Is there a part of God's Word you find difficult to obey at the moment? Share it with your family and pray about it together.*

Prayer Stop: Thank God for His Word and for the power it has to change lives. Pray for the areas you are finding difficult to obey right now.

Practical Application: Why not make a chocolate cake this week and take it to a friend who needs cheered up?

DAY 13

On the Way: David knows with great certainty that it is God who guides, saves, and directs him through every circumstance in life. He knows that nothing can separate him from the love of God. It is my prayer that as we study the Psalms together, we can experience God in our own lives as David did.

READ PSALM 27

> *Yet I am confident I will see the LORD's goodness while I am here in the land of the living* (v13).

Checkpoint: We do not know exactly when David wrote this psalm, but he seems to be in some trouble. He starts by stating his confidence in God no matter what. He moves on to say how deeply he really wants to praise God and asks God to rescue and guide him. David has experienced God's rescuing of him on previous occasions and knows that God is his guide, his rescuer, and his protector. He is confident in this.

Sometimes when we face problems, we forget what God has done for us in the past. We worry about what will happen and become scared that God is not aware of our situation. Learn from David. Remember what God has done for us in the past. Praise Him for it and ask Him for help with the present problem. We can be confident in God. He wants to be our guide, rescuer, and protector. He wants us to be as confident in Him as David was.

In verse 14, David encourages us to wait for God. This is hard, but it shows that we trust Him with our problem if we are willing to wait for Him and not take matters into our own hands. David had to learn this the hard way. Perhaps we can learn from his experience and trust God right from the start.

- *What things can we do when trouble comes to help us put our confidence in God? Look at verses 4, 6, and 14.*
- *What do you think it means to wait for the Lord?*

Prayer Stop: Praise God that He knows when we are going through hard times and is able to guide, rescue, and protect us. Pray for anyone you know who is going through difficult times just now. Pray that they will have confidence in God and wait on Him to deal with the problems.

DAY 14

On the Way: Today's psalm shows us the results of confessing our sin to God. David shares a time when he did not confess his sin right away and encourages us (again) to learn from his experience.

READ PSALM 32

> *Yes, what joy for those whose record the LORD has cleared of guilt, whose lives are lived in complete honesty!* (v2).

Checkpoint: Have you ever done something wrong and not admitted it? Perhaps you thought saying nothing would help you avoid trouble. In verses 3–5 of this psalm, David tells us of a time when he tried to do this with God. He did not avoid trouble though, did he? He felt ill, lost weight, and had no strength! God had a way of reminding him that his sin needed to be dealt with.

When we sin, we often feel bad inside. Guilty feelings can be God's way of telling us something is not right. We can choose to ignore those feelings or put things right. If we ignore our conscience, God may show us in other ways that things are not right. He may challenge us through His Word or at church, etc., reminding us that we need to confess our sin to Him.

David tells us that when he confessed his sin, God forgave the guilt, and David knew joy in his life (Psa. 32:1–2). These opening verses tell us how good it is to be forgiven by God. We can know this feeling of joy in our own lives if we confess our sins.

- *In what other ways might God remind us of sin in our lives?*
- *Do you think that we need only to confess our sins to God? Explain your answer.*
- *Read 1 John 1:8–9. What verses in Psalm 32 would you relate these to?*

Prayer Stop: Take some quiet time with only you and God and ask Him to show you if there is anything in you that needs to be confessed to Him or perhaps to others. Ask His forgiveness and His help if you need to put things right with other people. Take time to thank Him for His forgiveness and rejoice in the joy that this gives you.

DAY 15

On the Way: Today's psalm is believed to be written by David when he was pretending to be insane so that the king of Gath would not hand him over to King Saul, from whom he was running.

READ PSALM 34

> *I prayed to the* Lord *and he answered me. He freed me from all my fears* (v4).

Checkpoint: This is a song of praise and thanks to God for rescuing David from King Saul. David recognizes that God heard his prayer and enabled him to escape alive. He starts off by saying that he will always give God glory and encourages those who are in trouble to do so with him. He has set us the example of praising God when we have difficulties. Most of us find this hard to do and might not know where to start. David answers this problem for us in verse 3: "let us exalt his name together." We can use the words of David to help us praise God when we find it hard and don't know where to start.

Throughout this psalm, David reminds us that when we draw near to God, He hears us, He answers us, and He delivers us. Verses 18–19 remind us that He does not stop us from having troubles but that He is close to those who are hurting and feeling that things are too much for them, and He rescues them from feeling that circumstances are too much. It is such a comfort to know that God cares so much for us that He will not turn us away but will give us a way out when life gets to be too hard. God is good.

- *Does God always solve our difficulties the way we expect Him to? How can we then say He delivers us from them? Read Philippians 4:6–7. What does this verse tell us about God's rescuing us from our troubles?*
- *Think of some things you can thank God for even when things are difficult. Sometimes it is good to think of these things when we are not going through a tough time so that we can be prepared!*

Prayer Stop: Take time to thank God for the things on your list today. Pray for anyone you know who is going through a hard time. Perhaps you are too. Bring this to God.

DAY 16

On the Way: Yesterday in Psalm 34, we saw that God rescues His children from difficulties. Not always in the way we would expect, but He gives us the strength to face hard times. In today's psalm, we are again reminded of this but on a bigger scale. We see that God is in control of world events.

READ PSALM 46

> *Be still, and know that I am God! I will be honored by every nation. I will be honored throughout the world* (v10).

Checkpoint: Today's psalm reminds us that God is in control of the huge things involving this world too and not just our own individual troubles. When we stop to think of this, it is amazing how great our God is. We can run to Him when things in this world are scary and uncertain. He is our protection from this.

As I write this, our news channels are talking of a global recession. Banks around the world are collapsing, and people are scared about their future. Verses 1–2 are such a comfort in such times. We don't need to be afraid; we don't need to panic, because God is our help and God is in control (Psa. 46:8–9). Our key verse reminds us of this too. When we panic, our minds bring up all the bad things that might happen, and we spend our time worrying and often making ourselves ill. God says, "Be still." We don't need to do anything. It is God who is in control of all these world events; we don't need to panic as His children. He asks us to keep still and come to Him for protection and strength.

- *What things are happening in the world today that perhaps make you feel a little scared? What can we do about it? Look at 1 Peter 5:7.*

- *Verse 11 is a repeat of verse 7. Why do you think this verse is so important? What does it mean for you and me today?*

Prayer Stop: Pray about events in the world today, perhaps wars or earthquakes. Pray for the people involved in them and for those trying to help. Thank God that He is in control and knows all about it. If you are worried by these events, tell Him and ask Him to help you be still.

DAY 17

On the Way: While we may not know why each psalm was written, they can teach us great things about God's plan for saving us. Psalm 49 is one of those psalms. It talks about the fact that we are unable to save ourselves. It is amazing to see God teaching this to His people in the Old Testament before Jesus came into the world.

READ PSALM 49

> *But as for me, God will redeem my life. He will snatch me from the power of the grave* (v15).

Checkpoint: The person writing this psalm tells us that all humanity is the same. Though one may be rich, poor, famous, or ordinary, there really is no difference. In the end, we all have to face dying, and it is only God who can make the difference. Verse 7 sounds a bit hopeless, saying that no one can pay God enough for his life to make things right. There is nothing that anyone can do. So being rich does not matter in the end. However, in verse 15 the writer gives us the hope we need. He says that God will put it right. "God will redeem my life," he says.

Verse 16 tells us not to be dismayed by those who are rich. Sometimes we can think those who have more money than we do or those who are famous deserve our respect more than others do. But God's Word tells us that there is no difference in God's eyes. God treats us all the same. If we have money or fame but no wisdom and do not accept God's salvation, then all those good things do us no good in the end.

- *What is God's plan of salvation for mankind? Why do you think some people find this hard to accept?*
- *Do you think it is more difficult for rich or famous people to accept God's gift of salvation? Why/why not?*
- *What did Jesus have to say about it? (Matthew 19:24)*

Prayer Stop: Pray for some celebrities today, that they will find Jesus and accept Him as their Savior. For example, some pop stars, actors, or people in government. Pray for those who already know Jesus too. Pray for anyone you know who finds it hard to accept God's gift of salvation.

DAY 18

On the Way: Today's psalm was written when David was king. He was going through the desert, perhaps when he was running away from Absalom. It would have been a difficult time for him. He would not have had any of the comforts of his palace, and yet we see him praising God.

READ PSALM 63

Your unfailing love is better than life itself; how I praise you! (v3).

Checkpoint: David was travelling through the desert. He probably did not want to be there. It would have been dry and hot with not much water. He may not have had much companionship. However, this psalm shows us that he still kept his relationship with God alive. He tells us that he is "thirsty for God." He might have felt sorry for himself but instead he turns his thoughts to praising God. He remembers worshipping God in the temple (Psa. 63:2) but he knows that God's love reaches beyond that, and he is determined to praise God in his situation now. He knows what it is like to be well fed, but he says that just now his soul will be well fed even if he hasn't great food in the desert. He is determined to praise God in his tough situation.

Sometimes when we face things that we don't really want to, we forget to praise God, and we end up feeling sorry for ourselves. Let's learn from David, who was used to lots of good things but praised God even when things were harder.

- *What does David mean in verse 1 when he says, "My soul thirsts for you"?*
- *Are there things in your life about which you tend to complain? How can you turn these into things about which to praise God?*
- *Are you going through something you would rather not be facing right now? Perhaps it is an illness or moving to a new area, or perhaps some friends are teasing you about being a Christian. What have you learned about God in the past that you can use to praise Him for now?*

Prayer Stop: Take time to praise God that He is with us through the hard times and ask Him to help you face the times that are more difficult without complaining. Pray for others you know who are going through things they would rather not be.

DAY 19

On the Way: Today's psalm is full of praise to God. Its title is "A song." It is full of God's amazing deeds and praise to Him for those. Sometimes we find it hard to remember the things God has done for us, but we find it easy to remember the words of the latest pop songs! The people who wrote the book of Psalms knew this and wrote about what God had done in songs so that the people would not forget so easily.

MEMORY VERSE

Come and see what our God has done, what awesome miracles he performs for people!

~ Psalm 66:5

READ PSALM 66

Checkpoint: The person who wrote this psalm is encouraging others to praise God (Psa. 66:1, 8). He is reminding them of things that God has done and is giving them words to use with which they too can praise God. There are people who write songs for us today like this. We are able to use their words to sing our praise to God in church with others or on our own. It is important to think about the words we are singing and not just enjoy the tune!

In verse 16, the writer wants to tell others what God has done for him, that He has answered his prayers. He thinks God's deeds are so awesome that he cannot keep them to himself. This is a challenge for us. Sometimes we don't tell others about what God has done for us. We forget to praise Him for answering our prayers and forget that it is amazing that He hears our prayers in the first place.

- *Has God answered any prayers for you for which you have forgotten to praise Him? Sometimes it takes us a while to realize that God has answered our prayers! Why is it good to tell other Christians about what God has done for us?*

Prayer Stop: Take time today to think of as many things as you can to praise God for. Make a joyful noise about it!

Practical Application: Perhaps you could write a song or poem to praise God for what He has done for you or your family.

DAY 20

On the Way: Psalm 85 seems to have been written after the children of Israel return from exile in Babylon. It tells of how glad they are to be back in their land, they are aware that they have sinned and now want to return to being faithful to God.

READ PSALM 85

You forgave the guilt of your people—yes, you covered all their sins (v2).

Checkpoint: The children of Israel kept on forgetting about God. They would worship Him for a while and then be tempted to worship other gods. As a result, God sent the Babylonians to capture their land and he took some of them away to live in Babylon. This was only for a while, they did return and in today's psalm, we hear their prayer when they return. They realized they had sinned and that God had shown them great favor by allowing them to return to their home. He had forgiven their sin and taught them that He was to be their God. Although they had forgotten God, He had not forgotten them, and He was not going to be angry with them forever. God is a forgiving God. He does not hold our sin against us forever. He has given us a way through Jesus by which we can have our sins forgiven. However, sometimes like the Israelites, we forget and we keep on sinning. God has to remind us the hard way and bring some hard times into our lives to remind us of His love for us and that He wants us to obey Him.

- *Have you ever had a time like this? How did you react to God reminding you that you are His child? If you cannot remember any time like this, think about how you would like to react when it does happen.*

- *What does it mean that God covered all their sins in verse 2? How has God covered our sins?*

- *What was the reaction of those in the psalm today? What should our reaction be?*

Prayer Stop: Pray that God would help you to be faithful and obedient so that He doesn't have to keep reminding you that you are His child. Praise God that He has forgiven our sins and given us a way of salvation.

DAY 21

On the Way: The title of today's psalm is "A song. For the Sabbath day." It is full of happiness and praise.

READ PSALM 92

> *You thrill me, LORD, with all you have done for me! I sing for joy because of what you have done* (v4).

Checkpoint: You can imagine the joy and happiness as the Jewish people met together on the Sabbath day and sang this song together. It proclaims how great God is. It reminds them that even though it may seem evil people are doing well, in the end they will face God's judgment. Verse 12 uses a picture of those who please God as being like strong cedar trees. These are very big and strong trees. Lebanon was famous for its cedar trees. It gives a picture of those who live right before God being strong and permanent, not being easily uprooted. The picture used for the evildoer is of grass (Psa. 92:7). Not quite the same as a strong cedar tree! As we read this psalm and imagine the people singing it together, we are reminded of one reason it is good to go to church. We too need to remember it is good to praise God. We need to remember that those who do not live God's way will be judged by Him, and if we live to please Him, we will be strong like the cedar trees of Lebanon.

This song gives the impression of lots of noise and happiness. It talks of praising God in the morning and in the evening. It is good to have a day to meet with other Christians to remind ourselves how great God is and of all He has done. If we miss this, it often becomes too easy to focus on the things that those who are against God are doing, and then we become discouraged.

- *What things do you focus on in church? According to this psalm, what should we focus on?*

- *Why is it important to meet with other Christians and focus on what God has done (Psa. 92:4–5) and what He is like (Psa. 92:15)?*

Prayer Stop: Pray that God will help us to focus on Him when we go to church. Pray for those you know who are not Christians, that they would put their trust in God.

DAY 22

On the Way: Psalm 103, which we will read today, is another one written by King David. It is a call to praise God and remember what He has done for us. So many psalms remind us to praise God, even those that talk about troubles. As God's children, we can learn to praise God even in the tough times.

READ PSALM 103

The Lord has made the heavens his throne; from there he rules over everything (v19).

Checkpoint: In verses 1–5 of this psalm, David is reminding himself of all that God has done for him on a personal level, and in the rest of the psalm he goes on to think of all that God has done for everyone. Sometimes it is easy to remember to praise God for what He does for us personally, but we forget to look further than that. We forget that God is in control of everything and that He directs the paths of nations as well as individuals. We forget what He has done for all of humanity. As our key verse today reminds us, His kingdom rules over all.

Verses 9–10 remind us of how deep God's forgiveness is. He does not bear grudges or treat us as we deserve. Instead, He has removed our sin from us because He loves us so much, even though compared to His greatness we are as insignificant as dust! This alone should make us want to praise God!

- *What world events can you pray for God to direct at the moment? Are there any world events that you can see God's hand in?*

- *Verse 2 tells us not to forget the good things God has done. What do you need to remember to praise God for today?*

- *Read verses 11–12 again. Talk about how far God's love reaches to us. How does this make you feel? What will your response be to this today?*

Prayer Stop: Pray for those events you mentioned in the first question above. Take time to praise God for all the things you talked about in the second question above. Pray that God would help you to respond in a right way to what He has done for all of us.

DAY 23

On the Way: We cannot look at Psalms without looking at the longest psalm written: Psalm 119. It has 176 verses (we will not read them all today.) It is primarily a study on the Word of God and has a lot to teach us regarding how God's Word can affect every area of our lives. It is written as an acrostic poem using the letters of the Hebrew alphabet, so it would have easily stayed in the minds of those who studied it in its original form. There are many verses in it that we would benefit from memorizing too. Perhaps you could see how many you can memorize in a month!

READ PSALM 119:9–16

I have hidden your word in my heart, that I might not sin against you (v11).

Checkpoint: In today's reading, we see a couple of the benefits of God's Word in our lives. By it we can keep our lives pure (Psa. 119:9) and not sin against God (Psa. 119:11). However, it is not just by having it in our home or reading a few lines that these things will happen in our lives. Verse 9 says we must live according to God's Word, and to do this we must know it well. This involves looking deeply into it and practicing what we see there. In verse 11, the writer says he has hidden God's Word in his heart. This involves a deeper sense of knowing. It is what we do when we memorize God's Word. It is ready at any time in our minds and hearts to help us when we are tempted or when things are tough. We do not need to wait until we have a Bible at hand when we have hidden God's Word in our hearts.

- *What other things can God's Word teach us according to the following verses: verse 41, verse 66, verses 89–91, and verse 105?*

- *Verse 10 says, "I have tried hard to find you." How can God's Word help us to do this? In what other ways can we do this?*

Prayer Stop: Pray that God will help you to live according to His Word. Ask God to show you anything you may need to change in your life.

DAY 24

On the Way: The psalm for today was written by Solomon, King David's son. He is well known for his wisdom. At the beginning of his reign, God gave him the opportunity to ask for whatever he wanted. He asked God for wisdom to rule his people wisely. God blessed him and granted his request (see 1 Kings 3:4–15).

READ PSALM 127

Unless the LORD builds the house, the work of the builders is wasted (v1a).

Checkpoint: Solomon is writing about our home, our work, and our family in this psalm. Verse 1, our key verse, summarizes the whole psalm in a line. It is teaching us that we must keep God the focus of all we do—otherwise our efforts are useless. If we do it in our own strength and for our own reputation, we do it all for nothing. Verse 2 speaks of someone working long hours in order to get food on the table; it gives the picture of worry and anxiety, but if God is in control, we need not worry about this. We must do our work for God and work honestly, and God will supply what we need. The end of verse 2 speaks of God-given rest. It does not mean that we don't need to work for our home or family but that we need not worry if we are doing it in God's way and for His glory. God wants us to rest in Him, not worry over our home and families. He wants us to see that all we have is a blessing from His hand.

- *Read Matthew 6:25–27. What good does worrying do us? How do these verses relate to what we have talked about today?*

- *Psalm 127 teaches that our home, our work, and our family are gifts from God. How does this change the way you view these things in your life?*

Prayer Stop: Pray that you will treat your home, work, and family in a way that gives God glory. Ask God to help you change any wrong attitudes. Pray for those you know that have family concerns just now. Pray that they will know peace that comes from God in them.

DAY 25

On the Way: Today's psalm is a call to worship. It would appear to be meant for public worship: the congregation responds with the constant chorus of "His love endures forever." If you are reading this as a family, it would be good to read it in this way. Have one person read the verses and the rest respond with the chorus.

READ PSALM 136

Give thanks to the God of heaven. His faithful love endures forever (v26).

Checkpoint: The constant repetition of the line *"His love endures forever"* through-out this psalm may seem a little over the top! The psalm starts with a call to praise God because He is good and His love endures forever. Verses 4–9 speak of God's work in Creation; verses 10–16 of His dealing with His children in bringing them out of Egypt; verses 17–22 of His involvement throughout their history.

The psalm reminds us that through each of these stages, God's love lasts forever. It has not changed from Creation through all the history of God's people right up until today. If we had to continue the psalm on from the point it left Israel's history, it would be the same. He sent His prophets to teach His ways. *His love endures forever.* He gave His only Son, *His love endures forever.* You could carry this on right up to your own life, and still God's love endures forever; it does not change. It is steadfast. Everything that God has done in the past, is doing, and will do in the future is related to the fact that His love endures forever.

- *How does this make you feel? Things around us are constantly changing; take some time to talk/think about what this phrase means in your life today.*

- *How is God's steadfast love different from the love we often experience?*

Prayer Stop: Take time to stop and praise God for all that He has done and that no matter what, *His love endures forever.* Pray that you will be able to show how different God's love is from what we see in the world around us.

DAY 26

On the Way: Today we will look at Psalm 145. This is a praise psalm written by King David. Verses 3–7 speak of God's greatness; verses 8–16 tell of His special care for others, and verses 17–20 remind us of God's righteousness.

READ PSALM 145

Great is the LORD! He is most worthy of praise! No one can measure his greatness (v3).

Checkpoint: Our key verse today sums up this psalm very well. No one can work out God's greatness or His compassion or righteousness. They are far above all that we as human beings can ever work out. When we think of God's greatness in all that He has made, it makes us want to praise Him more. His love and compassion reach beyond anything we can ever imagine. Everything we have comes from Him (Psa. 145:15–16).

As we think about these things and let them sink into our hearts, we see that we can trust God to act in a right and just way toward all that He has made. When we call on Him, He is near to us and hears what we say; when we feel down or have made mistakes, He gives us joy in our hearts and forgives us; He feels so deeply about us. Verses 8–9 tell us how patient God is with all He has made; there are people in this world who have been created by God and yet choose to ignore Him or even worse, speak against Him. Verse 9 tells us God has compassion on *all* He has made. This is hard for us to understand but shows how great our God is. He wants everyone to respond to Him; however, He will punish those who continually reject Him and His plan of salvation (Psa. 145:20).

- *According to verse 9, how does God feel about those who reject Him? How does this make you feel?*

- *In verses 3–7, what things should we tell our family or those younger than we are about? Why?*

Prayer Stop: Praise God for His greatness, compassion, and justice even though we cannot understand it fully. Pray for anyone you know who has rejected God's way of salvation so far.

DAY 27

On the Way: Today we reach the end of our walk through Psalms. We have seen a whole lot of different feelings experienced by those who wrote the psalms in this book. These feelings are ones that we too can feel from time to time. I hope it has been helpful to see how these people handled their feelings. All of the psalms we have looked at have in some way ended up praising God, even when the writer was having a hard time. This is what we want to do today by looking at the last psalm (Psalm 150) which is a psalm of praise.

READ PSALM 150

Let everything that breathes sing praises to the LORD! (v6).

Checkpoint: This very joyful psalm calls all of God's creation to praise Him at the end of this "song book" of the Bible! Verse 1 tells us where we should praise God: in His sanctuary. That was at Jerusalem in the Old Testament days. However, this is a call to God's people to praise Him in His house, which for us today would be together with other Christians in church. The verse goes further than this to show us that we don't need to wait until Sunday at church to praise God but that wherever we are in the universe, we can praise God. There is no excuse for not praising God!

Verse 2 tells us why we should praise God, and verses 3–5 explain how we should praise God. It doesn't sound like a very quiet affair, does it? It involves a whole orchestra here! This takes us to our key verse, verse 6, which tells us who should praise God. Everything that has breath should praise God. That leaves us without excuse. We have seen some of the writers of Psalms go through some hard times in their lives, but this last psalm is a reminder that no matter what, we should praise God as long as we are alive.

- *When do you find it hardest to praise God?*
- *What can the book of Psalms teach us about this?*

Prayer Stop: Take time to praise God today for all He has done.

Practical Application: Write a psalm of praise to God and use it in your prayer time today or after you have finished it.

PROVERBS

The book of Proverbs is part of what we call the "wisdom books" in the Bible, along with Job and Ecclesiastes. Proverbs is a collection of wise sayings mainly written by King Solomon, but some are also linked to other wise men of his day. They were written to give guidance and values for living, particularly to the young. The first nine chapters teach the difference between wisdom and foolishness; the chapters following are a collection of short sayings on various subjects concerning everyday life. We will spend the next seven sessions looking at some of the subjects covered in the book.

DAY 28

On the Way: In the first nine chapters of Proverbs, Solomon often addresses his statements to "my child," emphasizing that this is instruction for the young to teach them how to gain wisdom for life and avoid the sad consequences of foolish decisions. Proverbs 1:2 tells us that these were written to teach wisdom and discipline, so the first topic we will look at today is wisdom.

MEMORY VERSE

Fear of the LORD is the foundation of true knowledge, but fools despise wisdom and discipline.

~ Proverbs 1:7

READ PROVERBS 1:1–7, 28–33

Checkpoint: The purpose of these Proverbs is clearly stated in the first seven verses of our reading today. Although we have mentioned they are meant for young people mostly, the introduction does not specifically mention this. It mentions another two types of people that they are helpful for: the simple (Prov. 1:4) and the wise (Prov. 1:5). That covers just about everyone! No matter who we are, we can learn something from this book. The last section of our reading shows us the consequences of rejecting the ways of wisdom in our lives. It does not sound very happy and is totally opposite to the consequences we read of in verse 1–7.

Throughout the first nine chapters, we are shown the difference between making wise and foolish choices in life. Often it seems easier to follow the crowd, but we must beware as Christians that doing so will often lead us into trouble. We can avoid trouble by following the things we learn in today's reading and the others we will learn from Proverbs over the next few sessions.

- *According to verse 7, how can we start out gaining wisdom?*
- *Gaining wisdom will save us from what? (Proverbs 2:12–19)*
- *Talk about the choices you are facing or will have to face in your life. How can you be sure you will make wise decisions for these? Our key verse may give you some pointers for discussion.*

Prayer Stop: Pray for wisdom concerning any choices you have to make or will be making in the future. Do you know anyone having to make difficult decisions today? Pray for wisdom for them.

DAY 29

On the Way: As we mentioned in the last session, Proverbs was written for the readers to gain wisdom and discipline. We looked at wisdom in the last session, so today's topic is discipline. This is described in two ways in the dictionary: 1) to improve behavior or orderliness by training; 2) punishment. Both of these meanings are mentioned in Proverbs.

READ PROVERBS 3:11–12; 5:11–14

For the LORD corrects those he loves (3:12a).

Checkpoint: You get the feeling in reading today's verses that discipline is something we should want! We don't often think of it that way, but when we look at what the writer says in Proverbs 5:11–14, we don't want to feel like that when we get older either. Therefore, these verses in Proverbs encourage us not to reject the correction of others and not to reject hard work and training in God's way of living. It does not come naturally to us to be pleased at being corrected or punished for doing wrong, but Proverbs teaches us that it will be good for us. By accepting correction, we will become more like what God wants us to be, and we will not feel that we have wasted our lives as the verses in chapter 5 mention.

There are some verses in Proverbs that encourage parents to discipline their children—to punish them for doing wrong and train them in doing right. It is important that we do both for our children and not just punish for doing wrong. Often it is the training part of discipline that is hardest. As we want the best for our children, we remember that God wants the best for His children too. Therefore, we should want Him to correct us when we go wrong.

- *What do Proverbs 6:23 & Proverbs 10:17 teach us about the results of discipline?*
- *What do you find hard about discipline as parents? As children?*
- *How might punishing someone for doing wrong show love for that individual?*

Prayer Stop: Pray that you will be willing to accept correction from others and God. Pray for Christian families you know, that they will train their children to live God's way.

DAY 30

On the Way: Having looked at the topics of wisdom and discipline in Proverbs so far we are now going to look at *the fear of the Lord*. This is a subject mentioned numerous times in Proverbs. The results that are mentioned in the book of having the fear of the Lord would seem to make it important to study.

READ PROVERBS 2:1–5; 14:27

> *Fear of the LORD is a life-giving fountain; it offers escape from the snares of death* (14:27).

Checkpoint: When we hear the word fear, we immediately think of something that scares us. However, there is another meaning of fear, and that is to be in awe of something or someone—to have a special respect for them. When *the fear of the Lord* is mentioned in Proverbs, it does not mean that we should be *scared* of God but that we should have a special *respect* for Him. The verses we read in chapter 2 teach us that if we listen to correction and learn to make wise decisions, we will begin to know what this special respect for God is. Proverbs 1:7 tells us that having this respect for God is a good place to start in all of our learning because all wisdom and knowledge come from God.

Our key verse tells us that the fear of God helps us avoid becoming involved in evil. When we see the benefits of having this respect for God in our lives, it should make us want to work hard at having the right attitude to God.

- *How can we show in our lives that we fear God?*
- *Read Proverbs 19:23. We all experience different kinds of trouble in our lives: how can the fear of the Lord bring us security and protection from harm?*
- *How can the fear of the Lord be a life-giving fountain as mentioned in our key verse?*

Prayer Stop: Thank God for His Word and for all that it teaches us. Spend some time worshipping God and asking Him to help you show Him special respect in all you do.

DAY 31

On the Way: Proverbs has a lot to say on the more practical issues of daily life. It teaches about relationships, working, money and possessions, how we speak, and much more. We will look especially at these four subjects over the next four sessions. Today we will start with relationships. Proverbs teaches about family relationships and friendship. There is no one passage involving both, so we will read several verses throughout the book.

READ PROVERBS 1:8–9; 14:26; 17:6; 27:6

> *Those who fear the LORD are secure; he will be a refuge for their children* (14:26).

Checkpoint: Our key verse is the starting point for all our relationships. If we as parents fear the Lord and are faithful to Him, our children will be secure in their relationship with us, will learn the fear of the Lord themselves, and will therefore have the basis for building strong family relationships and friendships as adults. In Proverbs 1:8–9, we are encouraged to pay attention to both our parents. Their godly teaching will be something that we can "show off" in our lives as we grow up. It will help us to be the children God wants us to be. It will teach us to be good friends and in turn will enable us to teach our own children, who will then be a special blessing to their grandparents.

As we look after our ageing parents/grandparents, we will continue to show their teaching in our family lives and in our friendships (Prov. 17:6). The way we learn to relate to our families will affect the way we relate to our friends. The fear of the Lord will not only affect our family life but every relationship we have.

- *Explain what you think Proverbs 27:6 means. Can a friend who deliberately hurts us be a true friend?*

- *In what ways can having a good relationship with our family help us be a good friend?*

- *How can grandchildren be the crowning glory of their grandparents?*

Prayer Stop: Pray for your parents/grandparents. Pray that as a family you will be a blessing to them as they get older. Thank God for our friends and family. Ask God to help you be a true friend.

DAY 32

On the Way: The next topic we are going to look at is work. Proverbs has much to say about the way we work and about those who choose not to work. It is right that we provide for our families in any way we can, and it is important that our attitudes are right as we do this. In our youth, we may not earn a living, but as we study we can focus on our attitude to work so that when the time comes, we have a godly approach to earning our living.

READ PROVERBS 24:27, 30–34

A lazy person is as bad as someone who destroys things (Proverbs 18:9).

Checkpoint: Proverbs uses quite strong language to describe those who choose not to work. Verses 30–34 do not create a very pretty picture in my mind! It seems like these peoples' lives are a bit chaotic and out of control; things have become too much for them to handle because they are not making wise decisions. Our key verse says that if we are not working as hard as we can, we are compared to those who destroy things.

The fields in verses 30–34 would seem wasted; they need a lot of work to make them grow good things again. If we are too lazy to work, then we too will need to make a lot of effort to put things right in our lives. By not producing our best either in schoolwork or for our employers, we affect our "business": either our future prospects of employment or our current employer. Proverbs 24:27 teaches that it is right to work in order to provide for our living requirements.

- *It would be unusual to be able to save enough money to buy/build a house completely. How can we apply Proverbs 24:27 to our lives today?*

- *There are some circumstances that make it impossible for us to provide for our families. Can you think of any? Proverbs 13:23 will give you one reason. What should our reaction be to these people? (Proverbs 14:31)*

Prayer Stop: Take some time to reflect on your own attitude to work. Ask God to help you have the right attitude. Pray for anyone you know who is unemployed at the moment.

Practical Application: Invite an unemployed friend for a meal this week.

DAY 33

On the Way: In the last session, we talked about working and providing for our families. Today we are going to look at what Proverbs says about our attitude to the money we earn.

READ PROVERBS 11:4, 24–28

> *Trust in your money and down you go! But the godly flourish like leaves in spring* (v28).

Checkpoint: The Bible does not teach that being rich is wrong, but it has a lot to say about our attitude to our wealth. No matter how little we have, we can be generous with it. Generosity is an attitude. The man mentioned in verse 24 is not identified as being rich, just generous. By being willing to share what we have, we will find we have plenty, but if we are selfish and store up what we have for ourselves, often we end up with nothing. This is because we are putting our trust in our wealth, hoping it will save us. Verses 4 and 24 tell us that it is not our wealth that will save us but our living to please God—our righteousness. If we live to please God, we should be thinking of ways we can bless others, and this will include being generous with what we have.

Proverbs 22:16 talks of those who try to increase what they have by hurting others less fortunate than themselves and by bribing those already rich; they think they can use their money to increase their position in life. This verse describes them as poor. Their attitude to their wealth is selfish, and they will not know the joy that being generous can bring.

- *Read Proverbs 3:9. How can we apply this to our lives today in our work situations?*
- *Do you think it is biblical to save money? Can Proverbs 13:11, 22 help us with this answer?*
- *Reflect on what your family's attitude toward money is. Do you need to change how you think and give?*

Prayer Stop: Thank God for all He has given you and pray for a generous heart to help others. Ask God to show you who He wants you to help and be willing to obey Him.

DAY 34

On the Way: Our mouth is a very important part of our body. By using it, we can feed ourselves and so keep ourselves healthy, and we can also communicate with others to build relationships. In Matthew 15, Jesus says the words that come out of our mouths come from our heart and show what we are really like on the inside. Let's look at what Proverbs says about it.

READ PROVERBS 10:11–14, 18–21

> *Those who control their tongue will have a long life; opening your mouth can ruin everything* (Proverbs 13:3).

Checkpoint: We see many contrasts in the verses we read today. The contrast between the wise and foolish person and how they use their mouths is demonstrated. The wise person's words bring life; they build people up and are precious like silver. The wise person speaks only from what he has learned and knows when not to speak. Contrast this with the foolish person in these verses. His words are ruled by violence; they bring him trouble and are full of hatred and slander. He does not know when to stay silent, and what he does say is of little value. As we mentioned earlier, Jesus said that the words that come out of our mouths show others what we are really like. Therefore, we must watch what we say, as our key verse encourages us to do. We can use words to encourage others or to bring them down. We can use words to bring peace or stir up trouble. The choice is ours.

- *Often we say things before we think about them. How can we guard our lips? How does the psalmist do it in Psalm 141:3–4?*

- *In what situations do you find it hard to "hold your tongue"?*

- *Proverbs 10:19 says, "Too much talk leads to sin." Why do you think this is the case?*

Prayer Stop: Thank God for His Word to us; it is full of wisdom and guidance for our lives. Pray for your family, that God would help you all to "watch your lips."

ECCLESIASTES

This book, part of the wisdom books of the Bible, was written by someone older who had many different life experiences. He is reflecting on all that he has learned and comes to the conclusion that life is meaningless when not centered on God.

Bible scholars believe that Solomon wrote this book, although it is not specifically mentioned in the book.

DAY 35

On the Way: The first few chapters of this book describe how the teacher set about finding the meaning of life. If we read only the first few chapters, it seems pretty gloomy; he seems to be saying that everything is meaningless! A look at the whole book reveals that the theme of the book is in fact that life, when not centered on God, is meaningless. It is God who makes the difference.

READ ECCLESIASTES 2:1–11

> *But as I looked at everything I had worked so hard to accomplish, it was all so meaningless—like chasing the wind* (v11a).

Checkpoint: In verses 1–3, the writer describes trying to find meaning in having endless fun and in drinking wine, but without success. In verses 4–9, he undertakes great building and landscaping projects as well as acquiring slaves and wealth; he found the life of luxury meaningless too.

Around us, we can see people spending time and money on those signs of success. They spend weekends going to parties and getting drunk; they spend a lot of money on doing their houses and gardens up and a lot of time working to make money to spend on these things. Their lives seem to be centered on attaining their version of success, but what good does it do them? In the end, such things do not make people happy and do not take away from the fact that one day they will die. No matter how important we are or how much money we make in this life, we will all face death. To find meaning in this life, we must accept the gift of eternal life that God has provided for us. Success and material possessions are not necessarily wrong, but they cannot make us completely happy.

- *Why do you think the trappings of success cannot make us truly happy?*
- *Why do you think people spend so much money, time, and effort trying to find happiness when all the time God has provided a way to true happiness?*
- *How can you help them?*

Prayer Stop: Thank God for His gift of eternal life and for giving us a way to live meaningful lives here. Pray for those you know who perhaps spend most of their time chasing things to try to make them happy.

DAY 36

On the Way: Having tried to find real happiness in all the things that he could do for himself, the writer now moves on to realize that it is indeed God who makes the difference. It is only when we give Him the proper place in our lives that we can be truly satisfied in our lives.

READ ECCLESIASTES 3:1–14

> *He has planted eternity in the human heart* (v11b).

Checkpoint: Yesterday we saw the teacher try all sorts of different ways to find true happiness; in the end, he found it all meaningless. Today he realizes that true happiness comes as a gift from God (Eccles. 3:13). It comes when we go about our days with our thoughts firstly centered on God. As we saw yesterday, working hard and spending money are not wrong; there is a right time for everything as we read today. Our key verse says, "[God] has planted eternity in the human heart." This means that God has made us for more than just living in this world, in this time. We need to prepare to live beyond time in the way He has provided; then we will know true happiness in doing all that God has given us to do while we are here. We must realize that God is in control of everything, that what He does lasts forever, not just for the time we are here on earth. He sees all of life, from beginning to end, more than we can ever begin to understand. This should cause us to worship Him.

- *How can we prepare for living in eternity? How has God provided for us to do this?*
- *In what way will this make a difference to how we feel about the things that happen to us in this life?*
- *How does verse 11 help us to accept the hard things that happen to us?*

Prayer Stop: Praise God that He is in control of everything that happens. Pray that knowing this will make a difference to how you react to circumstances this week. Pray for anyone you know who is finding this hard to accept.

DAY 37

On the Way: We have talked about all the different ways people try to find true happiness, and we discovered that true happiness can only come from God. We must live our lives on earth focusing on God and preparing for life beyond this earth. This brings us to the point the teacher talks about in chapter 5: that even our worship can be meaningless.

READ ECCLESIASTES 5:1–7

> *Talk is cheap, like daydreams and other useless activities. Fear God instead* (v7).

Checkpoint: What is our attitude about church attendance? Today the teacher warns us to "keep our ears open and our mouths shut!" Some people go to church to be seen so that others will think them "holy." Others go because they can be heard saying great prayers or preaching great sermons. The teacher warns us to go to listen to God rather than to be foolish and sin in the things we say and do. It is not wrong to pray or preach in church, but our focus should be on God and not on ourselves. When we go to God's house, we should realize that God is in control of everything. This should make us be silent before Him! Verses 4–6 warn us not to be too quick to promise God we will do something. We must take all that we say to Him seriously; dreaming up some good idea and saying we will do it is meaningless if we do not intend to carry it out. Be careful what you tell God you will do, and watch out for a wrong attitude when you go to church. We need to always remember how glorious God is.

- *How do you feel about going to church? Do you ever think about your attitude about church? Are there things you may need to change?*

- *If you are asked to take part in a service, how can you prepare to make sure you have the right attitude?*

- *Why do you think it is difficult to sit in silence and focus on God?*

Prayer Stop: Pray for those who lead your church services, that they will focus on God and lead others to worship God. Use Psalm 139:23–24 to ask God to show you attitudes in your heart that may need changed.

DAY 38

On the Way: The writer continues to study different areas of life: wealth, wisdom, loyalty, and many others. His studies conclude that these things are meaningless if they are not related to God, and that people cannot understand the things that happen in the world. He reminds us again that all we do depends on God and we cannot know how our lives will turn out, whether good or bad. Today we reach his conclusion.

MEMORY VERSE

Here now is my final conclusion: Fear God and obey his commands, for this is everyone's duty.

~ Ecclesiastes 12:13b

READ ECCLESIASTES 12:1, 8–14

Checkpoint: Having reached the conclusion in chapter 9 that whether we are good or bad, rich or poor, we all end up at the same point—we all die—the teacher challenges us to focus on God when we are young, before we become old and frail. If we spend our lives chasing after happiness in all the worldly things we have talked about, we will be wasting our lives because those things have no meaning on their own. If we focus on God when we are young and have life ahead of us, we will discover a true happiness and joy in all that we do. God will give meaning to the things that are otherwise meaningless! When we are old and frail and perhaps unable to do many of the things we have talked about, we will be able to reflect on God and be thankful that our lives are in His hands. Verse 11 teaches us to pay attention to these words, as they will direct us in life: they are like the stick the shepherd uses to bring his sheep to where he wants them. So having looked at life and all that it involves, verse 13 offers the teacher's conclusion, and we use it as our memory verse for Ecclesiastes.

- *In what way is God's Word like a shepherd's stick? How should it affect us?*
- *What does it mean to fear God?*
- *What is the main lesson you have learned from Ecclesiastes?*

Prayer Stop: Praise God for His Word to guide us. Think of two things you have learned in Ecclesiastes and thank God for them, asking Him to help you put what you learned into practice.

SONG OF SOLOMON

This book is a love song written either by Solomon himself or written about Solomon. It is a collection of love poems showing that true love between a man and a woman is right and to be treasured. Sometimes the book is thought of as being a picture of how much God loves His people.

DAY 39

On the Way: This book has a lot to do with love; it is a collection of very intimate love songs. God obviously thinks very highly of love between husbands and wives because this has been included in the Bible. We learn lots from it about how to keep our marriages strong. Children may feel too young to think about this, but when we learn God's idea for a happy marriage when we are young, it will help us start off married life with a godly attitude.

READ SONG OF SOLOMON 2:1–7

He escorts me to the banquet hall; it's obvious how much he loves me (v4).

Checkpoint: This couple thinks a lot of each other. Each sees the other as standing out from the crowd (e.g., Song 2:2). In verses 3–4, they enjoy being in each other's company alone and in public. The love of the man is clear to see. In the last verses, we read they also had time to be alone together, treating each other as special in ways that no one else is part of.

Such loving behaviour is part of what makes a marriage happy; it is not the *only* thing but is a good start! It is important to see one's spouse as special and to say so. The lovers in this book do not stop telling each other how special each sees the other. Others will be aware of how special we think our spouses are because our love will be displayed, not in unreal ways, but in ways that show respect for our spouse. When we spend time alone, that time will also be ruled by respect and building each other up rather than selfishness.

We cannot make love happen. Verse 7 tells us that love will happen when the time is right. True love takes time and effort; we cannot pretend.

- *Think about some ways we can show that we respect our spouse. How do you think it is easy to tell if these actions are genuine? (To whom should they bring attention?)*

- *Do you think it would be difficult to treat someone that way all the time? If so, why?*

Prayer Stop: Pray for married people you know, that their marriages will honor God. Pray that God will help those who find that difficult.

DAY 40

On the Way: We saw in the last passage how this couple felt about each other; they were happy in each other's company and happy to show others how much they loved each other. Their love develops through this book, and in chapter 3 they seem to get married (Song 3:11). The way they continue to express their love for each other becomes more intimate.

READ SONG OF SOLOMON 8:6–7

Many waters cannot quench love, nor can rivers drown it (v7).

Checkpoint: After we marry someone, we continue to get to know that person; we are able to get to know each other in a closer, more intimate way. If each partner follows the guidelines in God's Word, then their love for each other should grow deeper and stronger. Verse 6 mentions love being as strong as death. Death never gives up the things it has taken: once someone has died, they do not live again on earth. Marriage that grows in God's way provides a love as strong as this—a love that is committed to loving and not giving up, a love set alight by God that cannot be snuffed out by the things that flood against it, a love that cannot be bought by any amount of wealth.

Sadly, because of sin in this world, marriage can sometimes be difficult and sad. If we can learn to love and relate to each other using God's guidelines, then we can have the kind of marriage He means us to have. The man and the woman in this book were committed to each other; it took both of them to make it work. We can see from this that marriage is meant to be teamwork. Marriage is created by God to provide a love that is stronger than any other in this world. God has given us a picture of the strength of His love for us.

- *What sort of things may happen in life that would perhaps "wash love away"? (Perhaps there have been events in your own family you could discuss here.)*

- *As Christian families, how can we help guard against our love being "put out"?*

Prayer Stop: Pray for couples/families who are experiencing difficult circumstances (it may be your own family); pray that their love will grow deeper and stronger and that nothing will put it out.

THE PROPHETS

The last seventeen books in the Old Testament are called the Prophets. The prophets were men who were especially chosen by God to take His message to His people. As we go through each book, we will discover the time in the history of Israel when the prophets were around. We will discover what God was telling the nation at that time and also what we can learn from their message.

ISAIAH

Isaiah was a prophet in Jerusalem around the time of 700 B.C. His message calls God's children to return to Him, speaking of God's judgment but also telling of God's salvation through the Messiah.

DAY 1

On the Way: As we read in the History Books of the Bible, Israel as a nation continually turned away from God. In the first few chapters of this book, Isaiah sets out how God feels about their sinful behaviour. God is going to punish them for constantly turning against Him. However, Isaiah also mentions that God will give them a way to be cleansed from their sin, giving them hope instead of hopelessness.

MEMORY VERSE

"Come now, let's settle this," says the LORD. *"Though your sins are like scarlet, I will make them as white as snow."*

~ Isaiah 1:18a

READ ISAIAH 6:1–8

I saw the Lord. He was sitting on a lofty throne (v1b).

Checkpoint: Isaiah tells us of what happened to him when God called him to be His messenger. He tells us that when the king of Judah was dying, he saw the Lord seated on a throne: the Heavenly King. The verses we read give us a picture that is almost too difficult to imagine. I think that what Isaiah saw was so amazing that he just did not know how to describe it! He was given a very special vision of God: as a result of that, he becomes very aware of his sin. However, God cleanses him from his sin, and Isaiah then offers to be God's messenger.

Before we can serve God effectively, we need to have a relationship with Him and, like Isaiah, recognize that He is King. As we grow closer to God, we become more aware of our sin but also more aware of just how much God is willing to forgive us. This should make us excited, like Isaiah, to go tell others of what God wants to do for them.

- *Try to imagine what Isaiah saw in his vision. (You could try to draw it!) How does that make you feel about God?*
- *How would you describe how you see God at the moment?*
- *Ask your youth leader, pastor, or a missionary how they experienced God's calling.*

Prayer Stop: Take time to worship God for how holy and awesome He is. Pray that your pastor/leader would also have a fresh vision of God to encourage them to keep serving Him.

DAY 2

On the Way: In the next few chapters (7–13), we read of God's promise to rescue His children from destruction. The Israelites were being invaded by the Assyrian army. God gave His message through Isaiah that they should turn to Him and trust Him, and He would be their rescuer. However, His message is much wider than that.

READ ISAIAH 9:6–7; 11:1–5

> *And he will be called: Wonderful Counselor, Mighty God, Everlasting Father,*
> *Prince of Peace* (v6b).

Checkpoint: In these verses, we see the birth of Jesus being foretold. Although God would rescue His children from the Assyrians, Jesus was to be the Israelites' ultimate rescuer: He would set them free from their sin. Not only for them but also for many more people, as we see in verse 7, His rule will not stop.

As a result of this, you and I can be part of God's kingdom. Isaiah's message is as much for us today as it was for the Israelites when he preached it! Isaiah was telling them of a King who would rule in a very different way from what they were used to—a King who would look out for the poor and unfairly treated and would not rule just by how things appear. These verses help us remember that God is in control now as well as in Isaiah's day and that we too can look forward to a day when Jesus will return and will judge all the unfair treatment and wickedness in the world. He is indeed the King of Kings. This was a message of hope to the Israelites when they were being invaded, and it is a message of hope for us today when we experience unfair treatment because of our faith in God.

- *Why do you think the judgment of God is different from the way our leaders judge?*
- *Look at the names in our key verse: what do they mean for you today?*

Prayer Stop: Pray that God would help you treat others fairly and reflect His love for them. Thank God that He sent Jesus to be our rescuer.

DAY 3

On the Way: Having given the Israelites a real message of hope along with the message of God's judgment and coming punishment for their sin, Isaiah goes on to give God's message to all the surrounding nations in chapters 13–23. God does not make a difference between nations; each one is answerable for all that they have done.

READ ISAIAH 24:1–6; 26:1–9

> *You will keep in perfect peace all who trust in you, all whose thoughts are*
> *fixed on you!* (26:3).

Checkpoint: Isaiah has spent the last few chapters telling the nations what God will do to them as judgment for rejecting Him. Now he summarizes these messages. He says that God's judgment is definitely coming. In chapter 24, we read that God will not show favoritism. Everyone, no matter who they are, will face judgment the same. He not only tells of people facing God's judgment but also the earth itself. It all sounds very depressing. BUT . . . then we get to chapter 26. Here is a different picture. As we have said before, God provides a way for His children to come back to Him and when we do, this is cause for real happiness. When we trust in God, it affects our minds: we do not need to give in to constant worry; our minds will be focused on God rather than on the destruction that is around us. When you feel afraid because of things that are happening in the world remember our key verse today.

- *"The earth suffers for the sins of its people" (24:5a). In what ways do you see the earth being destroyed by the people? How does this make you feel?*

- *In some countries, Christians live in fear for their lives. How do you think that Isaiah 26:3–4 could be a comfort to them? How can it help us live in our sinful world?*

Prayer Stop: Ask God to help you find ways to look after His world. Pray for those who deliberately destroy it. Pray for our Christian brothers and sisters who live in fear. Pray that they would know God's perfect peace.

DAY 4

On the Way: Isaiah continues to preach God's message. He warns the children of God not to be stubborn and follow their own ways but to remember that God wants to save and guide them. He looks forward to a time when the children of God will listen and will know joy again. Having been called to ministry the year king Uzziah died, we now move two kings further on, to King Hezekiah. Hezekiah is unwell and receives visitors from Babylon. Isaiah gives him a message from the Lord, telling him that one day the Israelites will be captured by Babylon. We take up reading today with God's message of comfort to His children in exile.

READ ISAIAH 40:25–31

> *The LORD is the everlasting God, the Creator of all the earth* (v28b).

Checkpoint: The Israelites were in captivity in Babylon and feeling that God had forgotten them. Today's reading is a reminder to them of how awesome their God is. It is a message of hope in a time of despair for them. Do you ever feel like God has forgotten you? Then think about what these verses tell us about our God and be encouraged. He is everlasting. He does not stop being but is the same forever. He does not get worn out like us, and we are unable to work out His ways. Because of this greatness, He is able to give us strength when we are weary—not just add to the strength we have but renew it completely. When we remember to trust in the Lord at such times, then we can do more than we could ever imagine. So be encouraged. God does not forget His children. He wants us to trust in Him.

- *Think of a time before when perhaps you have felt tired and weary: How did God encourage you and strengthen you at that time?*

Prayer Stop: Pray for someone you know who is feeling weary just now. Thank God that He never grows tired and that He is so great we cannot begin to understand His ways.

Practical Application: Consider sending the person you just prayed for a card, e-mail, or text of verse 31 to encourage them.

DAY 5

On the Way: God's message of hope to His children continues. He reminds them that they are very special to Him, that He chose them and will provide a way out of their captivity. He reminds them of His great power to which nothing compares. When we remember that this God is also our God, it should make us want to worship Him more. Sometimes we can be a bit like the Israelites though . . . and take all God's greatness for granted. God's message for them was that they would be rescued from Babylon, but it was also much deeper than that. God was going to send a rescuer that had a much wider mission, a mission to the world. The verses in our reading point to Jesus.

READ ISAIAH 49: 1–7

> *I will make you a light to the Gentiles, and you will bring my salvation to the ends of the earth* (v6b).

Checkpoint: God had appointed the Messiah to bring salvation to the world. This was God's plan for Him even before he was born. God prepared Him for all He was to do. Yet in verse 4, we see God's servant feeling frustrated because it feels like He is expending a lot of energy and not seeing any results in His ministry.

As servants of God today, we too can sometimes feel frustrated at what God has called us to do when we don't see results. The end of verse 4 reminds us it is God who gives us our reward and gives us the strength we need to carry on. Keep your focus on Him, and He will lead us on to do amazing work for Him.

- *Read Ephesians 6:7–8. How can this help us if we feel discouraged in what we are doing for God?*

- *Think about how God prepared others for the plans He had for them: Moses, Joseph, Paul, etc. Think about how God is preparing you to serve Him.*

Prayer Stop: Praise God that He has a special task for each of us to do for Him. Pray that you would keep focused on God and not on the results of what you do. Pray this for your church leaders and any missionaries you know.

DAY 6

On the Way: Having described the way God prepared His servant and gave Him the special task of bringing salvation to the whole world, God continues to call the Israelites to remember His call to them as His chosen people. He urges them to seek Him and accept His gift of salvation. He tells them more about what the mission of the Messiah will be when He comes. We read part of this today.

MEMORY VERSE

But he was pierced for our rebellion, crushed for our sins. He was beaten so we could be whole. He was whipped so we could be healed.

~Isaiah 53:5

READ ISAIAH 53:1–7

Checkpoint: This chapter points us to the trial and death of Jesus. Sometimes we are so used to hearing the Easter story that we forget just how much Jesus suffered for us so that we might be forgiven for our sin. These verses tell us that there was nothing attractive about Him; He was treated as an outcast by others. Verse 3 mentions that He was treated like someone that others would hide from. We don't like it when we are made to feel like an outcast among others, yet we forget that Jesus was not among the most popular group; He was mocked and lied about. He can be our example when we feel left out or when others make fun of us. Verse 7 tells us He did not open His mouth. When we think of how much He suffered for us, it helps us to see the things we find hard to cope with in a different light and can perhaps help us react in a different way. How we react can be a witness for what Jesus has done in our lives.

- *How do you react when others make fun of you or you feel left out?*
- *How can these verses help us to cope with that?*
- *Why did Jesus do this? (Hebrews 12:2) How can this encourage us?*

Prayer Stop: Take time to worship Jesus for what He suffered for us. Pray for those who make life difficult for you. Ask God for strength to help you cope with them.

DAY 7

On the Way: God has promised not only that freedom from captivity will come in time but also that He will send His Messiah to bring salvation to all the world. Over the last few chapters of this book, God's message is that He will come to judge the earth. Those who choose to follow His ways will see God's greatness and glory but those who continue in their sin will see His punishment.

READ ISAIAH 66:1–6

> *Heaven is my throne and the earth is my footstool* (v1b).

Checkpoint: God's message to His people at the end of this book is clear: "There is nothing you can do for me that is greater than I can do myself, and yet there are those who continue to try to 'get in my good books' by being seen offering me sacrifices and worshipping me even though they continue to do things that don't please me." Verse 2 tells us that it is those who are humble and repent of their sin that God will bless. Repeatedly throughout the Bible, we read that it is not what we do or don't do that bothers God; it is the attitude with which we do it. So often we think that we need to read our Bible every day, pray for a certain time, be kind to our neighbors, or do so much at church to be accepted by God. This is far from what the Bible teaches: God loves us and simply wants us to love Him too. If we truly love Him, then we will automatically do things to please Him, not deliberately do things that don't please Him, like the people in our reading today.

- *In what ways do you see people trying to be accepted by God today?*
- *How does verse 6 bring comfort to those who truly worship God and are perhaps ridiculed for doing so?*
- *What do you do because you are a Christian? Reflect on why you do what you do. Is it only because you are a Christian or because you love God?*

Prayer Stop: Ask God's forgiveness for the wrong attitudes you may have in serving Him. Praise God for His greatness.

JEREMIAH

Jeremiah preached in Judah about one hundred years after Isaiah. He is known as "the prophet of doom" or the "weeping prophet." He was a priest who was very concerned about the sin of his people. He wanted them to turn back to God and often uses actions or symbols to explain God's message to them. He brings them the message that God will judge them because of their continued sin, but there is also a message of hope and restoration in the end.

DAY 8

On the Way: Jeremiah was a priest; he came from a family of priests and would have had a specific role in serving God in the Temple. It would have been as he was carrying out his daily routine, serving God, that the Word of God came to him very specifically.

READ JEREMIAH 1:1–15

Before you were born, I set you apart (v5b).

Checkpoint: Today we read of God's call to Jeremiah and also the message that he was to give to the people. However, we are not going to focus on his message but on the fact that God had been preparing Jeremiah for this purpose from before he was even in his mother's womb! Having been told this amazing fact, Jeremiah says to God, "I can't do that, I am too young!" God patiently answers him, encouraging him with the promise that He will be with him and as with Isaiah, God touches his mouth, giving him the words to say.

God has plans for each one of us, plans that He had from before we too were even thought of! We can be like Jeremiah and choose to carry out those plans, or we can be like the children of Israel and choose to turn our backs on God and do our own thing. However, God loves us so much that if we choose to turn away from Him, He will send His messengers to us to urge us to turn back to Him. These messengers can be people, like Jeremiah, that God calls to give us warning, encouraging us to turn again to God. Sometimes these "messengers" can be events that make us think about God. If God is asking you to do something for Him, let me encourage you to do it, no matter what age you are!

- *Can you think of other people in the Bible who made excuses to God when He asked them to do something?*

- *What excuses do we hear people making today?*

- *Why do you think it is important for Jeremiah that God touched his mouth? How does God confirm what He has asked us to do today?*

Prayer Stop: Praise God that He knew us before we were even born! Pray that you will know what God is calling you to do and be willing to do it.

DAY 9

On the Way: Gods sends Jeremiah to preach His message in Jerusalem. He challenges the people about why they have turned away from God. They have started to worship idols made by man instead of the mighty Living Creator God, and because they continued to do this, God will bring punishment on them from the nations around. Jeremiah weeps at having to bring such a message to the people because they refuse to listen to God. They are bringing this punishment on themselves.

READ JEREMIAH 13:1–12

> *"As a loincloth clings to a man's waist, so I created Judah and Israel to cling to me says the LORD. . . . but they would not listen to me"* (v11).

Checkpoint: Here is one action Jeremiah used to show the people what God was saying to them. Often when we see a picture of something, it helps us understand it better. God was saying that the people of Israel and Judah were like this loincloth. At first, they were kept close to God, as a belt is round the body. It looks good when it is being used for the purpose it was made for. However, once it has been left stuck in rocks for a while, not at all what it was meant for, it becomes useless. God's message to the people was that they had stopped doing the things they were created for; they had stopped worshipping God and refused to listen to Him.

When we stop listening to God, we begin to let other things come into our lives that do not please Him. When this happens, we are not able to do the things God wants us to: we become like this belt, unable to do what we are made to do. This is what had happened to the Israelites and God sent His messengers, the prophets, to warn the people to turn back to Him.

- *Who has God used in your life to remind you to follow Him?*
- *Why do you think God used objects to show the people His message?*
- *What objects do we have as Christians today to remind us of how special we are to God?*

Prayer Stop: Thank God for those people in our lives who encourage us to follow Him. Pray that you will be willing to listen to God's warnings.

DAY 10

On the Way: Jeremiah continues to plead with the people to listen to God. Again he brings them the message that if they do not stop worshipping idols, God will have to punish them. The people just ignore this message, and Jeremiah weeps because they are so stubborn. Do we listen to those God sends to teach us His Word?

READ JEREMIAH 18:1–12

As the clay is in the potter's hand, so are you in my hand (v6b).

Checkpoint: Here is another object lesson from Jeremiah. When the potter discovered the pot he was making had a fault in it, he was able to start again with the clay and make it into something else. This is a message of hope for the people. God says, "It is not too late, turn back to me; I am able to give you a purpose because I am the Living God." God is supreme, able to do what He sees is best. If, after hearing His warning, the nations turn back to Him, He is able to change the course of destruction they were set on. The opposite is true too (Jer. 18:10).

This is a picture of how amazing God's grace and mercy are. Mercy is God holding back from the punishment we deserve. Grace is God giving to us that we do not deserve. If we believe in His Son, God holds back the punishment we deserve for our sin and instead gives us the gift of eternal life. God is willing to change His actions if we change ours. If we turn away from God, it is not too late to turn back to Him. He loves us so much that He wants us to be molded into something beautiful and worthwhile, just like the pot in today's reading.

- *How do you think Jeremiah felt when God gave him this message for the people?*
- *How do you think he felt in verse 12?*
- *How do you feel when people don't listen to the good news of Jesus?*

Prayer Stop: Praise God for His mercy to us. Pray for those you share His message with, that they will listen.

Practical Application: Perhaps you could make a clay pot and paint or write today's verse on it.

DAY 11

On the Way: The people do not like Jeremiah's message and plan to get rid of him. They had priests who told them what they wanted to hear and chose to listen to them. However, when Babylon attacked, the king suddenly wanted God to rescue them with miracles, but God had given them the chance to repent, and because they refused, they had to take the consequences. After they had been captured, Jeremiah wrote them a letter telling them to settle down but to remember the Lord now. There would come a time when God would bring them back to the land they left. They had lost hope, but God was giving them hope.

MEMORY VERSE:
If you look for me wholeheartedly, you will find me.

~ Jeremiah 29:13

READ JEREMIAH 32:36–44

And I will make an everlasting covenant with them (v40a).

Checkpoint: Psalm 30:5a tells us, "[God's] anger lasts only a moment, but his favor lasts a lifetime." We see this in action in today's reading. God had punished His people for turning against Him, but He was now giving them a message of hope, promising they would be restored to their land and promising His great blessing on them. They felt like they were being destroyed by famine and war, but God was telling them to look beyond that to a time when He would make a new promise to them, when they would look for Him and find Him.

Sometimes we find it hard to forgive ourselves for sin we commit. God does not want us to focus on that but to remember and accept His promise of forgiveness. He wants us to seek Him with all our heart and remember that His promises last FOREVER.

- *How do you feel when you are punished for something you have done?*
- *How do you think the Israelites were feeling in Babylon?*
- *Describe the feeling of being forgiven.*

Prayer Stop: Now thank God for His forgiveness and the hope He gives us in life. Pray for anyone you know who finds it hard to accept God's gift of forgiveness.

DAY 12

On the Way: Because Jeremiah was speaking words that no one wanted to hear, he was kept under arrest in the courtyard of the guard. Although this was not exactly prison, it restricted his movements greatly. This did not stop his relationship with God: he was still able to hear and speak what God was saying to him and the people.

READ JEREMIAH 36:1–8, 15–16, 21–25

I am a prisoner here and unable to go to the Temple (v5b).

Checkpoint: Jeremiah continued to be faithful to God, giving the people God's messages. He was not popular, as we said earlier; he was restricted in what he could do so that he wouldn't cause too much "damage" to morale by what he said. This did not stop him from obeying God.

Sometimes when we are restricted, perhaps by illness (or as teenagers grounded by our parents), instead of listening to what God is saying to us, we become frustrated at our restraint. We can learn from Jeremiah. He continued in his ministry even though he was restricted. He asked Baruch to help him.

The king was not interested in God's message because it meant that he would have to change his ways. He chose instead to listen to the prophets who told him only good things. This meant he could carry on as he wanted and pretend everything was going to be okay.

We do not like being told we are wrong, but it is best to deal with corrections as we are made aware of them. Otherwise, we can be in danger of ignoring the truth and bringing difficulties on ourselves that could have been avoided.

- *Can you think of others in the Bible who did not listen to God and met with difficulties that could have been avoided?*

- *Can you think of others who were restricted in their movements but still carried on obeying God?*

- *What is the challenge to your life from today's passage?*

Prayer Stop: Pray for those who are in prison or restricted because they are spreading God's Word. Pray that God would make you willing to accept when others correct you.

Practical Application: You can find out some more about prisoners of faith from organizations such as Release International.

DAY 13

On the Way: After the king had burned the scroll, the Lord told Jeremiah to write another one. He did this, but this time the Lord added more to the words because the king had destroyed the first one. As Nebuchadnezzar, king of Babylon, invaded Jerusalem, he appointed another king there, Zedekiah. Zedekiah ignored God's message through Jeremiah, yet he sent a message to him asking him to pray for them. For a while, the Babylonian army withdrew from Jerusalem to fight the Egyptians, but this was not to last. They would return.

READ JEREMIAH 37:11–21

> *"That's not true!" Jeremiah protested. "I had no intention of doing any such thing"* (v14a).

Checkpoint: Jeremiah was carrying on his daily life, going to see some land that God had told him to buy earlier (Jer. 32), but he was arrested on the way and falsely accused of defecting to the enemy. As a result, he was harshly treated and put in prison. In the next chapter, we see an attempt to kill him. Jeremiah pleads his case to the king and is given permission to stay in the palace prison, where he would be given bread.

There are some countries and cultures today that do not want to hear the truth of God's Word spoken, and they put those who are Christians into prison. In some places, Christians' lives may be at risk because of their faith. Often the people who arrest them tell lies to have them put into prison, just as we read in Jeremiah today. If you are living in such a culture, be encouraged by those in the Bible who have gone through this before you. God's promise is that He will always be with you. If you live in a culture in which you are free to worship God, pray faithfully for those don't.

- *How do you think Jeremiah felt when the officials told lies about him?*
- *How do you think you would react in such a situation?*
- *What can we learn from the way Jeremiah reacted?*

Prayer Stop: Pray for those who are in prison because others have told lies about them, pray that God would give them strength and grace. Pray that God would help the authorities to listen to them and see the truth.

DAY 14

On the Way: Jeremiah survives an attempt on his life by the officials and is questioned again by King Zedekiah: this time the king hears what Jeremiah is saying. The king of Babylon marches into Jerusalem, as God had said through Jeremiah; Zedekiah and his army try to escape, but the Babylonians chase and capture them. They treat the king and his family harshly but give some of the poor people vineyards and land.

Jeremiah was set free when Jerusalem was captured. As the Babylonian army overpowered Jerusalem, the army captains and the few people left asked Jeremiah to ask God what they should do. Again, they did not like what they heard and disobeyed. This made God angry, telling them through Jeremiah that they would be destroyed if they did not obey. Jeremiah continued to preach God's Word to all the nations around.

READ JEREMIAH 1:5, 17–19; 29:10–13

> *"For I know the plans I have for you," says the* Lord (29:11a).

Checkpoint: Jeremiah's story does not seem to have a happy conclusion. The people still refused to listen to God. Jeremiah continued telling them God's message, but it was not what they wanted to hear. In chapter 1, we read of the plans God had for Jeremiah: he carried these out faithfully even though it was very difficult. In chapter 29, we read of God's plan for the nation; however, the nation refused to listen to God and had to take the consequences.

God has plans for each one of us and also for nations today. His plans are always for our good because He loves us. However, like we saw in Jeremiah's story, these plans may not always be easy, but as with Jeremiah, God promises to be with us in them. God gives our nations and us the choice to obey Him or not, and we must remember the choices we make will have consequences.

Can I encourage you today to put Jeremiah 29:13 into practice and pray that God would provide leaders in our nations to do the same?

- *Why does God give us the choice to obey Him or not?*
- *What consequences do you notice today that are the result of people ignoring God?*

Prayer Stop: Pray that God would provide godly leaders for our nation. Pray for God's wisdom to make the right decisions in your life.

LAMENTATIONS

This book follows Jeremiah, and although we are not told who wrote
it, there is a possibility that it was the prophet Jeremiah himself. It was
written when Babylon had destroyed Jerusalem and captured its people
and shows that God suffers when His children suffer.

DAY 15

On the Way: Chapter 1 takes us to the streets of Jerusalem. They have fallen to the enemy and are deserted. There is no one to comfort those who are left, and they are suffering. The Lord has allowed this to happen because the Israelites refused to listen and would not turn back to Him. Jeremiah describes how he has cried to God because of the trouble his nation is suffering. He says he has never seen such sorrow and yet because he knows God, he knows there is hope.

READ LAMENTATIONS 3:19–33

> *The faithful love of the Lord never ends! His mercies never cease. Great is his faithfulness; his mercies begin afresh each morning (vs22–23).*

Checkpoint: There seemed no hope for Jerusalem, but then Jeremiah remembered the things he knew about God. God never stops showing His love and faithfulness to His children. Even though the suffering and homelessness they faced seemed such a huge problem, they needed to remember that God never forgot about them. He longed for them to turn back to ask Him for help.

Verse 23 tells us that God's kindness to us starts new every day. It does not depend on what we did yesterday or in the past. We have the chance to turn to God at the start of each new day and ask His forgiveness no matter what we have done, because He wants to show us kindness each day. Sometimes we need to be reminded of that. Verse 25 tells us that it is good to take time to think about what God is teaching us even when we are young. As we do this, we will demonstrate the kindness of God in the way we live.

- *When you see suffering, what is your reaction? Does it make you cry for the people who suffer?*
- *What suffering do you see in the world around you at the moment?*
- *What practical things can you do to help those in need?*

Prayer Stop: Praise God that He wants to show His kindness to those who are suffering. Pray that you will be His hands and feet in this. Pray that God would give you His compassion for those who suffer.

EZEKIEL

Ezekiel was among the Jews living as captives in Babylon. He was called by God to preach to the Jews living there with him. He was to remind them that even though they were God's chosen people, God would not overlook their sin. They were in captivity because they refused to listen to God.

DAY 16

On the Way: As we mentioned in introducing Ezekiel, he was a Jew who lived in Babylon, having been taken there as a captive when Babylon destroyed Jerusalem. He came from a family of priests and was serving as a priest to the Jews in Babylon. It was during this time that he had a vision from God, and God called him to preach His special message to the Jews in Babylon.

READ EZEKIEL 1:1–9, 26–28 (If you have time, read the entire chapter.)

This is what the glory of the Lord looked like to me. When I saw it, I fell face down on the ground, and I heard someone's voice speaking to me (v28b).

Checkpoint: This first chapter describes what Ezekiel saw when he had a vision from God. It all sounds very strange, and we cannot imagine some of the things we read. However, we need to remember that this was a vision of heaven. It seems that the things Ezekiel saw were almost too amazing for words, and he struggles to find a way to describe it so that others will understand. This helps us to remember just how awesome our God is: we often think that what we see and know on earth is all that there is; however, there is so much more to God than we could ever start to explain.

Ezekiel was called to preach after he had seen this vision. God has something for each one of us to do, but we need to have a personal experience of Him in our lives before we set out to serve Him. We will not all have such amazing visions as Ezekiel, but each personal experience of God is special.

- *Ezekiel had explained what the glory of God looked like to him; what does it look like to you? Think of ways you can describe it. How does this make you feel? What effect did it have on Ezekiel?*
- *Talk about some of the ways God has spoken to you recently.*

Prayer Stop: Take time to worship our awesome God, using some of the ways you mentioned in the first discussion point.

DAY 17

On the Way: Having had such an amazing experience of the glory of God, Ezekiel fell down in worship. However, God wanted him to get up and go with His message to the Jews in captivity in Babylon. It is not a terribly encouraging call, as we will see. But God wants the Jews to hear His message anyway and has called Ezekiel to deliver it! God gives Ezekiel lots of pictures to act out His message to the people in the following chapters. The first one, however, is a picture for Ezekiel himself; he is given a scroll with God's Word on it to eat.

READ EZEKIEL 3:4-15

Then he added, "Son of man, let all my words sink deep into your own heart first. Listen to them carefully for yourself" (v10).

Checkpoint: The description we get of Ezekiel's call is not terribly exciting: "Go to give these people my message, Ezekiel, but they won't listen because they are so stubborn. Don't worry though; I have made you as stubborn as they are!" We can understand why in verse 14 Ezekiel feels bitter and confused.

Some of the work that God asks us to do is not terribly exciting and could be extremely difficult, but God promises to help us do what we need to do, as He did for Ezekiel. It is important that we obey God even though others may not want to listen. Before he could go, Ezekiel needed to do his part. He had to make sure he knew the Word of God and made it part of his life. We need to do the same. Before we can tell God's Word to others, we need live it out.

- *Have you ever felt annoyed at something God wanted you to do? How would Ezekiel's experience of God so far help him in the task he was given? How can your relationship with God help you?*
- *Why is it important to live God's Word yourself before you take it to others?*

Prayer Stop: Thank God that He has a special task for each one of us. Pray that, regardless of circumstances, you will be willing to obey God.

DAY 18

On the Way: Pictures and drama often help us learn things that are sometimes a little difficult. God uses both drama and pictures in Ezekiel's ministry. God asks him to do some funny things so that the Jews would perhaps understand more of the message. He had to draw a map, cut and weigh his hair, lie on his side for over a year, and pack his bag and dig a hole through the city wall. Even after all this, the leaders still come asking for a message from God. They do not like what they hear from Ezekiel; they want some good news. Instead, the news gets worse for Ezekiel.

MEMORY VERSE
God is our merciful Father and the source of all comfort.

~ 2 Corinthians 1:3

READ EZEKIEL 24:15–27

Then they will know that I am the LORD (v27b).

Checkpoint: All through his ministry, the pictures and drama used by Ezekiel do not have an effect on the people. So imagine how Ezekiel felt when he heard the message from God that his own wife would die and that his reaction to this tragedy would also be an object lesson for the people. The fact that he does obey God in this shows us what a close relationship of trust Ezekiel had with God. We see him demonstrate the strong character that God had given him for his ministry.

Serving God does not protect us from suffering tragedy or pain in our lives, but our reaction to these events may cause others to ask where we get our strength. When Ezekiel was obedient to God in his grieving, the people started to ask what was going on. They started to take notice of what God was saying.

- *What difference does having hope in God make to us when tragedy happens? (1 Thessalonians 4:13)*

- *Can you think of others in the Bible who faced tragedy and showed great faith in God?*

Prayer Stop: Pray for anyone you know who has had a close relative die recently. Pray that they will know God's strength.

Practical Application: Perhaps you could take the bereaved person or family a meal or invite them to your home for a meal to encourage them.

DAY 19

On the Way: It would seem that Ezekiel has no message from God for the Jews for a while after this event, but instead he receives messages to deliver to the surrounding nations. When Jerusalem is finally destroyed and a messenger comes to Babylon to tell him, God gives him a message again for the people but also a challenge for himself.

READ EZEKIEL 33:1–11

> *I am making you a watchman for the people of Israel. Therefore, listen to what I say and warn them for me* (v7b).

Checkpoint: God charged Ezekiel with a serious task: he was responsible for making God's message clear to the people so that they understood it. If they chose to ignore it, that was their own fault, but God wanted to make sure that they were given the chance to turn back to Him. God described His task as that of the lookout on the wall who ran to tell the king that the enemy was coming. Ezekiel had to tell the people that there was a way for them to be rescued from the effects of their sin. If they ignored it, they would face God's punishment, but if they listened, they would be rescued. If Ezekiel did not give them the message, then their death would be his responsibility.

As Christians, we are responsible for telling others that God has given a way for them to be rescued from their sin. We, like Ezekiel, have been made watchmen for our friends and family who do not love Christ. We need to tell them of God's great love for them and desire for them to accept His free gift of eternal life. We need to remember that, like the Israelites, others will choose whether to accept the message or ignore it.

- *Read 1 Corinthians 9:22–23. What did Paul do to make sure people heard the gospel? How can you put this into practice in your life?*

- *How does it make you feel when those you love refuse to listen to your message? What can you do about that?*

Prayer Stop: Thank God that Jesus died for our sins and praise Him for helping us tell others about it. Pray that you would be able to share this good news with someone this week. Pray for those you know who need to trust Jesus.

DAY 20

On the Way: Ezekiel tells the people that God is fair and wants them to turn back to Him. He also has a strong message for the leaders of Israel: God calls them the shepherds of His people, and they have not been looking after their flock well. They have been more interested in themselves. God tells them He will now shepherd the people, and He will give them back the good things in their land and give them the right attitude to please Him. God gives Ezekiel another vision of how He will restore His people.

READ EZEKIEL 37:1–14

> *I will put my Spirit in you, and you will live again and return home to your own land* (v14a).

Checkpoint: God gives Ezekiel a vision of hope for the people. At the moment, their nation and people are as the dead, but God is going to restore them. This gives them hope; life seems so hard. Everything has been destroyed, but God gives them this message. They simply need to trust in Him and turn back to Him.

This message of hope goes further than just the nation of Israel at the time Ezekiel was preaching. As God's children today, we can know the new life God wants to give us by the power of His Spirit when we trust Him as our Savior.

First Corinthians 15:22 says that everyone who belongs to Christ will be given new life. This new life came into the bones after hearing the Word of the Lord. God told Ezekiel to call on the winds to put breath in them so they would live. It is through hearing God's Word and prayer that we too can be given this new life from God.

- *How do you think Ezekiel felt when he saw this vision? How do you feel when you think about the new life God wants for us? Have you received this new life?*

- *Read 1 Thessalonians 4:16–18. What hope do these verses give us of the resurrection?*

Prayer Stop: Thank God for the gift of new life He has for all of us. Pray for people you know who need to hear God's Word and trust Him.

DAY 21

On the Way: Ezekiel continues to preach that God is going to restore the land to the people, that they will return to God, and that Israel and Judah, the two parts of the kingdom, would be together again. God also gave Ezekiel a vision of the Temple where the people would come to worship. He saw the glory of God, as he did at the start of his book, and he fell face down to worship. In his vision, God took him up and placed him in the Temple, where he saw the glory of God fill the Temple again. God gave him clear instructions for the people to follow in the Temple and of how to divide the land for the tribes again.

READ EZEKIEL 47:1–9

Life will flourish wherever this water flows (v9b).

Checkpoint: This river is a picture of the good news of Jesus. It gives life wherever it goes. When we look at it, we notice, first of all, it flows out of the Temple—out of the place of worship. The more we worship God, the more we too will want to share this good news. The further out it goes, the deeper it gets. As we look more into God's Word, we learn more about this good news. At the start of our journey, we learn the basic truth of God's Word (ankle deep); then as we grow deeper, we realize that it is a message that we can never reach the bottom of. It is so awesome we will never fully understand it. This river brings life to places that no life has been. Ezekiel was surprised at how much life surrounded this river. The gospel brings eternal life to people who have no hope. Sometimes we too may be surprised at the difference it can make in other people's lives or even in our own life.

- *Have you ever been surprised by the way someone has reacted to the good news of Jesus?*

- *Read John 4:14. Where does Jesus say this water comes from? Why might it make a difference if it comes from inside rather than being provided from somewhere else?*

Prayer Stop: Praise God for the effect the good news of Jesus has around the world. Pray that you may be able to share this good news with someone who needs to hear it this week.

DANIEL

Daniel, a young man from a noble family in Jerusalem, was taken captive by the king of Babylon and taken to his city. There, along with some others, he was given special treatment and training to prepare for important positions in the Babylonian government. Daniel had faith in God. Even though he was in captivity, he still trusted God and His promises. Because of this, he and his friends were given the death sentence; however, in this book we read how God rescued them and gave Daniel His message.

DAY 22

On the Way: The God-promised invasion of Jerusalem took place, and King Nebuchadnezzar took some sacred objects from the Temple and took them back to Babylon. His army also captured some of God's people. The king ordered his official to bring some of the young, strong, healthy, handsome, and well-educated men who had been captured and train them for three years to know the ways of Babylon so that they could work in the royal palace. They would dine on the king's food and wine every day.

READ DANIEL 1:6–20

But Daniel was determined not to defile himself by eating the food and wine given to them by the king (v8a).

Checkpoint: Daniel and his friends had made up their minds beforehand to be faithful to God, so when he was offered the king's food, which would have been blessed by a heathen ritual, Daniel decided to take a stand and ask to be given only vegetables and water. He did not want to defile himself by eating such food. He had thought about it beforehand and was able to stick to his convictions because of that. It is easier to stand firm if we have thought about it before and are sure of what we believe.

God was with these young men; He had given them a special place in the royal court of this foreign king, and He gave them the ability to learn all they needed to learn. God has a place for each one of us. It may be that He wants us to train and work among those whose lives do not honor God. As He did with Daniel and his friends, He will give us what we need to honor Him in that situation if we, like Daniel, make our minds up to honor God regardless of circumstances.

- *Are there things you may face that, like Daniel, you would want to change because you want to honor God? (E.g., school reading materials)*
- *How can you be prepared when faced with situations that may be against what you believe is pleasing to God?*

Prayer Stop: Praise God that He helps us to honor Him among people who perhaps do not. Ask God to give you strength to stand up for what pleases Him. Perhaps you are facing a specific situation. Pray for that now.

DAY 23

On the Way: One night king Nebuchadnezzar had a dream that disturbed him. When his wise men could not tell him the dream he ordered them all to be executed. However, Daniel and his friends prayed, and God revealed the dream to Daniel. He told the king that no man could do as he had asked but that God in heaven had shown him the answer. The dream concerned the future of Nebuchadnezzar's kingdom. Daniel and his friends were promoted. The king built a huge statue of himself and ordered that all his officials bow down to worship it or be thrown into a blazing furnace! It was reported that Daniel's three friends had not bowed down to it. The king became furious and had them brought to him.

READ DANIEL 3:16–30

There is no other god who can rescue like this! (v29b).

Checkpoint: Shadrach, Meshach, and Abednego continue to show that they have made up their minds to honor God regardless of the danger. This decision put them in a tricky situation. They did not know if God would rescue them; they knew He could, but they had to trust Him no matter the outcome.

Sometimes when we make a stand for God, it makes us stand out from others, which is not always comfortable. However, like these young men, we need to stand firm in what we believe, regardless of the outcome; it may not always be a happy conclusion. Those three young men could have died, but they were willing to take that risk. As a result of standing firm, God's amazing power was shown, and the king declared there was no other God like Him.

Are you prepared to take the risk to stand up and stand out for God?

- *How do you think Shadrach, Meshach, and Abednego felt after this event? How would it have affected the rest of their lives?*

- *Are you facing a situation where you need to make a stand for God? How does this passage give you strength?*

Prayer Stop: Praise God that "there is no other God who can rescue like this." Pray for the courage to stand up for God when you need to. Pray for those who are perhaps suffering because they took a stand.

DAY 24

On the Way: Chapter 4 is a letter from King Nebuchadnezzar to his people, telling them about the power of the God of Heaven. It tells part of his story. He had another dream: this time he explained it to his wise men, but they still could not interpret it. The dream was of a tall strong tree providing food for all the world and shelter for animals. A messenger from heaven comes and shouts that the tree should be cut down, leaving just a stump. The messenger shouts that this stump will live for a while like an animal so that everyone will know the power of God. Daniel interprets the dream for the king. The tree is the king.

READ DANIEL 4:24–37

All his acts are just and true, and he is able to humble the proud (v37b).

Checkpoint: King Nebuchadnezzar had experienced the power of God in his life before. In chapter 2, he told Daniel that his God was the greatest of gods because Daniel was able to tell and interpret his dream. In chapter 3, he stated that "no other god can rescue like this," and he declared that those who said anything against God would be punished severely. He still does not admit that God is his own ruler, though. Verse 30 of our reading today shows that even though the king had these experiences, he still thought he achieved everything by his own power.

Many people believe that God exists and that He is able to do miracles, but knowing this has no effect on anyone's life until that individual knows God personally as Savior. If you have not already asked God to save you through Jesus, perhaps you would like to do that now. Sometimes God will go to extreme measures, as with the king in today's reading, so that we may turn to Him.

- *If you have trusted Jesus as your Savior, what was it that made you take the last step to commit to Him?*

- *Why do you think the king wrote this letter to his people? Who needs to hear you tell about what God has done for you?*

Prayer Stop: Thank God for not giving up on us. Pray for those you know who believe God exists and believe He is powerful but need to know Him personally.

DAY 25

On the Way: We meet a new king in chapter 5: Belshazzar. He held a great feast and used the sacred cups Nebuchadnezzar had brought from the Temple in Jerusalem. While they were all drinking, they saw a finger writing on the wall. The king was terrified and promised a great reward to any wise man who could interpret the writing. None of them could tell him. His mother remembered Daniel, and so the king summoned Daniel. God gave Daniel the meaning of the message; Daniel told the king that as he had not humbled himself as Nebuchadnezzar had done, his reign would come to an end. That night the king was killed, and Darius the Mede took over.

READ DANIEL 6:1–9

He was faithful, always responsible, and completely trustworthy (v4b).

Checkpoint: Here we are several years after we first met Daniel. He is perhaps around eighty years old now, still serving faithfully in all he is asked to do. He is working among those who do not know or honor God and who in fact worship other gods, but Daniel has been consistent through it all, being faithful to God and trustworthy in all he does. He is rewarded by his master by being given the top job in the government. Others are jealous of him and his good reputation.

As Christian people working or studying among people who do not know God or who may worship another god or no god at all, we are called to be faithful, trustworthy, and responsible in all we do so that others can see the difference God makes in our lives. We need to remember we represent God to those we work/study beside.

The officials couldn't find anything about Daniel's work life to criticize, so they created a new law to trap him. If others criticize you because of your faith, continue to live, as Daniel did, in a way that pleases God.

- *Do your fellow students/workmates know you are a Christian? In what ways can you be God's representative to them?*

- *How do you respond when others criticize your faith? What can we learn from Daniel's response? (Daniel 6:10)*

Prayer Stop: Pray for your school/workmates that they will see the love of God through your life. Pray the same for your boss/teachers.

DAY 26

On the Way: As Daniel keeps his faith in God, God continues to look after him and rescues him from the lion's den. The second half of the book of Daniel tells us of the dreams and visions that God gave Daniel during the reign of King Belshazzar and Darius. Some of these were frightening for Daniel, and he had to ask God what they meant. They were dreams of things that would happen far in the future, dreams of God's everlasting kingdom.

In chapter 9, as a result of reading God's Word through Jeremiah, Daniel learned that Jerusalem would be under siege for seventy years, so Daniel prays for the people, that God would forgive their sins.

MEMORY VERSE

But the Lord our God is merciful and forgiving, even though we have rebelled against him.

~ Daniel 9:9

READ DANIEL 9:4–19

Checkpoint: As a result of reading God's Word and understanding it, Daniel realizes that the exile in Babylon was actually God's promise being carried out. Through the prophets we have studied already—Jeremiah and Ezekiel—God had warned His people to turn back to Him and had also warned of the Babylonian army coming. The people did not listen, so God carried out His consequences.

As we have seen, Daniel has been faithful to God even in a place where others did not worship God. We have seen how he prayed continually. Daniel 9:2 tells us he read God's Word. These are good habits for any Christian to have. It is through praying and reading God's Word that God speaks to us and can help us make sense of the situations we are in. When Daniel understood why his nation was in captivity, he turned to prayer straight away, asking God to forgive him and his people.

- *What does Daniel mention about God's character in his prayer?*
- *What are the things that concern Daniel as he prays?*
- *When you pray, what are the things that concern you most?*

Prayer Stop: Thank God that He speaks to us through the Bible and that we can pray to Him. Pray that you would hear and obey the things He wants to say to you.

HOSEA

Hosea was a prophet to the Northern kingdom of Israel around the same time as Isaiah. His story is a sad romance with a happy ending. The first few chapters describe Hosea's circumstances. The rest urges God's children to return to Him. Hosea's personal story is a picture of God's relationship with His children.

DAY 27

On the Way: God told Hosea to marry a woman who would not be faithful to him as a wife. This was to be a picture for people to understand how Israel had treated God. God had loved Israel, but the nation had insisted on following other gods. Israel was unfaithful to God, just as Hosea's wife was unfaithful to him. When Gomer, Hosea's wife, had been unfaithful to him and gotten herself in a shameful situation, God told Hosea to go and buy her back and live with her as his wife again. This must have been a difficult thing to do, but again it was to be a picture of God's willingness to completely forgive His children.

READ HOSEA 6:1–6; 14:1–7

Bring your confessions, and return to the LORD (14:2a).

Checkpoint: The Israelites had continually turned away from God ever since God brought them out of Egypt. No matter how good God was to them, they were tempted by the gods of the nations around them and turned to follow them. When trouble came, they would often turn back to God and ask for His help. In chapter 6, we see the people thinking this way; trouble hits them and they think that God will rescue them if they turn back to His ways. But in verse 6, we see God saying that He is not interested in their religious actions; He wants their attitude to be right. In chapter 14, we see a different attitude: a confession of sin and a realization that they cannot do anything without God. God is then able to bring them back to a close relationship with Him.

So often, we can be distracted from loving God with all our hearts. We too can start to give other things the priority God should have in our lives. God wants us to confess this to Him and return to Him so we can have that close relationship with Him again.

- *How do you think Hosea felt about his situation? How does God feel when we are unfaithful to Him?*
- *What things can take God's place in our lives sometimes?*
- *What things can we do to make sure this doesn't happen?*

Prayer Stop: Praise God that He forgives us when we confess our sins. Pray that God would show you anything in your life that has the wrong priority.

JOEL

We don't really know anything about the prophet Joel as a person; he does not seem to be mentioned anywhere else specifically. There is also some doubt about when this message was written, but not knowing does not change the message. Joel sees an enormous army of locusts come and destroy the crops of Judah; he sees this as a sign of God's judgment and calls on the people to repent. His message has hope for those who repent but contains a reminder of how terrible the judgment of God will be for those who do not.

DAY 28

On the Way: Judah had become a wealthy nation with plenty of crops and cattle. However, it would seem that the people had become smug and had forgotten God provided all they possessed. God had sent a swarm of locusts and a drought, which had destroyed all of the crops. Joel saw this as a sign of God's judgment on the people and cried out to them to repent.

READ JOEL 2:1–2, 11–14, 23–25, 32

> *But everyone who calls on the name of the Lord will be saved* (2:32a).

Checkpoint: Joel's message was for everyone in the land. The verses we read describe how awful this event was, but Joel's message gives the people hope, telling them God wants to give them back what they have lost if they will turn back to Him. The people of Judah had many religious practices. One was that when they were mourning, they tore their clothes to show their grief. In verse 13, God says He is not interested in seeing that display, because it is only a show on the outside; God prefers that they change the attitude of their hearts.

Verse 32 tells us that everyone who turns to God will be saved. Joel's message was for everyone, and God wanted everyone to respond. Joel's message is for us too. The New Testament tells us Jesus is coming back again and will judge those on earth, just as the message of Joel teaches. God wants us to turn to Him and be saved while there is time. He wants us to know the true happiness of following Him, and He has given us the chance to do this. Sometimes we become so comfortable with this message that we forget that we may have friends and family who have not yet turned to God. We need to be like Joel and tell them that God has given them a chance to be saved.

- *God sent the locusts as a warning to the people. What things does God use today to warn us to turn to Him?*

- *Why did God tell the people not to tear their clothes (Joel 2:13)?*

Prayer Stop: Thank God that He wants us to turn to Him and has made it possible for us. Pray for a chance to tell someone about the good news of Jesus this week.

AMOS

Amos was not a priest like many of the other prophets; he was a shepherd and fig farmer. However, he was faithful to God, and God gave him a message for the nation of Israel in the form of visions. He spoke against Israel turning away from God and worshipping false gods, giving in to greed, and dealing dishonestly.

DAY 29

On the Way: God gave Amos messages of judgment for the nations around Israel. He was also given messages for the people of Judah and Israel because they had sinned against God. In chapter 2, Amos mentions how the people of Israel treated the poor cruelly, their relationships were not right, and they tempted others to do what they vowed not to. They had sinned, and God was angry with them. He tells them how God has tried to call them back to Him, but they have not listened. So again, God uses Amos to call His children back.

READ AMOS 5:4–7; 7:7–15

> *I will test my people with this plumb line. I will no longer ignore all their*
> *sins (7:8b).*

Checkpoint: God knows what His children have been doing but still calls them to come back to Him. This shows us God's great mercy toward us. He does not write us off because we sin but calls us and keeps calling us to follow Him. Amos has been given this message to tell the people of Israel again, just as other prophets had before him. God gave Amos the vision of a plumb line, a measure used when building to make sure that the walls are put up straight and not at an angle. This was a picture of how God would measure what His children did against His standards, and if they were not in line, God would have to punish them. He had given them many chances to move back into line, but they had not listened. God used Amos to tell them this message. He was a faithful shepherd, not a priest.

Sometimes God asks us to do something for which we are not trained, something very different for us. Like Amos, we should be willing to obey God and follow His plans for us.

- *Read Romans 3:23–24. What is God's plumb line for us, and how has He made sure we can measure up?*
- *What/who does God use to show you when you have fallen short of His standard?*
- *How do you usually respond to this? How does God want us to respond?*

Prayer Stop: Praise God that He shows us mercy and forgives us. Ask Him to forgive you for any sin in your life. Pray that those who preach God's message will do so faithfully.

OBADIAH

We do not know much about Obadiah, and it is a bit uncertain when this book may have been written. However, this is a strong message from God for the nation of Edom. They had been happy when Israel had been captured. They were descendants of Esau, Jacob's brother, and should have helped Israel, but instead they helped in their destruction.

DAY 30

On the Way: The Lord gave Obadiah a message for Edom, and verses 10–14 give us a clear picture of all that the people of Edom had done that caused the Lord to give them such a message. They stood and watched while their relatives in Israel were invaded. They did nothing to help them and in fact seemed to help Israel's enemies. These verses show us that not only did they stand back, but they were a bit smug about what was happening to Israel. God has a lesson for us in these verses.

READ OBADIAH 1:2–4, 7, 10–12, 15

> *The day is near when I, the LORD, will judge all godless nations!* (v15a).

Checkpoint: Edom was in a safe and secure area in the mountains; the nation had become smug because of this and felt secure because of their safe position. When things are going well for us, it can be tempting to become secure in the good things that are happening to us. We might look at other churches and families having difficulties and feel that we are better than they are because we have better control of our life and situation. We might even think we are closer to God than they are.

God's message to Edom was that they should have helped their relatives. This is His message to us too. When we see other Christians in difficulties, we should do what we can to help and encourage them. They should be able to rely on us to support them, not kick them when they are down. We need to remember that God will one day judge us for all we have done.

- *What things can make us feel secure? What should we think about these things?*
- *When churches/families are having a difficult time, what actions may encourage them? What might not encourage them?*
- *What can you do to encourage someone in this situation this week?*

Prayer Stop: Pray that God would help you have the right attitude when things are going well for you. Pray for the person/church you choose to encourage this week.

JONAH

Jonah was a prophet who was born in Israel. God gave him the job of going to Nineveh to tell the people there to repent so that God would not destroy them. They were part of the most powerful empire around in those days and had the reputation of being very violent to those they captured. Israel was in their path of destruction.

DAY 31

On the Way: God told Jonah to go to Nineveh to announce God's judgment on them because they were wicked, but Jonah went in the opposite direction! He didn't want to go to Nineveh and tried to get away from God by setting sail for Tarshish. When he was on his way, God sent a huge storm, making all the sailors afraid that they were going to drown. They started to cry to their gods and throw the cargo overboard, but it did no good. Meanwhile, Jonah was asleep in the hold.

READ JONAH 1:6–17

What should we do to you to stop this storm? (v11b).

Checkpoint: The people of Nineveh had a terrible reputation, and Jonah was afraid to go and give them God's message, so he tried to get away. Sometimes we can be scared of what God asks us to do, but we need to remember that God has promised to go with us and never leave us to do these things alone. Jonah had forgotten that because he was scared.

While he was asleep on the boat, the sailors were fighting for their lives. His actions had put the sailors' lives in danger. When we run away from God, it will have an effect on other people around us even though we may not want to admit it.

Jonah seems to have told the sailors that he was running away from God. They are now seeing the power of Jonah's God at work, and they are afraid. Jonah does not seem too afraid in the storm. Even though he was disobeying God, he told others about Him, and the sailors believed. (We don't know if Jonah ever found out that they believed, because he was in the fish by that time.) Even though this was a hard lesson for Jonah and he had no way of knowing that God would rescue him, he was willing to risk his life so that the sailors would be saved.

- *What are you willing to risk so that others may come to know God?*
- *Read Romans 8:28. How can we see this at work in Jonah's life?*
- *How have you seen this at work in your own life?*

Prayer Stop: Praise God that we cannot change His plans. Pray that God will help you be obedient and ask Him for courage.

DAY 32

On the Way: Jonah is now inside a big fish! He had tried to control his escape from God but that proved impossible: he is now sailing in a big fish and he has no idea where he will end up or even if he will survive. He is there for three days and nights. It cannot have been a pleasant experience. There is nothing else for him to do but turn to God. So he prays.

READ JONAH 2:1–10

As my life was slipping away, I remembered the LORD (v7).

Checkpoint: In this prayer, Jonah tells us about his experience once he was thrown overboard. As he was sinking in the waves, he called out to God. He knew that he had been running away from God, but now God had put him in a position where God was his only hope of rescue. He had to run back to God in order to save his life. God will not let us run away from Him without giving us an opportunity to turn back to Him, no matter how desperate we might be! So God heard Jonah and sent along a fish to swallow him. I'm sure that Jonah had no idea what was happening at the time, but as he came to his senses inside the fish, he realized he now had time to pray. Perhaps it was at this time he vowed that if he survived this situation, he would obey God (Jon. 2:9). The fish was God's rescue plan for Jonah. It also gave Jonah some time to think things through.

When we have disobeyed God and turn back to Him, we need to take time to think and pray about what happened. Then we can ask God to show us the way forward. God is full of mercy and will forgive us if we truly turn back to Him.

- *What things might Jonah have been thinking as he was being thrown overboard?*
- *His prayer tells us a little of his thoughts inside the fish. What do you think Jonah felt when he ended up on the beach?*
- *Who else in the Bible was given a second chance? How does this make you feel?*

Prayer Stop: Praise God that He does give us second chances and ask Him to help you be obedient to Him no matter what.

DAY 33

On the Way: Because of God's mercy, Jonah ended up on a beach instead of dying inside the fish. Afterwards, God gave Jonah the same instructions: go to Nineveh with His message. This time, Jonah obeyed.

MEMORY VERSE

For there is only one God and one Mediator who can reconcile God and humanity—the man Christ Jesus. He gave his life to purchase freedom for everyone.

~ 1 Timothy 2:5–6a

READ JONAH 3:3–10

The people of Nineveh believed God's message (v5a).

Checkpoint: This time, Jonah does as God asks him. He goes to Nineveh and gives them the message from God. The message he gave did not give the people any hope of rescue. It simply said that God was going to destroy them. As soon as Jonah started preaching, the people responded, turning to God and showing that they were sorry for the things they had been doing. Everyone, from the king to the lowest in the land and even the animals, was made to fast.

Sometimes we don't feel comfortable sharing the good news of Jesus with people. We don't really want to tell people that they are sinners or that God will judge everyone on earth one day. The message Jonah had was not gentle, yet the people responded. As Jonah had learned, we must learn to obey God no matter what and leave the outcome to Him.

Although the Bible teaches that we must treat people with love and so tell them the good news of Jesus in love, we must not change the good news of Jesus to make it sound easier. We just need to obey God; the results are His responsibility, not ours! Unlike Jonah's message, our message has hope. The Bible tells us God wants everyone to be saved (1 Tim. 2:3–4).

- *Read 1 Corinthians 3:6–7. How can this verse encourage us when we share the good news of Jesus with others?*

- *In what ways do you see the good news being changed today to make it "easier" for folks to listen to? Why is this dangerous?*

Prayer Stop: Thank God for every chance you have had to share His good news with others. Pray that they will respond to God's message and that you will tell it as God wants you to.

DAY 34

On the Way: The people of Nineveh listened to Jonah and showed God by their actions that they were truly sorry for the wicked things they were doing. When God saw they were sorry, He forgave them and did not destroy them. Seeing God having mercy like this is an awesome thing, or so you would think . . . but Jonah was not happy.

READ JONAH 4:1–11

I knew that you are a merciful and compassionate God (v2b).

Checkpoint: Having been through all he had been, you would think Jonah would be happy that God showed mercy to the people of Nineveh. After all, he had just experienced God's amazing mercy and rescue in his own life. He was given this second chance to obey God, and now he sees God's mercy toward others. But Jonah is angry with God. He wanted the people of Nineveh to suffer; that was what his message had been, and that is what they deserved.

Somehow, Jonah did not understand that they were not the only ones who disobeyed God; he had done so as well. He had repented and been given a second chance, and now God was giving the Ninevites a second chance. It seems that Jonah thought he was better than they were.

God does not show favoritism. He treats everyone the same so that all who call on the name of the Lord will be saved. Jonah knew about God's nature (Jon. 4:2), and he had seen it in action—not only in his own life but also in the lives of others.

It is so easy to find fault with other people and to forget that we have the same faults and need God to forgive us every bit as much. Sometimes the things that annoy us most about others are the things we are weakest in ourselves, just as Jonah was annoyed at Nineveh being given a second chance.

- *Read Matthew 7:1–5. How can we apply this to the story of Jonah?*
- *Why was Jonah so angry that God took the plant away?*
- *Have you ever been angry because of something God has done?*

Prayer Stop: Thank God that He does not have favorites. Pray that you will see the faults that God wants to change in your life and ask Him for help to change.

MICAH

Micah was a prophet to Israel and Judah around the same time as Isaiah. He called the leaders and priests to confess their sin before God. He warned the people that God would judge them for their sin but that He would forgive them if they repented. God gave His children many chances to turn back to Him.

DAY 35

On the Way: During His ministry, Micah received visions from God concerning the rebellion of Israel and Judah. Because of their constant sin, God was going to bring judgment on them. He was going to destroy the cities if they did not turn away from doing evil. He called on them to show sorrow for all they had done.

READ MICAH 2:1–8

If you would do what is right, you would find my words comforting (v7b).

Checkpoint: Micah spoke out against those who planned evil on others. These were wealthy people planning how they could gain more from those in their own nation, taking advantage of those who were poorer or less powerful. When we are in a position of authority over others, we need to make sure that we treat others as God would want. When He blesses us with good things or positions of leadership, we are responsible for how we act. God wanted His people to do what was right; He sent messengers to keep reminding them, but they refused to listen. They did not want to hear what God's messengers were saying to them.

God will always let us know if we are disobeying Him. He wants us to obey Him and gives us every chance to do that, just as He kept sending prophets to warn the Israelites. If we keep on refusing to listen, He will have to discipline us, just as He did Israel and Judah.

God warns us so that we will turn away from sin and not need to face His discipline. He is always willing to forgive us if we come sincerely to Him.

- *Are you aware of powerful people in your nation who treat others unjustly?*
- *How might God speak to your nation concerning wrongdoing? Is God asking you to take any action concerning that?*
- *How does God correct us if we are sinning?*

Prayer Stop: Praise God that He always gives us a chance to change and that He is willing to forgive us. Pray that your nation's leaders will take heed to God's ways.

DAY 36

On the Way: Even though the people in Samaria and Jerusalem continued to sin against God, He gave them a message of hope. Even though He would have to punish them for their sin, one day God's blessing would return to them; He would bring them back to the land that He had given them and would make a leader rise from among them who would bring them peace. This was a message concerning the birth of Jesus (Mic. 5:2–3).

READ MICAH 6:3–8; 7:18–20

> *You will not stay angry with your people forever, because you delight in show-ing unfailing love* (7:18b).

Checkpoint: In verse 3 of our reading today, God asks why the people have become tired of serving Him. He reminds them of all the goodness and faithful-ness He has shown them over the years, yet they no longer care to serve Him. We sometimes may become tired as Christians, weary of living for God and thinking that we are the only ones who work as hard. When we start to think like that, we need to look back and remember all the good things God has done for us, all He has provided for us, and most of all how He has given us the chance to be His children because of what Jesus did. By remembering these things, we will start to respond to God by being grateful and more willing to obey. We will respond from our hearts and not just out of duty. This is the response that God wants. He does not want us to go through religious motions; He has shown us from His Word how He wants us to respond. As we think about all He has done for us, we will want to please Him because we love Him.

As we turn back to God, we can praise Him because we know that no other god can forgive sin, no other god shows kindness and compassion to his children by keeping his promises through every generation.

- *Why do we become weary serving God today?*
- *How can verse 8 help us to focus on the right things when we feel weary?*

Prayer Stop: Use the passage from Micah 7:18–20 as a guide to praise God. Pray for those you know who may be feeling weary today; pray that God will help them focus on Him.

NAHUM

Nahum's message was to warn Nineveh that God was going to judge them for all the violence and cruelty they showed against Samaria. They had destroyed the city and taken its people captive. This message would also be a comfort for the people of Judah; they would know that God was going to bring justice to their enemies.

DAY 37

On the Way: This warning is sent to Nineveh well after Jonah had been sent to warn the city that God was going to destroy it. They had repented then and been spared God's judgment, but it seems they did not carry on in that repentance attitude but returned to their violent ways, attacking and destroying Judah. Now God gave Nahum a message for them.

READ NAHUM 1:1–8

> *The LORD is slow to get angry, but his power is great, and he never lets the guilty go unpunished* (v3a).

Checkpoint: The people of Nineveh were enemies of God's children and so enemies of God, and God was going to judge them. God deeply loves His people and will defend them. He will not let anyone keep on doing evil. It might seem to us that those who do evil often get away with it, but we need to remember that God is slow to get angry. He is not like us. When we see evil happening, we want to put it right immediately; we want to see justice done. God is a God of compassion, even for His enemies. He will always give them a chance to put things right. He had already done that with Nineveh through Jonah. God treats everyone with justice. God's justice is a warning to those who are doing evil, so they will have time to turn from wrongdoing. God's justice is comforting for His children; they know they can trust God to deal fairly with those who are against them.

As God's children, we too have sinned against God. He is patient with everyone who sins against Him, giving everyone a chance to come to Him. That is why it sometimes seems that God is slow to act against evil; He wants everyone to have that chance to repent. One day, He will punish those who have refused to listen to His warnings. We can see from our reading today what a terrible thing that will be.

- *Do you ever feel frustrated because you feel God is ignoring evil? Read Romans 2:4. How does God's justice make you feel?*
- *How can you put Jesus' teaching in Matthew 5:44–45 into practice?*

Prayer Stop: Praise God that He is slow to get angry and full of compassion. Pray that you will learn to show His compassion and mercy to your enemies.

HABAKKUK

We are not told much about Habakkuk as a person except that he was a prophet. His book is not a message to anyone in particular but a record of what he said to God concerning the evil that he saw happening in Judah and around. God's response to him is also recorded.

DAY 38

On the Way: Habakkuk brings his concern to God, but it seems that God is not listening to him; all he sees around him is violence and evil. God tells him that He is going to bring the Babylonians against His people because they keep on sinning. Babylon is a strong nation, determined to do evil. Habakkuk is concerned about this too. Why is God going to allow such an evil nation to have victory over His people?

READ HABAKKUK 2:1–4, 9–14

For as the waters fill the sea, the earth will be filled with an awareness of the glory of the LORD (v14).

Checkpoint: Habakkuk is a prophet with some questions for God. We take up the reading after he has asked God his second question concerning why God is using an evil nation like Babylon to bring about His plans. Sometimes we have questions for God; we may feel that He is not answering our prayers, or we may not understand His answers. God doesn't mind us asking questions! However, we need to be prepared to accept His answers.

When Habakkuk asked God his second question, he took himself up to his watchtower, away from other people and to a place where he could have time to listen to God. Often when we pray, we do not take the time to listen to God for His answer. We need to make sure that we are listening, that we have taken time away from others to spend with God.

When Habakkuk was given his answer, he was told it would happen in the future. Are we prepared to wait for God to work out His plans? Perhaps we are like the people in verse 4 who are too proud to wait for God, who trust in their own answers and take things into their own hands. The end of verse 4 says that those who do right will have faith in God; they are the ones who will see God's glory fill the earth as they wait on God.

- *What was Habakkuk told to do with the answer? (Habakkuk 2:2) It is good to take note of God's answers so we can look back and praise.*

- *What do you do to listen to God?*

Prayer Stop: Praise God that His timing is perfect. Pray for patience to wait for God's answers.

DAY 39

On the Way: Habakkuk continues to pray after God answers him again. It is a good habit to keep praying and praising God. We should not just come to God when we want an answer to something, but we should make it a habit to talk to God as we see Habakkuk doing here.

READ HABAKKUK 3:1–2, 16–19

Yet I will rejoice in the LORD! I will be joyful in the God of my salvation (v18).

Checkpoint: Habakkuk has heard God's answer and is filled with awe at all God is going to do. When God answers us, we should respond to Him. We should take the time to think about what God has said and how we are going to respond. Habakkuk accepted God's answer; he did not try to stop God but instead asked for help through the difficult time ahead. He remembered all that God had done for His people in the past, and his prayer is that God will do the same for His people now. Although God is angry and the people have not repented, Habakkuk asks God to show them His mercy again. He does not ask God to look at anything they have done but to act in His great mercy (not treating them the way they deserve). When we face difficult times, it is always good to look back and remember what God has done for us.

At the end of his prayer, Habakkuk is overcome by the greatness of God, trembling at the thought of what lies ahead but willing to accept God's answer to his questions. He says that no matter how bad it gets, he will be joyful in God, knowing that it is God who gives him strength. When God allows hard times to come into our lives, do we accept them from Him, being determined to be joyful in Him as we trust Him through them?

- *How have you seen God's mercy in your life?*
- *How do you respond to God when He answers your prayers? What if the answer is not what you want it to be?*

Prayer Stop: Use your answer to the first question above as points for praise. Pray that you will learn to be joyful in God no matter what is happening.

ZEPHANIAH

Zephaniah was a prophet in Judah not long before the Babylonians destroyed it. Judah had totally abandoned following God and worshipped false gods. Zephaniah's message was an attempt to alert them to the fact that God would bring punishment on them because they had disobeyed Him. There is always a message of hope for God's people though, and God told the people through Zephaniah that they would be brought back to their land and to God again.

DAY 40

On the Way: God's judgment was coming for Judah. They refused to honor God; even their priests had started to worship false gods. God was about to punish the leaders and everyone who took part in worshipping these false gods. Zephaniah calls the people to repent before God's judgment begins, while there is still time.

READ ZEPHANIAH 3:1–5, 8–13

But the Lord is still there in the city (v5a).

Checkpoint: As we have read from the prophets at the end of the Old Testament, we have seen over and over again that the Lord tried to warn His children to turn back to Him. He gave them many chances, but they would not listen. Now God's judgment was going to come.

Often we can be like that too. As children, sometimes we push our parents to the limit, and then they have to take action (normally unpleasant) to help us learn to obey them. This punishment does not last forever; when we learn our lesson, we can enjoy the company of our parents again without any bad feeling between us. God told Israel that this is what was going to happen to them; after His judgment, those who trusted in Him would return to their land.

God has the same message for us. The Bible tells us that God will judge the whole earth. We have the chance to put things right with Him and ask Him to forgive our sins. Make sure you take the chance He is giving you today. No matter how far the Israelites had turned away from God, He was still "in that city" wanting them to turn back to Him. No matter how far you feel from God, He still calls you to follow Him.

- *Acts 17:31 says that God has set a day for judging the world with justice. How does this make you feel?*

- *How can you make sure you are ready for that day? If you aren't sure, who can you talk to about it?*

- *How does it make you feel when you think that one day everyone who has ever trusted God will be together praising Him?*

Prayer Stop: Praise God that He gives us many chances to return to Him. Pray for your friends and family who need to turn to God.

HAGGAI

Haggai was a prophet in Jerusalem shortly after some of the Jews had returned from exile in Babylon and had started to rebuild the Temple with Zerubbabel in charge. This was a little while before Nehemiah returned to rebuild the walls. The Jews seemed to have stopped rebuilding the Temple, so God gave Haggai a message for them.

DAY 41

On the Way: The problem in Jerusalem was that the Jews had returned from exile and started rebuilding the Temple; however, some of the local governors taunted them, and eventually the work had stopped and the Jews left the Temple half finished. Haggai, along with the prophet Zechariah, came along and encouraged the people to start working on the project again.

READ HAGGAI 1:1–11

> *Why are you living in luxurious houses while my house lies in ruins?* (v4).

Checkpoint: These Jews had changed their minds about what was important to them. God had tried to show them that they had the wrong priorities, but they had not realized their mistake. So God sent Haggai with a clear message for them. They had left God's house half finished to concentrate on building their own houses—not just to get a roof over their heads but to add luxury with all the extra bits. They were also busy working, trying to make more money by working in the fields. Their focus was all wrong.

Today, we see people doing the same. They spend a lot of time working, trying to make more money so that they can buy more things or have a bigger house, but they never seem to have enough. They are never content with what they have. We need to remember that all we have comes from God; He gives, and He can take it away from us, as He did with the Jews. This should serve as a reminder to put God first in our lives. We need to remember that as Christians we are called to build *God's* kingdom, not our own. Having lovely possessions is not wrong, but when that becomes more important to us than God and His kingdom, our priorities are messed up.

- *Read Luke 12:29–31. How can this help us work out our priorities in life?*
- *Are there possessions that are more important to you than God right now?*
- *What do you need to do to put that right?*

Prayer Stop: Praise God that He is patient with us as we learn to put Him first. Pray that you would be wise in the way you spend your time and money.

ZECHARIAH

Zechariah was a priest as well as a prophet. He preached at the same time as Haggai, encouraging the people to start building the Temple again. The book was written in two parts: Chapters 9–14 were written around 30–40 years after the first half of the book. Zechariah also has a message for the future in his book.

DAY 42

On the Way: Zechariah gives the people a message of hope, not only for themselves but also for the future. Again, God calls His people to return to Him, promising them that He will also return to them. Zechariah reminds them that all God said to their ancestors had come true, and he encourages them to listen and obey God's message. Zechariah has some visions from God to tell the people. These are also a message for us and our future as God's children.

MEMORY VERSE

Who then will condemn us? No one—for Christ Jesus died for us and was raised to life for us, and he is sitting in the place of honor at God's right hand, pleading for us.

~ Romans 8:34

READ ZECHARIAH 1:7–17

And the Lord spoke kind and comforting words to the angel who talked with me (v13).

Checkpoint: God uses picture language to help us understand His Word sometimes. Here, Zechariah has a vision of horses in a valley of trees. One of the riders is separate from the rest. Zechariah talks to the angel in his vision and asks for an explanation. The angel tells him that the Lord sent the riders to patrol the earth. These riders were from God and have been looking at what is happening on earth. It is comforting to know that God has His messengers watching over us as His children. When they report to the angel what they have seen, this angel immediately prays to the Lord. This reminds me of our memory verse on day 33: we have someone in heaven who is pleading with God on our behalf, and that is Jesus Christ. The message that God gave the angel in the vision was that God would bring about justice for His children. God's message for us is the same. One day He will bring justice for all of His children.

- *What do you find comforting about Jesus being at God's throne praying for us?*
- *Will this change the way you pray? Or the way you live?*

Prayer Stop: Thank God that Jesus is praying for you and that He watches over His people. Pray for those who need God's comfort today.

DAY 43

On the Way: Zechariah saw a man measuring Jerusalem in his vision, and a second angel came to give him a message. This message was that Jerusalem would one day be so full of people again that some of them would live outside the city wall; there would be no room for all of them, but God would protect the city. So he called everyone still living in Babylon to come home.

READ ZECHARIAH 3:1–10

> *See, I have taken away your sins, and now I am giving you these fine new clothes* (v4b).

Checkpoint: Zechariah has a vision about the high priest, Jeshua. He would have known him well because he worked with him, but in his vision, he was standing before the angel of the Lord. Satan was there as well. As a high priest, Jeshua would have worn some very fine garments, but in this vision, he was wearing filthy, ragged clothes. This is a picture of sin and of how God would see him, not how others would see him. However, God does not send him away but gives him fine new clothes to wear. This is also a picture of how God sees us with our sin; He does not send us away either but has given us a way to be cleansed so that we can be His children.

Verses 8–9 talk about Jesus coming as Messiah. The priests were also a picture that God had given His children. They offered sacrifices for the people's sin and stood before God for them. They had to keep doing this though. God was going to send His servant to remove the sins of His people in one day. We know that this servant was Jesus and that by dying on the cross, He both has power over Satan and has removed our sins once and for all.

- *Revelation 12:10 tells us that Satan accuses us before God. Read Romans 8:1. How can this encourage us when we feel Satan accusing us?*
- *What day do you think verse 9 is talking about?*

Prayer Stop: Praise God for that day that Jesus defeated sin and Satan. When you feel Satan accuse you, resist him. Then he will flee from you.

DAY 44

On the Way: Zechariah continues to have visions concerning the future of Jerusalem and the people of God. These messages encourage the people to complete the Temple they had started to rebuild, they tell of how God is going to restore Jerusalem not only immediately after the exile but in the future. God's servant will serve as a priest and reign as a King: we know this is Jesus who came many years later. Zechariah's message also reaches to us as he talks of the day of the Lord: a day yet to come when Jesus will reign over all the earth.

READ ZECHARIAH 14:3–9

> *And the LORD will be king over all the earth. On that day there will be one LORD—his name alone will be worshipped* (v9).

Checkpoint: The Jews had been in exile in Babylon for seventy years and were coming back to Jerusalem. God sent His messengers to them to encourage them to turn back to God completely and worship Him. These messages also told them of a future when God would send His servant to deal with sin once and for all. Then they would not need to continue making sacrifices to God. Zechariah's message told of a day further on from that, a day that we have yet to experience—when Jesus will return to earth, this time to reign as King over all the nations.

We read about this in the New Testament too; Jesus talks about it, and in Acts when Jesus goes back to heaven, the angel says that He will come again the same way that He went. Revelation is a vision given to John about the same thing. As we look back and see how all that God said would happen to His children did happen—he told them about the Messiah coming and He did, just as God's Word said He would—we can now look forward knowing that Jesus *will* come again just as God promised in His Word because God always keeps His promises.

- *Read Revelation 21:22–26. What things are similar to what we read in Zechariah today? How do these verses make you feel?*

- *How can knowing this change the way we live today?*

Prayer Stop: Praise God that He always keeps His promises. Think of two reasons to worship Him from the reading today.

MALACHI

After the people had rebuilt the Temple upon their return from Babylon, the priests began to serve there again as they were meant to. However, after a few years, the people forgot again all that God had done for them. They started letting their faith in God slip and did not live as they should. So God sent them Malachi to bring them His message.

DAY 45

On the Way: The Jews were beginning to do as they pleased again in worshipping God; they had started to take God for granted and forget all that He had done for them in the past. They forgot the things He required of them and started doing things their own way.

READ MALACHI 1:6–14

> *"For my name is great among the nations," says the* LORD *(v11b).*

Checkpoint: This is God's message to the priests, to those who were meant to lead the people and teach them about true worship. They had let their standards slip and were not keeping the requirements of God. It seems that they were not even aware of what they were doing wrong (Mal. 1:6b). They were respectful of others in their human relationships but did not honor God; they were offering sacrifices that were not perfect on the altar. God had fallen down their priority list.

We should always pray for our church leaders, that they will keep God at the center of all they do and honor Him. It had become so bad that God wished they did not bother to offer any sacrifice at all. God told them that other people honored Him more than His own children did.

Often today, we can take God for granted; we forget all that it cost Jesus to make us His children, and we do not give God our best. We don't spend time with Him, our attitude may be wrong, or we don't give our best effort as we serve Him. We may be more concerned with what other people think than what God thinks. Sometimes those who are not Christians have a better idea of how we should worship God than we do.

- *Have any of your non-Christian friends or family ever reminded you what you should do as a Christian?*
- *In what ways do we let the way we treat God "slip"?*
- *Are there things you need to change after today's reading?*

Prayer Stop: Pray that God would show you anything that needs to be changed in your life. Thank Him for His Word that teaches us how to honor Him.

DAY 46

On the Way: God's Word to the priests continues. He pleads with them to make the right decision to honor His name. If they do not do this, He will have to act in judgment on them. He had chosen them to be an example to the people and to teach them how to live according to His Word but they had left God's paths and led the people into sin.

READ MALACHI 2:10–17

So guard your heart: do not be unfaithful to your wife (v16b).

Checkpoint: Malachi's message continues to show God's people how their family life has affected their walk with God. God wanted His children to marry those who worshipped Him so that they could serve God together. God was not against marrying people from another nation—after all, Boaz married Ruth from Moab—but He didn't want His children marrying those who worshipped other gods. This would take their hearts away from God, as we saw with Solomon. As Christians, we should marry someone who loves and serves God as a priority in their lives. Then we can encourage each other to live in a way that pleases God. Our spouse is the closest human relationship we will have, and we need to be able to share the things that are closest to us with them. As Christians, that is our faith in God.

The people wondered why God seemed not to hear their prayers. God told them it is because they had not been faithful to their wives. We cannot just do as we please and expect God to hear and answer our prayers. Every part of our lives, including our family lives, need to be committed to Him. The way we treat our spouse is important to God because marriage is also a picture of God's relationship with His children.

- *Read 1 Peter 3:7. How does this verse relate to our reading today?*
- *How is a husband's love for God shown in the way he loves his wife?*
- *How can we guard our hearts to make sure we are faithful to our spouse?*

Prayer Stop: Pray for people you know who are married, that they would live to please God. Pray for Christians who are not married, that they will not be tempted to compromise their faith in God.

DAY 47

On the Way: At the end of chapter 2, the people ask where the God of justice is. God gives the answer at the start of chapter 3. God says He will send His messenger, and then the Lord will come to the Temple. These verses tell us of John the Baptist coming to tell people about Jesus and of Jesus Himself coming.

READ MALACHI 3:6–15

> *"Now return to me, and I will return to you," says the* Lord *of Heaven's Armies* (v7b).

Checkpoint: God wanted His children to return to Him. He has not changed and will not change; He always wants His children to return to Him and gives them many chances to do so. The people Malachi preached to did not realize that they had turned from God. They were not worshipping false gods, but they were not worshipping God either. They had kept some of what they should have given to God for themselves: they thought they might not have enough food if they gave all they should to the Temple.

Sometimes we may feel that we do not have enough money to give an offering to God. My family did that once, but we soon learned that if we gave our offering to God first, before we spent anything on ourselves, we were able to give and live! We have never had much money, and sometimes we have had to go without some extra things, but we have always had what we needed, and often God gives us extra as a surprise! It is a good lesson to learn to make giving our offerings to God a top priority in our worship. God wants to bless His children; He always has done and always will do. He does not change.

- *Read Hebrews 13:7–8. What things could the Jews have learned from their past about God? What can you learn from your past or your parents or leaders' past?*

- *Have you ever experienced God giving you what you need by a surprise or miracle? How did it change your relationship with Him?*

Prayer Stop: Thank God that He never changes and always wants to bless His children. Pray that you would obey Him completely.

THE GOSPELS AND ACTS

Today we start looking at the Gospels and Acts. Matthew, Mark, Luke, and John wrote these. They are an account of the life, ministry, death, and resurrection of Jesus. We will look at all four Gospels together, as some events are recorded in more than one. At the end of the Gospels, we will look at the book of Acts—the story of the beginning of the church. Acts seems to have been written by Luke, although his name is not mentioned in it. It is an account of the start and growth of the Christian church. It begins with Jesus being taken up to heaven after His resurrection.

DAY 1

On the Way: As we arrive in the New Testament just before the birth of Jesus, we see the way being prepared for Him. The prophet Isaiah prophesied hundreds of years before about the ministry that John the Baptist would have before Christ (Isa. 40:3–5). He had also prophesied about the birth of Jesus (Isa. 7:14). In today's reading, God sends another messenger to prepare the people for the coming of His Son.

MEMORY VERSE

The Word gave life to everything that was created, and his life brought light to everyone. The light shines in the darkness, and the darkness can never extinguish it.

~ John 1:4–5

READ LUKE 1:5–20, 38

Although reading in Luke, our key verse is from John. We will also use this as our memory verse for this section.

Checkpoint: Zechariah got the fright of his life as he went to worship God. There was the angel Gabriel standing before him and telling him that he and Elizabeth were going to have a baby. His response was one of doubt. "How can I be sure?" he asked. Although he was a priest and worshipped God, leading the people in worship and teaching them the Scriptures, he reacted with doubt.

Gabriel also appeared to Mary with some surprising news. Mary was a young girl engaged to be married. When she was told she would have a child by the will of God, her reaction was one of surprise and acceptance (Lk. 1:38).

You would think that Zechariah, a man of God, would have had no problem taking God at His Word. It seems he did not understand it. Sometimes as we get older, our doubts take over, so let us learn from Mary and simply take God at His Word and be prepared to obey Him without question.

- *Talk about the promises in God's Word for His people; which promises are you familiar with? Can you name others in the Bible who found it hard to believe? What about those who accepted God's promises without doubt?*
- *How easy do you find it to accept God's Word and not doubt?*

Prayer Stop: Thank God for the promises in His Word and pray that you will accept these without doubt. Pray for anyone you know who is finding it hard to hold on to God's promise to them. Pray that they will have faith to stand firm.

DAY 2

On the Way: Mary went to stay with Elizabeth, who by this time was expecting the promised baby. They praised God together for His promises. It must have been nice for Elizabeth to have someone to praise the Lord with, as Zechariah would not be able to do that for a while yet! It is encouraging to praise God with other Christians and to share in their happy experiences with them.

READ LUKE 1:57–66; MATTHEW 1:18–25

The one who is the true light, who gives light to everyone, was coming into the world (John 1:9).

Checkpoint: The promised babies are born. Zechariah praises God out loud for His promises and for the "true light that was coming into the world." In his song of praise, he shows a full understanding of God fulfilling Scripture through the birth of Zechariah's son, John.

Sometimes it takes a while for us to be able to praise God for events in our lives. When it is hard to understand God's ways, doubts come in, and it is hard to praise. Mary, however, went straight away to her cousin and shared her joy with her. She knew Elizabeth would understand. She left Joseph for God to deal with! He did have doubts about marrying Mary, but when God spoke to him in a dream, he obeyed. When others close to us don't share our faith in God's promises, it is best to let God deal with them in His way. He knows the best way to speak with them. When they have heard God's will for themselves and are willing to obey, we can praise God with them, as we see Mary and Joseph doing at the end of today's reading.

- *At what point do you react to God's promises in your life: after they have come about, like Zechariah, or do you praise Him in faith, as Mary did, for what He has said He will do?*
- *How do you think we can overcome our doubts and learn to praise God in faith? Philippians 4:10–13 may help in your discussion.*

Prayer Stop: Praise God for the promises He has given you. Ask Him to help you learn to praise Him in faith. Ask God to strengthen us so that we may live and act in faith as Joseph did.

DAY 3

On the Way: We left the story yesterday after the birth of Jesus. I'm sure you know of the angels appearing to the shepherds in the fields and giving them the fright of their lives. The angels told the shepherds of Jesus' birth and where they would find Him. Matthew's Gospel tells of the wisemen who traveled from the East to bring gifts and worship Jesus. He also tells of how Jesus' family had to escape to Egypt for a while to be safe from King Herod. After Herod's death, they returned to Nazareth, where we take up the reading today.

READ LUKE 2:40–52

> *There the child grew up healthy and strong. He was filled with wisdom, and*
> *God's favor was on him* (v40).

Checkpoint: Jesus had to grow up as we all do. He would have cut teeth as a baby, learned to walk, eat, talk, and live in a family just as we do. We see Him taking part in family worship, going with His parents to the Passover. It is encouraging to realize that our Lord Jesus knows what it is like to be part of a family and to take part in family life and worship. He would have had other brothers and perhaps sisters by this time in His life. He knows the frustrations that can cause. He knows what it is like to have parents worry about Him.

In all of this, we read in verse 52 that Jesus had to grow in wisdom. He would have learned like any other boy His age. He knows exactly what it means to be a young boy growing up in a growing family.

- *What do you find difficult about being part of a growing family?*
- *Jesus seemed surprised that His parents didn't know where to find Him. Sometimes as we are growing up, our parents forget we are no longer babies! Have you experienced this? Share it with the family now.*

Prayer Stop: Thank God for your family and pray that God would help you to grow in wisdom, both parents and children! Pray that God would give you wisdom to deal with those difficult areas you have just talked about.

DAY 4

On the Way: We are not told anything of Jesus' life as a teenager or in His twenties, nor are we told anything of John's life growing up. However, as in yesterday's key verse where we learned that Jesus grew in wisdom and that God's favor was on Him, so in Luke 1:80 we also learn that John grew and became strong in spirit. This was God's preparation for his future ministry. At God's chosen time, John set out to preach the Word of God and to prepare people to accept the Messiah.

READ JOHN 1:19–28

God sent a man, John the Baptist, to tell about the light so that everyone might believe (Jn. 1:6–7).

Checkpoint: John is speaking with the religious leaders of Jerusalem in today's reading. He is explaining who he is and the purpose of ministry. He clearly tells them that he is not the Messiah but that he is preaching in preparation for the coming of God's Messiah, who he says was among them already. John was sure of who he was and of his purpose in his ministry. This seemed to confuse the leaders he was speaking with.

When we explain our faith in Jesus as our Savior to others, it may not make sense to them, and it may seem to confuse them. However if we, like John, are sure of our faith and our purpose, then we need not be anxious. God will honor our efforts when we are ready to stand up for Him.

- *Discuss the following verses: 1 Peter 3:15, 1 Corinthians 16:13–14, Ephesians 6:14–15. How can these verses teach us something of God's purpose for our lives? How do they encourage us to be like John?*
- *Talk about things you can do to help you be ready to share your faith with others.*

Prayer Stop: Pray for each member of the family that they will be ready to share their faith when God gives the opportunity. Pray for those serving God in other countries as missionaries. Pray that they will know God's courage and strength when things are difficult for them.

DAY 5

On the Way: At the outset of Jesus' public ministry, He approaches John the Baptist and asks him to baptize Him in the Jordan River. John at first refuses, realizing that it should be the other way around. However, the purpose was to show that Jesus had been set apart by God and that He identified fully with us. This was also the time when John announced publicly that Jesus was the Messiah. If you have not been baptized yet, perhaps you might want to think about it. This is a picture for others to see that we are committing our life to following Jesus.

READ MATTHEW 4:1–11

Then the devil went away, and the angels came and took care of Jesus (v11).

Checkpoint: After His baptism, Jesus was led out to the desert, where He was tempted by the devil. Jesus overcame every temptation by repeating the Word of God to Satan. Satan cannot stand against the power of the Word of God. That is why it is important we keep God's Word in our hearts so we can fight the devil when he tempts us or gives us doubts.

It is comforting to know that Jesus knows what it feels like to be tempted. He can give us strength to overcome temptation. Often when we experience a special time in our spiritual lives, like baptism, we very soon afterwards experience a time of tempting. Satan does not like to see us grow in our faith and will try anything to distract us. We must be on our guard.

- *Look at 1 Peter 5:8–10; how can we "stay alert and stand firm" in order to resist the devil?*

- *Have you or any member of your family ever experienced being able to use God's Word in the same way that Jesus did in today's reading?*

Prayer Stop: Pray for those finding the Christian life difficult. Try to find a way of encouraging them with the Word of God. Praise God for the power of His Word to overcome Satan. Make it a priority as a family to memorize the special memory verses in these readings.

DAY 6

On the Way: Returning from the desert, Jesus went to Galilee and began preaching. John had been put in prison, and Jesus knew that it was time for Him to begin His ministry. He didn't sit around feeling sorry for Himself for having had such a difficult time in the desert. (I'm sure I may have been tempted to do this!) He got up and set about the purpose He knew God had for Him.

READ MARK 1:14–20

Jesus called out to them, "Come, follow me, and I will show you how to fish for people!" (v17).

Checkpoint: Jesus was alone at the start of His ministry. He knew that He would need others to help Him, but He did not let this delay Him from getting started doing what God had sent Him to do. He knew God would guide Him to those who would become His disciples.

We may sometimes feel alone when God asks us to start something for Him. However, He may want us to be willing to start, and once we have started, He will bring those we need to help us.

Today we meet the first four disciples, called as they were carrying out their normal jobs. As they fished, Jesus called them to follow Him, to give up what they were doing and start out on a new adventure with Him. God may ask us to do something different for Him. We might not feel that we are able to handle it, but He just wants us to be willing to start and, like the men in today's reading, immediately follow Him.

- *What things do you think would have been difficult for Simon, Andrew, James, and John to leave immediately and obey Jesus? What things would you find hard to leave if God called you to do something different for Him?*
- *Is there anything that you as a family, or even just on your own, feel that God is asking you to do but that you find difficult to start out on your own?*

Prayer Stop: Pray for anyone you know or have heard of who have left the things they are comfortable with to start out on a new adventure with God. Pray that each person in your family will have the confidence and trust to obey God completely.

DAY 7

On the Way: Jesus traveled throughout Galilee and the area around it. He taught in the synagogues. Large crowds followed Him and brought sick people to Him to be healed. When He saw the crowds, He went up a hillside, called His disciples to Himself, and taught them the meaning of God's Word. Our reading today is the start of what is known as "The Sermon on the Mount." The people knew the Laws of Moses and the requirements that their religious leaders put on them, but here Jesus taught something greater than they had ever heard before, something that brought a deeper meaning to the laws that they knew. Over the next few days, we will study some of Jesus' teaching.

READ MATTHEW 5:1–16

> *Let your good deeds shine out for all to see, so that everyone will praise your heavenly Father* (v16b).

Checkpoint: The first section in our reading is known as "The Beatitudes." Jesus teaches about having the right attitudes that are pleasing to God. By living these out, Jesus says we will be "blessed," i.e., deeply happy and content. It seems impossible to achieve that on our own, but Jesus says, "Happy are the poor in spirit for theirs is the kingdom of heaven." The "poor in spirit" are those who realize they cannot reach these goals without the Lord's help and therefore rely on Him to show them how to have the right attitudes.

Verses 13–16 teach that as God's children, we must have an effect on those around us. Salt and light make a difference wherever they are used. If we are looking to God to help us live our lives with the right attitudes, then these attitudes will make a difference to those around us.

- *What will be the result be when we live with the right attitude? (Matthew 5:16) How does this make you feel?*

- *Think about being salt and light. What does salt do? How can we be salt on the earth? What about light?*

Prayer Stop: Pray that God would create right attitudes in your heart. Pray for each other that you will let Him do it! Pray that God's love would show in your life this week and that others would praise Him as a result.

DAY 8

On the Way: Jesus continued teaching, challenging those listening to be concerned about their thoughts more than their actions. Jews were very concerned about being seen doing the right thing (and we can be also). They focused on what they did rather than what they thought. Jesus taught that our thoughts are often more important to God than our deeds, and He challenged them to take control of their thinking. This is a challenge for us today also.

Jesus continued to teach about having a relationship with God and we read about His teaching on prayer today.

READ MATTHEW 6:5–15

Your Father knows exactly what you need even before you ask him (v8b).

Checkpoint: Jesus' teaching would have shocked most of the Jewish leaders. He taught that it is not our words but our attitude that is important when we pray. Some of these leaders loved to be heard praying and made a big show of it so others would think they were great people. Jesus said, "Pray to your Father."

It is God who answers your prayers, not other people. This is a lesson we can learn today. Sometimes it is easier to pray when others are there. We "pray to the audience" and forget that it is really to our Heavenly Father we are speaking.

You don't need to use fancy words or methods—just tell Him what is on your heart. He already knows your needs; He just wants to hear it from you. Jesus gives an example of how we can pray in what has become known as "The Lord's Prayer."

- *Look at verses 9–13 and list the things Jesus taught we should include in our prayers.*
- *What words would you use to describe the attitude in which we should come to prayer?*
- *Why do you think Jesus taught forgiveness as such an important attitude? How easy do you find it to forgive those who have hurt you?*

Prayer Stop: Use the example Jesus gave in your prayer time today. Use the list you made in the first question above to help you pray.

DAY 9

On the Way: We have discovered that God is more interested in what is in our hearts than in our appearances and actions. It is easy to pretend to others, but God knows our heart; we cannot pretend to Him.

Today we are going to look at Jesus' teaching concerning our possessions.

READ LUKE 12:22–34

Wherever your treasure is, there the desires of your heart will also be (v34).

Checkpoint: What things are important to you? It may be your new computer or some designer clothes you bought. How would you feel if those things were damaged? Perhaps a parent's concerns are slightly different. Do you worry about paying bills or how you are going to buy the kids clothes they need (or want)? In our reading today, Jesus is saying that these things are His concern. They don't need to be ours. When we feel worried about the things in this life that will get damaged and waste away, or when our concern is where we will get the money to pay for the things we need, Jesus says, "Look around you. Look at the beautiful creation and think about who gave it all its beauty. Do you think God would neglect you if He looks after all of His other creation?" If we spend time worrying about the things we have or need, we will not be concerned for God's kingdom in the way we should be. Our hearts will be concerned with the wrong things.

- *What attitude does Jesus want us to have toward our possessions? (Luke 12:32–34)*
- *Sometimes parents struggle to have enough money to provide for their children. What would your attitude in the past have been if this had happened to you? After reading the verses today, will your attitude change the next time?*

Prayer Stop: Pray that you will have the attitude Jesus wants you to have to those things you consider precious. Pray that God will provide your needs and the needs of others who may have concerns about what they will eat or wear at the moment.

Practical Application: Is there anything you could do to help such people? Perhaps you could invite them for a meal. Do you have clothes you no longer wear that are in good shape?

DAY 10

On the Way: As Jesus taught around the region, many people followed Him and listened to His teaching. At times He would teach the crowds who congregated around Him. Often He would take His disciples to a quiet place to explain the Word of God in a deeper way. Some of the teaching they seemed to be able to accept and understand without a problem; other teachings seemed too difficult for them to take in. Our reading today takes us to one of those times.

READ LUKE 17:1–10

Show us how to increase our faith (v5b).

Checkpoint: Jesus taught His disciples that they will always face the temptation to sin. He urges them to look out for each other and encourage each other to behave in the right way. This message is for us too if we are Jesus' disciples today. If someone hurts us and asks for our forgiveness, we must be willing to forgive them. If they do it again, we must forgive them again and again and again!

I think the disciples knew it was a hard thing they were being asked to do, because they asked Jesus for more faith to be able to do it. Jesus tells them that no matter how small their faith is, they can exercise it and God will honor it, but He gives them (and us) a warning. When we have behaved as He has taught us to, we must not get bigheaded about it. We must remember we are His servants, and servants obey their masters. They don't get extra rewards for being obedient. It is what we are expected to do.

- *When someone keeps on doing something that hurts you, do you ever think, "I'm not letting you get away with that again"? What does Jesus' teaching tell us about that attitude?*
- *What should make us want to obey Jesus' teaching?*

Prayer Stop: Thank God for the things He has done for you that make you want to serve Him. Pray that God would give you a heart that is ready and willing to forgive others.

DAY 11

On the Way: Jesus spent a lot of time teaching people about the kingdom of God. His teaching was different from what their rabbis taught. He also warned about things that would tempt them away from that kingdom.

MEMORY VERSE

But the Holy Spirit produces this kind of fruit in our lives: love, joy, peace, patience, kindness, goodness, faithfulness, gentleness and self control. There is no law against these things!

~ Galatians 5:22–23

READ MATTHEW 7:15–29

Just as you can identify a tree by its fruit, so you can identify people by their actions (v20).

Checkpoint: How do you recognize an apple tree . . . or a strawberry plant? Can you imagine looking at a tree ripe with strawberries? It would appear a little out of place! Jesus was saying that our attitudes and behavior reveal whether we are truly His children or not. He warns His disciples that some people will appear to be genuine when really they are teaching lies. Jesus calls them "false prophets and evildoers." This is very strong language. Jesus is completely opposed to what such people are teaching.

Jesus says the miraculous signs and wonders performed by these men do not make them genuine. It is easy to see why people think such men are from God. They were doing the same things as Jesus, but it is important that we do not look at their actions but at the attitude in which they are doing it. Look at the fruit they bear. Look at their lives. Does it agree with the rest of Jesus' teaching? There will be people like that in our communities, and we must watch carefully that we are not tempted to follow them because of the things they are doing; instead, we must look at their attitudes and motivation. Jesus says, "Beware."

- *Look at Galatians 5:22 and John 13:34–35. What fruit should be seen in our lives if we are true disciples of Jesus?*

- *How can we tell whether people are teaching the truth of God or teaching lies? Have you had experience with any groups/people like that?*

Prayer Stop: Thank God for the truth taught in His Word. Ask Him to help you bear His fruit in your lives. Pray for any groups in your area that seem to be teaching truth but are not.

DAY 12

On the Way: Often as Jesus traveled around, the Pharisees would send groups to try to catch Him out by asking awkward questions! They loved to criticize what He was doing and tried to show the people that His teaching was not in keeping with the law. Jesus always brought them back to the Law of God and showed them where they were getting things mixed up with their own tradition. You can imagine they were not very happy about this!

READ MARK 7:1–15

And so you cancel the word of God in order to hand down your own tradition (v13a).

Checkpoint: The Pharisees had come to think that the rules they lived by were God's Law and that anyone who broke them broke God's Law. Sometimes they would use their own rules to make excuses for not obeying the bits of God's Law they found too hard. Jesus showed them how the rules they were living by were things made up only by men and not actually written in God's Law.

Again we see Jesus teaching that it is our attitude that is important, not what rules we keep or what others see us doing. Sometimes we have traditions in our homes and churches that we live by without thinking about their origins. Such traditions are not necessarily wrong. They often point us very clearly to God's Word. However if they become more important to us than what God's Word teaches, they become wrong. If we use them as our rules to live by and not God's Word, we risk becoming like the Pharisees.

- *Think about the traditions you have in your home and church. It is important that we see them as tradition and not as God's Law. Are there any that you need to change your attitude toward? Which ones show us God's teaching clearly?*
- *How can we be sure that our traditions are not taking the place of God's Word in our lives? Use Psalm 119:9–11 to help you think about this.*

Prayer Stop: Pray that God would help you to live by His Word and not the rules made by man. Thank Him for the rules and traditions that have been wisely made and point us to His Word.

DAY 13

On the Way: Today we come to the end of our study of Jesus' sermons. We will continue to look at more of His teaching through the stories He told. We have learned a lot about the difference between Jesus' teaching and that of the Jewish leaders. God is interested in our hearts' attitude and not simply in the things we do. Jesus does not expect us to manage this on our own, He tells us of the way to do this.

READ JOHN 15:1–17

You cannot be fruitful unless you remain in me (v4b).

Checkpoint: Jesus tells us in today's reading that we can bear fruit for Him (the fruit we talked about a few days ago) if we remain in Him. He uses the picture of a vine to show that unless a branch stays on the vine, it will not grow grapes. We too as His disciples will only be able to "produce" the fruit of the Spirit if we stay "in Him." This means that we need to be joined to Him and take our spiritual nourishment from Him as a branch is nourished by a vine.

It is great that God does not expect us to produce our own fruit. If I was left to do that, I would produce lots of anger, pride, and all sorts of things that would not look like Christ. God gives us the right food so we can produce the right fruit. Some branches on a vine are stronger than others and will produce more fruit. As we grow older and stronger, we too will produce more fruit. God will "prune" us to make us produce more fruit because He really loves us and wants us to be like Him.

- *What can we do to remain in Jesus?*
- *What things might God do to prune us as branches in the vine?*

Prayer Stop: Thank God that He does not leave us on our own to produce fruit but gives us the right food so that we might give Him glory. Pray that God would help you to be faithful to Him and bear the right fruit.

DAY 14

On the Way: Over the next five days, we will look at some parables Jesus told. Parables are stories that did not actually happen, but Jesus used them to teach the people more about what following Him really meant. They were stories about things the people came across in everyday life and could understand. The first one we will look at is called the parable of the farmer.

READ MARK 4:1–9

Anyone with ears to hear should listen and understand (v9b).

Checkpoint: Jesus explains the meaning of this parable to His disciples in verses 13–20. He tells them that the seed the farmer sews is a picture of the Word of God. As some people hear the Word of God, they have different reactions to it, like the different ground that the seed falls on in the parable. Jesus was making His disciples aware that not everyone would respond in a positive way when they heard the Word of God.

This is not a story that was only relevant in Jesus' time; it is every bit as true today. What different responses do people you know have to the good news of Jesus? In verse 9, Jesus encouraged those who heard the Word to respond to it in a way that would bear fruit. It seems a funny thing to say because everyone has ears, but often we choose not to respond to what we hear. Then it becomes as if we did not hear in the first place.

- *Look at verse 17. What do you think Jesus means by those who "have no root"?*
- *How could worries and wealth "crowd out" the Word (Mark 4:19)?*
- *What other reactions to God's Word do you note in verses 13–20?*
- *What kind of crop does the Word produce in those who accept it? (Mark 4:20)*

Prayer Stop: Pray for anyone who knows the good news of Jesus but for some reason has not accepted it yet. Pray for yourselves, that you would produce good fruit in your lives. Thank God for His Word and what it teaches us.

DAY 15

On the Way: During Jesus' ministry, the religious leaders often tried to trick Him by asking awkward questions. Today's parable is told in answer to one of those questions. A ruler came to Him and started to discuss what he should do to gain eternal life. Among other things, Jesus told Him that he should "love his neighbor as himself." Thinking to catch Jesus out, the ruler asked, "Who is my neighbor?" We will read Jesus' reply.

READ LUKE 10:30–37

> *Now which of these three would you say was a neighbour to the man who was attacked by bandits?* (v36a).

Checkpoint: In the story, there is only one sensible answer to this question. Of course, the man was not going to suggest that the priest or Levite were neighbors to the man; they had ignored him. It had to be the Samaritan. There was one problem with this: Jews and Samaritans hated each other very much. The Jews thought Samaritans were worse than dogs. Under normal circumstances, the Jewish victim would not have wanted the Samaritan near him, but when his own people passed by (and not just ordinary people but religious leaders), he would have had no choice but to accept help.

Jesus taught that when it comes to loving our neighbors, it is not just those next door to us, or those we like, that matter but everyone, even those we count as enemies. This would have been a hard lesson for this Jewish expert to learn. Often it is hard for us too. We don't mind helping our friends or people we think are respectable, but when it comes to the tramp in the street or perhaps someone who is openly nasty to us, we often feel differently. Did you notice that the Samaritan in the story did not just do the bare minimum for the man? He did everything he could to help, even spending his own money to do it.

- *Why do you think Jesus chose a Samaritan to be the one who helped in the story?*
- *What kinds of people would you find hard to help?*
- *How do you think the ruler felt when Jesus told him to go and do as the Samaritan did?*

Prayer Stop: Pray that God would show you those who need your help this week and ask Him to make you willing to help, no matter who they are.

DAY 16

On the Way: The parables Jesus used always involved things that the listeners could relate to. It made it easy for them to understand what He was teaching and left them without an excuse if they did not act on it. In the parable we read today, Jesus is teaching about what is important in life.

READ LUKE 12:13–21

Life is not measured by how much you own (v15b).

Checkpoint: People saw Jesus as a good teacher, treating everyone fairly. So the man in today's reading comes and asks Jesus to make his brother treat him fairly. Quarrels like this were normally settled by rabbis. Jesus did not choose to sort the actual dispute but rather went straight to the point that was causing the dispute in the first place. Jesus saw the root of the problem as greed and addressed the issue with a parable. The man in the parable spends his time thinking about how he can save all his grain to make himself richer and richer and so retire a wealthy man and enjoy a life of luxury.

Does this picture ring any bells about people today? Some people do spend a lot of time and energy working only to make themselves rich, and like the man in the parable, they do not give any thought to God. What does God call the man in verse 20? This is very strong language! But it gives us a clear picture of what God thinks of those who have this attitude. God holds our life in His hand.

Today's key verse teaches that being rich does not necessarily make us a better person.

- *Was Jesus teaching that being rich was wrong? How could the man in the parable have used his possessions better?*
- *In verse 21, Jesus talks about being rich toward God. What do you think this means?*
- *Think about your own attitude to rich and poor people. Does it need to change any in the light of today's reading?*

Prayer Stop: Pray for those you know who are caught up in working only to make themselves rich. Pray that you would spend what you have wisely and in ways that honor God and that you would spend time and effort being "rich toward God."

DAY 17

On the Way: Forgiveness is a major theme in all of Jesus' teaching. That is because it is a major part of the ministry Jesus had and still has today: the forgiveness of our sin. The forgiveness Jesus wants us to show others is the forgiveness He has shown us. Today's parable explains this.

READ MATTHEW 18:21–35

Then his master was filled with pity for him, and he released him and forgave his debt (v27).

Checkpoint: Peter thought that forgiving someone seven times would be enough. It would seem that he might think it okay to bear a grudge against a person after that. When he asked Jesus about it, he may have been surprised by the answer!

Can you work out how many times Jesus says we should forgive someone? It's a lot! In fact, we would never be able to keep a record of forgiving someone that many times. I think that is the message Jesus was getting across: we need to keep forgiving and remembering that God keeps forgiving us. Jesus does not hold grudges against us if we keep getting it wrong. He forgives us even more than we deserve. The servant in the parable today only asked to be given time to pay his debt, but the master actually cancelled his debt. He did not owe anything after that. Sometimes when others do things that hurt us, we easily get angry at them. We forget that often we do things that unintentionally hurt others, and we don't like them getting angry with us. Let's try to treat others more fairly.

- *What kind of character do you think the master in today's parable had?*
- *What kind of character does the servant have?*
- *Which would you rather have? Is there anything that you need to put right with someone else to start on the road to being a forgiving person?*

Prayer Stop: Pray that God would help you forgive those who sin against you. Pray for the people you perhaps find it hard to forgive. Thank God for His forgiveness for you and for dying on the cross to pay the price for your sin.

DAY 18

On the Way: Although Jesus used many parables to teach His disciples about Himself, we will look at only one more. In today's parable, Jesus compares the kingdom of heaven to a wedding reception held by a king for his son.

MEMORY VERSE

I am overwhelmed with joy in the LORD my God! For he has dressed me with the clothing of salvation and draped me in a robe of righteousness.

~ Isaiah 61:10a

READ MATTHEW 22:1–14

For many are called, but few are chosen (v14).

Checkpoint: The first group of guests mentioned in today's reading is a picture of the nation of Israel. As a nation, they rejected God's way of salvation through Jesus, although there were some individual Jews who did believe. The next group of guests who eventually attended the wedding was a group of randomly invited people from the street! This is a picture of how God extends His offer of salvation to everyone, not just the Jews. This is how you and I are able to be part of God's kingdom.

We want to focus on the one man who was not wearing the right clothes. At first, the king's reaction seems a bit harsh. After all, he had just been brought in from the street! Tradition says that the king would have provided outfits for his guests, so they needn't have worried about not being dressed appropriately. This man must have insulted the king by refusing to accept the garment provided for him to wear. God has provided the correct "garment" for us to be able to attend His banquet. We must be sure we have accepted it.

- *According to the memory verse, what garment do we need to be able to be part of the kingdom of heaven?*

- *How do we obtain this garment? Read John 3:16 and John 14:6.*

- *Who do you think the man in the parable is a picture of?*

Prayer Stop: Thank God for providing a way for us to be part of His kingdom. Pray for those you may know who deliberately refuse to accept God's plan of salvation.

DAY 19

On the Way: Having looked at Jesus' birth, the start of His ministry, and some of His teaching, we are going to look at some of the miracles He performed. These events showed His great power and should have helped people recognize that He was God. Had the Jews reflected on the Scriptures, they would have seen how these things were foretold. However, the miracles of Jesus seemed to anger the Jewish leaders, and they refused to accept that He was God. The first miracle we will look at involves a Roman Centurion.

READ MATTHEW 8:5–13

> *Go back home. Because you believed, it has happened* (v13b).

Checkpoint: Here an important Roman soldier asked Jesus to heal his servant. Romans were people who worshipped many other gods and often did not care for their servants. If servants became ill, they would often be left at the temple or thrown into the street to beg. This centurion seems a bit different. He not only asks Jesus to heal his servant, but he also seems to understand that it is by great authority that Jesus has this power. He has obviously thought about the things he has heard about Jesus and now acts on what he has learned. Most Romans thought themselves greater than any Jew, but this man says to Jesus, "I do not deserve to have you come to my house." He realizes that Jesus is worthy of honor and gives it to Him publicly. He places himself under the authority of Jesus.

- *Why might it have been difficult for the centurion to do what he did?*
- *By healing this man's servant, what was Jesus showing those who were there?*
- *Sometimes we think we deserve to have Jesus bless us because of what we have done for Him. What can we learn from the attitude of this centurion? What was Jesus' response to his attitude? (See today's key verse.)*

Prayer Stop: Thank God that He does not show favoritism but loves us all the same. Pray that you will give God the proper place in your lives and so reveal His power to those around you.

DAY 20

On the Way: As we have already learned, Jesus traveled around and taught. As He did so, He affected other people's lives by healing them or showing them a better way to live. He did not have any barriers that would affect who He would help. Yesterday we saw Him with a powerful Roman soldier; today He deals with ten men who would not have been allowed to mix with other people because of their disease.

READ LUKE 17:11–19

> *One of them, when he saw he was healed, came back to Jesus shouting, "Praise God!"* (v15).

Checkpoint: These men had leprosy. They would have been put out of the families and communities they lived in and treated as unclean. They knew there was no one else who could help them, and they called to Jesus for help. Instead of praying for them or touching them or even telling them they would be healed, Jesus gave them a task to do. It was not until they were on their way to the priest that they realized they were healed. By obeying Jesus, they showed their faith in Him. Sometimes we need to just obey God and have faith that He is in control of the outcome.

The lepers did not know what would happen when they started on the road to the priest. However, only one of them came back to offer thanks. He came back praising God. This shows that he knew where Jesus' authority came from. Verse 16 tells us this man was a Samaritan, an enemy of the Jews. It is good to thank God for answered prayer.

- *Have you asked the Lord for help with something and yet don't seem to have an answer? Is He perhaps asking you to do something that you have not yet obeyed? Remember, it was as the men were on their way that they realized they were clean.*
- *Why do you think only one man came back to offer thanks?*

Prayer Stop: Take time to thank God that He hears and answers our prayer. Thank Him for any specific answers you have had recently. Pray that He would show you anything He wants you to do to be obedient to Him.

DAY 21

On the Way: Jesus had sent the twelve disciples out in pairs to preach and heal the sick (Mk. 6:7–13). In today's reading, we see them returning to Him to report all that they had done. This appeared to be impossible as so many people were coming to them that they didn't even have time to eat. So Jesus takes them away on their own to spend some time with them, but when they arrive at their intended destination, they discover the crowds have beaten them there!

READ MARK 6:34–44

They all ate as much as they wanted (v42).

Checkpoint: The disciples realized it was getting late and asked Jesus to send the people away to let them get something to eat. Perhaps they were a little tired and hungry themselves. Remember, they were meant to be having some time alone with the Lord, but over five thousand people had gate-crashed their meeting! However, instead of doing what the disciples asked, Jesus faces them with a task that probably made them laugh. Can you imagine what they thought when Jesus said, "You feed them"? They were probably still laughing when they told Jesus they had five loaves . . . oh, and two fish! This is added as an afterthought. You can imagine them sarcastically thinking, "Ah that will make all the difference." However, Jesus wants them to learn what can be done if the little we have is will-ingly given to Him. I'm sure they were laughing with joy and amazement by the end of the evening as they saw what Jesus did with the five loaves and two fish.

We may think we don't have much to offer God in our lives, but we can learn from this miracle. Be willing to do the little things and leave the big things to God. He can do amazing things with just a little if it is given with a willing heart.

- *Can you imagine the feeling of the person whose lunch was used to feed so many?*
- *Are there things that you could be doing for God just now that you think are too insignificant to bother about? Remember, you may be missing out in a miracle!*

Prayer Stop: Thank God for His power that can do mighty things from just a little. Pray that you will be willing to do even the little things for God and allow Him to show you His power at work.

DAY 22

On the Way: The miracles we have looked at reflected the different types of people affected by Jesus' ministry: enemies of the Jews, the Jewish people themselves, and those who were outcasts from society. So often these miracles angered the Jewish leaders, but there were those who believed. We read of one today.

READ MATTHEW 9:18–26

Don't be afraid. Just have faith (Mark 5:36b).

Checkpoint: Although we read the account of this miracle in Matthew, there is a much fuller account in Mark 5:21–43. Jairus would have been well known by those around and regarded as a dignified person, yet he was so desperate for Jesus to touch his daughter that he came and fell at His feet publicly. That other Jewish rulers were strongly against Jesus did not faze him. Jairus knew his daughter was in desperate need and went to seek help personally. (He could have sent a servant.) Can you imagine how he felt when Jesus stopped to speak with the woman who had touched Him? Then his disappointment when the messengers came to say his daughter had died? Jesus' message to him was what we read in our key verse in Mark: "Don't be afraid. Just have faith." In effect, Jesus was reminding Jairus that he had faith to come and ask Jesus to heal his daughter; now he must continue to believe that Jesus will do as He said. It may not be going as smoothly as Jairus would have liked; it may appear to have gone horribly wrong, but Jesus tells him to keep believing.

We must keep believing too when things we have prayed about don't seem to be working out. We must remember the outcome of today's miracle. Jairus expected his daughter to be healed but instead witnessed something far greater: his daughter raised from the dead!

- *Why was it so important for Jesus to stop to speak with the woman?*
- *Have you prayed about something, and now it seems worse or that God has forgotten? Remember Jairus's miracle.*

Prayer Stop: Pray for faith to keep on believing even though we don't understand what God is doing. Thank God that He is able to do more than we can ever ask or imagine (Eph. 3:20).

DAY 23

On the Way: The last miracle we are going to look at involves only Jesus' disciples and takes place after Jesus has risen from the dead. We can imagine the disciples feeling a bit down and confused after all that had happened, perhaps not quite sure what to believe anymore. However, Jesus meets them on the beach to encourage them.

READ JOHN 21:1–12

Then the disciple Jesus loved said to Peter, "It is the Lord!" (v7a).

Checkpoint: Peter decides to go fishing. He knew how to do that; that was his job before he met Jesus. Now that circumstances have left him confused, he goes back to his boat, and the others go too. However, even this didn't help. They caught no fish. How do you think they were feeling?

Jesus knew where they were and went to meet them. They were so wrapped up in their sadness and confusion that they did not recognize Him. It wasn't until after the miracle catch that they recognized Him. You can almost sense the relief in the disciples as they realize that they have not been abandoned by their Lord. He is there. Even better, He encouraged them when they were down and provided for them too, even preparing breakfast for them.

Sometimes we can spend so much time thinking about our confusing circumstances that we do not recognize when God sends us encouragement, and we forget His promises. Remember, He has said, "I will never leave you." He knows where we are and how to encourage us.

- *Look at verse 12. How do you think the disciples were feeling?*
- *What had made the difference?*
- *Are there circumstances in your life that are confusing and make you think that God has forgotten you? Talk about your reaction to these circumstances.*
- *Are there others you know facing hard times? What can you do to encourage them?*

Prayer Stop: Thank God that He never leaves us, even when we feel He has. Pray for those you know facing difficult circumstances, that they may see God working things out and be encouraged.

DAY 24

On the Way: Over the next few sessions we will look at some of the people Jesus met during His ministry and how their meeting with Him changed their lives. The first group we meet are the Pharisees.

READ MATTHEW 15:1–20

> *It's not what goes into your mouth that defiles you; you are defiled by the*
> *words that come out of your mouth* (v11).

Checkpoint: The Pharisees were a group of religious leaders who studied the Law of Moses. They added so many rules to this law themselves, making it impossible for anyone to live by them. They were exceptionally good at seeing when others did not keep the rules and pointing it out to them! They were so focused on keeping their own rules (traditions) that they failed to recognize when their traditions actually broke God's Law. One of these rules concerned washing in a certain way before eating. In today's reading, Jesus teaches them that it doesn't really matter if your hands are clean or not. It is the condition of your heart and actions that matter. There is no point in having spotless hands if the things we do are against God's Law. There are often things that we do traditionally without giving much thought to them, but if they are taking our focus away from the things that are really important to God, then we must get rid of them and change our ways. Verse 12 tells us that the Pharisees were offended by Jesus' teaching. By meeting Jesus, their rules were being challenged and shown up for what they really were.

- *Think of some traditions you have in your church or family. Are they helping or hindering your focus on God's will for your life? Perhaps some of them will need to change.*

- *How does having to change some of these make you feel? Are you offended like the Pharisees or willing to change to be in line with God's will?*

- *Read Psalm 141:3–4. How can we make sure our attitudes and actions are pure?*

Prayer Stop: Use Psalm 141:3–4 as a prayer for yourself and your family today. Thank God that He helps us to live in a way that pleases Him.

DAY 25

On the Way: Jesus' ministry touched the lives of people from every area of society. He healed the sick, spoke to the poor and outcast, and mixed with those who were ignored by respectable people. His life and ministry also affected those in religious leadership as we saw yesterday, whether as individuals or as a group. Today Jesus meets a rich young man.

READ MARK 10:17–31

"Then who in the world can be saved?"... "Humanly speaking, it is impossible. But not with God. Everything is possible with God" (v26b–27).

Checkpoint: Here is a man who has all he needs in life, keeps the commandments as he knows them, and as a result is respected in society. He comes to Jesus to ask what he has to do to gain eternal life. He sees himself in a position of being able to do whatever it takes to gain it. He has wealth and position. By asking Jesus this question, he either feels that the answer he gets will indeed put the spotlight on his "good living," or it could be that he genuinely feels his keeping the commandments is not enough to gain eternal life. Whatever the reason, Jesus' answer immediately highlights the thing that is standing between this man and God: his wealth. His security lies in his wealth, and he leaves Jesus sad because this is too hard for him to give up. Jesus wanted him to see that there is nothing we can do that is great enough to receive eternal life. It is a gift to us from God. Today's verse highlights this. If it was up to us, it would be impossible for anyone to have eternal life, but God in His love for us has provided a way through the death and resurrection of Jesus.

- *What things today keep people separated from God?*
- *What attitude was keeping this man from God?*
- *Why do you think it was hard for him to do what Jesus asked?*

Prayer Stop: Pray for anyone you know who is finding it hard to accept the gift of eternal life from God. Think of anything that might be coming between you and God right now and pray that God would help you to be obedient to Him.

DAY 26

On the Way: The Pharisees and the rich young man found Jesus' teaching offensive and difficult. The next two people we will look at are people who responded in a positive way to Jesus' teaching. The first is a woman with whom no respectable person would associate.

READ LUKE 7:36–50

Your faith has saved you; go in peace (v50b).

Checkpoint: Jesus was invited to dinner at a Pharisee's home. According to verse 44, Simon did not even offer Jesus water to wash His feet with on arrival. This was common hospitality in those days as the roads were so dusty. The woman in today's reading had obviously heard Jesus preach and knew that her life could be changed by this man. She came to Simon's house to worship Jesus because of this. Simon could see only what the woman was on the outside. He knew she led a very sinful life and felt that if Jesus was such a great prophet, He should know that about her and banish her from His presence. However, Jesus knew Simon's thoughts and demonstrated that although she had lived a sinful life for everyone to see, she was now changed and forgiven. Her act of worship was out of gratefulness for the forgiveness and change that Jesus had brought to her life.

Because Simon lived a life of keeping rules made by man to try to please God, he did not realize that he was in as much need of forgiveness. Jesus' statement to the woman in verse 50 reinforces that it is not keeping rules and living what appears to be a good life that makes us right with God. It is our faith in who Jesus is and what He came to earth to do that saves us.

- *How do you think Simon felt when he saw the actions of this woman in his home? Are there people that you find it hard to accept can come into Jesus' presence? What do you think Jesus would say about that?*
- *Read Psalm 139:23–24. How did Jesus show He knew the hearts of Simon and the woman in our reading?*

Prayer Stop: Take time to think about your acts of worship. Ask God to show you the things that are done only to be seen. Take time to worship Him truly for the gift of forgiveness.

DAY 27

On the Way: The last person we will look at is a Jewish leader called Nicodemus. He came to speak to Jesus at night. I wonder if that was so no one would see him. Jesus clearly explains to him God's plan of salvation as we read in today's reading.

MEMORY VERSE

God sent his Son into the world not to judge the world, but to save the world through him.

~ John 3:17

READ JOHN 3:1–21

Checkpoint: Nicodemus was a member of the religious rulers in Jerusalem. He had been watching Jesus and thinking about what His ministry meant. He seemed to realize that the things Jesus did and said were done through the power of God. Jesus knew Nicodemus did not need more information; he had all the learning he needed. What he lacked was a changed life from accepting God's way of salvation.

Sometimes we can get too involved in discussions with people when all they need to hear is a clear message of God's plan for salvation. Jesus mentions the snake Moses lifted in the desert; the Israelites had to look to the bronze serpent for healing from snakebites caused by their rebellion against God. Nicodemus, as a religious scholar, would know this well and would perhaps then understand that unless he accepts God's plan of salvation, he cannot be saved, just as the Israelites had to look to the raised snake to be healed. We are not told of Nicodemus' response to Jesus' words but as we read further in John's Gospel, we can see evidence of his life being changed (Jn. 7:50–51; Jn. 19:39).

Sometimes people take time to think about God's gift of salvation, while others respond immediately. Either way, it is the evidence of a changed life through faith in Jesus that is important. Jesus does not judge us by how quickly we respond. It is what is in our hearts that matters to Him.

- *What could be some reasons for Nicodemus taking time to respond to Jesus' message? Think about his position in society.*
- *Think about ways that you can explain the message of the gospel clearly to your friends, e.g., Jesus using the example of the snake to Nicodemus.*

Prayer Stop: Pray for those you know who are thinking about their response to Jesus. Pray for opportunities to share the gospel story with your friends.

DAY 28

On the Way: Having looked at Jesus' ministry and teaching and their effect on different groups, we now come to the climax of the gospel story. Our last five studies in the Gospels will cover the death and resurrection of Jesus. Today we start with the first event that occurred before His arrest. Jesus is heading into Jerusalem with His disciples.

READ MARK 11:1–11

> *Rejoice, O people of Zion! Shout in triumph, O people of Jerusalem! Look, your king is coming to you He is righteous and victorious, Yet he is humble, riding on a donkey* (Zechariah 9:9a).

Checkpoint: Today's reading is the fulfillment of the prophecy in Zechariah that we have used for our key verse. It is the event that we traditionally celebrate as Palm Sunday in the Christian calendar. The Jews were looking for a Messiah, a mighty warrior who would come and rescue them from the Roman Empire. Instead, Jesus entered riding on a donkey, which had never been ridden before. This is in keeping with animals dedicated to the Lord according to the Law of Moses. It is also thought that in Bible times a royal person arriving on a donkey was a sign of peace.

Jesus' actions here were understood by every member of society. The leaders would have known the prophecy was being fulfilled, and the general public would have known the symbolism of a king entering in peace. The message that Jesus is King was being proclaimed in a very public way. The leaders and the people would see Him coming in peace, not as a warrior king. Those who were there worshipped Him. Jesus' message is still for everyone in all areas of society. It is a message of peace. Jesus has come that we might have peace with God.

- *How can we make sure we reach everyone in the society around us? Talk about specific ways that we can demonstrate that Jesus is King to those around us.*

- *Those with Jesus worshipped Him. What is your reaction to Jesus coming so that we might have peace with God?*

- *What is the reaction of those around you?*

Prayer Stop: Pray that you would be able to share the message that Jesus is King with someone this week. Pray for those you know who refuse to accept Jesus as the way to have peace with God.

DAY 29

Note: At the end of today's reading, you may wish to be prepared to celebrate communion together.

On the Way: Jesus prepares His disciples for when He will be arrested and killed. In Jerusalem, He cleared the temple courts of the market stalls and taught about God's house being a house of prayer. This angered the leaders, making them look for a way to kill Him. In today's reading, Jesus celebrates what has become known as the Last Supper with His disciples.

READ MATTHEW 26:17–30

> *For this is my blood, which confirms the covenant between God and his people.*
> *It is poured out as a sacrifice to forgive the sins of many (v28).*

Checkpoint: Jesus is with His disciples eating the Passover meal. He tells them that one of them will betray Him. This grieves them, and they question Jesus in disbelief. Even Judas says, "Surely not me." He had already thought about this and planned to turn Jesus over to the authorities as soon as possible (Matt. 26:14–16).

Jesus knew Judas' heart. We may be able to fool others and even ourselves into thinking that we are living right with God, but we cannot fool God. He knows what we truly feel.

At the end of supper, Jesus shares bread and wine with His disciples. This was a normal part of the Passover meal, but Jesus gave it a new meaning. This was a new promise that God was making with His children, a promise that our sins can be forgiven through Jesus' body and blood shed for us on the cross. He was using the bread and wine as a picture by which we can remember the reason He died and rose again. When we celebrate communion with other Christians, we use Jesus' words to remind us of His death and the reason for it.

- *How do you think Judas felt as he shared supper with Jesus?*
- *Read 1 Corinthians 11:27–28. As Christians, what should our attitude be as we celebrate communion?*
- *Why do we need to constantly remember Jesus death? Look at 1 Corinthians 11:26.*

Prayer Stop: Spend time in prayer, remembering Jesus' death and worshipping Him for His willing sacrifice.

Practical Application: We do not need to be in church to celebrate communion. We can share it with other Christians anywhere. If you are able, perhaps you would like to share together as a family now.

DAY 30

On the Way: After sharing the Passover meal, Jesus and His disciples went to the Garden of Gethsemane. He took Peter, James, and John to pray with Him. He knew that His time to die was near and needed to pray for strength to face what was ahead. He wanted the three disciples to pray too, but they were very tired and fell asleep, unaware of what was about to happen. We can sense the anguish in Jesus' words as He announces to them that His betrayer has come.

READ MARK 14:42–54, 66–72

> *Suddenly Jesus' words flashed through Peter's mind . . . And he broke down and wept* (v72b).

Checkpoint: Try to imagine the scene. The sleepy disciples, trying to keep their eyes open but finding it hard to concentrate, are suddenly faced with a noisy crowd coming to take Jesus away. How do they react? (John 18:10 tells us Peter cut a servant's ear off.) How do you think they felt when they saw Judas with the crowd?

In verse 31, Peter boldly stated that he would never disown Jesus and would even die with Him. By verse 54, Peter is already distancing himself from Jesus. He is not at His side as he said he would be.

Often when we are under pressure, we react to situations without thinking. Peter was afraid and tired. He had already overreacted by cutting the servant's ear off and was now distancing himself from Jesus. We cannot guess what was going on in Peter's mind as he denied he knew Jesus, but as soon as he heard the rooster crow, he knew he had let his Lord down. Again we see Peter's emotional reaction. It seems as if it is slowly dawning on him that Jesus had been preparing them for this time.

- *How do you think Peter felt as he heard the rooster crow?*
- *Can you think of a time when you had a chance to speak for Jesus but you backed down? How did you feel?*
- *Read John 21:15–17. Why do you think Jesus asked Peter the question three times?*
- *What does Jesus' command to Peter show us?*

Prayer Stop: Pray that you will have the courage to speak for Jesus whenever the chance arises. Thank God for His gift of forgiveness and grace that gives us a second chance.

DAY 31

On the Way: While Peter dealt with his betrayal, Jesus was taken to the high priest's house. There the soldiers made fun of Him and beat Him. He was then taken to the Jewish leaders and elders for questioning. When Jesus affirmed that He was the Son of God, they were enraged and took Him to the Roman governor, Pilate, to have Him sentenced to death. Pilate tried to release Him, but the crowd, stirred up by the leaders, shouted, "Crucify Him!"

READ LUKE 23:26–56

Suddenly the curtain in the sanctuary of the Temple was torn down the middle (v45b).

Checkpoint: "He was despised and rejected—a man of sorrows, acquainted with deepest grief . . . But he was pierced for our rebellion, crushed for our sins" (Is. 53:3–5a). These verses in Isaiah are fulfilled in the reading we covered in Luke today. This is the climax of God's plan for our salvation. The Old Testament pointed toward the coming of Jesus. The Law and the prophets taught about Him. As Jesus dies on the cross, God shows the world a picture of what this means by the curtain in the Temple being torn in two. The curtain was to separate the holiest place in the Temple from the rest. Only the high priest could enter behind it, and that occurred only once a year.

God's presence is so holy that we cannot come into it on our own. When Jesus died, He made that sacrifice for all of us, that we might be able to come directly into God's presence by trusting in Him as our Savior. It is because of His wounds that we can be made pure and so come into God's presence.

- *Read Isaiah 53:3–7. Talk about the different events in today's reading that fulfill this prophecy.*

- *Who mocked Jesus? Who trusted in Him?*

- *What is your response to His death?*

Prayer Stop: Praise God for His plan of salvation.

DAY 32

On the Way: Imagine how Jesus' disciples were feeling after the events in our last reading. The person they had put their hope in had died, and they were now on their own. They were afraid and without hope. They were so overwhelmed with grief that they didn't remember Jesus teaching that these things would happen, and they didn't fully understand the teaching in Scripture.

READ JOHN 20:1–23

"Mary!" Jesus said (v16a).

Checkpoint: Today's reading is really exciting. Everyone is sad and lost because of Jesus' death on the cross. Then there is joy at the sudden realization that Jesus has truly risen from the dead. It is beginning to dawn on them who Jesus really is. On seeing the empty tomb, the disciple who Jesus loved, believed. All the teaching of Jesus and the Scriptures he knew sank in, and he believed. It took Mary a little longer. She stayed behind and wept when Peter and John left. It was while she was crying that Jesus came to her and changed her sorrow to joy. He used her name.

It was a very personal meeting with Jesus. Jesus wants to meet each of us in a personal way. He knows our names and calls us to believe that He rose from the dead so that we may one day be with Him in heaven. As Jesus appeared to the disciples in a locked room, He came to give them a job to do. He was going back to His Father and it was up to them to continue His teaching. Their lives would never be the same. Because Jesus was alive, they did not need to be afraid. He gave them the strength to do what He asked them.

- *Read Romans 4:25. Use your own words to explain why Jesus died and rose again.*
- *Put yourself in the room with the disciples as Jesus appeared. How do you think they reacted?*
- *Jesus turned the disciples' sorrow to joy. How can knowing Jesus is alive today turn our sorrow to joy? Is this the same as being happy?*

Prayer Stop: Thank God that He turns our sorrow into joy. Pray for those you know who may be afraid or sad today and ask God to give them His joy.

DAY 33

On the Way: Jesus had risen from the dead. This had caused a great stir in Jerusalem, and the disciples were afraid of the Jewish leaders. However, Jesus had a special task for them. He didn't want them to stay hidden behind locked doors. Our reading tells us how He helped them to have courage.

READ ACTS 1:1–11

> *But you will receive power when the Holy Spirit comes upon you. And you will be my witnesses, telling people about me everywhere . . . to the ends of the earth* (v8).

Checkpoint: After rising from the dead, Jesus spent forty days teaching and encouraging His disciples before ascending into heaven. They were beginning to fully understand now who Jesus really was, remembering His teaching and the Law they had learned growing up and understanding now how it all tied together. Jesus had a very special task for the apostles. He tells them of it in our key verse today. It is encouraging that Jesus does not just expect them to go alone but is going to provide them with a very special and powerful helper: the Holy Spirit. He warns them not to go until the Holy Spirit had come.

The Holy Spirit is our helper too. God has given us the same help and encouragement He gave His first disciples so that we can carry on the task He gave to them: to be His witness all over the earth.

Imagine the surprise they felt when they saw Jesus suddenly taken up into heaven. It is no wonder they just stand there looking into the sky! It seems that two angels were sent to remind them to get on with what Jesus had left them to do, to "bring them back to earth," we could say. We often need to be reminded to keep going, to continue to do what God wants us to do.

- *Talk about the different feelings the disciples might have had in today's reading.*
- *Do you know anyone who has gone to another country to be a witness for Jesus? To what countries have they gone?*
- *Can you think of any country in which it is difficult to be a witness for Jesus?*

Prayer Stop: Thank God for the Holy Spirit who helps us be His witness. Pray for Christians in the countries where it is difficult to be a witness for Jesus.

DAY 34

On the Way: The disciples returned to Jerusalem, to the place where they were staying. They continued to have prayer meetings with all the believers, and Jesus' mother and brothers met with them. During one of those gatherings, Matthias was chosen as an apostle to replace Judas, who had betrayed Jesus. Matthias had been with the disciples and Jesus all through the time Jesus was on earth.

READ ACTS 2:1–16

> *And we all hear these people speaking in our own languages about the wonderful things God has done!* (v11b).

Checkpoint: What an exciting day! From verses 17–36, Peter explains to the people from the books of the Prophets what was happening and how the Scriptures had taught about Jesus. At the end of the day, verse 41 says that about three thousand people were added to their number. I'm sure the apostles were feeling very excited and perhaps even a bit surprised. God had sent the Holy Spirit as promised and—WOW! People from miles around were hearing the good news of Jesus in their own languages. They would travel home to their own country and start to share what they had learned with others, and the good news of Jesus started to reach the ends of the earth.

Peter was a fisherman; he was not raised to be a public speaker addressing huge crowds. However, the Holy Spirit gave him courage and helped him remember what he knew of God's Word to teach it to the people. God gave the results.

The Holy Spirit is in each one of us if we are Christians and will give us courage and help us remember what we have learned from God's Word too. God will use us to be His witnesses just as He did with the apostles.

- *Can you think of a time you felt afraid to witness for Jesus? How did you feel when you did it anyway?*

- *Can you remember any promises in God's Word that give you courage when you feel afraid like this?*

- *Make it your aim to tell at least one person about Jesus this week.*

Prayer Stop: Thank God for the gift of the Holy Spirit. Pray you will have the courage to tell someone about Jesus this week.

DAY 35

On the Way: Before the Holy Spirit came, the disciples were hiding for fear of being targeted for death as followers of Jesus, but when God sent the Holy Spirit, there was no need for them to hide in fear. They had seen the marvelous things God was doing by bringing thousands of people into His kingdom. So it would seem that, to some extent, normal life carried on. In today's reading, we meet with Peter and John on their way to pray at the temple, as they would have normally done.

READ ACTS 3:1–10

I don't have any silver or gold for you. But I'll give you what I have (v6b).

Checkpoint: Peter and John were going about their normal daily business. Three o'clock was one of the appointed times for prayer in the Jewish faith. It would have been normal for them also to see beggars sitting outside the temple gates, hoping that those going to pray would give them money. I can imagine people perhaps throwing some coins onto their rug without looking at them. However, verse 4 says that Peter and John looked straight at the man. This may have worried him, as he would have been unused to receiving such attention. However, Peter also speaks directly to him, telling him to do something that he has never been able to do.

Can you imagine how the man felt? This was more than he could ever have imagined. In the course of an ordinary day, Peter and John were used by God to do something extraordinary for one man, which resulted in the message of Jesus being shared with many more people (Acts 3:11–26). God can also use us to do extraordinary things for Him as we live our daily lives so that others may see His power and turn to Him.

- *Do you know anyone who doesn't receive much attention from others? How can you help them know the love of Jesus?*

- *God can use ordinary people doing ordinary things to do extraordinary things for Him. How does this make you feel?*

Prayer Stop: Pray for those you know who don't have many friends and ask God to show you how you can be a friend. Pray that you will use every chance God gives you to share the gospel message.

DAY 36

On the Way: The healing of the man in our last reading brought Peter and John a lot of attention. They used this opportunity to continue to share the good news of Jesus, explaining that they did not do these miracles in their own strength but in God's strength. Their teaching disturbed the religious leaders who had them put in prison. Before they were released, they were told to stop speaking in the name of Jesus. Peter said they could not stop. When they got out of prison, they met with believers who praised God and prayed with them. Those in the church began to share all they had with each other. They willingly sold land and used the money to help those in need. It is at this point that we read of Ananias and Sapphira.

READ ACTS 5:1–11

You weren't lying to us but to God! (v4b).

Checkpoint: Ananias and Sapphira saw that the believers were selling their land to help others. They wanted to be part of this but came up with a plan to keep some of the money for themselves while pretending that they were giving all their money to help others. This would make them appear great in front of everyone. However, God knew the truth. They did not seem to understand that God knows what is in our hearts. God knew they were deceiving other people to make themselves appear better than they were. Peter gave them the chance to be honest, since the money was theirs to do with as they pleased. However, Ananias insisted in keeping up the pretense.

As a result of this deceit, both Ananias and his wife died. This seems quite dramatic to us today. However, God wanted to teach His children at the very start of the church that pretending to God was not an option. He knows exactly what goes on in our hearts and our motives for the things we say and do.

- *Can you think of some examples of people doing good things for the wrong reasons today?*
- *Read Psalm 139:1–4, 23–24. How can knowing these verses help us have the right attitude about the things we do?*

Prayer Stop: Use verses 23–24 of Psalm 139 as a prayer. Ask God to forgive you for any wrong attitudes you may have.

DAY 37

On the Way: The apostles continued to preach the good news of Jesus. Nothing held them back; many people were healed from diseases, and more and more men and women believed in the Lord Jesus, causing the church—the body of believers—to grow. However, the leaders of the synagogue did not like their message and had the apostles put in prison. God sent an angel to set them free, and they continued to preach about Jesus. Nothing stopped them from spreading the good news about Jesus, not even being beaten by the authorities. In today's reading, we meet a man called Stephen. He was a godly man who had been chosen to help to look after the widows in the church, overseeing the distribution of food among them with six other men.

READ ACTS 6:8–15; 7:51–8:1

> *None of them could stand against the wisdom and the Spirit with which*
> *Steven spoke* (v10).

Checkpoint: Stephen had been given a job to do in the church. He also served God in other ways; he continued to do miracles and teach about Jesus. He showed great wisdom in all he said, and the religious leaders could not argue with him. This made them so angry that they stoned him to death because of his faith in Jesus.

When people die because of their faith, we call them martyrs. Stephen was the first Christian martyr. In some countries today, being known as a follower of Jesus can be dangerous. Some people are in prison because of it, and some are put to death for it. God gave Stephen special strength as the people were throwing rocks at him. We read in the last few verses that Stephen was aware of God being with him. He was even able to pray for those who were stoning him.

- *What do you think Stephen did when others told lies about him?*
- *How would knowing Deuteronomy 31:6 perhaps have helped Stephen at this point?*
- *What do you find difficult when telling others about Jesus? How can Stephen's story help us? How can Deuteronomy 31:6 help us?*

Prayer Stop: Pray for Christians who are in prison because they follow Jesus. Pray that God would free them and protect their families. Pray that God would help us to be bold in telling others about Him.

DAY 38

On the Way: At the end of our reading yesterday, we saw Saul watching Stephen being stoned. He was a very highly trained Jewish leader and was known in the area for his violence against the followers of Jesus, taking them prisoner and even having them killed. Today's reading begins with him heading to Damascus to continue his mission.

READ ACTS 9:1–19

> *But the Lord said, "Go, for Saul is my chosen instrument"* (v15a).

Checkpoint: I am sure Saul had not given any thought to following Jesus himself! His mission was to stop those who believed in Jesus from spreading their faith. So I am sure it came as a mighty surprise when a great light suddenly shone around him. Then he heard the voice of the Lord. There was no mistaking that God was also on a mission to meet with Saul that day. Saul had no option but to take notice; the light had been so bright that he had lost his sight. He could not have carried on as normal even if he wanted to.

When God calls us to follow Him, we cannot ignore Him. He does not give up on us. God had a very special task for Saul: He has a special task for each one of us too.

Ananias lived in Damascus and had certainly heard of Saul's reputation. So when God told him to go and visit Saul, we can understand him having a few questions. This Ananias obviously knew God well and trusted Him completely, because he did go and visit Saul as instructed. He then discovered with great happiness and relief, I am sure, that God has the amazing power to completely turn people's lives around. Imagine the amazement Jesus' followers would have felt when they heard Ananias' story. God still has the same power to change people's lives today.

- *Talk about some of the awesome things you have experienced or heard of God doing. Why do you think, like Ananias, we sometimes find it hard to believe?*

- *Are there people among your family or friends who seem like they will never become followers of Jesus? Mention them by name to God in your prayer time today.*

Prayer Stop: Pray for those you mentioned in the discussion points. Pray that you will hear and obey when God asks you to trust Him for something difficult.

DAY 39

On the Way: In Acts 10, we meet a Roman centurion called Cornelius. He gave to the poor and prayed regularly. One day as he was praying, he saw an angel of God who told him to send for a man named Peter, who was staying in Joppa. So he sent three men to fetch Peter. Cornelius did not know it, but Peter was Jesus' disciple whom we met earlier in Acts. Our reading today concerns Peter's own vision just before the men arrive at his door.

READ ACTS 10:9–23

> *Do not call something unclean if God has made it clean* (v15b).

Checkpoint: Peter was Jewish and had lived by Jewish tradition all his life. Jews were very strict about the food they could eat and the people they could meet. So when Peter had this vision, he found it hard to understand what God was telling him. But when three Gentile men arrived at his door, it soon became very clear to him. God is not interested in what nationality we are or our traditions; He is only interested in our hearts. Cornelius feared God; however, he did not know that God had given him a way to become His child. God wanted Peter to go and tell Cornelius the good news of Jesus. First, Peter had to learn that God wanted *all* people to come to Him, not just the Jews. This was why God had given him the vision. He realized that it is the sin in our hearts that makes us unclean, not our nationality.

We all have traditions and rules that we live by; it could be things we don't watch on TV or places we don't go; it could be not doing certain things on a Sunday or even not eating certain food for whatever reason. Not all tradition is bad, but we do need to be aware that sometimes it may stand in the way of our being obedient to God. Are you willing, like Peter, to have your way of life challenged in order to spread the good news of Jesus?

- *Cornelius lived a devout (religious) life but he did not know God initially. How can religion stop people from being true followers of Jesus?*

Prayer Stop: Pray that God would show you the things in your lives that may hinder others from hearing the gospel.

DAY 40

On the Way: Peter continued to tell everyone the good news of Jesus, and the church grew. Saul (now known as Paul) also became well known among the churches as a special teacher. He was sent out on a journey round the churches with a man named Barnabas, teaching all the new Christians more about the Scriptures. The government and Jewish leaders did not like the spread of the gospel. On several occasions, the apostles were put in prison. Today we join Paul in prison with another Christian named Silas.

READ ACTS 16:16–34

Believe in the Lord Jesus and you will be saved (v31a).

Checkpoint: The masters of the slave girl were making money from her being possessed by an evil spirit and telling people what was going to happen to them. Even though what the girl said concerning Paul and Silas was correct, Paul did not want the truth of the gospel to be mixed up with any "magic" fortune-telling and commanded the spirit to leave her. Angry at losing their money-making power, the girl's master had Paul and Silas thrown in prison. Paul and Silas stood firm in doing what was right and yet ended up in prison. However, they did not let this prevent them from praising God and praying.

As they were worshipping God, the other prisoners heard. When the earthquake struck, the prison officer saw the power of God at work. He and others became followers of Jesus as a result of this. Sometimes we don't understand why we need to endure difficult situations, but if we trust God and continue to praise Him in these situations, He can use them to bring glory to His name.

- *In what ways can the truth of the gospel be confused today?*
- *What is the difference between praising God in a situation and praising Him for something? How can we then praise God at difficult times?*

Prayer Stop: Ask God to give you wisdom to know when the truth is being confused or mixed up with things that are not right. Pray for anyone you know who is facing difficulties, that they may still be able to praise God.

DAY 41

On the Way: Paul and Silas continued to travel, teaching the good news of Jesus wherever they went. Many Jews and Gentiles believed in Jesus, but as usual, there were others who did not and were intent on harming them. It was Paul's custom to go and teach in the synagogue wherever he went. Today, he meets a man from Italy.

READ ACTS 18:1–4, 18–28

He proved to be of great benefit to those who, by God's grace, believed (v27b).

Checkpoint: Paul met Aquila and his wife Priscilla when he went to Corinth. They had recently come from Italy. Since they had the same trade as Paul, he was able to stay with them and work with them. I am sure that was a time when Paul would have taught them a lot about the Scriptures and following Jesus. By the time Paul was moving on, they would have understood a lot more about the Scriptures and what it meant to follow Jesus. When they heard Apollos preaching, although he knew the Scriptures, they saw that he did not fully understand the way of God. They were able to teach him more of what the Scriptures meant. They did not get into an argument because he was not quite right; they just explained the Scriptures to him more fully, as Paul had done for them. This meant that Apollos then went on to teach these things to others. So we see the Word of God spreading by others teaching the gospel now, not just the apostles.

- *Who has taught you about the Bible and following Jesus?*
- *Aquila and Priscilla treated Apollos in a loving way and taught him more of the Scriptures. How do you think Apollos would have felt after this?*
- *What was the result of this? (Acts 18:27–28)*
- *Can you think of attitudes that may make it difficult for others to learn from us?*

Prayer Stop: Thank God for those who have taught you about Jesus and His Word. (Use their names as you thank God for them.) Pray that you will share what you have learned so that others will get to know God better. Pray that you will have the right attitude as you do this.

DAY 42

On the Way: Paul continued traveling, teaching people about following Jesus and encouraging those in the churches. He encountered many difficulties. There were riots in Ephesus; in Jerusalem he was arrested and had to stand trial; the Jews also plotted to kill him; he was sent to the Roman governor; and as he was sailing to Italy, they encountered storms, long delays, and an exciting shipwreck. In every circumstance, Paul always made sharing the good news of Jesus his priority. Eventually, still under guard, he arrived in Rome.

READ ACTS 28:17–31

Some were persuaded by the things he said, but others did not believe (v24).

Checkpoint: Paul had seen God do some amazing things on his journey to Rome. He was traveling as a prisoner to appeal to Caesar because of his arrest. However, this did not prevent him living his life for God. Paul continued to share the gospel every chance he had.

Sometimes we can let circumstances discourage us, and we forget that our priority is to let others know of Jesus regardless. We can show others Jesus' love and power by our attitudes and the way we react to difficult circumstances.

When he arrived at Rome, Paul took the opportunity to meet the Jews there and explain to them from their Law that Jesus was the Messiah. Our key verse tells us that some believed and some didn't. When we share the gospel with others, some will believe but often, as Paul experienced, others will choose not to. We must just be faithful to God, telling the truth of Jesus to everyone. It is the Holy Spirit who can open peoples' hearts to believe.

- *Paul did not let being a prisoner stop him from sharing the gospel. What things might we feel could be a hindrance to our telling others about Jesus? (For example, being sick)*
- *How do you think Paul felt when some people didn't believe his message? Have you ever felt this way?*

Prayer Stop: Pray that you will have the courage to tell others about Jesus in every situation. Pray for those you know who have chosen not to believe in Jesus so far.

LETTERS OF THE NEW TESTAMENT

Most of the books in the New Testament are letters to churches and people from Apostle Paul and some other apostles. They were written for many different reasons—some to encourage others, some to teach them what God's Word taught about living to please God, and others to correct mistakes or wrong teaching.

ROMANS

Paul wrote this letter to the church at Rome, which had mainly Gentile Christians in it. He wrote to them to explain the way of salvation, to tell them how this should affect their lives and to explain how God had a plan for salvation for both Jews and Gentiles.

DAY 1

On the Way: Paul introduces himself as he starts this letter. He then introduces the good news of Jesus and the fact that the apostles preach this message faithfully not only to the Jews but now also to the Gentiles. These Christians were among those Gentiles.

READ ROMANS 1:1–10, 18–22

> *And you are included among those Gentiles who have been called to belong to Jesus Christ* (v6).

Checkpoint: Paul starts his letter by letting the Roman Christians know of his great love for the good news of Jesus and his love and care for them too. In verses 1–5, he tells them he has a special task to share that good news with those who are Gentiles, and in verse 9 he tells us he preaches the gospel with his whole heart. He puts all his energy into it. He also prays for them at all times, not just at certain times; they seem to be constantly in his thoughts and prayers.

God has a special job for each one of us. Whatever it is, we should do it with our whole heart, making the good news of Jesus a top priority in our lives. We should pray constantly for those things that are on our minds and not just let our thoughts drift.

Paul moves on from his introduction to explain why people need God's salvation. He states that if people looked, they could see all the evidence they needed for God, but instead they choose to look to the things they make themselves. They know about God but have tried to make God fit into their thinking instead of worshipping Him because He is so far beyond our understanding. Verse 18 talks about God showing His anger because of this. God is not angry like we are, but He is so holy that He cannot look at sin. Our sin separates us from Him. Paul explains later on how God has given us an answer to this problem.

- *What are the top priorities in your life at the moment?*
- *In your experience, how have people tried to make God fit their thinking today?*

Prayer Stop: Pray that God will help you make His good news top priority in your life. Worship God for how great He is and for how He shows us that.

DAY 2

On the Way: Paul continues to write about how everyone has sinned and therefore deserves punishment. The Jews are not exempt from this because they have a special Law from God; they break this Law and so are as guilty of sin as everyone else. At the end of chapter 2, Paul writes that actually keeping the Law will not save us because we are not able to keep every part of it. He says that God is more interested in our change of heart.

MEMORY VERSE

For everyone has sinned; we all fall short of God's glorious standard. Yet God freely and graciously declares we are righteous. He did this through Christ Jesus when he freed us from the penalty of our sins.

~ Romans 3:23–24

READ ROMANS 3:21–31

Checkpoint: Let's give a little thought to the meaning of our memory verse. As in the first two chapters, Paul continues to tell the Romans that it doesn't matter who you are, Jew or Gentile; no one can reach God's standard by keeping rules alone. In our reading, he starts to tell them of the way that God has provided for everyone to become right with God. It starts with verse 22: we need to believe and have faith in Jesus Christ. (Faith is being absolutely sure of what we hope for even though we cannot see it (Heb. 11:1).

When we put our faith in Jesus, then we can be made right with God. Grace is the blessings God gives us even though we don't deserve them. We do not deserve to be right with God, but because of what Jesus has done, we can be. So, by being sure that Jesus is the Son of God and believing in Him, we are made right with God through Jesus rescuing us from our sin. This is not what we deserve but a blessing from God.

- *Wow! How does that make you feel?*
- *The Jews tried to please God by obeying rules. What things do people try to please God with today?*

Prayer Stop: Thank God for His grace to us: giving us what we do not deserve. Thank God for sending Jesus so that through Him we can have our sins forgiven.

DAY 3

On the Way: Having written about having our sins forgiven through faith in Jesus, Paul writes about Abraham. The Jews used Abraham as an example of someone who was friends with God because of what he did. However, Paul explains to them that the Scriptures say Abraham believed God; that is why he could have his sins cancelled. It was not because he kept the Jewish rules. In fact, God promised to bless him before those were even written!

Paul wrote this so that the Jews meeting with the Roman church did not try to make them follow their rules as well.

READ ROMANS 5:1–8

When we were utterly helpless, Christ came at just the right time and died for us sinners (v6).

Checkpoint: Having made sure that the church in Rome understood fully that no one can do anything by themselves alone to make themselves right with God, Paul tells us of the solution in our key verse: when we were still sinners, Christ died for us. Not because we had already started to put things right ourselves, but before we could do anything about it, God put the answer in place. God's love is so great for us. Being sure of this amazing love, we can praise God for all He has done for us—not only for the good things but also for when we face difficulties. We know that God is in control and that the problems we face are able to change us to become more like He wants us to be. He can use problems for good in our lives if we let Him.

- *God wants to use the hard times we face to help us grow more like He wants us to be. How might knowing that change the way we react to problems?*

- *How does it make you feel to know that Jesus took the punishment for your sin?*

Prayer Stop: Pray about any difficulty you or someone you know is facing just now. Ask God to help you/them see how He can use it for good. Thank God for sending Jesus to die for our sin.

DAY 4

On the Way: Paul goes on to explain that as we are all affected by sin because Adam sinned in the beginning, so we can all be made right with God through faith in Jesus, His death, and His resurrection. This does not mean that we can all just continue to sin as we please.

READ ROMANS 6:1–7

Since we have died to sin, how can we continue to live in it? (v2b).

Checkpoint: God is willing to forgive us. When we commit our lives to Him, the influence sin has on us is broken, and we don't want to keep disobeying God. Our life has become new, like the new life that Jesus had after He rose from the dead. When people became Christians in Paul's day, they usually were baptized quickly after that. The two events seemed to be joined together. Baptism was when the person was put under the water (briefly) and brought back up again. Paul explains that baptism is a picture of what happens when we become Christians. We are buried from our old life of sin (under the water) and then we rise again to a new life with Jesus. We leave our old sin nature behind. That is what baptism demonstrates.

- *Some of the Romans were saying that because of God's grace, it didn't matter if they kept on sinning. How did Paul explain to the Romans that this was not right?*

- *Sometimes we find it hard to do what pleases God even though we are Christians. Why do you think this might be?*

- *If you have not been baptized since accepting Jesus as your Savior, you may want to think about doing this.*

Prayer Stop: Praise God that sin does not control us when we are Christians. God is willing to forgive our sins. Pray that God will help you understand more about what it means to be a Christian.

DAY 5

On the Way: In the rest of chapter 6, Paul continues to tell the Roman Christians that because they have a new life in Jesus, they should not let sinful things rule them. He encourages them to do what pleases God, which leads to holiness and eternal life. He tells them that the Law was given so that they would know what was sinful. If we did not have a commandment saying, for example, "Do not covet," then we would not know that being jealous of others' possessions is sinful.

READ ROMANS 7:14–24

> *For I want to do what is right, but I don't do it. Instead, I do what I hate* (v15b).

Checkpoint: In our reading, Paul continues to show us how God's Law is good but can only show us sin in our lives; it cannot rescue us from that sin. Paul tells the Romans that he struggles with doing things that he really doesn't want to do. It is as if something else is working in him.

This is comforting for us. I know that at times I find myself doing things, saying things, or thinking things that I know do not please God, and I am sure that you do too! Paul explains that this is sin at work in us. Our minds want to please God, but the sinful nature in us does something different. This is not an excuse to sin. In verse 25, Paul shows us that we can be rescued through Jesus. This has been his message thus far in this letter to the Romans: Jesus can rescue us from the effects of sin in our lives. The end of verse 25 says that in our minds we become a slave to God's Law. That means that we become determined to live as God's Word directs. However, we must understand what is happening when we do sin so that we know where to turn to put it right.

- *If we let sin rule our lives, what is the result? (Romans 6:23)*
- *Give some examples from your own life of verse 15.*
- *How can we let God's Law rule our minds?*

Prayer Stop: Pray that God would show you any sin in your life and then ask God to forgive you. Pray that you would know God's Word and let it rule your mind.

DAY 6

On the Way: In chapter 8, Paul tells us that Christ sets us free from the death that sin brings. As we said yesterday, the Law could only point out the sin in us, but Jesus can set us free from it. He talks about those who let sin rule in them, having their minds fixed on sinful things, but if we have our mind fixed on what pleases God, then we will know peace in our life. As Christians, God's Spirit lives in us and makes us children of God. Because of this, we have some very special privileges.

READ ROMANS 8:18, 26–27, 34–39

And I am convinced that nothing can ever separate us from God's love (v38a).

Checkpoint: The first privilege is that no matter how difficult things are here on earth, we can look forward to sharing in God's glory when we get to heaven. When we are suffering difficulties, we can focus on what God has in store for us; this is our hope. Just as He helps us when we are suffering, so He helps us when we are tempted to do wrong (Rom. 8:26).

Sometimes things in life are very confusing, and we do not know how to pray. We can take comfort in knowing that the Spirit of God prays for us at these times. Verses 37–39 remind us that when we suffer or when we feel we don't know what to do, we can be confident that we will overcome this because nothing at all, no matter how big, can ever put us beyond the reach of God's love. How amazing is that? To know without a doubt that there is nothing in heaven or earth that can take God's love from us.

- *How do you feel, knowing that we can't be separated from God's love and that the Holy Spirit speaks for us when we don't know how to pray?*

- *How does it help you face the things that are difficult in your life?*

- *Have there been times when you did not know how to pray about something? How can verses 26–27 bring comfort to us in those times?*

Prayer Stop: Thank God for the privileges we have as His children, for the hope of heaven, and for the comfort of His continued love.

DAY 7

On the Way: Over the next few chapters in Romans, Paul talks about how he really wants the Jews to know Jesus as their Savior. He highlights the fact that they are very religious, trying to keep the rules. However, in Romans 10:9, he explains that it is not keeping rules that makes you right with God, but believing and telling others that Jesus is your Lord and knowing that God raised Him from the dead. Having spent a lot of time explaining God's plan for salvation, Paul now moves on to explain how this should affect our lives.

READ ROMANS 12:1–10

And so, dear brothers and sisters, I plead with you to give your bodies to God because of all he has done for you (v1a).

Checkpoint: Paul says that as a result of all he has taught concerning God's salvation, we now need to take action. Jews offered sacrifices at the temple for various reasons according to the Law of Moses. One sacrifice was not enough to cover a lifetime of sin.

However, Paul is encouraging the Christians (and us) to think of our lives as a sacrifice to God, not as a one-time event but as a continual, living sacrifice. As long as we are alive, we can give glory to God in all we do. Paul goes on to say that each individual has been given different jobs to do. We all are not meant to offer the same service to God; we are to do what He has given us the gifts and talent to do as individuals and encourage others to do so as well.

- *How does verse 2 tell us we can be changed? What do you think this means in practice?*

- *Why is this so important for us as Christians?*

- *How can we put verse 10 into practice? Perhaps you could carry out one of your ideas this week.*

Prayer Stop: Thank God that we are part of His family and that He has given each of us a special gift to serve Him. Pray that God would help you to know His will for your life and pray that God would help you put others before yourself.

DAY 8

On the Way: Having written about continually giving God glory in the way we live our lives, Paul gives practical examples of how we can accomplish this at the end of chapter 12. He mentions actions that go against what might seem normal and acceptable to others who are not Christians. He talks about sharing what we have with those who have less, not retaliating when hurt, about being happy to mix with those who may be less popular. This chapter deals with how we treat the people we are in contact with daily. In chapter 13, he moves on to talk about our attitude to those who are in charge of us.

READ ROMANS 13:1–8

> *For all authority comes from God, and those in positions of authority have been placed there by God* (v1b).

Checkpoint: Our Christian life does not just affect those to whom we are close. Paul writes in this chapter that it should also affect our attitude to those in charge of us. These verses do not mean that we need to agree with everything our government says. That would be impossible because we—and they—are sinful human beings! Submitting to their authority means obeying their laws. Paul writes that we should obey them because having rulers was God's good idea to keep order in society.

Paul is not teaching that rulers will always do what is right—we all know that there are some who definitely do not rule well—but he is talking about God's ideal example of rulers and what our attitude and behavior should be toward them. So often we hear people complain about having to pay taxes or parking fines. These things are in place to help keep order, and we should show respect for that as Christians.

- *Even though we do not break the law, in what ways might our attitude not honor our leaders?*
- *Are there any ways you could improve your attitude toward your government?*
- *We know of governments today that persecute Christians. Do you think it's possible for Christians in these nations to disagree with and yet still respect their leaders? (Perhaps Acts 4:18–19 and 5:29 may help.)*

Prayer Stop: Pray that God will help you show respect to your government. Pray for Christians who live in countries whose leaders persecute them. Pray for their protection and witness in that land.

DAY 9

On the Way: At the end of chapter 13, Paul keeps encouraging the Christians to focus on the fact that Jesus is coming back; their lives should be very different from those around who do not follow Jesus. The challenge is the same for us today.

Paul finishes the letter to the Romans by reminding Christians to accept one another and not be harsh with those who are weaker in their faith. Some Christians were criticizing others because they refused to eat certain foods. Paul says we need to show understanding toward each other.

MEMORY VERSE

Therefore, accept each other just as Christ has accepted you so that God will be given glory.

~ Romans 15:7

READ ROMANS 14:19–15:7

Checkpoint: Some people require certain things to help them stay strong in their faith. For others, that same thing may not be so important. Often we are tempted to criticize those who think differently from us. We need to remember that everyone has areas in their faith that they are strong in as well as areas of weakness. In verse 19, Paul tells us we need to concentrate on building each other up, accepting that some things are important to others that may not be so important to us and vice versa. If we know that drinking wine or taking part in certain activities causes our fellow Christian difficulty, then we should not boast about the fact that we have no problem with it. This builds on what Paul wrote in chapter 13 when he taught that we should think more of others than ourselves. So instead of criticizing others for what they do or do not do as Christians, we should praise God with them for what we can share together: the fact that Jesus has saved us.

- *What are some of the things that you criticize other Christians for doing? What do you do that others may criticize? (We mentioned two examples in Checkpoint.)*
- *What can you do this week that will help you remember to accept the way others think?*

Prayer Stop: Pray that God will make you aware of any wrong attitude toward other Christians. Pray that your relationship with other Christians will bring praise to God.

1 AND 2 CORINTHIANS

The letters of Paul to the church at Corinth were written because Paul had heard of difficulties that had come into the church—disagreements and false teaching. He wrote them a letter to help and encourage them to start putting things right.

DAY 10

On the Way: Paul starts his first letter to Corinth by thanking God for all that the Christians there have because they follow Christ. He reminds them that they have every gift they need from God and that He is faithful. He then immediately starts to deal with the problems he has heard of. When we face difficulties, it is good to be reminded of God's faithfulness to us. It is also necessary to deal directly with difficulties and not avoid them. He starts by mentioning the divisions that have appeared in the church.

READ 1 CORINTHIANS 3:1–15

For we are both God's workers. And you are God's field. You are God's building (v9).

Checkpoint: Christians in Corinth were arguing about whether Paul or Apollos was greater. This was causing division and jealousy. Paul writes to say that they are focused on the wrong thing. It is not the human leaders but God who should be our focus. Our church leaders are servants of God, doing what God has called them to do. We must learn from them but allow God to change us through the power of His Spirit in us. This means that we can then serve God with the gifts He has given us, bringing praise to God and encouragement to our leaders. By growing in this way, we build on the foundation that is laid in our lives when we become Christians. By being taken up with worldly arguments, the Corinthian Christians were not building anything that will last in their lives.

It is tempting sometimes to put our Christian leaders on a pedestal. However, Paul reminds us that it is God who should take that place in our lives so that we grow to be mature Christians.

- *What evidence can you see in churches today of the divisions Paul was talking about?*
- *What can you actively do to help overcome this?*
- *How are you building on the foundation of Christ in your life?*

Prayer Stop: Thank God that you are the temple of the Holy Spirit (1 Cor. 3:16). Pray that you will allow God to challenge and change you so that you fully accomplish His plans for you. Pray for your church leaders.

DAY 11

On the Way: Paul continues to challenge the Corinthians not to think more highly of some Christians than others and not to worry about what other Christians think of what they do. It is what God thinks that matters. He mentions that Timothy is coming to visit them to remind them of his teaching. At the end of chapter 4, he writes that God's kingdom is not just about talk and power; it is about seeing the evidence of God at work in our lives. He moves on to challenge sexual sin in the church.

READ 1 CORINTHIANS 5:9–13; 6:18–20

> *You do not belong to yourself, for God bought you at a high price. So you must honor God with your body (6:19b–20).*

Checkpoint: Sexual immorality occurs when we behave in a way that disrespects and dishonors other people and our own bodies in a very intimate and personal way. God has given very clear guidelines in His Word for how we should treat our own and other people's bodies. If we go against this, then we are sinning. Those who are not Christians may not have this high standard of respect for intimacy; we cannot be responsible for their behavior. However, Paul is writing to those who are Christians and warns that those in the church should never be connected to such behavior.

If we know of someone who is involved in sexual immorality, then that individual must be made aware that his or her behavior is sinful. Paul goes as far as to say that we must have nothing to do with people who continually live in this way. As Christians, we have the Holy Spirit living in us; if we are involved in sexual sin, then we are destroying not only our respect for our own and others' bodies but also our relationship with God.

- *What kinds of sexual temptations do we as Christians regularly come across?*
- *First Corinthians 6:18 tells us to run away from sexual sin. How can you put this into practice?*
- *How can meditating on our key verse today help us overcome sexual temptation?*

Prayer Stop: Pray that God would help you and other Christian friends to be pure in the way you think and behave toward others. Check out your thinking. Ask God to forgive you and help you to stop if you find that you are thinking impure thoughts about others.

DAY 12

On the Way: Having corrected some of the problems in Corinth, Paul now answers some of their questions. He writes about marriage and about whether it is right to eat meat sacrificed in the Temple. He says that those who teach God's Word should be given enough to live on and reminds us to think about how God has acted in the past when His children sinned against Him and let that be a warning to us. Chapter 10:11–13 remind us that God will always help us find a way out when we are being tempted to sin. Paul moves on to teach the Corinthians about their worship.

READ 1 CORINTHIANS 11:17–33

That is why you should examine yourself before eating the bread and drinking the cup (v28).

Checkpoint: It seems that when the church at Corinth met for communion, it had become a big selfish party. Some folk were eating and drinking too much, while others were not getting anything to eat; they all seemed to be thinking only of themselves. Paul reminds them that Jesus pointed to His death when He shared this supper with His disciples, and when we share it together, we should also remember Jesus' death for us. Communion is not as much about celebrating but about remembering. So Paul recommends that we take a look at what is going on in our hearts before we take part in communion. When we share communion, we are telling the story of Jesus' death, remembering the sacrifice Jesus made for us personally and remembering that we are part of the Church, the body of Christ. As Christians, we are all part of that body, and our behavior when we meet together should reflect that.

- *In what ways can we take communion "unworthily"? (1 Corinthians 11:27)*
- *What things distract you when you meet for communion? How can you overcome this?*
- *How did Paul encourage the church at Corinth to recognize the body of Christ at communion? Can you think of ways that we can do that in our churches?*

Prayer Stop: Take time to thank God for sending Jesus to die for us. Pray that your heart and mind will not be distracted when you meet with the church for communion.

Practical Application: If you are reading this with others, you may want to share communion together.

DAY 13

On the Way: Paul is aware the Corinthians used to worship idols and were now concerned about how they would know the Word of God. In chapter 12 Paul tells them to look at what their teachers taught about Jesus, and then they would know the truth. We too can use this test. He mentions how God's Spirit gives each Christian different gifts and abilities in order to help His church and continues his theme of the body of Christ.

READ 1 CORINTHIANS 12:12–27

All of you together are Christ's body, and each of you is a part of it (v27).

Checkpoint: The picture of the church being a body is brilliant. Our bodies are made up of thousands of different parts, some very obvious and some not so noticeable, but each part has a vital function in our daily life. As Christians, we are all different, like the parts of the body. Some folks have very obvious roles in the church, and some not so noticeable, but all are very necessary if the church is to work as God intended.

Some of the things in our body seem so small and insignificant, yet if they are not there or are hurting, our whole body cannot function right. Have you ever had a toothache? A small hole in a small tooth can make you feel so bad. So it is with the body of Christ; we all need each other. Those in public roles cannot do their job right if those with less public roles are not doing theirs right. We must be ready and willing to do the job God has called us to do and remember that He sees us doing it even if no one else does. The effects of us serving God well, even if it seems a small role to us, will be felt in every area of the church.

- *Think about which part of the body you would be, e.g., are you someone who helps out? You could be a hand. Do you sing? Then you may be a mouth.*

- *Think about your own body not having that part; how would it affect you?*

- *How can you encourage others to play their part in the body of Christ?*

Prayer Stop: Thank God for the gifts He has given you. Pray that you would be faithful in serving God.

DAY 14

On the Way: Paul closes this first letter to the Corinthian church by reminding them of the gospel and the effect it should have on their lives and worship. He reminded them that Jesus rose from the dead and is coming back again and how that should spur them on to live their lives to please Him. In chapter 13, Paul deals with the fact that no matter what we do, if we do not have love in our lives, it all means nothing.

READ 1 CORINTHIANS 13:1–13

But love will last forever (v8b).

Checkpoint: This chapter tells us what love is, what love is not, and that if our lives are not motivated by love, then all we do and say is worthless.

So often we value people by what they do or how popular they are. If we see them doing good things or having lots of friends, we think they are great. This chapter tells us the opposite. It mentions that no matter how heroic our actions are, if we do not act with the motive of love, then there is no point to our heroic actions at all!

The word used for love in this chapter shows that we should be completely concerned with the needs of others and not ourselves. It is a decision we make, not a feeling we have. As a result, it will not matter if those to whom we show love do not return the compliment; it will not affect our behavior toward them. This is true love, the love that Jesus loved us with, and it is what we are called by God to do if we truly follow Him and want to make a difference for Him.

- *Look at verses 4–8 again. How does the love we hear about in the media today differ from the love we read of here? (Be specific.)*

- *What areas of true love is God challenging you with today?*

- *Why is love the greatest of "faith, hope, and love"?*

Prayer Stop: Thank God for His unfailing love for us. Pray that God will work in your life to help you love others more as He wants you to love them.

DAY 15

On the Way: Today we start the second letter to Corinth that Paul wrote. This was as a result of false teachers coming into the church and teaching that the things Paul taught were not true. Paul urges the Christians there to remember the life-changing message he had preached and to see how his life lived up to it. Sometimes when others put doubt in our minds, it is good for us to remember the life-changing message of the gospel.

READ 2 CORINTHIANS 1:3–11

We have placed our confidence in him (v10b).

Checkpoint: Paul thanks God for the comfort he has received from the Holy Spirit during times of hardship. He realizes that because of this, he has been able to bring comfort to others as they have suffered. He encourages the church at Corinth to understand this too. In verses 8–9, we can see they faced enormous fear and dangers, and yet they knew God protected them. Paul could see that they faced these huge dangers in order that they would depend on God and not themselves. They did not know and could not control the result of these sufferings, yet they were not overcome by anxiety.

Sometimes when we face hard times, we panic and become very anxious. Paul encourages us to have a *firm* hope in God. When we experience the peace He gives at such times, we are able to tell others what God has done for us, encouraging them when they face difficulties to trust in God too. When we know others have prayed for us, as the Corinthians had for Paul, it is good to share the answer to their prayer with them. When we see that God has answered our prayers for others, we can praise God and be encouraged to continue to pray for others.

- *When have you been aware of God's comfort and strength in your life?*

Prayer Stop: Praise God for His comfort and protection. Pray for the person you are going to encourage this week.

Practical Application: Think of specific ways you can encourage others who face difficulties. Pick one and use it to encourage someone this week.

DAY 16

On the Way: Paul mentions that he wants to come and visit Corinth again but has had to change his plans. This gives them a chance to put right the things he had to write to them about previously and so will mean his visit will be happy. He reminds them that they need to forgive those who have repented from doing wrong, not hold their sin against them forever. He also reminds them that the message they speak is truth and that God is using it to change people's lives. He points to God's greatness and man's weakness.

MEMORY VERSE

We now have this light shining in our hearts, but we ourselves are like fragile jars of clay containing this great treasure. This makes it clear that our great power is from God, not from ourselves.

~2 Corinthians 4:7

READ 2 CORINTHIANS 4:1–12

Checkpoint: As a servant of God, Paul does not try to trick anyone into believing the gospel message. He sets the truth out plainly and does not boast about himself in his preaching. He understands that it is God's glory that is important. In those days, it was normal to keep treasure in clay jars so that it did not attract attention to the treasure. Paul is likening himself to a clay jar, saying that it is the amazing power of God that calls people to follow Him, nothing to do with Paul himself. When we tell others about Jesus, we must not draw attention to ourselves but to Him.

Paul continues to write about how they face troubles constantly but do not give in because God never abandons them. These troubles give God an opportunity to demonstrate His great power at work. They give us opportunity to demonstrate faith in God. Difficulties bring us opportunities to grow and share the good news of Jesus.

- *In what ways might we be tempted to draw attention to ourselves rather than Jesus when we share the gospel?*

- *How can difficulties help us demonstrate our faith?*

- *Can you think of some examples of false teachers today?*

Prayer Stop: Praise God that He gives us opportunities to share the gospel. Pray that you will always speak more of Jesus than yourself at these times.

DAY 17

On the Way: Paul writes that, through every trial, he keeps his heart focused on God. He realizes that no matter what happens to his body here on earth, one day in heaven he will have a new body that will not suffer pain. This helps him to focus on sharing the gospel, no matter how difficult it becomes. His focus is on pleasing God, not others.

READ 2 CORINTHIANS 6:24–7:1

Don't team up with those who are unbelievers (6:14a).

Checkpoint: In Bible times, farmers ploughed their fields by binding teams of oxen together with a special wooden harness called a yoke. This kept the oxen working together at the same speed and in the same direction. Then the field became ready to plant with crops. There were teachers coming into the church in Corinth who were not teaching the truth, and Paul urged the believers not to team up with these men because they did not have the same goal in mind. Those men were looking for important positions, but Paul had reminded the Christians that it was only God and His work that was important and deserved all their attention. So he used an example of something they knew about to explain why they should not work closely with those people.

If we are working as a team to share the good news of Jesus with others, it is important that we have the same goal and the same principles as those with whom we are working. If we don't, this will lead to confusion and in turn will take the attention away from God.

- *The Christians in Corinth would understand about teams of oxen. What examples of working as a team are relevant to our lives today? (Think of sports teams, etc.)*

- *What are the important things to have in common when we are part of a mission/ outreach team?*

- *Does this mean that we can never team up to do anything with those who are not believers? (1 Corinthians 5:9–11 may help you think about this.)*

Prayer Stop: Pray that God would help you know the right people to team up with in sharing His good news. Pray for unity in mission/outreach teams that you know of or are part of.

DAY 18

On the Way: Paul encourages the Corinthians to stay focused on the truth. He is also encouraged by them because he has heard that they have put into practice the things he had previously written to them. This shows they were growing in their faith. He is happy to see this and wants them to keep on growing in their faith. Until we reach heaven, we will never arrive at a point where we don't need to grow. So Paul encourages the Corinthians to keep going.

READ 2 CORINTHIANS 9:6–15

> *You must each decide in your heart how much to give* (v7a).

Checkpoint: This church seems to be a very generous church. Paul is encouraged by the way they are so happy to give to others even though they don't have much themselves. It is God who supplies all that we have and blesses us with good things. We should be willing to share what we have with others so that they will be blessed and will in turn give thanks to God.

Paul does not offer rules about how our giving should affect our bank account, only how it should affect our heart. Again we see the principle that God is more interested in our attitudes than in our actions. If our attitudes are right, our actions will be right. In the New Testament, there is no given amount that we are told is right to give. Jesus mentions the widow who gave all that she had, and Paul mentions in chapter 8 about the Corinthians being extremely poor yet giving more than they were able. So we should follow what God has put on our hearts, remembering that if our attitude in giving is right, then the action of our giving will be right as a result of that.

- *What does verse 11 tell us about our attitude to being rich? How is this different from the world's view of wealth?*

- *What are the results of generosity? (Verses 12–14 may help you answer this question.)*

Prayer Stop: Pray that God would help your attitude toward giving to be cheerful and generous.

Practical Application: Ask God to show you someone who needs something that you can supply this week. Bless that person with a generous gift.

DAY 19

On the Way: As we come to the end of the letters to the church in Corinth, Paul is keen to emphasise that it is God he is serving; all he achieves he does because God gives him the ability to do so, not because he has the strength himself. He does not want the believers to follow the false teachers who really want the people to follow them rather than God. He warns the Corinthians quite sternly against all that those men say and do.

READ 2 CORINTHIANS 13:1–10

> *We are glad to seem weak if it helps to show that you are actually strong. We pray that you will become mature* (v9).

Checkpoint: Paul was preparing the Corinthian Church for his next visit. He writes very strongly that he wants to find them growing in the truth and living for God. He reminds them of all that he has been through so that they might hear and believe the truth. His own reputation is not important to him. His prayer is for them to grow in their faith; this is what he wants most of all.

Paul writes to them in the same kind of way that a Christian dad might write to his son or daughter who has gone away to university and has been tempted to become involved in a lifestyle not in keeping with the Christian life in which they were raised. Paul encourages the Corinthians to look at their own hearts to see if they truly are following Christ, not just by what they say, but also by their attitude.

- *Having seen the Corinthians being tempted to follow false teachers, what things can we do to make sure that we are not also tempted to stray?*

- *How do you think Paul felt when he heard of the things the Corinthians were saying? How did he react?*

- *How do you feel when others criticize your godly leaders? How should we react?*

Prayer Stop: Pray for those young adults you know who have moved away from home. Pray that they will become stronger in their faith. Pray for wisdom to know when others are not teaching the truth.

GALATIANS

Paul wrote this letter to the churches in Galatia because there were those who were telling the Gentiles who became Christians that they were not saved unless they kept the Jewish laws too. Paul encouraged them to be free from this.

DAY 20

On the Way: Paul writes to the Galatians and reminds them that God called him to preach the gospel; he was not doing it for any other reason. He reminds them that the only way to God is through faith like they were taught at the start, not through religious rules, as some were teaching them. He mentions how religious he was himself before he was a Christian and lets them know that these things have been discussed among the church leaders, who agreed that it is not Jewish law that saves a believer but only faith.

READ GALATIANS 2:11–16

For no one will ever be made right with God by obeying the law (v16b).

Checkpoint: Having reminded the Galatians that it is not keeping rules that saves us, Paul mentions a disagreement he had with Peter over just such behavior. This incident shows us that no one is above being corrected. Peter was an apostle, a leader in the church, and yet he was behaving in a way that showed he was afraid of what people thought of him. In Acts 10, we read how God had shown Peter clearly there was no difference between Jews and Gentiles, but now Peter was behaving as if there was! He was trying to please people instead of living by God's truth.

If this can be true for a great leader like Peter, it can also be true for you and me. We can behave in ways that others expect us to, and yet these may not be things that please God. We need to remember that others are watching the way we live and may follow us as they did Peter. God is not interested in our rule-keeping; He is interested in us believing in Him and loving Him. This is what makes us acceptable to Him.

- *How do you think Peter felt when Paul corrected him?*
- *When someone points out wrong behavior in you, what is your reaction?*
- *Are there any "rules" you live by as a Christian that are perhaps only manmade?*

Prayer Stop: Pray that God would protect you and your Christian leaders from being hypocrites. Pray that God will show you any manmade rules you live by and be willing to change.

DAY 21

On the Way: Paul is really concerned that the Galatian Christians are being misled into believing that they can win God's approval by keeping the Law. If this is the case, he says, then Jesus died for nothing. He did not need to die if we could win God's approval by simply keeping the Law. Paul reminds them that Abraham believed God and received the promise, not because he did anything; he simply believed.

READ GALATIANS 3:26–4:7

Now you are no longer a slave, but God's own child (4:7a).

Checkpoint: Our reading today focuses on the fact that as Christians we have become sons and daughters of God. We are part of His close family. The way a son behaves in a family is far more relaxed and familiar than a servant would behave in the same family. If you have ever viewed a period drama film, you will notice the way a servant behaves in the household. The family knows the individual and may respect him or her. The servant knows a lot of close details about the family; however, there is always a distance between them, a line that is rarely crossed.

Not so in God's family. We are not servants, but sons and daughters. God has made it so by giving us the gift of His Holy Spirit in our hearts; it is because of that, that we can address God as "Abba" Father. This is a term used to describe a very close, loving yet respectful relationship with a father. This is the kind of relationship God has given us with Himself as His children. When we have a close and respectful relationship with our Father, we do not spend our day focusing on the rules we must keep to stay part of the family. No! Instead, we know what pleases our Father, and because we love Him, we want to please Him. This is how God wants it to be with us.

- *Think of some other ways a servant is treated differently from a son.*
- *Do you think being reminded of this would change the Galatians thinking about keeping the "rules"?*
- *Does it change your thinking?*

Prayer Stop: Praise God that we are His children and not just His servants. Thank Him that He has made this possible.

DAY 22

On the Way: The Galatian Christians were turning back to keeping the Law in order to please God. Some people were teaching this. Paul was hurt and frustrated by it. Instead of growing stronger, they were being diverted in their faith. Paul mentions Abraham's story again to remind them that it was God's promise, not Abraham's action, that made the difference. He tells them again that Christ died to set us free, urging them to stay free, to live their lives by the Spirit of God, not trying to please their old natures but allowing God's Spirit to produce good fruit in them.

READ GALATIANS 6:1–10

So let's not get tired of doing what is good. At just the right time we will reap
a harvest of blessing if we don't give up (v9).

Checkpoint: If we allow God's Spirit to work in us, it will affect how we treat others and what we do. Paul encourages us to look out for other Christians who may have been tempted to sin. He asks us to gently help them see their sin, remembering that it could so easily have been us needing the correction. We need to constantly watch our own behavior, not comparing it to others but to what God wants us to do.

As we do so, we should not become tired or weary of doing the good that God asks of us. Weariness is more than just being tired; it is when things become difficult to do because we are "fed up" or bored with them. If we focus on the things we are doing rather than our relationship with God our Father, then we are in danger of becoming weary. Our key verse tells us that we will see results if we keep on going. We should not miss any chance to do good. Even if we do not see the reward we expect, we will know that we are pleasing God, and this should help us want to carry on.

- *Are there things you are involved in that make you feel weary?*
- *How can you change this? (Sometimes we may be weary with something because it is not what God wants us to do.)*

Prayer Stop: Pray for those you know who are perhaps weary; maybe you could share what you have learned from this passage with them.

EPHESIANS

This is a letter written by Paul to the church that met at Ephesus. It does not mention any specific help that the church needed but instead helps the Christians there to understand better the reason we have the church.

DAY 23

On the Way: Paul had spent three years working with the church in Ephesus. He was very close to them, and as he was unable to be with them, he sent them this letter to encourage them in their faith. He sent it while he was in prison at Rome. Paul starts his letter by reminding the Christians about all the good things we have because of Jesus.

READ EPHESIANS 1:3–10

He has showered his kindness on us, along with all wisdom and understanding (v8).

Checkpoint: Even before the world was made, God chose us to be His children. Not only before we were born, but also before the world was created, God had plans for you and me. (That is a lot of planning!) These words remind us that we cannot do anything to save ourselves. God's plan was to send Jesus into the world, and it is only through accepting God's plan that we can be saved. God did not need to do that, but these verses tell us that He wanted to.

Verse 3 tells us God has blessed us with every spiritual blessing, and verse 8 says that He has showered His kindness on us. When we think of the words Paul uses here, we get a picture of God being so generous, not just sharing one blessing to each of us, but giving us everything and pouring it out on us. When we think about this, it should make us very thankful to God for all He has done for us.

- *Think about verses 3 and 8. What are the spiritual blessings God has given you? What kindness has He showered on you?*

- *Although we are all saved through faith in Christ alone, God does show His kindness to us in ways that suit us as individuals. Why do you think this is? (The last part of our key verse is a clue.)*

- *Talk about how you feel when you think that God understands you.*

Prayer Stop: Praise God that He fully understands us more than anyone does. Praise Him today for all the blessings He has given you.

Practical Application: Perhaps you could share one of His blessings with someone you meet this week.

DAY 24

On the Way: Having written about all the blessings we have from God, Paul goes on to tell the Ephesian Christians that he thanks God for them and has been praying for them. He reminds them that as Jews and Gentiles, they are all part of God's one family. It doesn't matter that they come from different backgrounds, because Jesus died for everyone. This is so amazing because Jews and Gentiles did not mix at all socially. When Paul thinks about this and of how God has used him to bring these two groups of people together, it makes him worship God in prayer and continue to pray for the Ephesians.

READ EPHESIANS 3:14–21

> *Now all glory to God, who is able, through his mighty power at work within us, to accomplish infinitely more than we might ask or think* (v20).

Checkpoint: We may pray regularly for our Christian family, but it is sometimes difficult to know exactly what to pray. We can take some ideas from the passage today. What does Paul pray for the Ephesians? In Ephesians 1:17 he prays for spiritual wisdom for them, and in today's reading, he prays that God would give them great inner strength through His Spirit.

What an amazing thing to pray for others. Instead of asking God to "bless" them or keep them safe or give them all they need, we can pray that our Christian brothers and sisters will experience the power of God in their lives and that they will experience how amazing God's great love is. If we start praying for our Christian family to know God more and see His mighty power at work, then we will start seeing results greater than we could ever have imagined, as our key verse today says.

- *Look at Ephesians 1:17–18 and today's reading (Ephesians 3:16–18). Why does Paul pray these things for the Ephesian church?*

- *Think about what our churches would be like if we prayed like that for all our church family. Now talk about it after reading verse 20 again.*

Prayer Stop: Think about some Christians you are close to, perhaps your church leaders, family, or friends. Pray the prayers of Paul for them today.

Practical Application: Send a card or e-mail to let those you prayed for know that you prayed for them.

DAY 25

On the Way: Paul goes on to encourage the Ephesians to live and act in a way that is worthy of what God has done for them. He reminds them that God has given each Christian a gift that they should use to grow and help others grow closer to God. Paul warns them not to live as those who don't believe, but instead to change their behavior to live as children of God.

MEMORY VERSE

Instead, let the Spirit renew your thoughts and attitudes. Put on your new nature, created to be like God—truly righteous and holy.

~ Ephesians 4:23–24

READ EPHESIANS 4:20–32

Checkpoint: In the verses we read today, Paul encourages the Ephesian Christians to live their lives in a way that is opposite to those around them. Our old way of life should be discarded, as if we are changing clothes. Instead, we need to put on a new way of thinking and behaving. We have to be active in "throwing away" and "putting on." We can only put on our new nature with the help of the Holy Spirit who, when we allow Him, will change us to be like God wants us to be. But first of all, we have to remove our old behavior. When we are Christians, others should recognize that our behavior and attitudes are different from those around. We will not be perfect, and our sinful natures often creep up on us, so we must be active in rejecting sinful attitudes and behaviors when they do appear.

- *Paul gives some really practical advice about how we can make our new nature visible to those around us. Look at the passage and list the ways Paul mentions we can do this.*
- *How do you think you can "throw off" your sinful nature?*
- *What makes it hard to have the right thoughts, attitudes, and behavior?*

Prayer Stop: Pray that others would see God's love in our attitudes and actions. Praise God that He wants to change us to be like Him and for the gift of His Spirit who lives in us.

DAY 26

On the Way: As we come to the end of this letter to the Ephesians, Paul reminds them that there should not be even a hint of a sinful lifestyle among those in the church. To help them with this, he gives guidelines as to what family relationships should look like. God has set out an order for family that reflects His relationship with His church. He also deals with what our attitude should be toward those we work for and those who work for us.

READ EPHESIANS 6:10–20

> *Therefore, put on every piece of God's armour so you will be able to resist the enemy in the time of evil* (v13a).

Checkpoint: Paul finishes off his letter to the Ephesians by telling them to be ready for battle! When we become Christians, Satan does not like it at all and will try everything to stop us, hurt us, or trip us up as we follow Jesus. In verses 13–17, we are told of the battle equipment God has given us for the fight. No soldier uses only part of the equipment he is given when he goes to war; he uses all of it. It is the same with us as Christians. We must use all of the equipment that God has given us, and then we will have the power of God to stand against Satan.

We must also stay alert. When soldiers are distracted, it is easy for the enemy to attack. Satan knows this and will try to distract us from pleasing God. Paul could easily have been distracted from serving God at the time he wrote this letter because he was in prison, but he continued to pray for others, to encourage others in the truth by writing to them, and even to tell others the good news of Jesus. He made use of all the armor of God and stood against Satan's schemes.

- *Look at the items of God's armor in verses 14–17. How can we use each item in the fight against Satan?*

- *What things may distract us from using this armor properly?*

Prayer Stop: Praise God that He is powerful and helps us stand against Satan. Verse 18 tells us to keep on praying for all Christians everywhere. Pray that they would be able to stand firm against Satan.

PHILIPPIANS

Paul wrote this letter to the church at Philippi mainly to say thank you
to them for a gift they had sent him while he was in prison. He also
takes the opportunity to encourage them to remain joyful in their faith
even though others are persecuting them.

DAY 27

On the Way: Paul is thankful and full of joy when he thinks of and prays for the church in Philippi. He tells them about his situation and how he has been able to preach the gospel even though he is in prison. He encourages them to live their lives to show that they are part of God's kingdom.

READ PHILIPPIANS 2:1–11

> *You must have the same attitude that Christ Jesus had* (v5).

Checkpoint: Our attitude toward others and toward situations is the most important way we will show we are members of God's family. Paul is encouraging us to think about the attitude that Jesus had and to imitate it. When we look at Jesus' life on earth, we do not see Him struggling or striving to prove to others how great He was. He was God. The Bible tells us this in John 1:1 and in various other places, yet He did not insist on being treated with the greatness He deserved. He was willing to serve others, mix with those whom others would not go near, and face humiliation in order that we might be saved.

What are you willing to put up with in order that others might be saved? We tend to try to prove how important we are and complain if we are treated wrongly. Paul is saying to us here that we should remember how Jesus acted and follow His example. This may mean that we look for those who have no friends and show them what a true friend is. We may spend time helping those that other people ignore. This is what it means to think of others as more important than ourselves. It is easy to spend time with the people who are loveable, but this is not what Jesus did.

- *Think of some ways you could serve others this week to show them the love of God. Make a plan to do that.*

- *What was the result of Jesus' attitude? Read Matthew 5:11–12 and Ephesians 6:7–8. What is the result of our having the correct attitude toward serving others?*

Prayer Stop: Praise Jesus that He was willing to give up His high position to come to earth. Pray that God would help you to serve others this week.

DAY 28

On the Way: Paul continues to encourage the Philippian Christians to live their lives so that they shine like stars among those who are corrupt. He tells them he hopes to send Timothy to see them soon and that he is sending Epaphroditus back to them. They had sent him to help Paul, but he had become ill and nearly died. They were to be glad because of what God has done for them and to beware of folks telling them that they must do certain things in order to be saved. It is only faith that can save us.

READ PHILIPPIANS 4:1–9

> *Don't worry about anything; instead, pray about everything. Tell God what you need, and thank him for all he has done* (v6).

Checkpoint: Sometimes Christian people have disagreements. That is only natural as we are all human and therefore sinners! However, as Christians we should be able to work these differences out because we have the Holy Spirit in us. That does not mean we need to agree with everything other Christians say, but we should be able to accept another's point of view and show them love. We should find the things we can work together on and concentrate on that. This will show others that loving God makes a difference in relationships.

Our key verse shows that loving God makes a difference in our worries too. When we pray about everything, we will experience God's peace more than we are able to understand. When others see that we can have peace in our hearts even when we face worrying situations, this may move them to ask us what makes the difference in our lives.

- *What does verse 7 tell us God's peace will do? How does that make a difference to us?*
- *What can we do to help us think the way verse 8 encourages us to?*

Prayer Stop: Thank God for His peace when we are worried. Tell Him about anything that is worrying you. Pray about any disagreements you have with other Christians or any disagreement you know of and ask God for wisdom to resolve them.

COLOSSIANS

Paul wrote this letter to the church at Colossae to help them stand against some false teaching that others were trying to bring into the church. Some people were trying to teach a mixture of pagan beliefs with Christian truth, but Paul wrote to show them how great Jesus Christ was and that we have all we need and more in Him. There are some practices today that mix other people's ideas with Christian truth. So Colossians is also helpful for us today, to enable us to stand against false teaching.

DAY 29

On the Way: Paul is still in prison in Rome, but he encourages and challenges the Christians here to grow in their faith and not to be distracted by other teaching. He tells them that the good news is spreading all through the world and that he is praying for them, specifically that they would know wisdom and strength to honor God in all they do.

READ COLOSSIANS 1:15–23

But you must continue to believe this truth and stand firmly in it (v23a).

Checkpoint: Having encouraged the Christians, Paul reminds them of their amazing God and Savior, Jesus Christ. Focus on the verses that tell us Jesus is completely God. What involvement did He have in the Creation? What involvement does He have in the church? What involvement does He have in your life?

It is impossible for us to completely understand all this. Our God is so amazing. Paul wanted to remind the people in Colossi about this, and it is good for us to remember it too. As mentioned earlier, there were people teaching other ideas along with Christian truth in the church, as still happens today. We need to be sure of the truth of who Jesus is and what He has done for us so that we will not be distracted by false ideas. By thinking about what these verses tell us about Jesus, we remember that He is greater than any other power in this universe and that He is our God, interested in us personally, not just in the universe as a whole. Because Jesus died for us, we can come directly to God as if we had no sin in us. This is awesome, and we don't need any other ideas to mix with this. It cannot be any better!

- *When we talk of the Creation, we think of the things we can see. What do these verses tell us about the Creation? How does this make you feel?*

- *Talk about how these verses encourage you as a Christian.*

- *How can we show that these verses are true in our lives? (Colossians 1:23)*

Prayer Stop: Spend some time worshipping Jesus for all He is and means to you. Pray that you (and others you know) will be certain of all God's truth so that you will not be distracted from it.

DAY 30

On the Way: Paul is so convinced about the truth of Jesus that he worked hard, even when he was in prison, to make sure others heard and understood the good news. He had never met the church at Colossae but was desperate for them to be confident and sure of what God had done for them. He warns them not to be taken in by the ideas of men that others were teaching and not to become fanatical about keeping rules that do not change hearts. Instead, he tells them to avoid the evil deeds that do affect our hearts and let the attitude that God wants rule.

READ COLOSSIANS 3:12–25

> *Above all, clothe yourselves with love, which binds us all together in perfect harmony* (v14).

Checkpoint: In today's reading, we are reminded of how knowing Jesus should affect our lives. We are given a wardrobe to wear! When we put on clothing, it serves several purposes: to protect us from the environment, to identify us as part of a team, and to draw attention to us. It is the same with the wardrobe Paul mentions today. The clothes Paul tells us to put on will protect us from the attitudes in the world around us, which often encourage the sinful behavior mentioned in verses 5–9. The reason we have to put these on, Paul says, is because God has chosen us to be part of His "team." He has chosen us to be holy, and by displaying these attitudes, we are displaying the "team membership," if you like. When we do this, others will notice the difference. This will affect every area of our lives, our family lives, our school and work lives, and our life in the community.

- *By allowing the things in verse 12 to be part of our lives, how can they help us put verse 13 into practice?*

- *Think about how your family relationships may be changed if you put this into practice more.*

- *What is the one item that finishes off our "outfit"? (Colossians 3:14) Why do you think it seems to be the item that holds it all together?*

Prayer Stop: Thank God that He has chosen us as His children and pray that you will be able to show that you are His child in the way you live.

DAY 31

On the Way: Having reminded the church of how amazing Jesus is and of all He has done for them, having encouraged them to live by the right attitudes and not simply keep manmade rules that do not affect their hearts, Paul now finishes by encouraging the Colossians to pray and continue in their faith.

READ COLOSSIANS 4:2–6, 12–18

Devote yourselves to prayer with an alert mind and a thankful heart (v2).

Checkpoint: As Paul has prayed for the church, he now asks them to pray for him. He is in prison, but his freedom does not seem to be the most important thing on his mind. He asks them to pray that he will have many chances to preach and for courage to do so. When we find ourselves in difficult situations, we often ask people to pray that God would give us a way out. Paul's thoughts were not for his own comfort and freedom but that the good news of Jesus would continue. This is a challenge to us. What is most important to us when we are having a hard time? In verse 18, Paul does ask that they remember he is in jail. It is not wrong to recognize when we are in horrible situations, or to ask God for a way out, but when that is all we think of, we may miss chances to share the good news with others.

When our minds are alert (v2), we are able to notice things that are happening around us. We should pray for the things that we see happening around us and remember to give thanks to God for all He has done for us. Epaphrus in verse 12 reminds us that we should also pray for those in our church fellowship. Sometimes we find it hard to know what to pray for; here are some things that we can start with today.

- *Why do you think Paul mentions prayer at the end of this letter?*
- *How do you think Archippus felt when he heard his personal message from Paul? (v17)*
- *Who do you know that would appreciate being encouraged to keep going? Write them a letter this week to encourage them.*

Prayer Stop: Pray Epaphrus's prayer (v17) for this person and some situations you see around you. Don't forget to be thankful too!

1 AND 2 THESSALONIANS

Here is another letter from Paul, this time to the church at Thessalonica. He wrote to them so that they would grow mature in their faith and also to help them understand more about when Jesus would return to earth again: what we call the "Second Coming" of Jesus.

DAY 32

On the Way: This letter was from Paul, Silas, and Timothy. They had visited the church before to teach them about God, and the people there had believed the message. They accepted it as from God and not just human ideas. Paul and his friend were not trying to make more friends but to tell others the truth from God.

READ 1 THESSALONIANS 1:1–10

And now the word of the Lord is ringing out from you to people every-where (v8a).

Checkpoint: Paul prayed for these Christians regularly. As we mentioned in the last thought from Colossians, it is right that we pray for others. As he did this, he remembered the great things about them—not things that they themselves managed to do, but things that the Holy Spirit in them was doing. They were being faithful and loving in all they did, and it showed others the hope that they had in their lives because of Jesus. They heard the Word of God and believed it. It did not stop there. They began to let that message affect the way they lived, and other people were hearing about it and talking about it too. Not just their neighbors, but the whole area.

When we hear God's Word, it is important that we let it affect our lives in the way we do things, treat others, and look at life. Then others will be affected and will ask us why we act like we do. This gives us a chance to share the good news of Jesus with them. The Christians in Thessalonica were being missionaries to their own area and beyond, and we can follow their example as we live our lives for Jesus where we are.

- *Verse 10 mentions the Christians looking forward to Jesus' return. Do you ever think about that in your daily life? What difference would it make to you if you did?*

- *They obviously told others about it too. Is it something you would tell your friends about? Why or why not?*

- *How can you let God's Word affect your life more?*

Prayer Stop: Praise God that Jesus will return again one day and take His children to be with Him. Pray that you will be able to share the good news by the way you live.

DAY 33

On the Way: Having spent time with the Thessalonian church, Paul moved on. When he heard they were being persecuted, he desperately wanted to see them again to encourage them, but that did not work out, so he sent Timothy instead. Timothy was able to tell Paul that the Thessalonian Christians were still holding onto their faith and the teaching of God even though they were suffering. He continued to encourage them to live holy lives.

MEMORY VERSE

Christ died for us so that, whether we are dead or alive when he returns, we can live with him forever.

~ 1 Thessalonians 5:10

READ 1 THESSALONIANS 4:13–5:11

Checkpoint: Yesterday we thought about the difference Jesus' return may make to our lives. In today's reading, Paul mentions that Jesus' return should make a difference to the way we grieve when someone we love dies. He reminds us that because Jesus rose from the dead, we can be sure that whether we live or die on earth, we will live with Him forever. People in Thessalonica were worried that those who had died before Jesus came back again would not be in heaven. Paul comforted them by assuring them that those who had died will be with Jesus. This gives us comfort and hope when a Christian we love dies. We too can be sure that they are with Jesus and will be in heaven when we get there.

First Thessalonians 5:1 reminds us that we cannot know when Jesus will return. This should not worry us as Christians, but it should encourage us to keep serving God and living to please Him. If we remember that Jesus is coming back for us, this should help us through hard times.

- *How do you think the Thessalonians felt when they read this part of the letter?*
- *How does knowing that Jesus is coming back make you feel?*
- *How can remembering that Jesus is coming back help us through hard times?*

Prayer Stop: Praise God that when we know Him, He brings us comfort when we are grieving. Pray for those you may know who have had a relative die recently.

DAY 34

On the Way: Paul writes another letter to the church at Thessalonica because some people had misunderstood some things he had written the first time. They thought that if Jesus was coming back, they might as well just stop working and wait. However, that plan was causing problems, and Paul wrote to correct this. He starts off by praising them for the things they were doing well and encourages them to keep hold of the things they were taught.

READ 2 THESSALONIANS 3:6–15

Urge them . . . to settle down and work to earn their own living (v12b).

Checkpoint: Idle people are those who refuse to work even though they are able. The Bible has a lot to say about idleness. In today's reading, we can see that those who were refusing to work were causing problems for others (2 Thes. 3:11). When we have this attitude, it usually affects those around us and can ruin our relationships. Paul had urged them in his first letter to stay alert. However, they had become idle, just waiting for Jesus' return. They had not learned from Paul's example of working and had forgotten his teaching that if they wanted to eat, they would need to work! They were so focused on going to heaven that they seemed to have forgotten that they needed to live on earth first! Have you heard the saying, "They were so heavenly minded that they were of no earthly use"? People today can become so focused on heaven that they are unable to relate to the people that God has called them to live among on earth. Although we look forward to being with Jesus, we do need to live the life He has given us here first of all. Ask God to show you His will for you and do it with all your heart, but do not be idle.

- *Read Proverbs 12:27, 20:4, and Ecclesiastes 10:8. What is the result of idleness in a person's life?*

- *How can our idleness affect other people? What about our relationship with God?*

Prayer Stop: Thank God that He has work for us to do and pray you will be willing to do it. Pray that you will be able to relate to those you live around and be an example to them.

1 AND 2 TIMOTHY

Timothy was a young Christian leader who had worked with Paul. As Paul approached the end of his life, he wrote to Timothy to encourage him in his work as a Christian leader in the church and to keep strong in his faith. The first letter was probably written a couple of years before the second one.

DAY 35

On the Way: Paul had trained and taught Timothy in his faith, and now as Timothy is in Ephesus leading the church there, Paul writes to encourage him. He is facing many responsibilities and challenges, perhaps wondering how he will cope, and then he receives a letter from Paul. It is always a good thing to encourage young Christians in serving God.

READ 1 TIMOTHY 1:3–11

> *The purpose of my instruction is that all believers would be filled with love*
> *that comes from a pure heart, a clear conscience, and a genuine faith* (v5).

Checkpoint: We live in a world where people want their opinions to be heard. They think that what they have to say is worthwhile, and they want people to think they are important. Timothy was facing this in the church at Ephesus. There were people teaching things and talking about things that were meaningless; they did not have any effect on peoples' lives apart from wasting time talking. They were doing this in order to become famous. Paul tells Timothy to stop this happening because they are not helping people live lives of faith.

When we listen to others discussing or teaching God's Word, we should notice the effect it has on others and ourselves. Does the teaching encourage others or cause arguments? Does the teaching draw attention to the person themselves or to God? The motives we have when we speak about God or His Word should be only to build other people up, not to cause arguments or draw attention to ourselves, but to draw attention to God.

- *What things can help people lead a life of faith? Perhaps you could put one of your ideas into action this week to encourage someone.*

- *In verses 8–11, Paul mentions the Law. Why do you think he has done this after talking about people teaching meaningless things?*

- *What ideas may we be focused on today that may not be the best ideas to help lead a life of faith?*

Prayer Stop: Praise God for those who teach you to lead a life of faith. Pray for them. Pray for wisdom to spend your time wisely rather than talking about meaningless things.

DAY 36

On the Way: Having urged Timothy to stop those who were wasting time discussing and teaching meaningless things, Paul takes time to reflect how great God's mercy is because He has chosen someone like Paul, who used to persecute people for following Jesus, to take the gospel message around the world. He again urges Timothy to cling to his faith and keep doing what is right. Paul follows this with instructions for worship.

READ 1 TIMOTHY 2:1–10

> *I urge you, first of all, to pray for all people* (v1a).

Checkpoint: The first thing Paul mentions when speaking about worship is prayer for others. He mentions this as a top priority. We can pray to our Heavenly Father and know He hears us. These verses encourage us to use this privilege to pray for others, to stand between God and them and ask God to help them. This is something we can do for anyone. In verse 2, we are told to do this for the leaders of our country. We should pray that they would make wise decisions.

Our attitude in prayer is also important. Verse 8 reminds us that our relationships with others should be right; we should not be angry with others or be stirring up trouble when we come to pray.

Paul encourages Timothy to teach that women should not be obsessed with their appearance. It's more important to be known for the good we do for God. Today, there is as much pressure on guys to look good as there is for girls, so this is a lesson for everyone.

- *Why do you think Paul mentions prayer at the beginning of the section on worship?*
- *Why do you think our attitude is so important when we pray?*
- *Do you think Paul is saying it is wrong to look good? What difficulties do you face in keeping the balance right?*

Prayer Stop: Give thanks and pray for the leaders of your country and church today. Pray that God will show you the right priorities as far as looking after yourself is concerned.

DAY 37

On the Way: Paul wants Timothy to teach the church that the way they behave when they get together to worship God is important. The way they act should be different from the way those in the community around them act; then others will take notice. There should be respect among Christians in the church. As they do this, the church will grow closer to God and do what pleases Him. Paul then moves on to talk about the character of the people chosen as church leaders.

READ 1 TIMOTHY 3:1–13

> *For if a man cannot manage his own household, how can he take care of*
> *God's church?* (v5).

Checkpoint: Paul sets down clear guidelines for church leaders. These involve the way they live their life outside of church and in their own homes. Church leadership cannot be separated from the rest of our lives. How we live affects our ability to lead God's children. In other careers, like medicine, law, or management, how you live your life away from it perhaps is not so important. In church leadership though, it is the opposite; how you live your life is what gives you the qualification to have the position. Elders, those who look after the spiritual side of the church, and deacons, those who are involved in the practical care of the church, are both expected to have self-control in their personal lives and in their family so that they will have the same character when looking after God's family. This is a tall order, and we as church members should encourage our leaders, making sure they have the time they need with their families. Young Christians should work in the church and develop godly character in order that one day they may be able to lead God's children.

- *Why is it so important for church leaders to have self-control and discipline in their private lives?*
- *Why is it important that people outside the church speak well of them? (1 Timothy 3:7)*
- *How can you encourage your leaders to live godly lives?*

Prayer Stop: Thank God for your church leaders and pray for them that they will live according to God's Word. Mention each one by name.

Practical Application: Perhaps you could send your church leaders a card this week to encourage them in their role.

DAY 38

On the Way: Paul was writing these things to Timothy so he could teach the church when Paul was unable to be there. He hopes to be with them soon, but in the meantime, he encourages Timothy to keep teaching the truth and not to be sidetracked by those who did not teach what was in God's Word. As he nears the end of the first letter he writes to Timothy, Paul encourages Timothy to be an example.

READ 1 TIMOTHY 4:6–16

Train yourself to be godly (v7b).

Checkpoint: Paul encourages Timothy to keep teaching the church, to train himself to be godly, and to be an example to others. Timothy was younger than Paul, and perhaps some of the church elders were not taking what Timothy was saying seriously. Paul encourages Timothy not to let this bother him but instead to make sure that he is showing a good example by the way he lives and that he is devoted to teaching the truth.

You have likely heard the statement, "Do as I say, not as I do." This is an excuse for one's own bad behavior sometimes, but Paul was urging Timothy to "practice what he preached" instead. It doesn't matter what age we are, if we are not putting into practice what we are teaching, we cannot expect to have respect as a teacher or leader. We all need to make sure that we are living our lives as a good example of what it means to follow Jesus. Then others will notice the difference, and we will have a chance to share the gospel or teach them more of what it means to follow Jesus.

- *What can we do to "train ourselves to be godly"?*
- *How can we encourage others to do the same?*
- *Why might it be harder for a younger pastor to teach in a church?*

Prayer Stop: Pray that your life would be a good example to others and ask God to show you anything that you may need to change. Pray that your church leaders would be an example and would practice what they preach. Pray that they always teach the truth from God's Word.

DAY 39

On the Way: Paul has encouraged Timothy to watch the way he lives and to keep doing what God has called him to do until Paul comes to be with him. He now moves on to how we should treat each other in God's family and in our natural families too.

READ 1 TIMOTHY 5:1–8

But those who won't care for their relatives . . . have denied the true faith (v8a).

Checkpoint: In the first few verses, Paul is very clear about the way we should treat each other in God's family. He tells Timothy to treat people with respect to their age. If they are older, then they should be treated with the respect we would give our parents. If younger, as if they were our brother or sister. In our communities, we see a lot of disrespect in the way other people speak, especially to the elderly; in our churches, we should notice the difference. We are family and should treat each other like that. It seems that perhaps some folks were expecting the church to look after their elderly relatives. Paul has very strong words for those who were not taking responsibility for their own natural families. It is important that as our relatives get older, we look after them in whatever way is needed. It may be just by visiting regularly, but as they become more frail, they may need more care. Some Jewish people in Jesus' day thought that if they gave the money they had for caring for their parents to the synagogue instead, then they did not need to look after their parents. Jesus had some strong words for them too.

- *Look them up in Matthew 15:4–9. What traditions or activities may hinder us today from caring for elderly relatives?*

- *Do you have relatives who live alone or are older? When did you last see them or do something for them?*

- *Do you need to change some priorities so that your relatives have more of your time?*

Prayer Stop: Thank God for your family: your parents, grandparents, and other relatives. Pray for those who do not have family to look out for them. Pray that the church will show them God's love and include them in your church family.

DAY 40

On the Way: Paul gives special instructions for the way the church should treat widows. They need to be looked after, especially if they have no family. He advises Timothy not to show favoritism and also to look after his own health. As he closes his first letter, Paul talks about wealth and satisfaction.

MEMORY VERSE

For the love of money is the root of all kinds of evil. And some people, craving money, have wandered from the true faith and pierced themselves with many sorrows.

~ 1 Timothy 6:10

READ 1 TIMOTHY 6:6–10

Checkpoint: Some people constantly try to get more money and more gadgets: they want the latest fashions, and some borrow money they cannot afford to pay back so that they can keep up with all the latest trends. Sometimes those in the church can be guilty of love for money too. We get caught up with all the latest crazes.

In today's reading, Paul talks about being content with what we have (1 Tim. 6:8). When we stop trying to get bigger and better possessions, we can focus on the things that really matter. Paul says godliness with contentment is a really valuable thing. *Contentment* means being satisfied with what we have. We cannot be satisfied when we get whatever we want, because we will always find other things to want. God wants us to be content even if there are things we want in life. It is not wrong to want things or to have them, but when getting them becomes our main focus, then we are not focused on God as we should be and our priorities are wrong. This can lead us away from God.

- *Do you find it hard to be satisfied with what you have?*
- *Look at the second part of the memory verse: How does craving money (or things) affect our lives? What kind of troubles can this bring us?*
- *Think of some practical way that can show we are happy with what we have.*

Prayer Stop: Thank God for all that you do have and ask Him to help you be satisfied with that. Pray for those who do not have enough food or clothes.

Practical Application: Consider whether you can do something practical to help those near you.

DAY 41

On the Way: We start 2 Timothy today, which was probably written shortly before Paul's death, to encourage Timothy to stay faithful. In chapter 1, we learn that both Timothy's grandmother and mother had great faith and that Timothy had that same faith. Paul encourages Timothy to keep growing in faith and holding onto the truth. He is thankful for those who have visited him in prison.

READ 2 TIMOTHY 2:1–14

Be strong through the grace that God gives you in Christ Jesus (v1b).

Checkpoint: This is Paul's goodbye letter to Timothy because he knows he is about to die. He encourages Timothy to be faithful in teaching the truth that he had heard Paul teaching and to train others to do the same. As we get older, it is important that we train others up to continue to teach God's Word. Younger Christians should be willing to learn and help out so that they become mature enough to take these tasks over.

Paul uses three themes of soldiers, athletes, and farmers in verses 3–6 to show Timothy what being involved in this work for God will mean.

1. He needs to focus on the right things, like soldiers not being involved in civilian life.
2. He needs to be disciplined in training, like the athlete training for a race.
3. He can expect to see results, like the farmer.

Paul reminds Timothy that though he is in prison, the Word of God cannot be chained up. Even as a prisoner, Paul was able to share the good news with those around him, and the Word of God continued to spread. No matter where we are, we can share the good news of Jesus.

- *What things should we focus on as Christians that will help us serve God? What does verse 14 tell us about this?*
- *How can we train and be disciplined in God's service?*
- *Are you involved in learning from someone or training someone for ministry? Do you need to think about this?*

Prayer Stop: Thank God for those older Christians who can teach younger Christians God's truths (mention them by name). Ask God to help you be willing to learn.

DAY 42

On the Way: Paul gives Timothy guidance on the things he should avoid, things that cause worthless discussion and arguments. He urges him again and again to hold onto the truth of God's Word and to be faithful to it. He mentions a couple of people who have been distracted by other issues and have turned from the truth.

READ 2 TIMOTHY 2:19–26

But God's truth stands firm like a foundation stone (v19a).

Checkpoint: A foundation stone is the stone that supports the rest of the building. God's truth is like that. If we build our lives on the truth in God's Word, we will live lives that will not crumble when trouble comes. Like the story Jesus told of the wise man who built a house on the rock, when the storm came, it stood strong, unlike the man who built his house on sand; his house fell when the storm came.

Verse 22 is a running verse. We have to run away from things that will tempt us to sin and then run after things that will help us live to please God. We cannot focus on something that is behind us and something that is in front of us at the same time. So if we are actively running toward those things that please God, we will be focused on them; the things that tempt us to sin will not be so much in our minds when pleasing God is our focus.

Sometimes when people oppose God's Word, we end up in strong discussions and even arguments as to why we believe it is the truth. This can sometimes come across as arrogant and unkind. We need to be careful when we discuss God's Word with others. Paul gives clear instructions here about how we should conduct ourselves. This is not the first time he has mentioned pointless discussions in his letters!

- *What things do some people build their lives on today?*
- *How can we actively run after those things that please God?*
- *Think about what you might say to someone who does not believe the Bible.*

Prayer Stop: Thank God that He is the "rock that we can stand on." Pray for those you know who do not believe God's truth. Pray for the right way to speak to them.

DAY 43

On the Way: Paul warns Timothy that times will be hard before the Lord comes back again. People will look out only for themselves; they will laugh at God and be undisciplined. They will be selfish and cruel, loving a good time rather than loving God. But Paul warns Timothy to keep faithful regardless of what others do. He warns that others will come to teach lies, but he needs to remember that the entire Bible is God's Word, and that God uses it in our lives to help us serve Him.

READ 2 TIMOTHY 4:1–8

But you should keep a clear mind in every situation (v5).

Checkpoint: When we look at the people around us and listen to the TV, we can see the things that Paul mentions in verses 3–4 happening today. People don't really want to hear the truth of the Bible; they just want to believe nice things, ideas that they are comfortable with and that make them happy. There are many groups around that encourage people to find the good inside themselves by meditation and other techniques. Paul reminds Timothy to work at telling others the good news of Jesus in this situation.

We need to tell others the good news of Jesus today. In order to do that, we need to know the truth and not become confused by all that we see around us; we need to "keep a clear mind." If we make it a priority in our lives to learn and live the truth in the Bible, this will help us to be able to recognize the lies we hear around us and to patiently teach others the truth. Often the truth is not very comfortable for people; rather than showing the good inside us, it shows our sin. Until we deal with that, it can be uncomfortable.

- *What do you hear talked about that is not the truth of the Bible but that people choose to believe instead?*
- *How can you patiently correct and encourage people who believe such lies?*
- *How can we keep a clear mind?*

Prayer Stop: Praise God for the truth of His Word. Pray for those you know who prefer to believe the lies rather than the truth of the Bible.

TITUS

Titus, like Timothy, had spent some time with Paul and was now was the leader of the church in Crete. Paul wrote this letter to him to instruct him in some pastoral issues and to encourage him in his work there.

DAY 44

On the Way: Paul starts by reminding Titus why he had stayed behind in Crete: he was given the task to appoint elders in the churches around Crete. So Paul writes to him to remind him of the kind of people that should be appointed as elders. He warns Titus about false teaching in the church and encourages him to stand firmly against it, teaching the truth. Paul has some very strong words for those who teach what is false.

READ TITUS 2:1–15

We should live in this evil world with wisdom, righteousness, and devotion to
God (v12b).

Checkpoint: Having given Titus instructions on what characteristics church leaders should have, he moves on to talk about the character of anyone who believes. This includes you and me. There is some guidance here for every age group, from the oldest to the youngest. The older men are encouraged to live wisely. As we get older, sometimes we become less patient. Paul says here that these older men should be filled with patience. The older women have a responsibility to teach the younger women all about godly family life. They can teach from their own experience rather than Titus teaching this with little or no experience. The younger men are also encouraged to live wisely. Titus is included in this group, so Paul encourages him to be active in being an example. He must put into practice the things that he teaches. Then no one will have cause to complain about his teaching. Over all, verse 12 sums up what Paul is teaching through this chapter. No matter our age, we should be an example to those who are younger in the faith, and we should be willing to learn from those who are older.

- *Think about your own church family. How do you see this being put into practice?*
- *How do you think young men can live wisely?*
- *Why is it important to watch how we live at work (Titus 2:9–10)?*

Prayer Stop: Praise God for the older Christians who have been an example in your life. Pray that God would help you to grow in your faith and be a good example to those who are younger.

DAY 45

On the Way: In this last section of Paul's letter to Titus, he directs Titus to teach the church about their attitude to government. As he finishes, Paul writes a few personal notes, mentioning names of those he will send to help Titus and also those who need some help. Paul is not only concerned about the teaching in the church as a whole, but he is also concerned personally for the people who are in the church.

READ TITUS 3:1–8

> *He saved us, not because of righteous things we had done, but because of his mercy* (v5a).

Checkpoint: As human beings, we tend to forget what we should be doing. Titus is to remind the church that they have a godly responsibility to obey the government by keeping the law. It is easy to think that we are all good citizens and do not break the law of the land, but we need to remember that as Christians we are also required to obey God. Verse 2 reminds us that we should watch the way we speak about our government. That may be more of a challenge to us than keeping the speed limit!

Paul urges us to be gentle and kind to everyone. Why? Because before God saved us, we were exactly the same as those who do not know God, and we need to remember that. Sometimes we may be tempted to think that because we are Christians, we are better than our government or others who do not know God. Paul reminds us that we are only saved because of what God has done for us, not because we have done anything for ourselves. We are the same as anyone else; we can be saved only by God's grace.

- *Read Romans 13:1 and 1 Timothy 2:1–2. How do these verses help us with our attitude to government?*

- *What about governments who make Christianity a crime? Is it right to submit to them?*

- *How can you improve your attitude toward your government?*

Prayer Stop: Thank God for the leaders of your country. Pray for them by name that they will make wise decisions and turn to God. Pray for Christians working within the government.

PHILEMON

Paul wrote this letter to Philemon, who was part of the church in Colossae. He had a slave named Onesimus who had run away. Onesimus became a Christian when he met Paul, and now Paul was sending him back to his master with this letter, asking Philemon to take Onesimus back.

DAY 46

On the Way: Philemon had a church that met in his house, and he was known for his faith in the Lord and for having a great love for God's people. Paul had experienced comfort from the love shown by Philemon in the past and so is sure that as he asks him to accept Onesimus back into his home, Philemon will do so out of love rather than just because it is the right thing to do.

READ PHILEMON 1:10–22

> *It seems you lost Onesimus for a little while so that you could have him back forever* (v15).

Checkpoint: Onesimus was not a Christian when he ran away, although he was part of a Christian household where the church met. It was not until he met Paul while on the run that he became a Christian. Our faith has to be a personal decision. Even though we are a member of a Christian family, we may not have a personal faith. We need to make the decision to ask God's forgiveness and follow Him for ourselves. We don't need to go away to do this, but sometimes it is as we grow up and leave home that we realize our faith has been dependent on our parents. As parents, it is hard to watch our children leave home unsure of their faith; however, it may be that we have to let them go so that they have space to discover Jesus for themselves.

Now as a Christian servant, having been taught by Paul, Onesimus would have a new attitude to his work and to his master. As Christians, our attitudes at work and school should be noted as being helpful to those who are in charge of us. If we have a Christian boss, we have an extra responsibility to him or her as part of God's family. This does not mean we respect the individual any less as a boss.

- *How do you think Philemon felt when he got this letter?*
- *Are there some "dangers" to being brought up in a Christian environment? Why do you think it was after Onesimus ran away that he came to faith?*
- *Have you made a personal commitment to Jesus?*

Prayer Stop: Praise God for His forgiveness and ask Him to help you always be able to forgive others. Pray for anyone you know who needs to make their faith personal.

HEBREWS

We do not know who wrote this letter. It was written to Jewish Christians who were being persecuted and were wondering if they had done the right thing in leaving Judaism and following Christ. This letter shows how God's new promise in Jesus' death and resurrection goes much deeper than the Law of Moses that the Jews followed. The writer gives some examples of people in the past who followed God even though they were persecuted and so encourages the Jewish Christians to do the same.

DAY 47

On the Way: The Jewish Christians were doubting their newfound faith. As Jews, they still believed in God but were not persecuted as much for their Jewish faith as they were for their Christian faith. So the writer of this letter starts to show them how much greater Jesus is to all that they followed before. He uses the Scriptures the Jews would have known to explain how the Law of Moses pointed to Jesus being greater than the angels or Moses himself.

MEMORY VERSE

The Son radiates God's own glory and expresses the very character of God, and he sustains every thing by the mighty power of his command.

~ Hebrews 1:3a

READ HEBREWS 1:1–4; 3:1–6

Checkpoint: The Jews knew that God spoke to His people in the past through the prophets. Now the writer reminds them that God has spoken again, but this time through His Son Jesus, who is far greater than the prophets. The first passage we read reminds us that Jesus shows us God's character; it tells us of His great power. Because of all He has done, Jesus is even greater than the angels.

In the second passage, having shown the Jews how their Scriptures teach that Jesus is greater than Moses or the angels, the writer asks them to give Jesus some special thought. As Jews, Moses held a special place in their hearts. Hebrews 3:5–6 tells us that Moses was only a part of God's family, just as we are, but Jesus is the builder of God's family. It is because of what He has done that we are able to be part of it. The writer encouraged the Jews to realize that they should honor Jesus more than any of the prophets. When we think about what the verses we read today tell us about Jesus, we too should remember that He is the greatest, and He deserves all the honor and praise we can give Him.

- *What do the verses we read tell us about Jesus?*
- *In what ways is Jesus greater than Moses or the angels?*
- *How do you feel when you think about this?*

Prayer Stop: Praise God for His great power and for Jesus who came to die for us. Praise God that we can be part of His family. Pray for anyone you know today who is not yet part of God's family.

DAY 48

On the Way: The Jews are reminded that some of their ancestors did not see God's Promised Land (God's rest) because they disobeyed God. The writer warns them that only those who believe can enter God's rest today. God gave them a chance to have His "special rest," and we have that chance now if we believe in Him.

READ HEBREWS 4:14–5:3

> *So then, since we have a great High Priest who has entered heaven, Jesus the Son of God, let us hold firmly to what we believe* (v14).

Checkpoint: Hebrews 5:1–3 explains to us that the Jewish high priest was a man chosen from the rest of the priests to serve at the Temple in a special way. Once a year he was to go into the special holy place behind the curtain in the Temple and offer special sacrifices to God for the people. He had first of all to purify himself for this special task because he was human like us.

The verses we read in chapter 4 tell us that we now have a great High Priest, better than the rest, in Jesus. He is in the presence of God, in heaven, constantly, not just once a year. He sacrificed His life on earth by dying on the cross, and now we can keep coming into God's presence because Jesus is there all the time. We don't need to wait until the special time of year like the Jews did, so trusting Jesus is far greater than following the old Jewish religion. Because Jesus is there constantly, the writer encourages us to come with confidence into God's presence. As we do that, God will bless us with the things we do not deserve (his grace) because Jesus has taken our punishment for us.

- *How do you think the Jews felt when they understood that they did not need to depend on a human high priest anymore?*
- *Jesus is before God for all of us, not just the Jews. How does this make you feel?*
- *Jesus understands our weaknesses. Do you think this is an excuse for us not to try to overcome them? Why not?*

Prayer Stop: Praise God that Jesus has made it possible for us to come into His presence. Pray that others might understand what Jesus has done for them. Pray for some by name.

DAY 49

On the Way: The writer continues to show the Hebrew Christians that believing in Christ is far greater than the old way they followed. The old law was meant to point them to the new way God now provided in Jesus. The old way was not permanent; they had to keep on offering sacrifices. This new promise from God is permanent. Jesus died as our sacrifice, so we do not need to keep on offering sacrifices any more.

READ HEBREWS 9:11–12, 24–28

But now, once for all time, he has appeared at the end of the age to remove sin by his own death as a sacrifice (v26b).

Checkpoint: In the Jewish faith, the high priest had to enter into the special holy place in the Temple once a year to offer special sacrifices for the people. Every year they came back out again; they did not stay there! Jesus has entered into heaven and is there, in God's presence, all the time. He does not leave, and because of that, we have that constant access to God. We are saved from the result of our sin forever; Jesus' sacrifice made that possible.

Our Savior's death on the cross was different from the sacrifices the priests made. He was perfect and sinless, and so by dying that horrible death on the cross, He was able to put things right with God once and for all. We only need to believe that and trust Him so we can be saved. Everyone faces dying at some point; there is death in the world because there is sin in the world. We die once because of this sin, and so Jesus also died once to rescue us from that sin.

- *Why does Jesus not need to keep on dying for our sins?*
- *What was the Temple a picture of?*
- *How would this show the Hebrew Christians that the new way they were following was better than the old way?*

Prayer Stop: Praise God that Jesus is in heaven and that we can be saved once and for all. Pray that you will realize how big a sacrifice Jesus made for you and that you will be able to share this with others, that they too might believe.

DAY 50

On the Way: The person writing this letter goes on to explain the importance of Jesus' death by using the Jewish Scriptures, passages they would be familiar with but may not have understood until it was explained to them. He explains why the sacrifice of animals was not good enough to bring us to God and why after Jesus died there was no more need to keep sacrificing in the old way they were used to.

READ HEBREWS 10:19–29

> *Let us hold tightly without wavering to the hope we affirm, for God can be trusted to keep his promise* (v23).

Checkpoint: Having clearly explained to the Hebrew Christians why Jesus' death is more important than the sacrifices they made constantly in their old religion, the writer encourages them to grow in their new faith, reminding them that they do not need a priest to enter God's presence for them. Now, Jesus is there, and they can go straight to God themselves. He encourages them to keep holding onto God's promise because as the time for Jesus to come back again gets closer, they will need to encourage one another more.

Jesus is coming back again. His return is much closer now than it was when this letter was written, and so we need to make sure we are encouraging other Christians to keep believing God's promise.

Verses 26–29 are a warning for those who refuse to accept that Jesus' sacrifice is the only way to be saved. Sometimes we forget that when Jesus comes back, it will be terrible for those who have refused to believe in Him. These verses should help us to pray and be determined to share the good news of Jesus with people who do not yet believe.

- *Put verse 24 into practice. What can you do to motivate Christians you know to keep on loving and doing good to others?*
- *Why is it important to keep meeting with other Christians?*
- *When you think about Jesus coming back, how does this make you feel?*

Prayer Stop: Praise God for other Christians to encourage us in our faith and for your church family. Pray for those you know who have not accepted Jesus as their Savior yet.

DAY 51

On the Way: These Hebrew Christians were doubting because they were being persecuted. They wondered if their old way of life was not easier. The writer encourages them to remember how enthusiastic they were when they first heard the gospel and to keep on believing, to keep having that same faith.

READ HEBREWS 11:1–6, 32–40

Faith . . . gives us assurance about things we cannot see (v1).

Checkpoint: The whole of chapter 11 gives a great list of people in the Old Testament who lived and acted by faith in God. Right from the start of the universe until the present day, people have lived and acted by faith in God. This chapter gave the Hebrew Christians a long list of people from their Scriptures who had lived and acted by being sure that God would keep His promises even though they might not see the full result of them. The end of the chapter reminds us that there were people who suffered (and still do today) because they lived by faith. What they believed God had for them was greater than what they suffered.

It is not possible to please God unless we have faith (Heb. 11:6). To please Him, we need to believe He exists since we cannot see God in person; that requires faith—being sure of what we cannot see. By mentioning all those people, the writer was encouraging the Hebrew Christians to keep on in their faith.

We can become weary too when things get hard for us. When this happens, we can think about the people in this chapter and also about people in our own past who lived and acted by faith. This should encourage us to keep going. To remember that others have given their lives and suffered because they were so sure of God's promise should inspire us to keep on when things get tough.

- *Who in your life inspires you to keep living by faith?*
- *How can faith turn our weakness to strength? (Hebrews 11:34)*

Prayer Stop: Thank God for the gift of faith. Pray for those you know who are finding living as a Christian difficult just now. Pray for those who suffer because of their Christianity.

DAY 52

On the Way: As this letter to the Hebrew Christians comes to a close, the writer asks the people to look after one another, to listen to what God says to them, and to keep living the life of faith they began. Having explained to them why Jesus' sacrifice is greater than any they made in their old way of life, they are encouraged to keep their focus on Jesus and on learning from the experiences they have.

READ HEBREWS 12:1–13

> *Let us run with endurance the race God has set before us* (v1b).

Checkpoint: These Christians had become weary of being persecuted for their faith in Jesus. When we are given a hard time because of our faith, we can become weary too. Our key verse encourages us to "run . . . with endurance." When we endure something, we keep going through the difficulties to reach our goal. As Christians, our goal is heaven, to be with Jesus forever. When we face difficulties, we need to remember what Jesus did. Verse 2 tells us He endured the cross because of what was ahead. We need to remember what is ahead of us, not here on earth but in heaven. When we keep our minds focused on that, it will help us to keep going through the difficulties.

Some of the difficulties we face are nothing compared to others in this world. We should keep that in mind, also remembering what Jesus suffered for us when He died on the cross. The difficulties we face can be used by God to change us, making us more like He wants us to be, helping us to live to please Him. So when we face difficulties because of our faith in God or because we are persecuted, we need to hold on tighter to God and keep our eyes fixed on Jesus, thinking about all the good things He has promised us.

- *What practical things can we do to help us endure persecution and encourage others to do the same?*
- *How can we fix our eyes on Jesus?*
- *How do you feel when you think about heaven?*

Prayer Stop: Thank God that we will be with Him one day forever. Pray for those who are persecuted, imprisoned, or tortured because of their faith. Pray that they will stand firm and know God is with them.

JAMES

This letter was written to Jewish Christians who were living in other places. It was written by James, the brother of Jesus, who was a leader in the church in Jerusalem. In this letter, James encourages Christians to live their faith in practical ways. The Christian faith is one of action, not just words.

DAY 53

On the Way: James' letter contains lots of practical advice about living as a Christian in our community. The first chapter starts by encouraging Christians to see difficulties and troubles as a chance to grow in their faith. He tells us we can ask for wisdom from God and reminds us that all the good things we have come from God.

MEMORY VERSE

But if you look carefully into the perfect law that sets you free, and if you do what it says and don't forget what you heard, then God will bless you for doing it.

~James 1:25

READ JAMES 1:19–27

Checkpoint: The verses we read today tell us the effect that the Word of God should have on our lives. We need to accept it, do what it says, and allow it to affect what we say. When we allow anger to rule our hearts, we cannot live the way that pleases God, and so the Word of God is not given the right place in our lives. That is why we need to listen more than we speak. Someone said, "We have two ears and one mouth, so we should listen twice as much as we speak!" We need to make sure we are listening to the Word of God and obeying it before we speak it to others. There is no point in reading God's Word if we don't do what it says; verse 23 says it is as pointless as looking in a mirror and then forgetting what you look like!

Verse 26 also tells us that if we cannot control our tongue, then all we read in God's Word and all we do for God is pointless. These are very strong words. Often we forget how important our behavior is, not just to those who see us, but to God as well. Make sure you concentrate on doing what God's Word says.

- *Why do you think James mentions anger especially here as something that will hinder God's Word in your life?*
- *How does God's Law set us free?*
- *In what ways may the world try to corrupt us?*

Prayer Stop: Thank God for His Word and the power it has to save us. Pray that you would obey God's Word and not hinder God's work in your life.

DAY 54

On the Way: James warns that showing favoritism to anyone is a sin. We must not judge others but show them true kindness as God shows us. There is no point in saying you have faith if it does not show itself in what you do and in your care for others. Even the evil spirits believe in God, but we must show in our lives the difference that makes.

READ JAMES 3:1–12

But a tiny spark can set a great forest on fire (v5b).

Checkpoint: At the end of chapter 2, James says, "Faith without works is dead." In the verses we read today, the challenge is about our words. If we have faith in God, our faith must show in the way we speak. These verses mention the tongue and the effect it can have in our lives and the lives of others. James uses the picture of a horse and how it can be directed by a small bit in its mouth. He also uses the example of a ship being guided by a small rudder even in a storm. Our tongue is a small part of our body, but its use can direct our whole lives. What we say and how we say it can have an effect on so many situations. Think of all the people in public life who have said one thing out of turn and have had to resign.

Our tongues can also destroy; verse 5b talks about a tiny spark setting a whole forest on fire. Have you ever said one small thing that someone misunderstood? Once the words are out of our mouths, it is difficult to control, just as a spark in a forest can so easily get out of control. That is why we must always be careful what we say. If we go back to James 1:19, the advice is to be slow to speak and slow to get angry; we need to control what comes out of our mouths.

- *Jesus said, "Whatever is in your heart determines what you say" (Matthew 12:34b). How can we make sure we have the right attitude in our hearts?*
- *In what way can our tongue direct our lives? Think of specific examples.*
- *How can you make sure what you say has a good rather than a bad effect?*

Prayer Stop: Think of words you can use to praise God today. Use Psalm 141:3 as a prayer.

DAY 55

On the Way: James warns Christians against being bitter and jealous; these are not godly attitudes and will cause quarrels. Instead, he encourages us to be wise, peace-loving, and willing to put others first. Quarrels come from the evil desires in us; we fight to get what we want rather than ask God for it. Then James says when we do ask, it is only to satisfy our desires; the reasons we ask are wrong. Again, this shows us what is in our hearts.

READ JAMES 4:7-17

Humble yourselves before the Lord and he will lift you up in honor (v10).

Checkpoint: James has given very clear advice on how we should live our lives. As we grow closer to God, we become more aware of the sin in our lives. Until we deal with that sin, God cannot draw closer to us; there is no room in our hearts for sin and God! So we need to keep asking God to show us the things in our lives we need to change, and we need to obey His Word.

Our faith needs to affect even how we make plans. When we think about the future and what we would like to do, we need to remember that it is God who directs our lives. What may look sensible to us may not be what God wants for us. We need to remember that He sees the whole picture of our lives from start to finish, and His plans are best for us. So when you plan for your future, remember to ask God to direct your path as you push the doors of opportunity. He has promised to direct those who sincerely seek Him.

- *How can we resist the devil? (James 4:7)*
- *Read Proverbs 3:5-6 and 16:9. How have you or your family ever experienced God directing the plans you have made for your lives?*
- *Can you think of someone in the Bible who tried to change God's plans for them? What happened?*

Prayer Stop: Praise God that He has good plans for us and pray that you will always ask for Him to guide you as you plan. Pray for those who are trying to ignore God's plans for their lives. Mention anyone you know by name.

1 AND 2 PETER

The Apostle Peter wrote his first letter to the Jewish Christians in Asia Minor to encourage them in their faith. They were being persecuted and were suffering because of their faith in Jesus. His second letter is to Christians in general, reminding us that Jesus will return, which should affect the way we live now.

DAY 56

On the Way: Peter starts his letter with a positive and exciting message. He reminds us that even though we face difficult times in our lives, these are only for a little while. God is preparing us to live with Him forever, and this should make us rejoice even during great trials that some of these Christians were facing. He reminded the Jewish Christians that the gift of eternal life was what the prophets in the Old Testament preached about, though they didn't completely understand it.

READ 1 PETER 1:13–25

Your new life will last for ever because it comes from the eternal, living word
of God (v23b).

Checkpoint: As Christians, we have eternal life. This does not just mean that when we die or when Jesus returns we will go to heaven to live with Him forever; that is only part of it. As soon as we trust Jesus as our Savior, God gives us that gift of eternal life now. When we become Christians, our eternal life starts here and will continue forever, because it is given to us by God who is eternal.

In the verses we read, Peter encourages us to live our lives differently, to be holy as God is holy. That means that we should be noticed as being different—different in the priorities we have, in the way we treat people and react to things, and how we spend our time and money. We should not just try to be different for the sake of it but to let the power of God work in us and change us to be the people He wants us to be. Our life on earth is the start of eternal life. In the rest of his first letter, Peter tells us how we can live our lives to show the difference to those who do not have hope beyond this life.

- *How can we prepare our minds for action and self-control (1 Peter 1:13)? How will this make a difference to the way we live our lives here?*

- *What difference will knowing that eternal life starts now make to the way you live?*

Prayer Stop: Think about what God has done for you (1 Peter 1:18–20) and worship Him for that. Pray that you will show others by the way you live the difference God's gift of eternal life makes to you now.

DAY 57

On the Way: In his second letter, Peter encourages us to keep growing in faith. He reminds us to keep pleasing God and to obey what we read in God's Word. We need to remember that others will try to trick us by saying the Bible is not true. He encourages us to stand firm in our faith.

READ 2 PETER 3:1–10

A day is like a thousand years to the Lord, and a thousand years is like a day (v8b).

Checkpoint: When we wait for an exciting date to come, maybe Christmas or a birthday, we can feel our anticipation building as the day gets nearer. Imagine how you would feel if you knew a big family celebration was going to happen, but you were not told when; you just had to wait . . . and wait . . . until it happened. Maybe at first you would be excited, but if it didn't happen quickly, there would be days you might forget about it and stop looking for it.

Christians can be like that when thinking about Jesus' return. That will be a great day for all God's people, a day when we will live with Him forever, a day for us to anticipate. However, this has been promised for hundreds of years now. Even in Peter's day, there were people who were sick of waiting. They were beginning to believe that the Second Coming was not true and laughed at those who believed. Our reading today reminds us of God's patience and love. God wants everyone to be saved and gives everyone the chance to become His child. He is not ruled by time like we are, so what seems like a long time is not like that to God. We need to keep believing His Word and keep living for Him, remembering that one day He will return as He has promised.

- *Read 1 Thessalonians 4:16–18. Why do you think remembering that Jesus is coming back will encourage us as Christians?*

- *How can you keep remembering and looking forward to Jesus' return?*

Prayer Stop: Praise God that we will be with Him forever when Jesus returns. Pray that remembering this will make a difference to the way you live and pray for those you know who still need to trust Jesus.

1, 2, AND 3 JOHN

These letters were written by the Apostle John. The first one is written to Christians and the church in general. The second one seems to be written to a specific church, and the third one to a personal friend named Gaius.

DAY 58

On the Way: Some folks were coming into the church saying that Jesus was not actually real, but John makes it clear that he had seen Jesus with his own eyes, and he wanted others to know that his teaching was true. So he encourages them to keep walking in the light of God and with other Christians. Some people today will try to tell us the same, but we can encourage each other to keep believing God's Word.

READ 1 JOHN 1:5–2:6

> *God is light and there is no darkness in him at all* (1:5).

Checkpoint: When we walk into a dark room, we have no way of knowing what is inside or whether it is safe to enter. However, as soon as the light is switched on, we can see everything. If there is a tiny light in the room, it makes all the difference. As Christians, we are drawn to the light of God's character and His Word.

Darkness is a picture of sin and things without God. When we spend time with God, He shows us the sin in our lives so that we may stop sinning and let more of His light shine into and out of our lives. Knowing His Word and doing what it says reveals to us and others that we are walking with God. This does not mean that we will be perfect; the Bible teaches that none of us will be perfect on this earth, but John reminds us that Jesus will forgive us if we are walking with Him in the light of His Word. If we keep walking in darkness—doing things we know do not please God—then we are showing others that God's Word doesn't mean much to us. So it is important that we live out the things we read in God's Word.

- *How do you think our fellowship (friendship) with God affects our fellowship with other Christians?*
- *How does what we think about sin affect our fellowship with God and other Christians?*
- *How will we recognize those who are living to please God?*

Prayer Stop: Thank God for the light that His Word gives and that He is light to us, showing us the way. Be willing to confess your sin to God and repent from it. (Be specific!)

DAY 59

On the Way: The rest of the first letter of John urges us to love one another and watch out for those who would try to trick us by teaching things that are not the truth. John's second letter is written to "the chosen lady and her children." This is likely to be a church and those who attend it. It is short so we can read it all in one sitting.

MEMORY VERSE

Love means doing what God has commanded us, and he has commanded us to love one another.

~ 2 John 1:6a

READ 2 JOHN 1:1–13

Checkpoint: This short letter is like a summary of the first letter John wrote. After he spoke of living in the light of God, he encouraged the Christians to love one another, just as he does in this letter. He met some people from this church and was encouraged by their lives; they were living in God's truth. Our lives can be an encouragement to our leaders too when they see us living in God's truth and notice its effect on our lives. If we live in this manner, it will also have an effect on other people's lives.

The second part of this letter reminds the church to be careful of the teaching they hear. John tells them not to show any encouragement to those who teach lies. His command that they love one another should help to guard against this happening. If we encourage each other to live by God's truth, we demonstrate love to each other; "love is doing what God has commanded." By doing this, we are guarding the truth in our church and keeping it top priority. If it has such an important part in our church, then it will be difficult for people to wander away from it unless they do so deliberately. This will encourage people to keep a strong relationship with God.

- *In what way does your life encourage your leaders?*
- *How can we "remain in the teaching of Christ"? (2 John 1:9)*
- *How can we discourage those who teach lies and still show them love?*

Prayer Stop: Pray for those you know who have put their hope in a false religion. Ask God to help you tell them His truth and pray that they will listen.

DAY 60

On the Way: The third letter of John is a personal letter to his friend Gaius. John has been encouraged by hearing from others about how Gaius is living in God's truth, and he wrote to encourage him to keep going. Like 2 John, it is short, so we will read it all today.

READ 3 JOHN 1:1–15

> *So we ourselves should support them so that we can be their partners as they teach the truth* (v8).

Checkpoint: John has high praise for Gaius because of the way he looks after the traveling teachers. These men had given up their lives in order to teach the truth of God to the churches, and Gaius was helping them and blessing them by looking after them in his home. It seems that Paul stayed with him too (Rom. 16:23).

Then we meet Diotrephes. He is the opposite. He refuses to help the traveling teachers and also refuses to let others help them. We are not told why he is doing this, but we get a hint of it when John says Diotrephes loves to be leader: it seems he would like to be in control of everything and everyone. Whatever the reason, he is obviously missing out on blessing others and being blessed by them. Hebrews 13:2 says, "Don't forget to show hospitality to strangers, for some who have done this have entertained angels without realizing it!"

So let's be like Gaius: always be ready to share our homes and what we have with those who are serving God. Let's be ready to invite those who come to teach us God's Word into our homes. If there are missionaries home from abroad, why not invite them to come into our homes to share about their lives? We may not all be able to have people staying with us, but we can all show hospitality in some way. Remember the verse in Hebrews and do not miss the blessings God wants to give you when you show hospitality to others.

- *What are some ways you could show hospitality to those who teach you God's Word?*
- *John wrote to Gaius. Is there someone you could write to this week to encourage in how he or she serves God in your church?*

Prayer Stop: Praise God for those who teach you God's Word. Pray for the one you will write to this week.

JUDE

Jude was the brother of James and the half-brother of Jesus. He is writing to remind the church to keep a look out for people who would come in to teach them lies and to stand firm in the faith, encouraging others who were weaker in their faith.

DAY 61

On the Way: Jude wanted to write to believers about their salvation, but because of what was happening in the church, he felt it was more important to write about guarding their faith. There seemed to be some people among those in the church who were teaching that because of God's grace, they could live whatever way they wanted. Jude reminds them of all the people in the Old Testament who did whatever they wanted and of God's punishment on them. He warned them that Christians are no different. God would judge them for the things they had done and continued to do.

READ JUDE 1:12–23

But you, dear friends, must build each other up in your most holy faith (v20a).

Checkpoint: The first two verses of our reading do not give us a picture of anyone building anything up; in fact, it is the exact opposite. Jude warns the Christians that these ungodly people are determined to destroy the faith. They seem extremely discontent, and Jude says they are grumblers and complainers who only want to get their own way. As God judged people and nations in the past for disobeying Him, He will do so again, and we need to be wary so that we are not tricked by what false teachers say.

Jude calls Christians to be faithful by being active in their faith. This gives priority to the way we treat others. We must build each other up, pray, and show mercy to those who are weaker in faith by encouraging them. Our priority should be to tell other people the good news of Jesus. We need to *show* people love and compassion but at the same time let them know how much God hates their sin.

- *In what practical ways can we build each other up in our faith?*
- *How can we encourage those who are having some doubts in their faith?*
- *What can we do to show people love but not love the sin in their lives?*

Prayer Stop: Pray for your church, that God would protect it against false teaching. Pray for someone you can help and encourage in their faith this week.

REVELATION

The last book in the Bible was written by the Apostle John while he was a prisoner on the Island of Patmos. This book is not only a letter but an account of a vision John had while on the island. The first three chapters are letters written to specific churches in Asia to encourage them and correct them in some problem areas. In the rest of the book, John tells us of his vision, which is about God's final judgment of the earth.

DAY 62

On the Way: John had been sent to the Island of Patmos because he was preaching and teaching about Jesus, and the government did not like it. While he was there, he was given a vision from Jesus Himself. He writes to the churches in Asia to share what he saw.

READ REVELATION 1:9–20

And standing in the middle of the lampstands was someone like the Son of Man (v13).

Checkpoint: Much of what we read in Revelation is picture language that John uses to explain what he saw. His vision was so majestic that there were probably no words to describe it for us to clearly imagine. We understand that what he saw was beyond amazing, and this leads us to recognize the awesome majesty of God.

John was worshipping God. It was the Lord's Day, perhaps our Sunday when churches would normally meet to worship. Even though John was unable to be with other believers, he could still worship, and God met with him in an extra special way. When we are away from home and cannot meet with a church to worship God, we can still worship wherever we are.

Jesus came and spoke to John. John's reaction was to fall down in fear of God. Even though he knew God and had seen Jesus on earth, being in the presence of the risen Lord Jesus was awesome. Sometimes we can take being in God's presence for granted. We need to remember His power and majesty when we come to Him in prayer.

Jesus explains that the stars in His hand are the angels looking after the churches to which he was to send messages. The lampstands are the churches.

- *Read Matthew 5:14–16 and Philippians 2:14–15. Why is a lampstand a great picture for a church?*

- *In what ways does God's light shine from your church?*

- *How can John's vision bring comfort to our churches today? (Where was Jesus standing?)*

Prayer Stop: Take time to worship God for His majesty and power. Pray that we would be God's light in this dark world both as individuals and in our churches.

DAY 63

On the Way: Chapters 2 and 3 are letters written to each of the churches mentioned in chapter 1. They are messages from Jesus to them. Some of these words encourage them to keep going and growing in their faith even though they are suffering for it. Others have messages to correct what they are doing wrong. We will just read the first two letters.

READ REVELATION 2:1–11

> *Anyone with ears to hear must listen to the Spirit and understand what he is saying to the churches (vs7a, 11a).*

Checkpoint: The letters are addressed to the "angels" of each church—those in the Lord's hand in John's vision. They are likely to be the leaders of these churches. It is comforting to know that the leaders of our churches are held closely in the hand of our Lord. Each letter is sent from God to the churches, but each one is given a separate title for God. To Ephesus, it was from "the one who holds the seven stars and walks among the lampstands." This gives us a picture of how closely the Lord knows our churches. He holds the leaders close to Him and walks among the churches. Ephesus needed to remember how close God was to them.

Smyrna's letter was from "the one who is the first and the last, who was dead but is now alive." They were experiencing persecution, and the letter warned them of worse to come. They needed to know that God was in control. He was there at the start and will be there forever. Each church is encouraged to listen to what God's Spirit says to them and to understand and act on it.

Our Savior knows each one of us personally. He knows the things that please God and the things that we need to change in our lives and the lives of our churches. We need to listen, understand, and obey Him.

- *If your church were included in these letters, what name for God would be an encouragement for it? Why?*

- *What do you think might be included in a letter to your church?*

Prayer Stop: Thank God that He holds our leaders close to Him and watches over our churches. Pray that we would listen and obey His Word in our church and as individuals.

DAY 64

On the Way: After John has finished writing the messages from the Lord to the churches, he is taken in another vision up into heaven. He tries to describe what he sees, but it seems so awesome it is hard for us to understand. It was probably hard for him to describe in human language. He saw living beings worshipping God.

READ REVELATION 5:1–14

Look, the Lion of the tribe of Judah, the heir to David's throne, has won the victory. He is worthy to open the scroll (v5b).

Checkpoint: The way this vision is described makes it seem incredibly odd to us. We need to keep in mind that heaven is so glorious that no words can describe it. The verses we read today focus on a picture of Jesus. The first picture we are given is Jesus being called the *Lion of Judah*. When Jacob blessed his sons before he died, he told Judah that he was like a lion and that the royal sceptre would stay with his family until the one who ruled all nations would come. Here in heaven, John is being shown what those words of Jacob meant so long ago. Jesus is that one.

When John looked, he did not see a lion but a lamb that looked as if it had been killed. It was standing between the throne of God and the living creatures. This is a picture of how Jesus was the sacrifice for our sins. In the Old Testament, the Jews had to offer a lamb to God to pay for their sins. Jesus was that sacrifice for us. He died once and now lives in heaven so we can come to God through Him. When all the living creatures in heaven saw Him, they worshipped Him along with every creature on earth. Jesus is worthy of all of our praise.

- *Why do you think Jesus is shown as a lion and a lamb?*
- *What has Jesus death done for us? (Revelation 5:9–10)*
- *When those in heaven saw Jesus, they worshipped Him. What will you do today?*

Prayer Stop: Take some time to worship God, thinking about the pictures we read about today.

DAY 65

On the Way: We have come to the end of this study of the Bible. As the Lamb is being worshipped in heaven, He breaks the seals on the scroll one at a time. Each time, John sees a vision describing something from the scroll. These things are too difficult for us to deal with here, but they give us a picture of things that will happen before Jesus returns to earth. We cannot tell when that will be or know how it will happen, but we are given a promise that He will return.

MEMORY VERSE

He will wipe every tear from their eyes, and there will be no more death or sorrow or crying or pain. All these things are gone forever.

~ Revelation 21:4

READ REVELATION 21:1–7; 22:1–7

Look, I am making everything new! (21:5b).

Checkpoint: These two passages give us a little peek at heaven. They are verses that give us the feeling of victory and of God completing all His work on earth. I wonder what stands out to you the most. I find the phrase in verse 21:1 interesting: "and the sea was also gone." Does this mean there will be no sea in heaven? I cannot imagine that, but I am sure all that is there is so awesome we cannot start to describe it.

Verse 5 tells us that everything will be new; we will never have experienced any of heaven before, and the greatest thing is that God will be among us. God says, "It is finished." When Jesus was dying on the cross, He gave this shout too. Jesus had completed His work when He died as a sacrifice for our sins, and now we see God in heaven having completed His final work when He brings everything on heaven and earth under His rule. This day is still to come. As God's children, we can look forward to being with Him forever in heaven. For those who have refused to accept Jesus as their Savior, there will be God's judgment to face.

- *List the things these two passages tell us about heaven.*
- *Are you ready to meet God in heaven? Have you asked Jesus to be your Savior?*
- *How can these verses encourage those who are suffering today?*

Prayer Stop: Thank God for the hope that these verses give us as Christians. Thank Him also for His Word and all that it teaches us about Him. Pray for those you know who are not yet Christians.

INDEX OF TOPICS

KEY: FS: From the Start; HB: History Books of the Old Testament; PW: Psalms and Books of Wisdom; PR: Prophets; G: Gospels and Acts; L: Letters of the New Testament.

The initials are followed by the number of the day within that section.

U, V, W, X, Y, Z

Uncertainty: FS6

Wealth: HB62; PW17; G16; L40

Weariness: PR36; L22

Wisdom: HB57,91; PW28

Work: HB59; PW24,32; PR22; L34,46

World: PW16

Worries: PW9,16,24; G9; L28

Worship: FS4; HB 29,59; PW37; PR44

NOTES

For more information about
Carolyn Wells
&
Walking in the Word
please visit:

carolynwells@ntlworld.com
www.facebook.com/WalkingintheWord1
@chowsonwells

....

For more information about
AMBASSADOR INTERNATIONAL
please visit:

www.ambassador-international.com
@AmbassadorIntl
www.facebook.com/AmbassadorIntl